English-Chinese
Pinyin-Chinese-English

(Simplified-Mandarin)

Word to Word®
Bilingual Dictionary

Compiled by:
C. Sesma, M.A.

Translated by:
Lei Tang
Weixuan Liao

Bilingual Dictionaries, Inc.

Chinese Word to Word® Bilingual Dictionary
4th Edition © Copyright 2012

Published in the United States by:

Bilingual Dictionaries, Inc.
PO Box 1154
Murrieta, CA 92564
T: (951) 296-2445 • F: (951) 296-9911
www.BilingualDictionaries.com

ISBN13: 978-0-933146-22-8
ISBN: 0-933146-22-1
Printed in India

Preface

Bilingual Dictionaries, Inc. is committed to providing schools, libraries and educators with a great selection of bilingual materials for students. Along with bilingual dictionaries we also provide ESL materials, children's bilingual stories and children's bilingual picture dictionaries.

Sesma's Chinese Word to Word® Bilingual Dictionary was created specifically with students in mind to be used for reference and testing. This dictionary contains approximately 20,000 entries targeting common words used in the English language.

List of Irregular Verbs

present - past - past participle

arise - arose - arisen
awake - awoke - awoken, awaked
be - was - been
bear - bore - borne
beat - beat - beaten
become - became - become
begin - began - begun
behold - beheld - beheld
bend - bent - bent
beseech - besought - besought
bet - bet - betted
bid - bade (bid) - bidden (bid)
bind - bound - bound
bite - bit - bitten
bleed - bled - bled
blow - blew - blown
break - broke - broken
breed - bred - bred
bring - brought - brought
build - built - built
burn - burnt - burnt *
burst - burst - burst
buy - bought - bought
cast - cast - cast
catch - caught - caught
choose - chose - chosen
cling - clung - clung
come - came - come
cost - cost - cost
creep - crept - crept
cut - cut - cut
deal - dealt - dealt

dig - dug - dug
do - did - done
draw - drew - drawn
dream - dreamt - dreamed
drink - drank - drunk
drive - drove - driven
dwell - dwelt - dwelt
eat - ate - eaten
fall - fell - fallen
feed - fed - fed
feel - felt - felt
fight - fought - fought
find - found - found
flee - fled - fled
fling - flung - flung
fly - flew - flown
forebear - forbore - forborne
forbid - forbade - forbidden
forecast - forecast - forecast
forget - forgot - forgotten
forgive - forgave - forgiven
forego - forewent - foregone
foresee - foresaw - foreseen
foretell - foretold - foretold
forget - forgot - forgotten
forsake - forsook - forsaken
freeze - froze - frozen
get - got - gotten
give - gave - given
go - went - gone
grind - ground - ground
grow - grew - grown
hang - hung * - hung *
have - had - had

hear - heard - heard	**ring** - rang - rung
hide - hid - hidden	**rise** - rose - risen
hit - hit - hit	**run** - ran - run
hold - held - held	**saw** - sawed - sawn
hurt - hurt - hurt	**say** - said - said
hit - hit - hit	**see** - saw - seen
hold - held - held	**seek** - sought - sought
keep - kept - kept	**sell** - sold - sold
kneel - knelt * - knelt *	**send** - sent - sent
know - knew - known	**set** - set - set
lay - laid - laid	**sew** - sewed - sewn
lead - led - led	**shake** - shook - shaken
lean - leant * - leant *	**shear** - sheared - shorn
leap - lept * - lept *	**shed** - shed - shed
learn - learnt * - learnt *	**shine** - shone - shone
leave - left - left	**shoot** - shot - shot
lend - lent - lent	**show** - showed - shown
let - let - let	**shrink** - shrank - shrunk
lie - lay - lain	**shut** - shut - shut
light - lit * - lit *	**sing** - sang - sung
lose - lost - lost	**sink** - sank - sunk
make - made - made	**sit** - sat - sat
mean - meant - meant	**slay** - slew - slain
meet - met - met	**sleep** - sleep - slept
mistake - mistook - mistaken	**slide** - slid - slid
must - had to - had to	**sling** - slung - slung
pay - paid - paid	**smell** - smelt * - smelt *
plead - pleaded - pled	**sow** - sowed - sown *
prove - proved - proven	**speak** - spoke - spoken
put - put - put	**speed** - sped * - sped *
quit - quit * - quit *	**spell** - spelt * - spelt *
read - read - read	**spend** - spent - spent
rid - rid - rid	**spill** - spilt * - spilt *
ride - rode - ridden	**spin** - spun - spun

spit - spat - spat
split - split - split
spread - spread - spread
spring - sprang - sprung
stand - stood - stood
steal - stole - stolen
stick - stuck - stuck
sting - stung - stung
stink - stank - stunk
stride - strode - stridden
strike - struck - struck (stricken)
strive - strove - striven
swear - swore - sworn
sweep - swept - swept
swell - swelled - swollen *
swim - swam - swum
take - took - taken
teach - taught - taught
tear - tore - torn

tell - told - told
think - thought - thought
throw - threw - thrown
thrust - thrust - thrust
tread - trod - trodden
wake - woke - woken
wear - wore - worn
weave - wove * - woven *
wed - wed * - wed *
weep - wept - wept
win - won - won
wind - wound - wound
wring - wrung - wrung
write - wrote - written

**Those tenses with an * also
have regular forms.**

English-Chinese

Bilingual Dictionaries, Inc.

Abbreviations

a - article - 冠词
adj - adjective - 形容词
adv - adverb - 副词
c - conjunction - 连词
e - exclamation - 惊叹号
n - noun - 名词
pre - preposition - 介词
pro - pronoun - 代词
v - verb - 动词

A

a *a* 一（个、只、件等）

abandon *v* 放弃

abandonment *n* 放弃，
放弃的事/物

abbey *n* 修道院

abbot *n* 男修道院院长，方丈

abbreviate *v* 缩短，缩写

abbreviation *n* 缩写，缩写词

abdicate *v* 退位

abdication *n* 退位

abdomen *n* 腹部

abduct *v* 诱拐

abduction *n* 诱拐

aberration *n* 偏差，越轨

abhor *v* 痛恨

abide by *v* 遵守

ability *n* 能力

ablaze *adj* 燃烧的

able *adj* 能

abnormal *adj* 反常

abnormality *n* 反常性

aboard *adv* 在船上，在火车上，
在飞机上

abolish *v* 废除

abort *v* 流产，夭折

abortion *n* 流产，夭折

abound *v* 富于，充满

about *pre* 关于

about *adv* 大概

above *pre* 在……上

abreast *adv* 并列，并排

abridge *v* 删节

abroad *adv* 在国外，出国

abrogate *v* 废除

abruptly *adv* 突然

absence *n* 缺席，不在场

absent *adj* 缺席，不在场

absolute *adj* 绝对

absolution *n* 赦免

absolve *v* 赦免

absorb *v* 吸收

absorbent *adj* 能吸收的

abstain *v* 戒绝，节制

abstinence *n* 节制，禁食，戒酒

abstract *adj* 抽象的

absurd *adj* 荒谬的

abundance *n* 丰富，充足

abundant *adj* 丰富的

abuse *v* 滥用，虐待

abuse *n* 滥用，虐待

abusive *adj* 滥用的，辱骂的

abysmal *adj* 深不可测

abyss *n* 深渊

academic *adj* 学术的

academy *n* 学院

accelerate *v* 加快

accelerator *n* 加速器

accent *n* 重音，口音

accept *v* 接受

acceptable *adj* 可接受的

acceptance *n* 验收，接受

access *n* 接近，使用，进入的权利

accessible *adj* 可接近的，可进入的，可使用的

accident *n* 意外，事故

accidental *adj* 意外的

acclaim *v* 欢呼，称赞，喝彩

acclimatize *v* 使适应新环境，使服水土，服水土

accommodate *v* 容纳

accompany *v* 伴随着

accomplice *n* 共犯，帮凶

accomplish *v* 完成

accomplishment *n* 完成，成就

accord *n* 调和，一致，协议

according to *pre* 根据

accordion *n* 手风琴

account *n* 帐户

account for *v* 解释

accountable *adj* 应负责的，可解释的，有责任的

accountant *n* 会计师

accumulate *v* 累积

accuracy *n* 精度

accurate *adj* 准确的

accusation *n* 指控

accuse *v* 指责

accustom *v* 使习惯于

ace *n* 幺点，好手，高手，发球得分

ache *n* 疼痛

achieve *v* 达到，实现，完成

achievement *n* 成就，完成

acid *n* 酸

acidity *n* 酸度

acknowledge *v* 承认，认可

acorn *n* 橡子

acoustic *adj* 声学的，音响的

acquaint *v* 使熟悉

acquaintance *n* 熟悉，熟人

acquire *v* 获得，收购

acquisition *n* 获得，收购

acquit *v* 宣告无罪，开释

acquittal *n* 无罪释放

acre *n* 英亩

acrobat *n* 杂技演员，特技演员

across *pre* 穿越

act *v* 行动，演

action *n* 行动

activate *v* 激活，启动

activation *n* 激活，启动

active *adj* 活跃

activity *n* 活动

actor *n* 演员

actress *n* 女演员

actual *adj* 实际的

actually *adv* 实际上

acute *adj* 严重的，敏锐的，急性的，剧烈的

adamant *adj* 坚决的，坚强的，倔强的，坚定不移的

adapt *v* 适应

adaptable *adj* 适应性强

adaptation *n* 适应

adapter *n* 适配器

add *v* 添加，加上

addicted *adj* 上瘾的

addiction *n* 瘾

addictive *adj* 让人上瘾的

addition *n* 添加，加上

additional *adj* 额外的，附加的

address *n* 地址

address *v* 称呼，发表演说，提出，写地址，处理

addressee *n* 收件人

adequate *adj* 充足的

adhere *v* 紧粘，粘附，坚持，遵守

adhesive *adj* 粘的，有粘性的，带粘性的

adjacent *adj* 邻近的

adjective *n* 形容词

adjoin *v* 毗连

adjoining *adj* 毗连的

adjourn *v* 休会

adjust *v* 调整

adjustable *adj* 可调的

adjustment *n* 调整

administer *v* 管理

admirable *adj* 令人钦佩的

admiral *n* 海军上将

admiration *n* 钦佩

admire *v* 佩服

admirer *n* 崇拜者

admissible *adj* 容许的，可采纳的

admission *n* 加入许可，入场券，承认，坦白

admit *v* 允许进入，承认，接纳

admittance *n* 进入，通道，入场许可

admonish *v* 告诫

admonition *n* 告诫

adolescence *n* 青春期

adolescent *n* 青少年

adopt *v* 采取，收养

adoption *n* 采取，收养

adoptive *adj* 采用的，收养关系的

adorable *adj* 值得崇拜的，可敬重的，可爱的

adoration *n* 崇拜，爱慕

adore *v* 崇拜，爱慕

adorn *v* 装饰，佩戴

adrift *adv* 漂浮

adulation *n* 奉承

adult *n* 成人

adulterate *v* 搀杂，搀假

adultery *n* 通奸

advance *v* 前进

advance *n* 前进

advantage *n* 优势

Advent *n* 出现，到来

adventure *n* 冒险

adverb *n* 副词

adversary *n* 对手

adverse *adj* 不利的

adversity *n* 逆境

advertise v 广告

advertising n 广告

advice n 建议

advisable adj 可取的，明智的

advise v 建议

adviser n 顾问

advocate v 提倡，主张

aesthetic adj 美学的，审美的

afar adv 在远方，从远方

affable adj 和蔼可亲的

affair n 事务，暧昧关系

affect v 影响

affection n 影响，喜爱

affectionate adj 示爱的，爱的

affiliate v 使（个人、社团、机构等）隶属於一较大组织，使接纳为成员

affiliation n 加入，附属

affinity n 亲和力

affirm v 申明

affirmative adj 肯定的，表示同意的

affix v 粘上，贴上，系住，附上，固定

afflict v 折磨

affliction n 苦恼

affluence n 富裕

affluent adj 富裕的

afford v 负担得起，买得起

affordable adj 负担得起的，买得起的

affront v 公开侮辱，冒犯

affront n 公开侮辱，冒犯

afloat adv 漂浮着

afraid adj 害怕

afresh adv 重新

after pre 在……后

afternoon n 下午

afterwards adv 后来，然后

again adv 再次

against pre 反对

age n 年龄

agency n 经销，代理

agenda n 议程

agent n 代理人，经销商

agglomerate v 成团，结块，凝聚

aggravate v 加重，使恶化

aggravation n 加重，恶化

aggregate v 使聚集，总计达

aggression n 进攻，侵略

aggressive adj 侵略性的

aggressor n 侵略者

aghast adj 惊骇的，吓呆的

agile adj 敏捷的

agitator n 鼓动者

agnostic n 不可知论者

agonize v 感到极度痛苦，使极度痛苦

agonizing adj 让人极度痛苦的

agony n 痛苦

agree v 同意

agreeable adj 惬意的，使人愉快的

agreement *n* 协议
agricultural *adj* 农业的
agriculture *n* 农业
ahead *pre* 在前，向前
aid *n* 援助
aid *v* 援助
aide *n* 助手
ailing *adj* 患病
ailment *n* 病
aim *v* 瞄准，旨在
aimless *adj* 盲目的
air *n* 空气
air *v* 通风，公开表示
aircraft *n* 飞机
airfare *n* 机票费
airfield *n* 机场
airline *n* 航线
airliner *n* 班机
airmail *n* 空邮
airplane *n* 飞机
airplane *n* 飞机
airport *n* 机场
airspace *n* 领空
airstrip *n* 飞机跑道
airtight *adj* 不透气的
aisle *n* 过道
ajar *adj* 半开的
akin *adj* 类似于
alarm *n* 警报
alarm clock *n* 闹钟
alarming *adj* 惊人的，告急的
alcoholic *adj* 酒精的

alcoholism *n* 酒精中毒，酗酒
alert *n* 警报
algebra *n* 代数
alien *n* 外星人，外国人
alight *adv* 发亮的
align *v* 使结盟，使成一行，排列
alignment *n* 对齐，联合
alike *adj* 同样的
alive *adj* 活的
all *adj* 所有
allegation *n* 断言，辩解，申述，主张
allege *v* 断言，辩解，申述，主张
allegedly *adv* 据称
allegiance *n* 效忠
allegory *n* 寓言
allergic *adj* 过敏的，反感的
allergy *n* 过敏，反感
alleviate *v* 减轻
alley *n* 胡同，小巷
alliance *n* 联盟
allied *adj* 联盟的
alligator *n* 短吻鳄
allocate *v* 分配
allot *v* 分配
allotment *n* 分配，份额
allow *v* 允许
allowance *n* 补贴，津贴
alloy *n* 合金
allure *n* 引诱

alluring *adj* 诱人的

allusion *n* 暗示，暗指

ally *n* 盟友

ally *v* 联盟

almanac *n* 历书，年鉴

almighty *adj* 万能的

almond *n* 杏仁

almost *adv* 几乎

alms *n* 施舍，救济

alone *adj* 单独的

along *pre* 沿

alongside *pre* 在……旁边

aloof *adj* 疏远的，冷淡的

aloud *adv* 大声地

alphabet *n* 字母表

already *adv* 已经

alright *adv* 好吧

also *adv* 也，还

altar *n* 祭坛

alter *v* 改变

alteration *n* 改变

altercation *n* 争吵

alternate *v* 轮流，交替

alternate *adj* 轮流的，交替的

alternative *n* 替代或供选择的人或物

although *c* 虽然

altitude *n* 高度，海拔

altogether *adj* 总共

aluminum *n* 铝

always *adv* 总是

amass *v* 累积

amateur *adj* 业余的

amaze *v* 使惊奇

amazement *n* 惊奇

amazing *adj* 令人惊奇的

ambassador *n* 大使

ambiguous *adj* 有歧义的，暧昧的

ambition *n* 野心，雄心

ambitious *adj* 有野心的，有雄心的

ambivalent *adj* 矛盾的，摇摆不定的

ambulance *n* 救护车

ambush *v* 伏击

amenable *adj* 顺从的，服贴的

amend *v* 修改

amendment *n* 修订

amenities *n* 适意，舒适，便利设施

American *adj* 美国的，美洲的

amiable *adj* 和蔼可亲

amicable *adj* 和睦的

amid *pre* 在……中间

ammonia *n* 氨

ammunition *n* 军火，弹药

amnesia *n* 健忘症，记忆缺失

amnesty *n* 大赦，特赦

among *pre* 在……中间

amoral *adj* 不道德的

amorphous *adj* 无定形的

amortize *v* 摊还，摊销，分期偿还

amount *n* 金额，数量

amount to *v* 总计

amphibious *adj* 两栖的

amphitheater *n* 圆形剧场

ample *adj* 充足的

amplifier *n* 放大器

amplify *v* 放大

amputate *v* 截肢

amputation *n* 截肢

amuse *v* 逗乐

amusement *n* 娱乐

amusing *adj* 有趣的

an *a* 一（个、只、件等）

analogy *n* 类似，相似，类推

analysis *n* 分析

analyze *v* 分析

anarchist *n* 无政府主义者

anarchy *n* 无政府状态

anatomy *n* 解剖，解剖学

ancestor *n* 祖先

ancestry *n* 祖先，家世，门第，血统

anchor *n* 主播，船锚

anchovy *n* 鳀鱼

ancient *adj* 古老的

and *c* 和，与，并且

anecdote *n* 轶事

anemia *n* 贫血

anemic *adj* 贫血的

anesthesia *n* 麻醉

anew *adv* 重新

angel *n* 天使

angelic *adj* 天使般的

anger *v* 使愤怒

anger *n* 愤怒

angina *n* 心绞痛

angle *n* 角度

Anglican *adj* 圣公会的

angry *adj* 愤怒的

anguish *n* 痛苦

animal *n* 动物

animate *v* 使有生气，赋予生命，绘制（动画片）

animation *n* 动画

animosity *n* 敌意

ankle *n* 踝

annex *n* 附件，附属物

annexation *n* 附加，并吞，合并，附加物

annihilate *v* 歼灭

annihilation *n* 歼灭

anniversary *n* 周年

annotate *v* 注释

annotation *n* 注解

announce *v* 公布

announcement *n* 公告

announcer *n* 播音员

annoy *v* 烦扰

annoying *adj* 烦人的

annual *adj* 年度的

annul *v* 废止

annulment *n* 废止

anoint *v* 涂以油或软膏，施以涂油礼

anonymity *n* 匿名

anonymous *adj* 匿名的

another *adj* 另外，别的

answer *v* 回答

answer *n* 答案

ant *n* 蚂蚁

antagonize *v* 使对抗

antecedent *n* 前情，先行词

antecedents *n* 前情，先行词

antelope *n* 羚羊

antenna *n* 天线

anthem *n* 圣歌

antibiotic *n* 抗生素

anticipate *v* 预期

anticipation *n* 预期

antidote *n* 解毒剂

antipathy *n* 反感

antiquated *adj* 陈旧的，过时的

antiquity *n* 古代，古老

anvil *n* 铁砧

anxiety *n* 焦虑

anxious *adj* 着急的

any *adj* 任何

anybody *pro* 任何人

anyhow *pro* 不管怎样

anyone *pro* 任何人

anything *pro* 任何事/物

apart *adv* 分离，分开

apartment *n* 公寓

apathy *n* 冷漠

ape *n* 猿

aperitif *n* 开胃酒

apex *n* 顶点，最高点

aphrodisiac *adj* 催情的

apiece *adv* 每人，每个，各

apocalypse *n* 启示，启示录

apologize *v* 道歉

apology *n* 道歉

apostle *n* 使徒，传道者

apostolic *adj* 使徒的

apostrophe *n* 撇号

appall *v* 使惊骇或沮丧

appalling *adj* 骇人的，可怕的，低劣的

apparel *n* 衣服，服装

apparent *adj* 明显的

apparently *adv* 显然

apparition *n* 鬼，幻影，幽灵

appeal *n* 上诉，呼吁

appeal *v* 上诉，呼吁

appealing *adj* 有吸引力

appear *v* 看来，出现

appearance *n* 外观

appease *v* 安抚

appeasement *v* 平息，满足，缓和，姑息

appendicitis *n* 阑尾炎

appendix *n* 附录

appetite *n* 胃口

appetizer *n* 开胃食品

applaud *v* 鼓掌欢迎、喝彩等

applause *n* 掌声

apple *n* 苹果

appliance *n* 器具，用具

applicable *adj* 适用的

applicant *n* 申请人

application *n* 申请，应用

apply *v* 申请，适用

apply for *v* 申请

appoint *v* 任命

appointment *n* 任命，约定

appraisal *n* 评价

appraise *v* 评价

appreciate *v* 欣赏，感激

appreciation *n* 欣赏，感激

apprehend *v* 忧虑，逮捕，理解

apprehensive *adj* 担心的

apprentice *n* 学徒

approach *v* 接近

approach *n* 接近，办法

approachable *adj* 亲切的，可接近的，平易近人的

approbation *n* 认可

appropriate *adj* 适当的

approval *n* 赞成，批准

approve *v* 批准

approximate *adj* 近似的，大约的

apricot *n* 杏

April *n* 四月

apron *n* 围裙

aptitude *n* 资质，才能

aquarium *n* 水族馆

aquatic *adj* 水生的

aqueduct *n* 疏水道

Arabic *adj* 阿拉伯的

arable *adj* 可耕种的

arbiter *n* 仲裁者

arbitrary *adj* 任性的，任意的，专横的

arbitrate *v* 仲裁

arbitration *n* 仲裁

arc *n* 弧

arch *n* 拱

archaeology *n* 考古学

archaic *adj* 古老的

archbishop *n* 大主教

architect *n* 建筑师

architecture *n* 建筑

archive *n* 档案

arctic *adj* 北极

ardent *adj* 热心的，热情的

ardor *n* 热忱

arduous *adj* 艰巨的

area *n* 地区，面积，领域

arena *n* 竞技场，舞台

argue *v* 争辩

argument *n* 论据，争论

arid *adj* 干燥的，不毛的

arise *iv* 升起，产生，出现

aristocracy *n* 贵族阶级，上层社会

aristocrat *n* 贵族

arithmetic *n* 算术

ark *n* 方舟

arm *n* 手臂

arm *v* 武装

armaments *n* 军备，武器

armchair *n* 扶手椅

armed *adj* 武装的

armistice *n* 停战

armor *n* 盔甲

armpit *n* 腋下

army *n* 军队

aromatic *adj* 芳香的

around *pro* 在……周围，在四处，大约

arouse *v* 调动，激起

arrange *v* 安排

arrangement *n* 安排

array *n* 阵列，编队

arrest *v* 逮捕

arrest *n* 逮捕

arrival *n* 到达

arrive *v* 到达

arrogance *n* 傲慢

arrogant *adj* 傲慢的

arrow *n* 箭

arsenal *n* 军械库，兵工厂

arsenic *n* 砷

arson *n* 纵火，纵火罪

arsonist *n* 纵火者

art *n* 艺术

artery *n* 动脉

arthritis *n* 关节炎

artichoke *n* 朝鲜蓟

article *n* 文章，物品

articulate *v* 清楚地讲话，发音

articulation *n* 清楚的发音，表达

artificial *adj* 人工的

artillery *n* 大炮，炮兵部队

artisan *n* 工匠

artist *n* 艺术家

artistic *adj* 艺术的

artwork *n* 艺术品

as *c* 作为

as *adv* 一样

ascend *v* 上升

ascendancy *n* 优势，优越，权势

ascertain *v* 查明，弄清，确定

ascetic *adj* 苦行的

ash *n* 灰

ashamed *adj* 惭愧的

ashore *adv* 上岸，向岸，在岸上，在岸边

ashtray *n* 烟灰缸

aside *adv* 在旁边

aside from *adv* 除了

ask *v* 问

asleep *adj* 睡着

asparagus *n* 芦笋

aspect *n* 方面

asphalt *n* 沥青

asphyxiate *v* 窒息

asphyxiation *n* 窒息

aspiration *n* 心愿，渴望

aspire *v* 渴望

aspirin *n* 阿司匹林

assail *v* 袭击

assailant *n* 攻击者

assassin n 刺客，杀手
assassinate v 暗杀
assassination n 暗杀
assault n 攻击
assault v 攻击
assemble v 组装
assembly n 集会，大会
assent v 赞同
assert v 声称，断言，坚持
assertion n 声称，断言，坚持
assess v 评估
assessment n 评估
asset n 资产
assets n 资产
assign v 分派，指派
assignment n 分派，指派
assimilate v 吸收
assimilation n 吸收
assist v 协助
assistance n 援助
associate v 联想，把……联想在一起，使有联系
association n 联想，协会
assorted adj 各种各样的，混杂的
assortment n 分类，什锦物，各式各样的搭配
assume v 假设
assumption n 假设
assurance n 保证
assure v 保证
asterisk n 星号

asteroid n 小行星
asthma n 哮喘
asthmatic adj 哮喘的
astonish v 使吃惊
astonishing adj 惊人的
astound v 使吃惊
astounding adj 令人惊叹
astray adv 入歧途，迷途
astrologer n 占星家
astrology n 占星术
astronaut n 宇航员
astronomer n 天文学家
astronomic adj 天文的
astronomy n 天文学
astute adj 精明
asunder adv 碎，散
asylum n 庇护所
at pre 在
atheism n 无神论
atheist n 无神论者
athlete n 运动员
athletic adj 运动的
atmosphere n 大气，气氛
atmospheric adj 大气的
atom n 原子
atomic adj 原子的
atone v 补偿，赎罪，弥补
atonement n 补偿，赎罪，弥补
atrocious adj 残暴的
atrocity n 暴行
atrophy v 萎缩
attach v 附上

attached *adj* 附上的

attachment *n* 附件，依靠感

attack *n* 攻击

attack *v* 攻击

attacker *n* 攻击者

attain *v* 达到

attainable *adj* 可以实现的

attainment *n* 达到，获得，成就

attempt *v* 试图，企图

attempt *n* 试图，企图

attend *v* 参加，出席

attendance *n* 出席

attendant *n* 服务员

attention *n* 注意力

attentive *adj* 注意的，留意的

attenuate *v* 变薄，变小，弱化

attenuating *adj* 细的，薄的，减小的

attest *v* 证明，作证

attic *n* 阁楼

attitude *n* 态度

attorney *n* 律师

attract *v* 吸引

attraction *n* 景点，吸引力

attractive *adj* 有吸引力的

attribute *v* 属性

auction *n* 拍卖

auction *v* 拍卖

auctioneer *n* 拍卖人

audacious *adj* 大胆的，鲁莽的

audacity *n* 大胆，鲁莽

audible *adj* 可听见的

audience *n* 听众，观众

audit *v* 审计

auditorium *n* 礼堂

augment *v* 增加，增大

August *n* 八月

aunt *n* 姑、姨、舅妈、姊

auspicious *adj* 吉祥的

austere *adj* 苦行的，简朴的，简陋的

austerity *n* 节俭，苦行，朴素

authentic *adj* 真实的，正宗的

authenticate *v* 证实，验证

authenticity *n* 真实性

author *n* 作者

authoritarian *adj* 权力主义者的，独裁主义者的

authority *n* 权力，权威

authorization *n* 授权

authorize *v* 授权

auto *n* 汽车

autograph *n* 亲笔签名

automatic *adj* 自动的

automobile *n* 汽车

autonomous *adj* 自治的

autonomy *n* 自治

autopsy *n* 尸检

autumn *n* 秋季

auxiliary *adj* 辅助的

avail *v* 使用，利用

availability *n* 有供，可用性

available *adj* 可用的，有空的

avalanche *n* 雪崩

avarice n 贪财，贪婪
avaricious adj 贪婪的
avenge v 报仇
avenue n 大道
average n 平均
averse adj 厌恶的，反对的
aversion n 厌恶，反对
avert v 避免
aviation n 航空
aviator n 飞行员
avid adj 热衷的
avoid v 避免
avoidable adj 可以避免的
avoidance n 避免，避开
avowed adj 公开宣布的
await v 等待
awake iv 苏醒
awake adj 醒着的
awakening n 唤醒
award v 奖励
award n 奖，奖品
aware adj 知道的，注意到的
awareness n 意识
away adv 远离
awe n 敬畏
awesome adj 令人敬畏
awful adj 可怕的
awkward adj 笨拙的
awning n 雨篷
ax n 斧
axiom n 公理
axis n 轴

axle n 车轴

B

babble v 含糊不清地说，喋喋不休，潺潺作声
baby n 宝贝
babysitter n 婴儿保姆
bachelor n 学士，单身汉
back n 后面，背部
back adv 在后面，回
back v 支持
back down v 放弃，让步
back up v 后退，支持
backbone n 脊骨，骨干
backdoor n 后门
backfire v 逆火，适得其反
background n 背景
backing n 支持
backlash n 反冲
backlog n 积压待办事项，存货
backpack n 背包
backup n 备份
backward adj 向后的
backwards adv 向后
backyard n 后院
bacon n 熏猪肉
bacteria n 细菌

bad *adj* 坏的

badge *n* 徽章

badly *adv* 恶劣地，严重地

baffle *v* 使困惑，阻止

bag *n* 袋

baggage *n* 行李

baggy *adj* 袋状的，松垂的

baguette *n* 法式长棍面包

bail *n* 保释

bail out *v* 保释出来，跳伞

bailiff *n* 执行官，法警

bait *n* 诱饵

bake *v* 烘

baker *n* 面包师，烤炉

bakery *n* 面包店

balance *v* 平衡

balance *n* 平衡

balcony *n* 阳台

bald *adj* 秃头的

bale *n* 大包，大捆

ball *n* 球

balloon *n* 气球

ballot *n* 投票用纸，选票

ballroom *n* 舞厅

balm *n* 香油

balmy *adj* 温和的，芬芳的

bamboo *n* 竹子

ban *n* 禁令

ban *v* 禁止

banality *n* 平凡，陈腐

banana *n* 香蕉

band *n* 乐队

bandage *n* 绷带

bandage *v* 用绷带包扎

bandit *n* 强盗

bang *v* 用力关

banish *v* 流放，放逐

banishment *n* 流放，放逐

bank *n* 银行

bankrupt *v* 破产

bankrupt *adj* 破产的

bankruptcy *n* 破产

banner *n* 横幅，旗帜，大标题

banquet *n* 宴会

baptism *n* 洗礼

baptize *v* 施洗

bar *n* 酒吧，块

bar *v* 闩住，阻塞，封锁

barbarian *n* 野蛮人

barbaric *adj* 野蛮的

barbarism *n* 野蛮，暴行

barbecue *n* 烤肉，烧烤，烤架

barber *n* 理发师

bare *adj* 光秃的

barefoot *adj* 赤脚

barely *adv* 几乎不，仅仅

bargain *n* 便宜货，交易

bargain *v* 讨价还价

bargaining *n* 讲价

barge *n* 驳船

bark *v* 吠叫

bark *n* 吠声，树皮

barley *n* 大麦

barmaid *n* 酒吧女

barman *n* 酒保

barn *n* 谷仓

barometer *n* 晴雨表

barracks *n* 军营

barrage *n* 堰，弹幕，火力网

barrel *n* 桶

barren *adj* 贫瘠的

barricade *n* 路障，栅栏

barrier *n* 障碍

barring *pre* 除……以外

bartender *n* 酒吧侍者

barter *v* 物物交换，以货易货

base *n* 基地

base *v* 以，作基础

baseball *n* 棒球

baseless *adj* 无根据的

basement *n* 地下室

bashful *adj* 害羞的

basic *adj* 基本的

basics *n* 基础知识

basin *n* 盆地

basis *n* 依据

bask *v* 作者或躺着取暖

basket *n* 篮子

basketball *n* 篮球

bastard *n* 私生子/女

bat *n* 蝙蝠，球拍

batch *n* 一批

bath *n* 沐浴

bathe *v* 洗澡

bathrobe *n* 浴衣

bathroom *n* 浴室

bathtub *n* 浴缸

baton *n* 指挥棒，接力棒，警棍

battalion *n* 营

batter *v* 连续猛击

battery *n* 电池

battle *n* 战斗

battle *v* 战斗

battleship *n* 战舰

bay *n* 湾

bayonet *n* 刺刀

bazaar *n* 集市

be *iv* 是，存在

be born *v* 出生

beach *n* 海滩

beacon *n* 烽火，灯塔

beak *n* 鸟喙

beam *n* 梁，光线

bean *n* 豆

bear *n* 熊

bear *iv* 忍受

bearable *adj* 可承受的

beard *n* 胡须

bearded *adj* 有胡子的

bearer *n* 持有人

beast *n* 野兽

beat *iv* 打，打击

beat *n* 敲打，拍子

beaten *adj* 被打败的

beating *n* 打，打败

beautiful *adj* 美丽x

beautify *v* 美化

beauty *n* 美丽

beaver n 海狸
because c 因为
because of pre 因为
beckon v 召唤，示意
become iv 成为
bed n 床
bedding n 寝具
bedroom n 卧室
bedspread n 床单，床罩
bee n 蜜蜂
beef n 牛肉
beef up v 加强
beehive n 蜂箱
beer n 啤酒
beet n 甜菜
beetle n 甲虫
before adv 前
before pre 在……前
beforehand adv 事先
befriend v 交朋友
beg v 乞求
beggar n 乞丐
begin iv 开始
beginner n 初学者
beginning n 开始
beguile v 诱骗，诱惑
behalf (on) adv 代表
behave v 行为，表现
behavior n 行为
behead v 斩首
behind pre 在……后
behold iv 注视

being n 存在，生命，生物
belated adj 迟来的
belch v 打嗝，喷出
belch n 打嗝，喷出物
belfry n 钟楼
Belgian adj 比利时的
Belgium n 比利时
belief n 信仰
believable adj 可信的
believe v 相信
believer n 信徒
belittle v 轻视，贬低
bell n 铃
bell pepper n 柿子椒
belligerent adj 好战的
belly n 肚皮
belly button n 肚脐
belong v 属于
belongings n 财物
beloved adj 心爱的
below adv 下面
below pre 在……下
belt n 带子
bench n 长凳
bend iv 折弯
bend down v 弯下来
beneath pre 在……下方
benediction n 祝祷
benefactor n 恩人，捐赠者
beneficial adj 有利的
beneficiary n 受益人
benefit n 好处

benefit _v_ 使……受益，受益
benevolence _n_ 仁爱
benevolent _adj_ 仁慈的
benign _adj_ 良性的
bequeath _v_ 遗赠
bereaved _adj_ 丧失的
bereavement _n_ 丧亲，丧友
beret _n_ 贝雷帽
berserk _adj_ 狂暴的，狂怒的
berth _n_ 停泊处，锚位
beseech _iv_ 恳求
beset _iv_ 困扰
beside _pre_ 在……旁
besides _pre_ 此外，加之，而且
besiege _iv_ 围攻
best _adj_ 最佳的
best man _n_ 伴郎
bestial _adj_ 野兽般的
bestiality _n_ 兽性
bestow _v_ 授予，给予
bet _iv_ 打赌
bet _n_ 打赌
betray _v_ 出卖
betrayal _n_ 背叛
better _adj_ 更好的
between _pre_ 在……之间
beverage _n_ 饮料
beware _v_ 注意，提防，小心
bewilder _v_ 迷惑
bewitch _v_ 蛊惑，使着迷
beyond _adv_ 超越
bias _n_ 偏见

bible _n_ 圣经
biblical _adj_ 圣经的
bibliography _n_ 书目，索引，文献
bicycle _n_ 自行车
bid _n_ 出价
bid _iv_ 出价
big _adj_ 大的
bigamy _n_ 重婚
bigot _n_ 偏执的人
bigotry _n_ 偏执
bike _n_ 自行车
bile _n_ 胆汁
bilingual _adj_ 双语的
bill _n_ 账单
billiards _n_ 台球
billion _n_ 十亿
billionaire _n_ 亿万富翁
bimonthly _adj_ 双月一次的
bin _n_ 箱子
bind _iv_ 捆绑
binding _adj_ 有束缚力的
binoculars _n_ 双筒望远镜
biography _n_ 传记
biological _adj_ 生物学的
biology _n_ 生物学
bird _n_ 鸟
birth _n_ 出生
birthday _n_ 生日
biscuit _n_ 饼干
bishop _n_ 主教
bison _n_ 野牛

bit *n* 小片，小段等

bite *iv* 咬

bite *n* 咬

bitter *adj* 苦的

bitterly *adv* 苦涩地

bitterness *n* 苦味

bizarre *adj* 怪诞的

black *adj* 黑色的

blackberry *n* 黑莓

blackboard *n* 黑板

blackmail *n* 勒索

blackmail *v* 勒索

blackness *n* 黑度

blackout *n* 断电，灯火管制

blacksmith *n* 铁匠

bladder *n* 膀胱

blade *n* 刀片

blame *n* 责怪

blame *v* 责怪

blameless *adj* 无可责难的，
清白的

bland *adj* 和蔼的，温和的，
平淡的

blank *adj* 空白的

blanket *n* 毛毯

blaspheme *v* 亵渎

blasphemy *n* 亵渎

blast *n* 疾风，爆炸

blaze *v* 燃烧

bleach *v* 漂白

bleach *n* 漂白剂

bleak *adj* 荒凉的，萧瑟的

bleed *iv* 流血

bleeding *n* 出血

blemish *n* 污点

blemish *v* 玷污

blend *n* 混合

blend *v* 混合

blender *n* 搅拌机

bless *v* 祝福

blessed *adj* 被祝福的

blessing *n* 祝福

blind *v* 使盲目

blind *adj* 瞎的，盲目的

blindfold *n* 蒙眼物

blindfold *v* 蒙蔽

blindly *adv* 盲目地

blindness *n* 失明

blink *v* 眨眼，闪烁

bliss *n* 极乐

blissful *adj* 极乐的

blister *n* 水泡

blizzard *n* 大风雪，暴风雪

bloat *v* 膨胀

bloated *adj* 膨胀的

block *n* 街区，大块

block *v* 阻塞

blockade *v* 封锁

blockade *n* 封锁

blockage *n* 封锁

blond *adj* 金发的

blood *n* 血

bloodthirsty *adj* 嗜血的

bloody *adj* 血腥

B

bloom *v* 绽放
blossom *v* 开花
blot *n* 污点
blot *v* 污损，弄脏
blouse *n* 女衬衫
blow *n* 打击
blow *iv* 吹，打击
blow out *iv* 吹熄
blow up *iv* 爆炸
blowout *n* 爆裂
bludgeon *v* 用棍棒连续打，
　强迫
blue *adj* 蓝色的
blueprint *n* 蓝图
bluff *v* 虚张声势
blunder *n* 大错
blunt *adj* 直率的，钝的
bluntness *n* 直率，钝度
blur *v* 模糊
blurred *adj* 模糊的
blush *v* 脸红
blush *n* 脸红
boar *n* 公猪
board *n* 董事会，板
board *v* 上船，上车，登机
boast *v* 夸耀
boat *n* 船
bodily *adj* 肉体的，身体的
body *n* 身体
bog *n* 沼泽
bog down *v* 被耽搁，陷入困境
boil *v* 煮沸

boil down to *v* 归结到
boil over *v* 因沸溢出
boiler *n* 锅炉
boisterous *adj* 猛烈的，喧闹的
bold *adj* 大胆的
boldness *n* 大胆
bolster *v* 支撑，援助
bolt *n* 螺栓
bolt *v* 拴好
bomb *n* 炸弹
bomb *v* 轰炸
bombing *n* 轰炸
bombshell *n* 炸弹，意外事件
bond *n* 契约，有息债券
bondage *n* 奴役，束缚
bone *n* 骨
bone marrow *n* 骨髓
bonfire *n* 篝火
bonus *n* 奖金
book *n* 书
bookcase *n* 书架，书柜
bookkeeper *n* 记帐员
bookkeeping *n* 簿记
booklet *n* 小册子
bookseller *n* 书商
bookstore *n* 书店
boom *n* 景气
boom *v* 繁荣
boost *v* 推进，促进
boost *n* 推进，促进
boot *n* 靴
booth *n* 货摊，岗亭

booty *n* 赃物，战利品，缴获物

booze *n* 酒

border *n* 边境

border on *v* 接壤

borderline *n* 边界线

bore *v* 使枯燥

bored *adj* 无聊的

boredom *n* 无聊

boring *adj* 让人感觉无聊的

born *adj* 出生

borough *n* 自治的市镇，区

borrow *v* 借

bosom *n* 胸部，胸怀

boss *n* 老板

boss around *v* 颐指气使，把……呼来唤去

bossy *adj* 爱指挥他人的，跋扈的

botany *n* 植物学

botch *v* 笨拙地修补，糟蹋

both *adj* 两个

bother *v* 打搅

bothersome *adj* 令人讨厌的

bottle *n* 瓶

bottle *v* 装瓶

bottleneck *n* 瓶颈

bottom *n* 底部

bottomless *adj* 无底的

bough *n* 大树枝

boulder *n* 卵石，大圆石

boulevard *n* 林荫大道

bounce *v* 弹跳

bounce *n* 弹跳

bound *adj* 被束缚的，装订好的

bound for *adj* 前往

boundary *n* 边界

boundless *adj* 无限的

bounty *n* 慷慨，恩惠，宽大

bourgeois *adj* 中产阶级的

bow *n* 弓，虹，鞠躬

bow *v* 鞠躬

bow out *v* 退出

bowels *n* 肠

bowl *n* 碗

box *n* 盒子，箱子

box office *n* 票房，售票处

boxer *n* 拳击手

boxing *n* 拳击

boy *n* 男孩

boycott *v* 抵制

boyfriend *n* 男朋友

boyhood *n* 少年期

bra *n* 文胸

brace for *v* 做好准备

bracelet *n* 手镯

bracket *n* 托架

brag *v* 吹嘘

braid *n* 辫子

brain *n* 大脑

brainwash *v* 洗脑

brake *n* 制动器，刹车

brake *v* 制动，刹车

branch *n* 树枝，支流

branch office *n* 分支机构

branch out *v* 长出枝条，扩展范围

brand *n* 品牌

brand-new *adj* 全新

brandy *n* 白兰地

brat *n* 孩子，顽童

brave *adj* 勇敢的

bravely *adv* 勇敢地

bravery *n* 英勇

brawl *n* 争吵，打架

breach *n* 违约

bread *n* 面包

breadth *n* 宽度

break *n* 破裂，破碎，间隔，小憩

break *iv* 打破

break away *v* 突然离开，放弃，脱离

break down *v* 失败，故障

break free *v* 挣脱

break in *v* 闯入，打断

break off *v* 中断，断交突然停止

break open *v* 砸开

break out *v* 突发，突围

break up *v* 打碎，分裂，破裂，分手

breakable *adj* 会破的，易碎的

breakdown *n* 崩溃，故障

breakfast *n* 早餐

breakthrough *n* 突破

breast *n* 乳房

breath *n* 呼吸

breathe *v* 呼吸

breathing *n* 呼吸

breathtaking *adj* 激动人心的，惊人的，惊险的

breed *iv* 养育，繁殖

breed *n* 品种

breeze *n* 微风

brethren *n* 同胞，同堂，同会

brevity *n* 短暂，简洁

brew *v* 酿造

brewery *n* 啤酒厂

bribe *v* 行贿

bribe *n* 贿赂

bribery *n* 受贿，行贿，贿赂行为

brick *n* 砖头

bricklayer *n* 砖瓦工

bridal *adj* 新娘的，婚礼的

bride *n* 新娘

bridegroom *n* 新郎

bridesmaid *n* 伴娘

bridge *n* 桥

bridle *n* 马勒

brief *adj* 简短的，短暂的

brief *v* 作简报，节录，摘要

briefcase *n* 公事包

briefing *n* 简报

briefly *adv* 简短地

briefs *n* 短内裤

brigade *n* 旅

bright *adj* 明亮的，聪明的

brighten *v* 使明亮

B

brightness *n* 亮度
brilliant *adj* 灿烂的，有才气的
brim *n* 边缘
bring *iv* 带
bring back *v* 带回
bring down *v* 减少，推翻
bring up *v* 提出，培养
brink *n* 边缘
brisk *adj* 活泼的，敏锐的
Britain *n* 英国
British *adj* 英国的
brittle *adj* 脆弱的，冷淡的
broad *adj* 宽的，阔的
broadcast *v* 广播，播送
broadcast *n* 广播，播送
broadcaster *n* 广播电台，广播员，广播器
broaden *v* 加宽
broadly *adv* 宽广地，概括地
broadminded *adj* 心胸开阔的
brochure *n* 宣传册
broil *v* 烧烤
broiler *n* 烤器
broke *adj* 破产的
broken *adj* 坏掉的，断掉的
bronchitis *n* 支气管炎
bronze *n* 青铜
broom *n* 扫帚
broth *n* 肉汤
brothel *n* 妓院
brother *n* 兄弟
brotherhood *n* 兄弟关系

brother-in-law *n* 内兄，内弟，大伯子，小叔子，姐夫，妹夫
brotherly *adj* 兄弟的，兄弟般的
brow *n* 眉毛
brown *adj* 棕色的
browse *v* 浏览
browser *n* 浏览器
bruise *n* 碰伤，擦伤
bruise *v* 挫伤
brunch *n* 早午餐
brunette *adj* 浅黑色的
brush *n* 刷子
brush *v* 刷
brush aside *v* 刷去
brush up *v* 刷新，擦亮
brusque *adj* 唐突的，直率的
brutal *adj* 残忍的
brutality *n* 残忍的
brutalize *v* 残酷对待
brute *adj* 野兽，野兽般的
bubble *n* 泡沫
bubble gum *n* 泡泡糖
buck *n* 美元，雄鹿
bucket *n* 桶
buckle *n* 带扣
buckle up *v* 把……扣紧
bud *n* 芽，花蕾
buddy *n* 好友
budge *v* 稍微一动，动一动
budget *n* 预算
buffalo *n* 水牛
bug *n* 臭虫，小昆虫

build *iv* 建造，建设

builder *n* 建筑者，建设者，建筑工人

building *n* 建筑

buildup *n* 积累，聚积

built-in *adj* 内置的

bulb *n* 球茎，灯泡

bulge *n* 胀，膨胀

bulk *n* 大小，大批，体积

bulky *adj* 庞大的，体积大的，笨重的

bull *n* 公牛

bull fight *n* 斗牛

bull fighter *n* 斗牛士

bulldoze *v* 用推土机推

bullet *n* 子弹

bulletin *n* 简讯

bully *adj* 恃强凌弱者，恶霸

bulwark *n* 壁垒，防波堤

bum *n* 流浪汉，懒汉

bump *n* 撞击，肿块，表面隆起

bump into *v* 意外撞到

bumper *n* 保险杠

bumpy *adj* 颠簸的，崎岖不平的

bun *n* 小圆面包

bunch *n* 串，束，扎

bundle *n* 捆，包，束

bundle *v* 捆

bunk bed *n* 双层床

bunker *n* 燃料库，沙坑，煤仓，地下碉堡

buoy *n* 浮标

burden *n* 负担

burden *v* 负担

burdensome *adj* 沉重的，累赘的，难以负担的

bureau *n* 局

bureaucracy *n* 官僚主义

bureaucrat *n* 官僚

burger *n* 汉堡包

burglar *n* 窃贼

burglarize *v* 盗

burglary *n* 盗窃

burial *n* 埋葬，葬礼

burly *adj* 结实的，魁梧的

burn *iv* 烧

burn *n* 烧伤

burp *v* 打嗝

burp *n* 打嗝

burrow *n* 洞穴，藏身处

burst *iv* 爆炸，突发

burst into *v* 闯入，突然开始

bury *v* 埋葬

bus *n* 公共汽车

bus *v* 坐公交车

bush *n* 灌木

busily *adv* 忙碌地

business *n* 商务

businessman *n* 商人

bust *n* 半身像，胸部

bustling *adj* 活跃的，忙乱的

busy *adj* 忙碌的

but *c* 但是

butcher *n* 屠夫

B
C

butchery *n* 屠杀，屠场
butler *n* 男管家
butt *n* 靶子，屁股
butter *n* 黄油
butterfly *n* 蝴蝶
button *n* 按钮
buttonhole *n* 扣眼
buy *iv* 购买
buy off *v* 收买，贿赂
buyer *n* 买家，买方
buzz *n* 嗡嗡声，流言
buzz *v* 发出嗡嗡声
buzzard *n* 鹭
buzzer *n* 门铃，蜂鸣器
by *pre* 由
bye *e* 再见
bypass *n* 旁路，支路
bypass *v* 绕过
by-product *n* 副产物
bystander *n* 旁观者

C

cab *n* 驾驶室，出租车
cabbage *n* 大白菜
cabin *n* 客舱
cabinet *n* 内阁，储藏架
cable *n* 电缆

cafeteria *n* 自助餐厅
caffeine *n* 咖啡因
cage *n* 笼子
cake *n* 蛋糕
calamity *n* 灾难
calculate *v* 计算
calculation *n* 计算
calculator *n* 计算器
calendar *n* 日历
calf *n* 小牛
caliber *n* 口径，弹径
calibrate *v* 校准
call *n* 呼，呼喊，呼叫
call *v* 呼叫，呼喊
call off *v* 取消
call on *v* 拜访，请求，号召
call out *v* 出动，大声叫唤，
唤起
calling *n* 呼叫，召唤，职业
callous *adj* 冷酷无情的，麻木的
calm *adj* 平静的
calm *n* 平静
calm down *v* 冷静下来
calorie *n* 卡路里
calumny *n* 诽谤
camel *n* 骆驼
camera *n* 相机
camouflage *v* 伪装，掩饰
camouflage *n* 伪装，掩饰
camp *n* 野营，兵营，营地
camp *v* 扎营
campaign *v* 参加活动，作战

campaign *n* 战役，活动，运动

campfire *n* 篝火

can *iv* 能，能够，可以

can *v* 能，能够，可以

can *n* 罐头

can opener *n* 开罐器

canal *n* 运河

canary *n* 金丝雀

cancel *v* 取消

cancellation *n* 取消

cancer *n* 癌症

cancerous *adj* 癌症的，患癌的

candid *adj* 坦白的，率直的

candidacy *n* 候选资格

candidate *n* 候选人

candle *n* 蜡烛

candlestick *n* 烛台

candor *n* 公正

candy *n* 糖果

cane *n* 手杖，藤条

canister *n* 罐，筒

canned *adj* 罐装的

cannibal *n* 食人者，吃同类的动物

cannon *n* 大炮，加农炮，机关炮

canoe *n* 独木舟

canonize *v* 正式宣布（死者）为圣徒

cantaloupe *n* 香瓜，哈密瓜

canteen *n* 餐厅，食堂

canvas *n* 帆布，画布

canvas *v* 用帆布覆盖，用帆布装备

canyon *n* 峡谷

cap *n* 无边帽

capability *n* 能力

capable *adj* 有能力的，能干的

capacity *n* 容量，才能，能力

cape *n* 海角，披肩

capital *n* 资本，首都

capital letter *n* 大写字母

capitalism *n* 资本主义

capitalize *v* 资本化，利用

capitulate *v* 有条件投降，屈服

capsize *v* 弄翻，倾覆

capsule *n* 胶囊

captain *n* 队长，船长

captivate *v* 迷住，迷惑

captive *n* 俘虏

captivity *n* 囚禁

capture *v* 捕获

capture *n* 捕获

car *n* 汽车

carat *n* 克拉，开

caravan *n* 拖车，篷车，旅行队

carburetor *n* 化油器

carcass *n* 尸体

card *n* 卡

cardboard *n* 纸板

cardiac *adj* 心脏的

cardiac arrest *n* 心脏停跳

cardiology *n* 心脏病学

care *n* 注意，烦恼，照料

C

care v 关心
care about v 关心
care for v 关怀
career n 职业，生涯
carefree adj 无忧无虑的
careful adj 小心的，仔细的
careless adj 粗心的
carelessness n 粗心的
caress n 爱抚
caress v 爱抚
caretaker n 看守人，管理人
cargo n 货物
caricature n 漫画，讽刺画
caring adj 有爱心的
carnage n 大屠杀
carnal adj 肉体的，肉欲的
carnation n 康乃馨
carol n 颂歌，欢乐之歌
carpenter n 木匠
carpentry n 木匠业，木器，木工
carpet n 地毯
carriage n 马车，客车厢
carrot n 胡萝卜
carry v 携带，搬运
carry on v 进行
carry out v 执行
cart n 购物车
cart v 用车装载
cartoon n 卡通，漫画
cartridge n 弹药筒
carve v 雕刻

cascade n 小瀑布，串联
case n 案例，情况，案件
cash n 现金
cashier n 出纳员，收银员
casino n 赌场
casket n 首饰盒，棺材
casserole n 砂锅
cassock n 法衣，袈裟
cast iv 投，抛
castaway n 被抛弃的人
caste n 种姓制度，等级制度
castle n 城堡
casual adj 休闲的
casualty n 伤亡者
cat n 猫
cataclysm n 巨变，灾难
catacomb n 地下墓穴
catalog n 目录
catalog v 做目录
cataract n 大瀑布，白内障
catastrophe n 大灾难，大祸
catch iv 抓住
catch up v 赶上
catching adj 易传染的，迷人的，有魅力的
catchword n 标语，口号，流行语
catechism n 教义问答书，问答集
category n 类别
cater to v 迎合
caterpillar n 毛毛虫

C

cathedral *n* 大教堂
catholic *adj* 天主教的
Catholicism *n* 天主教
cattle *n* 牛
cauliflower *n* 菜花
cause *n* 原因，起因
cause *v* 引起
caution *n* 谨慎
cautious *adj* 谨慎的
cavalry *n* 骑兵，骑兵部队
cave *n* 洞
cave in *v* 塌陷
cavern *n* 大洞穴，巨窟
cavity *n* 洞室
cease *v* 停止
cease-fire *n* 停火
ceaselessly *adv* 不停地，持续地
ceiling *n* 天花板
celebrate *v* 庆祝
celebration *n* 庆祝
celebrity *n* 名人
celery *n* 芹菜
celestial *adj* 天的，天空的，天国的
celibacy *n* 独身，禁欲
celibate *adj* 独身的
cell phone *n* 手机
cellar *n* 地窖
cement *n* 水泥
cemetery *n* 公墓
censorship *n* 审查
censure *v* 责备

census *n* 普查
cent *n* 分
centenary *n* 百年纪念
center *n* 中心
center *v* 居中，使集中
centimeter *n* 厘米
central *adj* 中央的，中心的
centralize *v* 集中
century *n* 世纪
ceramic *n* 陶瓷
cereal *n* 谷物
cerebral *adj* 脑的，大脑的
ceremony *n* 仪式，典礼
certain *adj* 一定的，确定的，某
certainty *n* 确定性
certificate *n* 证书
certify *v* 认证
chagrin *n* 懊恼
chain *n* 链，连锁店
chain *v* 上链
chainsaw *n* 锯链
chair *n* 椅子
chair *v* 使入座，使就任要职
chairman *n* 主席
chalet *n* （瑞士的）木屋，小型度假屋
chalice *n* 杯，圣餐杯
chalk *n* 粉笔
chalkboard *n* 黑板
challenge *v* 挑战
challenge *n* 挑战
challenging *adj* 挑战性的

C

chamber n 室，枪膛，房间
champ n 冠军
champion n 冠军
champion v 保卫，拥护
chance n 机会
chancellor n 总理，首相，大臣，大法官
chandelier n 枝形吊灯
change v 改变
change n 改变
channel n 频道，渠道
chant n 圣歌，赞美诗，旋律
chaos n 混乱
chaotic adj 混乱的
chapel n 小礼拜堂
chaplain n 牧师
chapter n 章
char v 把……烧成炭灰
character n 性格，文字
characteristic adj 特有的，典型的
charade n 手势猜字
charbroil adj 用炭烧烤
charcoal n 木炭
charge v 索价，指控，充电
charge n 指控，冲锋，费用，电荷
charisma n 非凡的领导力，神授的能力，魄力
charismatic adj 神赐能力的，领袖魅力的
charitable adj 慈善的

charity n 慈善
charm v 吸引
charm n 魅力
charming adj 迷人的
chart n 图表
charter n 宪章
charter v 特许设立，发执照给
chase n 追
chase v 追
chase away v 驱赶
chasm n 深坑，裂口
chaste adj 贞洁的，正派的
chastise v 严惩，惩罚
chastisement n 严惩，惩罚
chastity n 贞洁
chat v 聊天
chauffeur n 司机
cheap adj 廉价的
cheat v 欺骗，作弊
cheater n 骗子
check n 支票
check v 检查
check in v 登记，报到
check up n 校对，检验
checkbook n 支票簿
cheek n 面颊
cheekbone n 颧骨
cheeky adj 厚颜无耻的
cheer v 欢呼
cheer up v 使振作
cheerful adj 快乐的
cheers n 干杯

C

cheese n 奶酪
chef n 厨师
chemical adj 化学的
chemist n 化学家
chemistry n 化学
cherish v 珍惜
cherry n 樱桃
chess n 国际象棋
chest n 胸口
chestnut n 板栗
chew v 嚼
chick n 小鸡
chicken n 鸡
chicken out v 退缩
chicken pox n 水痘
chide v 责备，责骂
chief n 领袖，领导，长官
chiefly adv 首要地
child n 儿童
childhood n 童年
childish adj 孩子气的
childless adj 无子女的
children n 儿童
chill n 冷
chill v 使寒心，冷冻
chill out v 冷静
chilly adj 寒冷的
chimney n 烟囱
chimpanzee n 黑猩猩
chin n 下巴
chip n 芯片，薯片
chisel n 凿子

chocolate n 巧克力
choice n 选择
choir n 合唱团
choke v 窒息，噎，阻塞
cholera n 霍乱
cholesterol n 胆固醇
choose iv 选择
choosy adj 挑剔的
chop v 剁
chop n 剁
chopper n 劈刀，斧头
chore n 家务杂事，零工
chorus n 合唱
christen v 洗礼
christening n 洗礼
Christian adj 基督的，基督教的
Christianity n 基督教
Christmas n 圣诞
chronic adj 慢性的
chronicle n 编年史
chronology n 年代学，年表
chubby adj 圆胖的
chuckle v 轻声地笑，暗自笑
chunk n 大块
church n 教堂
chute n 瀑布，斜道
cider n 苹果汁
cigar n 雪茄
cigarette n 香烟
cinder n 煤渣
cinema n 电影院
cinnamon n 肉桂

circle n 圈，圆圈

circle v 包围，环绕，盘旋

circuit n 电路

circular adj 圆的

circulate v 流通

circulation n 流通

circumcise v 割包皮，割阴蒂

circumcision n 割礼，割包皮

circumstance n 环境，事件，状况

circumstantial adj 偶然的，与情况有关的

circus n 马戏团

cistern n 水塔，蓄水池

citizen n 公民

citizenship n 公民身份

city n 城市

city hall n 市政厅

civic adj 市的，公民的，市民的

civil adj 公民的，民间的，国内的

civilization n 文明

civilize v 文明化

claim v 要求，声称

claim n 要求，声称

clam n 蛤蜊

clamor v 喧闹

clamp n 夹子，夹钳

clan n 氏族，党派，宗教

clandestine adj 秘密的，暗中的

clap v 拍手

clarification n 澄清

clarify v 澄清

clarinet n 单簧管

clarity n 明晰

clash v 冲突

clash n 冲突

class n 阶级，课，班

classic adj 经典的

classify v 分类

classmate n 同班同学

classroom n 教室

classy adj 上等的

clause n 子句，条款

claw n 爪

claw v 用爪子抓

clay n 粘土

clean adj 清洁的，干净的

clean v 清洁

cleaner n 清洁工

cleanliness n 洁净

cleanse v 清洗

cleanser n 清洁剂

clear adj 明确的

clear v 澄清

clearance n 清除

clear-cut adj 轮廓分明的

clearly adv 清楚地

clearness n 明亮，明晰

cleft n 裂缝

clemency n 仁慈，温和，宽厚

clench v 握紧

clergy n 神职人员

clergyman n 牧师

clerical *adj* 文书或办事员的

clerk *n* 文书，办事员

clever *adj* 聪明的

click *v* 点击

client *n* 客户

clientele *n* 客户

cliff *n* 悬崖

climate *n* 气候

climatic *adj* 气候的

climax *n* 高潮

climb *v* 爬

climbing *n* 攀登

clinch *v* 钉牢，紧抓，扭住对手，最终解决

cling *iv* 紧贴

clinic *n* 诊所

clip *v* 夹

clipping *n* 裁剪

cloak *n* 斗篷

clock *n* 时钟

clog *v* 阻塞

cloister *n* 修道院，回廊

clone *v* 克隆

cloning *n* 克隆

close *v* 关闭

close *adj* 靠近的，亲密的

close to *pre* 接近

closed *adj* 关闭的

closely *adv* 密切地

closet *n* 壁橱

closure *n* 关闭

clot *n* 凝块

cloth *n* 布

clothe *v* 穿衣

clothes *n* 衣服

clothing *n* 服装

cloud *n* 云

cloudless *adj* 无云的

cloudy *adj* 多云的

clown *n* 小丑

club *n* 俱乐部

club *v* 联合，协作，组成俱乐部

clue *n* 线索

clumsiness *n* 粗笨

clumsy *adj* 笨拙的

cluster *n* 串，群，丛

cluster *v* 丛生，成群

clutch *n* 离合器

coach *v* 辅导

coach *n* 教练

coaching *n* 训练

coagulate *v* 凝结

coagulation *n* 凝结物

coal *n* 煤

coalition *n* 联盟

coarse *adj* 粗糙的

coast *n* 海岸

coastal *adj* 海岸的，沿海的

coastline *n* 海岸线

coat *n* 大衣

coax *v* 哄骗

cob *n* 玉米棒

cobblestone *n* 鹅卵石

cobweb *n* 蜘蛛网

C

cocaine n 可卡因

cock n 公鸡

cockpit n 驾驶舱

cockroach n 蟑螂

cocktail n 鸡尾酒

cocky adj 狂傲的

cocoa n 可可粉

coconut n 椰子

cod n 鳕鱼

code n 代码

codify v 编成法典，编码

coefficient n 系数

coerce v 强制

coercion n 强迫，强制

coexist v 并存

coffee n 咖啡

coffin n 棺材

cohabit v 同居

coherent adj 连贯的

cohesion n 凝聚力

coin n 硬币

coincide v 同时发生

coincidence n 巧合

coincidental adj 巧合的

cold adj 冷的

coldness n 冷

colic n 绞痛

collaborate v 协作

collaboration n 协作

collaborator n 合作者

collapse v 崩溃

collapse n 崩溃

collar n 衣领

collarbone n 锁骨

collateral adj 并行的，并列的，附属的

colleague n 同事

collect v 收集

collection n 收藏

collector n 收藏家

college n 学院

collide v 碰撞

collision n 碰撞

cologne n 古龙香水

colon n 冒号，结肠

colonel n 上校

colonial adj 殖民的，殖民地的

colonization n 殖民

colonize v 拓殖

colony n 殖民地

color n 色彩

color v 上色

colorful adj 多彩的

colossal adj 巨大的

colt n 小马

column n 专栏，栏

coma n 昏迷

comb n 梳子

comb v 梳

combat n 战斗

combat v 战斗

combatant n 战斗员

combination n 组合

combine v 结合

combustible *n* 可燃物

combustion *n* 燃烧

come *iv* 来

come about *v* 发生

come across *v* 偶然碰到

come apart *v* 裂开

come back *v* 回来

come down *v* 下来，倒塌

come forward *v* 自告奋勇，提出

come from *v* z

come in *v* 进来

come out *v* 出来

come over *v* 过来，抓住

come up *v* 上升，出现

comeback *n* 恢复，复原

comedian *n* 喜剧演员

comedy *n* 喜剧

comet *n* 彗星

comfort *n* 舒适

comfortable *adj* 舒适的

comforter *n* 慰问者，羊毛围巾

comical *adj* 好笑的，滑稽的

coming *n* 来临

coming *adj* 就要来的，将来的

comma *n* 逗号

command *v* 命令，控制，指挥

commander *n* 指挥官

commandment *n* 戒律

commemorate *v* 纪念

commence *v* 开始

commend *v* 称赞，推荐，表扬

commendation *n* 称赞，推荐，表扬

comment *v* 评论

comment *n* 评论

commerce *n* 商业

commercial *adj* 商业的，商务的

commission *n* 佣金，委员会

commit *v* 委托，押往，犯罪

commitment *n* 托付，交托

committed *adj* 忠诚的，坚定的

committee *n* 委员会

common *adj* 共同的

commotion *n* 骚动，暴乱

communicate *v* 沟通，交流，通讯

communication *n* 沟通，交流，通讯

communion *n* 交流，共享

communism *n* 共产主义

communist *adj* 共产主义的

community *n* 社区

commute *v* 通勤

compact *adj* 紧密的，结实的，紧凑的，小巧的

compact *v* 压紧

companion *n* 同伴

companionship *n* 友谊，陪伴，伴侣关系

company *n* 公司，陪伴

comparable *adj* 可比的

comparative *adj* 比较的，相当的

C

compare v 比较
comparison n 比较
compartment n 区划，隔间
compass n 罗盘，圆规
compassion n 同情，怜悯
compassionate adj 有同情心的
compatibility n 兼容性
compatible adj 兼容的
compatriot n 同胞
compel v 迫使
compelling adj 强制的
compendium n 纲要
compensate v 补偿
compensation n 补偿，赔偿
compete v 竞争
competence n 胜任，能力，资格
competent adj 能干的
competition n 竞争
competitive adj 竞争的
competitor n 竞争对手
compile v 编写
complain v 抱怨
complaint n 投诉
complement n 补足物
complete adj 完整的
complete v 完成
completely adv 完全地
completion n 完成
complex adj 复杂的
complexion n 脸色
complexity n 复杂性

compliance n 服从
compliant adj 服从的
complicate v 复杂化
complication n 复杂，并发症
complicity n 同谋
compliment n 赞扬
complimentary adj 问候的，称赞的，免费赠送的
comply v 遵守
component n 组件，成分
compose v 作曲
composed adj 镇静的，沉着的
composer n 作曲家
composition n 组成，作文
compost n 混合物，堆肥
composure n 镇定
compound n 混合物，化合物，围场
compound v 增加，恶化，使化合
comprehend v 领会，理解
comprehensive adj 全面的
compress v 压缩
compression n 压缩
comprise v 包含，构成
compromise n 妥协
compromise v 妥协
compulsion n 强制
compulsive adj 强制的，强迫的
compulsory adj 被强制的，义务的
compute v 计算

computer *n* 计算机

comrade *n* 同志

con man *n* 骗子

conceal *v* 隐蔽，隐藏，隐瞒

concede *v* 让步

conceited *adj* 自负的

conceive *v* 构思

concentrate *v* 集中

concentration *n* 浓度，集中

concentric *adj* 同中心的

concept *n* 概念

conception *n* 概念

concern *v* 涉及，关系到

concern *n* 关注，关心，担心

concerning *pre* 关于

concert *n* 音乐会

concession *n* 特许，认可，让步

conciliate *v* 安抚，怀柔，驯服

conciliatory *adj* 安抚的，怀柔的

concise *adj* 简洁的

conclude *v* 结束，做结论

conclusion *n* 结束，结尾，结论

conclusive *adj* 决定性的，最后的，确实的

concoct *v* 调制，捏造

concoction *n* 调制，捏造

concrete *n* 水泥，混凝土

concrete *adj* 具体的

concur *v* 意见相同，一致

concurrent *adj* 并发的，一致的，协作的

concussion *n* 激动，震荡，冲击

condemn *v* 谴责，判刑，处刑，责备

condemnation *n* 谴责，非难

condensation *n* 压缩，液化，凝缩

condense *v* 浓缩，缩短，凝结

condescend *v* 谦逊，屈尊

condiment *n* 调味品

condition *n* 条件

conditional *adj* 有条件的，假定的

conditioner *n* 调节器，调理员

condo *n* 集合公寓

condolences *n* 哀悼

condone *v* 宽恕，赦免

conducive *adj* 有助的，有益的

conduct *n* 行为，指导，举动

conduct *v* 进行，传导

conductor *n* 指挥，导体

cone *n* 锥体

confer *v* 授予

conference *n* 会议

confess *v* 坦白

confession *n* 坦白

confessional *n* 忏悔室，告解室

confessor *n* 自白者，忏悔者

confidant *n* 密友

confide *v* 吐露，信托

confidence *n* 信心

confident *adj* 有信心的，有把握的

confidential *adj* 秘密的，机密的

confine v 限制，禁闭
confinement n 限制，禁闭
confirm v 确认
confirmation n 确认
confiscate v 没收
confiscation n 没收
conflict n 冲突
conflict v 冲突
conflicting adj 相矛盾的，冲突的
conform v 符合，遵守
conformist adj 因循守旧的
conformity n 一致性
confound v 混淆，挫败
confront v 使面对，遭遇，对抗
confrontation n 对抗，对峙
confuse v 搞乱，使糊涂
confusing adj 令人困惑的
confusion n 混乱，困惑
congenial adj 同性质的，意气相投的
congested adj 拥挤的
congestion n 拥挤，拥堵
congratulate v 祝贺
congratulations n 祝贺
congregate v 聚集，集合
congregation n 集合，会集，会众
congress n 国会
conjecture n 猜想
conjugal adj 结婚的，配偶的
conjugate v 结合，配合

conjunction n 连接词，关联，联合
conjure up v 使人脑海中浮现出，用魔术变出
connect v 连接
connection n 连接，关系
connive v 纵容
connote v 意味着，暗示
conquer v 征服
conqueror n 征服者
conquest n 征服
conscience n 良心
conscious adj 有意识的
consciousness n 意识
conscript n 征兵
consecrate v 奉献
consecration n 奉献
consecutive adj 连续的
consensus n 意见一致，共同看法，共识
consent v 同意
consent n 同意
consequence n 后果
consequent adj 必然的，当然的
conservation n 保存，守恒，保持
conservative adj 保守的
conserve v 保存，保藏
conserve n 防腐剂
consider v 考虑
considerable adj 可观的
considerate adj 体贴的

consideration *n* 考虑
consignment *n* 寄售
consist *v* 构成
consistency *n* 一致性
consistent *adj* 一致的
consolation *n* 慰藉
console *v* 安慰
consolidate *v* 巩固
consonant *n* 辅音
conspicuous *adj* 显著的，显眼的
conspiracy *n* 阴谋
conspirator *n* 共谋者
conspire *v* 密谋
constancy *n* 恒久
constant *adj* 持续的，坚持的
constellation *n* 星座
consternation *n* 震惊
constipate *v* 限制，使迟钝
constipated *adj* 患便秘症的
constipation *n* 便秘
constitute *v* 制定，构成
constitution *n* 宪法，构造
constrain *v* 强迫，抑制
constraint *n* 约束
construct *v* 建造
construction *n* 建设
constructive *adj* 建设性的
consul *n* 领事
consulate *n* 领事馆
consult *v* 咨询
consultation *n* 咨询

consume *v* 消费
consumer *n* 消费者
consumption *n* 消费
contact *v* 联系
contact *n* 联系
contagious *adj* 传染性的，会传播的
contain *v* 含有
container *n* 集装箱
contaminate *v* 污染
contamination *n* 污染
contemplate *v* 沉思
contemporary *adj* 当代的
contempt *n* 蔑视
contend *v* 竞争
contender *n* 竞争者
content *adj* 满意的
content *v* 使满意
contentious *adj* 好辩的，有争议的
contents *n* 目录
contest *n* 竞赛
contestant *n* 参赛者
context *n* 上下文，背景
continent *n* 洲，大陆
continental *adj* 洲的，大陆的
contingency *n* 偶然，偶发事件
contingent *adj* 偶然的
continuation *n* 延续
continue *v* 继续
continuity *n* 连续性
continuous *adj* 连续的

contour *n* 轮廓，等高线
contraband *n* 违禁品，走私品
contract *v* 订约，缩短
contract *n* 合同
contraction *n* 收缩
contradict *v* 与……矛盾，反驳
contradiction *n* 矛盾
contrary *adj* 相反的
contrast *v* 对比
contrast *n* 对比
contribute *v* 贡献
contribution *n* 贡献
contributor *n* 贡献者
contrition *n* 悔恨
control *n* 控制
control *v* 控制
controversial *adj* 引起争议的
controversy *n* 争议
convalescent *adj* 康复中的，调养的
convene *v* 召开
convenience *n* 方便
convenient *adj* 方便的
convent *n* 女修道院
convention *n* 大会，公约
conventional *adj* 常规的
converge *v* 聚合，连接
conversation *n* 交谈
converse *v* 交谈，谈话
conversely *adv* 相反地
conversion *n* 转换
convert *v* 转换

convert *n* 皈依者，改宗者
convey *v* 搬运，转让，传达
convict *v* 定罪
conviction *n* 信念
convince *v* 说服，使相信
convincing *adj* 使人信服的
convoluted *adj* 旋绕的，费解的
convoy *n* 护送，护卫
convulse *v* 使震动，使痉挛
convulsion *n* 痉挛
cook *v* 烹饪
cook *n* 厨师
cookie *n* 曲奇饼
cooking *n* 烹饪
cool *adj* 酷，冷
cool *v* 冷却
cool down *v* 降温，冷静
cooling *adj* 凉快的，冷淡的
coolness *n* 凉快，冷淡
cooperate *v* 合作
cooperation *n* 合作
cooperative *adj* 合作的
coordinate *v* 协调
coordination *n* 协调
coordinator *n* 协调员
cop *n* 警察
cope *v* 应付
copier *n* 复印机
copper *n* 铜
copy *v* 复制，拷贝
copy *n* 拷贝，复制，一份
copyright *n* 版权

cord *n* 绳子

cordial *adj* 诚恳的，亲切的

cordless *adj* 无绳的

cordon *n* 警戒线，防卫圈

cordon off *v* 封锁

core *n* 核心

cork *n* 软木塞

corn *n* 玉米

corner *n* 角落

cornerstone *n* 基石

cornet *n* 短号

corollary *n* 自然的结果，推断

coronary *adj* 冠的，冠状的，花冠的

coronation *n* 加冕

corporal *adj* 肉体的，个人的

corporal *n* 下士，圣餐布

corporation *n* 公司

corpse *n* 尸体

corpulent *adj* 肥胖的

corpuscle *n* 小体，微粒，光子，血球

correct *v* 纠正

correct *adj* 正确的

correction *n* 更正

correlate *v* 使互相关联，互相有关系

correspond *v* 符合，通信，协调

correspondent *n* 通讯记者，通信者

corresponding *adj* 相应的

corridor *n* 走廊

corroborate *v* 使坚固，确证

corrode *v* 腐蚀

corrupt *v* 腐败

corrupt *adj* 腐败的

corruption *n* 腐败

cosmetic *n* 化妆品

cosmic *adj* 宇宙的

cosmonaut *n* 宇航员

cost *iv* 花费

cost *n* 成本

costly *adj* 昂贵的

costume *n* 服饰

cottage *n* 村舍，小屋

cotton *n* 棉花

couch *n* 长沙发

cough *n* 咳嗽

cough *v* 咳嗽

council *n* 理事会

counsel *v* 劝告，提议

counsel *n* 律师，商议，劝告

counselor *n* 顾问，律师

count *v* 计数

count *n* 计数

countdown *n* 倒计时

countenance *n* 面容，支持，面部表情

counter *n* 计数器，柜台

counter *v* 反对，反驳

counteract *v* 抵消，阻碍，中和

counterfeit *v* 伪造，假装

counterfeit *adj* 假冒的，假装的

counterpart *n* 副本，配对物
countess *n* 伯爵夫人，女伯爵
countless *adj* 无数的
country *n* 国家，乡村
countryman *n* 同胞，乡下人
countryside *n* 农村
county *n* 县
coup *n* 政变
couple *n* 夫妇，两个
coupon *n* 优惠券
courage *n* 勇气
courageous *adj* 勇敢的
courier *n* 导游，信使
course *n* 课程，过程
court *n* 法院
court *v* 献殷勤，求爱
courteous *adj* 有礼貌的
courtesy *n* 礼仪
courthouse *n* 法院
courtship *n* 求爱
courtyard *n* 庭院
cousin *n* 堂兄弟姊妹，表兄弟姊妹
cove *n* 小海湾
covenant *n* 盟约
cover *n* 封面，盖子
cover *v* 盖住，包涵
cover up *v* 掩盖
coverage *n* 覆盖范围，新闻报导
covert *adj* 隐蔽的，偷偷摸摸的
cover-up *n* 企图掩盖

covet *v* 垂涎，渴望，贪图
cow *n* 奶牛
coward *n* 懦夫
cowardice *n* 懦弱，胆怯
cowardly *adv* 懦弱的，胆怯的
cowboy *n* 牛仔
cozy *adj* 舒适的
crab *n* 蟹
crack *n* 裂缝
crack *v* 爆裂
cradle *n* 摇篮
craft *n* 工艺，手艺
craftsman *n* 工匠
cram *v* 塞满
cramp *n* 夹钳
cramped *adj* 局促的
crane *n* 起重机
crank *n* 曲柄
cranky *adj* 胡思乱想的，发疯似的
crap *n* 拉屎，胡言
crappy *adj* 下贱的，品质低劣的
crash *n* 相撞
crash *v* 相撞
crass *adj* 粗鲁的
crater *n* 火山口
crave *v* 渴望
craving *n* 渴求
crawl *v* 爬
crayon *n* 蜡笔
craziness *n* 疯狂
crazy *adj* 疯狂的

creak *v* 发咯吱声
creak *n* 咯吱声
cream *n* 乳酪，面霜，奶油
creamy *adj* 奶油的
crease *n* 褶缝，褶痕
crease *v* 起褶痕
create *v* z
creation *n* 创造
creative *adj* 创意的
creativity *n* 创造力
creator *n* 创造者
creature *n* 人，创造物，动物
credibility *n* 可信度
credible *adj* 可信的
credit *n* 信用
creditor *n* 债权人
creed *n* 教义，信条
creek *n* 小溪
creep *v* 怕，蠕动
creepy *adj* 趴着走的，毛骨悚然的
cremate *v* 火葬
crematorium *n* 火葬场
crest *n* 冠，顶部，饰毛
crevice *n* 裂缝
crew *n* 全体船员，全体乘务员
crib *n* 婴儿床
cricket *n* 板球
crime *n* 犯罪
criminal *adj* 犯罪的
cripple *adj* 瘸子
cripple *v* 使瘫痪

crisis *n* 危机
crisp *adj* 脆的，清楚的
crispy *adj* 脆的
criss-cross *v* 十字交叉
criterion *n* 标准
critical *adj* 关键的
criticism *n* 批评
criticize *v* 批评
critique *n* 批评
crockery *n* 陶器
crocodile *n* 鳄鱼
crony *n* 密友
crook *n* 骗子，弯曲处
crooked *adj* 弯曲的
crop *n* 作物
cross *n* 使字架，混杂
cross *adj* 交错的
cross *v* 交错，越过
cross out *v* 划去
crossfire *n* 交火
crossing *n* 交叉，渡口，交叉点
crossroads *n* 十字路口
crosswalk *n* 人行横道
crossword *n* 纵横字谜
crouch *v* 蹲伏
crow *n* 乌鸦
crow *v* 啼，报晓
crowbar *n* 铁橇，起货钩，铁棍
crowd *n* 人群
crowd *v* 使拥挤
crowded *adj* 拥挤的
crown *n* 皇冠

crown v 加冕
crowning n 加冕
crucial adj 关键的
crucifix n 十字架
crucifixion n 在十字架上钉死
crucify v 在十字架上钉死
crude adj 天然的，粗糙的，未成熟的
cruel adj 残酷的，悲惨的
cruelty n 残酷
cruise v 巡航
crumb n 面包屑
crumble v 崩溃，破碎
crunchy adj 发嘎吱嘎吱声的，易碎的
crusade n 字军东侵，改革运动，宗教战争
crusader n 十字军战士，改革者
crush v 压碎
crushing adj 破碎的
crust n 外壳，面包皮
crusty adj 有硬壳的，脾气暴躁的，顽固的
crutch n 拐杖
cry n 叫声，大叫，哭声
cry v 哭，喊，叫
cry out v 痛哭，大声呼喊
crying n 叫声，大叫，哭声
crystal n 水晶
cub n 幼兽，年轻人
cube n 立方体
cubic adj 立方体的

cubicle n 小卧室
cucumber n 黄瓜
cuddle v 拥抱
cuff n 袖口，手铐
cuisine n 烹调风格，烹饪，烹调法
culminate v 到绝顶，达到高潮，达于极点
culpability n 苛责，有罪
culprit n 被控犯罪的人，罪犯，刑事被告
cult n 礼拜，祭仪，礼拜式
cultivate v 培养，耕作
cultivation n 耕作，耕种，养殖，栽培
cultural adj 修养的，文化的
culture n 文化，耕种，修养
cumbersome adj 讨厌的，累赘的，麻烦的
cunning adj 狡猾的，可爱的，巧妙的
cup n 杯
cupboard n 橱柜
curable adj 可治愈的
curator n 馆长
curb v 抑制，勒住，束缚
curb n 抑制，勒住，束缚
curdle v 凝结，变质，凝固
cure v 治愈
cure n 治愈
curfew n 晚钟，宵禁，戒严
curiosity n 好奇心

C
D

curious *adj* 好奇的
curl *v* 卷曲
curl *n* 卷曲
curly *adj* 卷曲的
currency *n* 货币
current *adj* 当前的
currently *adv* 目前
curse *v* 诅咒
curtail *v* 削减
curtain *n* 窗帘
curve *n* 曲线
curve *v* 弯曲
cushion *n* 垫子，靠垫，坐垫
cushion *v* 加垫褥，掩盖，缓冲
cuss *v* 乱骂，咒
custard *n* 蛋奶沙司
custodian *n* 看管人，监护人
custody *n* 监护，监禁，拘留
custom *n* 习惯，海关
customary *adj* 习惯的
customer *n* 顾客
custom-made *adj* 定做的
customs *n* 进口税，海关
cut *n* 削减，裁剪
cut *iv* 削减，剪，折断
cut back *v* 削减
cut down *v* 削减
cut off *v* 切断
cut out *v* 删去
cute *adj* 可爱的
cutlery *n* 刀，餐具，利器
cutter *n* 切割者，刀具

cyanide *n* 切割者，刀具
cycle *n* 周期
cyclist *n* 骑自行车的人
cyclone *n* 旋风
cylinder *n* 缸，圆筒
cynic *adj* 愤世嫉俗的
cynicism *n* 犬儒主义，冷嘲热讽，玩世不恭
cypress *n* 柏树
cyst *n* 囊肿
czar *n* 沙皇

D

dad *n* 爸爸
dagger *n* 短剑
daily *adv* 每日
dairy farm *n* 奶牛场
daisy *n* 雏菊
dam *n* 大坝
damage *n* 损坏
damage *v* 损坏
damaging *adj* 破坏性的
damn *v* 咒
damnation *n* 诅咒
damp *adj* 潮湿的
dampen *v* 使潮湿
dance *n* 舞蹈

D

dance v 舞蹈

dancing n 跳舞

dandruff n 头皮屑

danger n 危险

dangerous adj 危险的

dangle v 悬吊着或摆动不定

dare v 敢于

dare n 挑战，大胆，挑动

daring adj 大胆的

dark adj 黑暗的

darken v 变暗

darkness n 黑暗

darling adj 亲爱的

darn v 缝补

dart n 飞镖

dash v 猛冲，突进

dashing adj 活跃的，浮华的

data n 数据

database n 数据库

date n 日期

date v 约会，记日期

daughter n 女儿

daughter-in-law n 儿媳

daunt v 威吓

daunting adj 令人生畏的

dawn n 黎明

day n 天，日

daydream v 做白日梦

daze v 使茫然，使晕眩，发昏

dazed adj 目眩的，茫然的

dazzle v 使目眩，使眼花

dazzling adj 眼花缭乱的，耀眼的

deacon n 副主祭，公会会长，执事

dead adj 死的

dead end n 尽头，困境

deaden v 缓和，消除

deadline n 截止期限

deadlock adj 僵局

deadly adj 致命的

deaf adj 聋的

deafen v 使耳聋

deafening adj 震耳欲聋的

deafness n 聋，听不清

deal iv 应付，分配，处理，交易

deal n 交易

dealer n 经销商

dealings n 交往或关系

dean n 院长，主持牧师

dear adj 亲爱的

dearly adv 深深地，真挚地，昂贵地

death n 死亡

death toll n 死亡人数

death trap n 死亡陷阱

deathbed n 临死所卧之床，临终之时

debase v 贬低，降低

debatable adj 可争论的，未决定的，成问题的

debate v 辩论，争论，讨论

D

debate *n* 辩论，争论，讨论

debit *n* 借方，借

debrief *v* 询问执行任务的情况

debris *n* 碎片

debt *n* 债务

debtor *n* 债务人

debunk *v* 揭穿

debut *n* 首次露面，初次进入社交界

decade *n* 十年

decadence *n* 颓废

decaf *adj* 无咖啡因的

decapitate *v* 斩首

decay *v* 腐朽，腐烂，衰败

decay *n* 腐朽，腐烂，衰败

deceased *adj* 死去的

deceit *n* 欺骗

deceitful *adj* 骗人的

deceive *v* 欺骗

December *n* 十二月

decency *n* 得体，宽容，礼貌

decent *adj* 有分寸的，大方的，得体的

deception *n* 欺骗，诡计

deceptive *adj* 欺骗的

decide *v* 决定

deciding *adj* 决定性的，无疑的，果断的

decimal *adj* 十进位的，小数的

decimate *v* 成批杀死，大量毁灭

decipher *v* 破译

decision *n* 决定

decisive *adj* 决定性的，果断的，坚定的

deck *n* 甲板

declaration *n* 声明

declare *v* 申报，宣称

declension *n* 词尾变化，倾斜，格变化

decline *v* 下降，衰退，衰落，减少

decline *n* 下降，衰退，衰落，减少

decompose *v* 分解，使腐烂，被分解

décor *n* 装潢

decorate *v* 装饰

decorative *adj* 装饰的

decorum *n* 端庄得体

decrease *v* 减少

decrease *n* 减少

decree *n* 法令

decree *v* 下达法令

decrepit *adj* 衰老的

dedicate *v* 献，题献，致力

dedication *n* 奉献，献辞，致力

deduce *v* 推论，演绎出

deduct *v* 扣除

deductible *adj* 可扣除的

deduction *n* 减除，减除额，扣除

deed *n* 行为，契约

deem *v* 为，以为，视作

deep *adj* 深的

deepen *v* 深化

deer *n* 鹿

deface *v* 损伤外观，使失面子，丑化

defame *v* 诋毁

defeat *v* 打败

defeat *n* 失败

defect *n* 缺陷

defect *v* 逃跑，背叛，脱离

defection *n* 背叛，不履行义务，脱党

defective *adj* 有缺陷的，欠缺的

defend *v* 防护，防卫，辩护

defendant *n* 被告

defender *n* 防卫者，辩护者，拥护者

defense *n* 防守，国防

defenseless *adj* 无防御的

defer *v* 推迟

defiance *n* 蔑视，违抗，挑衅

defiant *adj* 违抗的，反抗的，藐视的

deficiency *n* 缺乏，不足

deficient *adj* 有缺陷的，不足的，缺乏的

deficit *n* 赤字

defile *v* 弄脏，损污，败坏

define *v* 定义，详细说明

definite *adj* 明确的

definition *n* 定义，清晰度，精确度

definitive *adj* 确切的

deflate *v* 放气，使缩小

deform *v* 变形

deformity *n* 畸形

defraud *v* 欺诈

defray *v* 支付

defrost *v* 除霜

deft *adj* 灵巧的

defuse *v* 除掉……的雷管，消除危险，缓和

defy *v* 藐视，挑衅，反抗

degenerate *v* 衰退，变坏，堕落

degenerate *adj* 衰退的，堕落的

degeneration *n* 退化

degradation *n* 降格，堕落，退化

degrade *v* 降低身份，有辱人格

degrading *adj* 有辱人格的

degree *n* 度数，程度，学位

dehydrate *v* 脱水

deign *v* 屈尊

deity *n* 神

dejected *adj* 沮丧的

delay *v* 延误

delay *n* 延误

delegate *v* 委派代表，授（权）给

delegate *n* 代表

delegation *n* 代表团

delete *v* 删除

deliberate *v* 深思熟虑

deliberate *adj* 故意的，深思熟虑的

delicacy *n* 精美，娇弱

delicate *adj* 易碎的，微妙的，精美的

delicious *adj* 美味的

delight *n* 喜悦

delight *v* 使喜悦

delightful *adj* 讨人喜欢的

delinquency *n* （少年）犯罪，失职

delinquent *adj* 有过失的，怠忽的，失职的

deliver *v* 投递交，发表

delivery *n* 投递，邮件，发送的货物

delude *v* 欺骗

deluge *n* 洪水

delusion *n* 错觉，谬见，妄想

deluxe *adj* 豪华的

demand *v* 要求，需要，询问

demand *n* 要求，需要

demanding *adj* 过分要求的，苛求的

demean *v* 贬低

demeaning *adj* 降低身份的，有辱人格的

demeanor *n* 行为，风度，举止

demented *adj* 疯狂的

demise *n* 死亡，转让房产

democracy *n* 民主

democratic *adj* 民主的

demolish *v* 拆毁

demolition *n* 破坏，拆除

demon *n* 恶魔

demonstrate *v* 论证，说明，示威游行

demonstrative *adj* 论证的，结论性的，明确的

demoralize *v* 使士气低落，使失去斗志

demote *v* 降级，降职

den *n* 兽穴，私室，秘密活动的场所

denial *n* 否认，拒绝

denigrate *v* 污蔑，诽谤

Denmark *n* 丹麦

denominator *n* 分母

denote *v* 意思是，表示，是…的标志

denounce *v* 谴责，指责

dense *adj* 密集的

density *n* 密度

dent *v* 弄凹，形成凹陷

dent *n* 缺口，凹痕

dental *adj* 牙齿的，牙科的

dentist *n* 牙医

dentures *n* 假牙

deny *v* 否认

deodorant *n* 除臭剂

depart *v* 离开，起程

department *n* 系，部门

departure *n* 出发

depend *v* 依靠

dependable *adj* 可靠的，可信赖的

dependence *n* 信赖，依赖

dependent *adj* 依赖的

depict *v* 描绘，描述

deplete *v* 耗尽，使枯竭

deplorable *adj* 应受谴责的，悲惨的

deplore *v.* 强烈反对，谴责

deploy *v* 部署

deployment *n* 部署

deport *v* 驱逐出境

deportation *n* 驱逐出境

depose *v* 废黜，罢免

deposit *n* 存款

depot *n* 仓库，栈房，火车或汽车站

deprave *adj* 使堕落，使恶化，使腐败

depravity *n* 堕落，恶习

depreciate *v* 贬值

depreciation *n* 折旧

depress *v* 压抑

depressing *adj* 令人沮丧的

depression *n* 抑郁，沮丧，不景气

deprivation *n* 剥夺

deprive *v* 剥夺

deprived *adj* 被剥夺的

depth *n* 深度

derail *v* 脱轨

derailment *n* 火车出轨

deranged *adj* 失常的

derelict *adj* 荒废的，遗弃的

deride *v* 嘲笑，愚弄

derivative *adj* adj. 引出的，系出的 n. 派生的事物

derive *v* 获取，得自，起源

derogatory *adj* 贬损的

descend *v* 下降，降临

descendant *n* 后裔

descent *n* 下降，下倾，斜坡

describe *v* 描述

description *n* 描述

descriptive *adj* 描述的

desecrate *v* 玷辱，亵渎

desegregate *v* 取消种族隔离

desert *n* 沙漠

desert *v* 遗弃，离弃，擅离职守

deserted *adj* 荒凉的

deserter *n* 逃犯（兵），逃亡者

deserve *v* 值得

deserving *adj* 值得的

design *n* 设计

designate *v* 指定

desirable *adj* 值得拥有的，可取的

desire *n* 渴望，愿望

desire *v* 渴望，向往

desist *v* 停止

desk *n* 服务台，桌子

desolate *adj* 荒凉

desolation *n* 荒凉

despair *n* 绝望

desperate *adj* 孤注一掷的，绝望的

despicable *adj* 卑劣的

despise *v* 鄙视

despite *c* 尽管

despondent *adj* 沮丧的

despot *n* 暴君

despotic *adj* 专制的，暴虐的

dessert *n* 甜品

destination *n* 目的地

destiny *n* 命运

destitute *adj* 贫困的

destroy *v* 摧毁

destroyer *n* 驱逐舰，破坏者

destruction *n* 破坏，毁灭

destructive *adj* 破坏性

detach *v* 使分离，拆卸，派遣

detachable *adj* 可拆卸的

detail *n* 详细

detail *v* 详述，详细说明

detain *v* 扣留

detect *v* 察觉，查明，侦查出

detective *n* 侦探

detector *n* 探测器

detention *n* 拘留

deter *v* 阻止，威慑

detergent *n* 洗涤剂

deteriorate *v* 恶化

deterioration *n* 恶化

determination *n* 决心

determine *v* 确定

deterrence *n* 威慑（力量、因素、物），震慑

detest *v* 憎恶

detestable *adj* 可憎的，令人厌恶的

detonate *v* 引爆

detonation *n* 爆炸（声）

detonator *n* 雷管

detour *n* 绕行的路，迂回路

detriment *n* 损害

detrimental *adj* 不利的

devaluation *n* 贬值

devalue *v* 贬值

devastate *v* 破坏

devastating *adj* 毁灭性的，令人震惊的

devastation *n* 毁灭

develop *v* 开发

development *n* 发展

deviation *n* 偏差

device *n* 装置

devil *n* 魔鬼

devious *adj* 不坦率的，狡猾的

devise *v* 设计，发明

devoid *adj* 全无的，缺乏的

devote *v* 献身

devotion *n* 奉献

devour *v* 吞食

devout *adj* 虔诚的

dew *n* 露水

diabetes *n* 糖尿病

diabetic *adj* 患糖尿病的，糖尿病患者

diabolical *adj* 恶毒的，狠毒的

diagnose v 诊断
diagnosis n 诊断
diagonal adj 对角线的，斜的
diagram n 图
dial n 拨号
dial v 拨号
dial tone n 拨号音
dialect n 方言
dialogue n 对话
diameter n 直径
diamond n 钻石
diaper n 尿布
diarrhea n 腹泻
diary n 日记
dice n 骰子
dictate v 口授，命令
dictator n 独裁者
dictatorial adj 独裁的
dictatorship n 专政
dictionary n 字典
die v 死
die out v 灭亡
diet n 饮食
differ v 不同于
difference n 差别
different adj 不同的
difficult adj 困难的
difficulty n 困难
diffuse v 扩散，传播
dig iv 挖
digest v 消化
digestion n 消化

digestive adj 消化的
digit n 数字
dignify v 使有尊严
dignitary n 权贵，高官，高僧
dignity n 庄严，尊严
digress v 偏离主题
dike n 堤防
dilapidated adj 破旧的，荒废的，毁坏的
dilemma n 困境
diligence n 勤奋
diligent adj 勤奋的，努力的
dilute v 稀释，冲淡
dim adj 昏暗的，朦胧的
dim v （使）暗淡，（使）模糊
dime n （美国、加拿大的）1分铸币
dimension n 方面，特点，尺寸
diminish v 变少，变小，降低
dine v 吃晚饭
diner n 吃饭的客人
dining room n 饭厅
dinner n 晚宴
dinosaur n 恐龙
diocese n 省（罗马帝国的行政区划），大主教管区
diphthong n 双元音
diploma n 文凭
diplomacy n 外交
diplomat n 外交官
diplomatic adj 外交的，老练的
dire adj 可怕的

direct *adj* 直接的

direct *v* 对准，指导

direction *n* 方向

director *n* 主任，导演

directory *n* 目录

dirt *n* 尘，土，污垢

dirty *adj* 肮脏的，下流的

disability *n* 残疾

disabled *adj* 残废

disadvantage *n* 不利，不利条件，损害

disagree *v* 不同意

disagreeable *adj* 不愉快的，厌恶的

disagreement *n* 不一致，争论

disappear *v* 消失

disappearance *n* 消失

disappoint *v* 使失望

disappointing *adj* 令人失望的

disappointment *n* 失望

disapproval *n* 不赞成

disapprove *v* 不赞成

disarm *v* 解除武装，裁军

disarmament *n* 缴械，裁军

disaster *n* 灾难，大祸

disastrous *adj* 灾难性的

disband *v* 解散

disbelief *n* 不相信，怀疑

disburse *v* 支付

discard *v* 抛弃

discern *v* 看出，察觉出，识别

discharge *v* 释放，排出，放电

discharge *n* 释放，排出，放电

disciple *n* 门徒

discipline *n* 纪律，学科

disclaim *v* 否认

disclose *v* 披露

discomfort *n* 不适，不安，困难

disconnect *v* 断开

discontent *adj* 不满

discontinue *v* 停止

discord *n* 不和，冲突

discordant *adj* 不一致的，不调和的

discount *n* 折扣

discount *v* 打折

discourage *v* 使泄气，劝阻

discouragement *v* 挫折，气馁

discouraging *adj* 令人泄气的

discourtesy *n* 无礼

discover *v* 发现

discovery *n* 发现

discredit *v* 败坏...的名声，怀疑

discreet *adj* 谨慎的

discrepancy *n* 相差，差异

discretion *n* 谨慎

discriminate *v* 歧视

discrimination *n* 歧视

discuss *v* 讨论

discussion *n* 讨论

disdain *n* 鄙视

disease *n* 疾病

disembark *v* 下船

disenchanted *adj* 不再抱幻想的，不再着迷的

disentangle v 解开

disfigure v 损毁（外貌），使丑陋

disgrace n 耻辱

disgrace v 耻辱

disgraceful adj 可耻的

disgruntled adj 不悦的

disguise v 乔装

disguise n 乔装

disgust n 厌恶，憎恶，反感

disgusting adj 令人厌恶的

dish n 碟子，菜

dishearten v 气馁

dishonest adj 不诚实

dishonesty n 不诚实，不法行为

dishonor n 耻辱

dishonorable adj 不光彩的

dishwasher n 洗碗机

disillusion n 觉醒，幻灭

disinfect v 消毒

disinfectant v 消毒剂

disinherit v 剥夺继承权

disintegrate v 瓦解

disintegration n 解体

disinterested adj 公正的

disk n 磁盘

dislike v 讨厌

dislike n 讨厌

dislocate v 错位

dislodge v 逐出，取出

disloyal adj 不忠的

disloyalty n 不忠

dismal adj 暗淡

dismantle v 拆除

dismay n 惊愕，沮丧

dismay v 使沮丧

dismiss v 辞退，解散

dismissal n 解雇

dismount v 卸下

disobedience n 不服从，违（反）抗

disobedient adj 不服从的

disobey v 违抗

disorder n 混乱，凌乱，骚乱

disorganized adj 紊乱的，无组织的

disoriented adj 分不清方向或目标的，无判断力的

disown v 声明断绝关系，否认

disparity n 不同，差异

dispatch v 分派，派遣

dispel v 驱散

dispensation n 分配，施与

dispense v 分配，分发，配（药）

dispersal n 疏散

disperse v 驱散

displace v 取代

display n 显示器，展示

display v 显示

displease v 使不高兴

displeasing adj 令人不悦的

displeasure n 不高兴，不快

disposable adj 可任意处理的，可支配的

disposal n 处置
dispose v 处置
disprove v 反证
dispute n 争端
dispute v 争端
disqualify v 取消
disregard v 不理会，漠视
disrepair n 失修，塌毁
disrespect n 不敬
disrespectful adj 不敬的
disrupt v 中断
disruption n 中断
dissatisfied adj 不满意
disseminate v 传播
dissent v 异议
dissident adj 有异议的，不同意的
dissimilar adj 不相似
dissipate v 消散
dissolute adj 放荡的，无节制的
dissolution n 解散，溶解
dissolve v 解散
dissonant adj 不和谐的，不协调的
dissuade v 劝阻
distance n 距离
distant adj 遥远的
distaste n 厌恶
distasteful adj 令人厌恶的
distill v 蒸馏
distinct adj 不同的，清楚的，明确的

distinction n 差别，区分，优秀
distinctive adj 有区别的，有特色的
distinguish v 区分
distort v 扭曲
distortion n 扭曲
distract v 分心
distraction n 分心
distraught adj 烦扰的
distress n 痛苦，忧虑，不幸
distress v 使痛苦（忧虑）
distressing adj 痛心
distribute v 分发
distribution n 分发，分配，分布
district n 区
distrust n 不信任
distrust v 不信任
distrustful adj 不信任的
disturb v 打扰
disturbance n 干扰
disturbing adj 令人不安
disunity n 不团结
disuse n 废弃
ditch n 沟
dive v 跳水，潜水
diver n 潜水员
diverse adj 多样
diversify v 多样化
diversion n 转移，转向，消遣
diversity n 多样性
divert v 分流

divide v 分开

dividend n 红利，股息

divine adj 神的

diving n 潜水

divinity n 神性，神

divisible adj 可分开的

division n 司，部门

divorce n 离婚

divorce v 离婚

divorcee n 离婚的女人

divulge v 泄露

dizziness n 头晕

dizzy adj 头晕的，眩晕的

do iv 做

docile adj 温顺的

docility n 温顺

dock n 船坞

dock v 靠船坞，扣除

doctor n 医生，博士

doctrine n 学说，教义，主义

document n 文件

documentary n 纪录片

documentation n 文件

dodge v 回避，逃避

dog n 狗

dogmatic adj 教条化

dole out v 少量地发放

doll n 洋娃娃

dollar n 美元

dolphin n 海豚

dome n 圆屋顶，穹顶

domestic adj 国内，家庭内部的

domesticate v 驯化

dominate v 支配，控制，占优势

domination n 支配，控制，统治

domineering adj 专制的

dominion n 统治，支配，控制

donate v 捐赠

donation n 捐赠

donkey n 驴

donor n 赠与人，捐赠人

doom n 厄运

doomed adj 注定的

door n 门

doorbell n 门铃

doorstep n 门阶

doorway n 门口

dope n 浓液，涂料，毒品

dope v 给某人吃或打兴奋剂

dormitory n 寝室

dosage n 剂量

dossier n 人事档案

dot n 点

double adj 双

double v 翻两倍

double-check v 复核，重新审查

double-cross v 出卖

doubt n 怀疑

doubt v 怀疑

doubtful adj 可疑的

dough n 面团，钱的俗称

dove *n* 鸠

down *adv* 向下（的），在下面

down payment *n* 预付定金，分期付款

downcast *adj* 垂头丧气

downfall *n* 下台

downhill *adv* 下坡

downpour *n* 倾盆大雨

downsize *v* 减小

downstairs *adv* 楼下

down-to-earth *adj* 脚踏实地

downtown *n* 市中心

downtrodden *adj* 被践踏的，被压制的

downturn *adj* 低迷

dowry *n* 嫁妆

doze *n* 瞌睡

doze *v* 打瞌睡

dozen *n* 十二个

draft *n* 草案

draft *v* 起草

draftsman *n* 绘图员

drag *v* 拖曳

dragon *n* 龙

drain *v* 流失

drainage *n* 排水系统，下水道，排水

dramatic *adj* 戏剧性的

dramatize *v* 戏剧化

drape *n* 悬垂

drastic *adj* 猛烈的

draw *n* 凹道，抽签

draw *iv* 绘画，引起

drawback *n* 缺点

drawer *n* 抽屉

drawing *n* 绘画

dread *v* 恐惧

dreaded *adj* 可怕的

dreadful *adj* 可怕

dream *iv* 梦见

dream *n* 梦

dress *n* 着装

dress *v* 着装

dresser *n* 服装员，碗柜

dressing *n* 敷料

dried *adj* 烘干的

drift *v* 漂移

drift apart *v* 失去联络

drifter *n* 漂流物，流浪者

drill *v* 演练，钻

drill *n* 演练，钻子

drink *iv* 喝

drink *n* 饮料

drinkable *adj* 可饮用的

drinker *n* 饮者

drip *v* 滴灌

drip *n* 滴灌

drive *n* 驱动

drive *iv* 驱动，开车

drive at *v* 径向

drive away *v* 逼走

driver *n* 司机

driveway *n* 车道

drizzle *v* 下毛毛雨

D

drizzle *n* 毛毛雨

drop *n* 辍学，一滴

drop *v* 辍学，放下

drop in *v* 来访

drop off *v* 放下

drop out *v* 辍学

drought *n* 旱灾

drown *v* 溺死

drowsy *adj* 昏昏欲睡

drug *n* 药物

drug *v* 用药物，拖

drugstore *n* 药店

drum *n* 鼓

drunk *adj* 醉

drunkenness *n* 醉酒

dry *v* 烘干

dry *adj* 干的

dry-clean *v* 干洗

dryer *n* 烘干机

dual *adj* 双的

dubious *adj* 半信半疑的

duchess *n* 公爵夫人，女公爵

duck *n* 鸭子

duck *v* 逃避，粘

duct *n* 管，输送管，排泄管

due *adj* 到期

duel *n* 决斗

dues *n* 应得物

duke *n* 公爵

dull *adj* 枯燥无味

duly *adv* 妥当地

dumb *adj* 沉默寡言，迟钝的

dummy *n* 傀儡，假人，仿制品

dummy *adj* 虚拟的，假的，虚构的

dump *v* 倾卸，倾倒，倾销

dump *n* 垃圾场

dung *n* 牛粪

dungeon *n* 地牢

dupe *v* 欺骗

duplicate *v* 复制，复印，重复

duplication *n* 重复，复制

durable *adj* 耐用的

duration *n* 期限

during *pre* 在期间

dusk *n* 黄昏

dust *n* 灰尘

dusty *adj* 多灰尘

Dutch *adj* 荷兰的

duty *n* 税，职责

dwarf *n* 矮子

dwell *iv* 纠缠，居住

dwelling *n* 住宅

dwindle *v* 缩小

dye *v* 给...染色

dye *n* 染料

dying *adj* 临终的

dynamic *adj* 动态的，生动的

dynamite *n* 黄色炸药，引起轰动的人（或物）

dynasty *n* 王朝

E

each *adj* 每

each other *adj* 对方

eager *adj* 渴望的

eagerness *n* 渴望

eagle *n* 雄鹰

ear *n* 耳朵

earache *n* 耳痛

eardrum *n* 鼓膜

early *adv* 早

earmark *v* 打上耳号，加上记号，指定

earn *v* 赚

earnestly *adv* 认真的

earnings *n* 盈利

earphones *n* 耳机

earring *n* 耳环

earth *n* 地球

earthquake *n* 地震

earwax *n* 耳蜡

ease *v* 缓解

ease *n* 舒适

easily *adv* 容易地

east *n* 东方

eastbound *adj* 东面

Easter *n* 复活节

eastern *adj* 东方的

easterner *n* 东方人

eastward *adv* 向东

easy *adj* 容易的

eat *iv* 吃

eat away *v* 侵蚀

eavesdrop *v* 偷听

ebb *v* 退潮，落潮，减少

eccentric *adj* 古怪的，怪癖的，异乎寻常的

echo *n* 回声

eclipse *n* 月食

ecology *n* 生态学

economical *adj* 经济实惠

economize *v* 节约

economy *n* 经济

ecstasy *n* 狂喜

ecstatic *adj* 欣喜若狂

edge *n* 边缘

edgy *adj* 锋利

edible *adj* 可食的

edifice *n* 大厦

edit *v* 编辑

edition *n* 版本

educate *v* 教育

educational *adj* 教育的

eerie *adj* 怪诞的，可怕的，奇异的

effect *n* 结果，影响

effective *adj* 有效的

effectiveness *n* 效力

efficiency *n* 效率

efficient *adj* 高效率

effigy *n* 肖像

effort *n* 努力，尝试

effusive *adj* 热情洋溢

egg *n* 鸡蛋

egg white *n* 蛋清

egoism *n* 利己主义

egoist *n* 利己的

eight *adj* 八

eighteen *adj* 十八

eighth *adj* 第八

eighty *adj* 八十

either *adj* 其中一个

either *adv* 要么

eject *v* 弹出

elapse *v* （时间）消逝，过去

elastic *adj* 有弹性的

elated *adj* 兴高采烈

elbow *n* 肘，（衣服的）肘部

elder *n* 长辈

elderly *adj* 老人

elect *v* 选出

election *n* 选举

electric *adj* 电动的，电的

electrician *n* 电工

electricity *n* 电力

electrify *v* 电气化

electrocute *v* 触电

electronic *adj* 电子

elegance *n* 优雅

elegant *adj* 优雅的

element *n* 元素，要素，成分

elementary *adj* 初级的

elephant *n* 大象

elevate *v* 提升，晋升，举起

elevation *n* 高度，晋升，高尚

elevator *n* 电梯

eleven *adj* 十一

eleventh *adj* 第十一

eligible *adj* 有资格的

eliminate *v* 消除

elm *n* 榆树

eloquence *n* 口才

else *adv* 否则

elsewhere *adv* 别处

elude *v* 逃避

elusive *adj* 难懂的，难捉摸的

emaciated *adj* 瘦弱

emanate *v* 发出

emancipate *v* 解放

embalm *v* 涂香油

embark *v* 上船（或飞机等），
（on）着手，开始工作

embarrass *v* 使尴尬

embassy *n* 大使馆

embellish *v* 美化

embers *n* 炭烬

embezzle *v* 盗用，挪用

embitter *v* 加苦味

emblem *n* 会徽

embody *v* 体现

emboss *v* 装饰

embrace *v* 拥抱，包围

embrace *n* 拥抱

embroider *v* 刺绣

embroidery *n* 刺绣

embroil *v* 波及

embryo *n* 胚胎

emerald *n* 绿宝石

emerge *v* 出现

emergency *n* 紧急

emigrant *n* 移民

emigrate *v* 移民

emission *n* 废气排放

emit *v* 喷出

emotion *n* 情感

emotional *adj* 有情感的

emperor *n* 皇帝

emphasis *n* 重点

emphasize *v* 强调

empire *n* 帝国

employ *v* 雇用，用，使用

employee *n* 雇员

employer *n* 雇主

employment *n* 就业

empress *n* 女皇

emptiness *n* 空虚

empty *adj* 空的

empty *v* 使空的

enable *v* 使

enchant *v* 迷惑

enchanting *adj* 迷人的

encircle *v* 包围

enclave *n* 飞地，被包围的领土

enclose *v* 附寄

enclosure *n* 围场，（信的）附件

encompass *v* 包含

encounter *v* 遇到

encounter *n* 遇到

encourage *v* 鼓励

encroach *v* 侵犯

encyclopedia *n* 百科全书

end *n* 完

end *v* 完结

end up *v* 结果

endanger *v* 危害

endeavor *v* 努力，尽力，尝试

endeavor *n* 努力，尽力，尝试

ending *n* 结尾

endless *adj* 不尽的

endorse *v* 赞同，签名于…背面

endorsement *n* 背书

endure *v* 忍受

enemy *n* 敌人

energetic *adj* 精力充沛

energy *n* 能源，精力

enforce *v* 强制执行

engage *v* 从事，订婚

engaged *adj* 忙碌的，使用中的，订婚了的

engagement *n* 参与，订婚

engine *n* 发动机

engineer *n* 工程师

England *n* 英格兰

English *adj* 英国的

engrave *v* 雕刻

engraving *n* 雕刻

engrossed *adj* 全神贯注的

engulf *v* 吞没

enhance *v* 提高，增加，加强

enjoy *v* 享受

enjoyable *adj* 愉快

enjoyment *n* 享受

enlarge *v* 放大

enlargement *n* 扩大

enlighten *v* 启迪

enlist *v* 赢得，征募

enormous *adj* 巨大

enough *adv* 足够

enrage *v* 激怒

enrich *v* 丰富

enroll *v* 报名

enrollment *n* 招生，报名

ensure *v* 确保

entail *v* 使承担，使成为必要

entangle *v* 纠缠

enter *v* 进入

enterprise *n* 企业

entertain *v* 娱乐

entertaining *adj* 娱乐的

entertainment *n* 娱乐

enthrall *v* 吸引

enthralling *adj* 吸引的

enthuse *v* 使热心

enthusiasm *n* 热情

entice *v* 诱惑

enticement *n* 诱惑

enticing *adj* 诱惑的

entire *adj* 整个

entirely *adv* 完全地

entrance *n* 入口

entreat *v* 哀求

entree *n* 进入，入场许可

entrenched *adj* 根深蒂固

entrepreneur *n* 企业家

entrust *v* 委托

entry *n* 参赛的人（物），进入，入口处

enumerate *v* 列举

envelop *v* 包围

envelope *n* 信封

envious *adj* 嫉妒的

environment *n* 环境

envisage *v* 设想

envoy *n* 特使

envy *n* 羡慕，嫉妒

envy *v* 羡慕，嫉妒

epidemic *n* 流行病

epilepsy *n* 癫痫病

episode *n* 插曲，集

epistle *n* 书信

epitaph *n* 墓志铭

epitomize *v* 代表

epoch *n* 世纪

equal *adj* 平等

equality *n* 平等

equate *v* 等同

equation *n* 方程

equator *n* 赤道

equilibrium *n* 平衡

equip *v* 装备

equipment *n* 设备

equivalent *adj* 同等的

era *n* 时代

eradicate *v* 根除

erase v 抹掉
eraser n 橡皮擦，擦除器
erect v 竖立
erect adj 笔直的
err v 犯错
errand n 差事
erroneous adj 错误的
error n 差错
erupt v 喷发，爆发
eruption n 喷发
escalate v 升级
escalator n 自动扶梯
escapade n 越轨行为，恶作剧
escape v 逃跑，逃避
escort n 护送
esophagus n 食道
especially adv 尤其
espionage n 间谍活动
essay n 杂文
essence n 本质
essential adj 根本的
establish v 建立
estate n 地产
esteem v 自尊
estimate v 估计
estimation n 估计
estranged adj 疏远的
estuary n 出海口
eternity n 永恒
ethical adj 有道德的
ethics n 道德
etiquette n 礼仪

euphoria n 幸福感
Europe n 欧洲
European adj 欧洲的
evacuate v 疏散
evade v 逃避，回避
evaluate v 评价
evaporate v 蒸发
evasion n 逃避
evasive adj 逃避的，难以捉摸的
eve n 前夕
even adj 均匀的
even if c 即使
even more c 更
evening n 晚上
event n 事件，大事，比赛项目
eventuality n 不测的事，可能
性，可能发生的事
eventually adv 最终
ever adv 曾经
everlasting adj 永恒的
every adj 每
everybody pro 人人
everyday adj 天天
everyone pro 人人
everything pro 一切
evict v 驱逐
evidence n 证据
evil n 邪恶，罪恶
evil adj 邪恶的
evoke v 呼应
evolution n 演变
evolve v 演变，（使）进化

exact *adj* 确切的
exaggerate *v* 夸大
exalt *v* 赞美，擢升
examination *n* 考试
examine *v* 审核
example *n* 举例
exasperate *v* 激怒
excavate *v* 挖掘
exceed *v* 超过
exceedingly *adv* 非常，极其
excel *v* 超越
excellence *n* 卓越
excellent *adj* 优秀的
except *pre* 除了
exception *n* 例外
exceptional *adj* 特殊
excerpt *n* 节录
excess *n* 过量，过度，超越
excessive *adj* 过多的，过分的
exchange *v* 交换
excite *v* 使兴奋
excitement *n* 兴奋
exciting *adj* 令人振奋
exclaim *v* 惊叹
exclude *v* 排除
excruciating *adj* 极痛苦的
excursion *n* 游览
excuse *v* 找借口
excuse *n* 借口
execute *v* 执行
executive *n* 主管，行政官，行政部门

exemplary *adj* 模范
exemplify *v* 举例证明
exempt *adj* 豁免
exemption *n* 豁免
exercise *n* 练习
exercise *v* 练习
exert *v* 施加
exertion *n* 努力，行使，活动
exhaust *v* 排气，消耗
exhausting *adj* 精疲力尽
exhaustion *n* 精疲力尽
exhibit *v* 显示（出），展出
exhibition *n* 展览
exhilarating *adj* 令人振奋
exhort *v* 力劝，勉励
exile *v* 流亡
exile *n* 流亡
exist *v* 存在
existence *n* 存在
exit *n* 出境
exodus *n* 大批的离去
exonerate *v* 免除，证明无罪
exorbitant *adj*（价格等）过高的，过分的
exorcist *n* 驱魔人
exotic *adj* 异国情调
expand *v* 扩大
expansion *n* 扩大
expect *v* 期望
expectancy *n* 预期
expectation *n* 期望
expediency *n* 权宜之计

expedient *adj* 适当的，权宜的
expedition *n* 远征
expel *v* 驱逐
expenditure *n* 支出
expense *n* 费用
expensive *adj* 昂贵的
experience *n* 经验，体验
experiment *n* 实验
expert *adj* 专家
expiate *v* 赎罪，补偿
expiation *n* 赎罪，补偿
expiration *n* 过期
expire *v* 到期
explain *v* 解释
explicit *adj* 明确
explode *v* 爆炸
exploit *v* 剥削，利用
exploit *n* 功绩，英勇行为
exploitation *n* 开发利用
explore *v* 探索
explorer *n* 探险家
explosion *n* 爆炸
explosive *adj* 易爆的
export *v* 出口
expose *v* 揭露
exposed *adj* 暴露在外的
express *n* 快递
expression *n* 表达
expressly *adv* 明确地
expropriate *v* 征用
expulsion *n* 开除
exquisite *adj* 精致的

extend *v* 延长
extension *n* 延长
extent *n* 程度，范围，限度
extenuating *adj* 情有可原的，使（罪行）减轻的
exterior *adj* 外部的，外面的，外表的
exterminate *v* 灭绝
external *adj* 外部的
extinct *adj* 绝迹的
extinguish *v* 灭绝
extort *v* 敲诈
extortion *n* 敲诈，勒索
extra *adv* 额外的
extract *v* 减去
extradite *n* 引渡
extradition *n* 引渡
extraneous *adj* 不相干的
extravagance *n* 奢侈
extravagant *adj* 奢侈的
extreme *adj* 极端
extremist *adj* 极端主义者，过激分子
extremities *n* 四肢
extricate *v* 解救
extroverted *adj* 外向的
exude *v* 流出，渗出
exult *v* 狂喜
eye *n* 眼睛
eyebrow *n* 眉毛
eye-catching *adj* 引人注目的，耀眼的

E

E
F

eyeglasses *n* 眼镜
eyelash *n* 睫毛
eyelid *n* 眼睑
eyesight *n* 视力
eyewitness *n* 目击者，见证人

F

fable *n* 寓言
fabric *n* 织物
fabricate *v* 杜撰
fabulous *adj* 极好的，极为巨大的，寓言中的
face *n* 脸
face up to *v* 面对
facet *n* 小平面，方面，刻面
facilitate *v* 便利
facing *pre* 面对
fact *n* 事实
factor *n* 因素
factory *n* 工厂
factual *adj* 事实
faculty *n* 能力，学院，教职工
fad *n* 时尚
fade *v* 淡出
faded *adj* 褪色
fail *v* 失败
failure *n* 失败

faint *v* 晕倒
faint *n* 晕倒
faint *adj* 晕倒
fair *n* 游乐场，集市，博览会
fair *adj* 公平
fairness *n* 公平
fairy *n* 童话
faith *n* 信仰
faithful *adj* 忠诚
fake *v* 假冒
fake *adj* 假冒的
fall *n* 秋天
fall *iv* 坠落
fall back *v* 退回
fall behind *v* 落后
fall down *v* 倒下
fall through *v* 落空，成为泡影
fallacy *n* 谬论
fallout *n* 非预期的收获，散落，放射性沉降[物]
falsehood *n* 虚假
falsify *v* 弄虚
falter *v* 犹豫
fame *n* 名利
familiar *adj* 熟悉
family *n* 家庭
famine *n* 饥荒
famous *adj* 著名
fan *n* 风扇，迷
fanatic *adj* 狂热
fancy *adj* 爱好，想象力，设想
fang *n* 犬齿

fantastic *adj* 神奇

fantasy *n* 幻想

far *adv* 远

faraway *adj* 远方

farce *n* 闹剧

fare *n* 票价

farewell *n* 告别

farm *n* 农场

farmer *n* 农民

farming *n* 耕作

farmyard *n* 农家场院

farther *adv* 更远

fascinate *v* 令人着迷

fashion *n* 时尚

fashionable *adj* 流行的，符合时尚的

fast *adj* 快

fasten *v* 紧固

fat *n* 脂肪

fat *adj* 胖

fatal *adj* 致命

fate *n* 命运

fateful *adj* 注定的

father *n* 父亲

fatherhood *n* 父权

father-in-law *n* 岳父

fatherly *adj* 象父亲般

fathom out *v* 理解，解释，领会

fatigue *n* 疲劳

fatten *v* 育肥

fatty *adj* 肥腻

faucet *n* 水龙头

fault *n* 缺点，错误，故障

faulty *adj* 错误的

favor *n* 好感，赞同，好事

favorable *adj* 有利

favorite *adj* 最爱

fear *n* 恐惧

fearful *adj* 可怕

feasible *adj* 可行

feast *n* 盛宴

feat *n* 壮举

feather *n* 羽毛

feature *n* 特点，专题

February *n* 二月

fed up *adj* 厌倦

federal *adj* 联邦

fee *n* 费用

feeble *adj* 软弱

feed *iv* 喂（养），向…提供

feedback *n* 反馈

feel *iv* 感觉

feeling *n* 感觉

feelings *n* 感情

feet *n* 脚

feign *v* 假装

fellow *n* 家伙

fellowship *n* 奖学金

felon *n* 重犯

felony *n* 重罪

female *n* 雌性动物，女子

feminine *adj* 女性的

fence *n* 围栏

F

fencing *n* 击剑

fend *v* 防卫

fend off *v* 避免

fender *n* 挡泥板

ferment *v* 发酵

ferment *n* 发酵

ferocious *adj* 凶猛

ferocity *n* 凶残

ferry *n* 渡船，渡口

fertile *adj* 肥沃

fertility *n* 生育

fertilize *v* 施肥，使肥沃，使丰富

fervent *adj* 热情的，强烈的，炎热的

fester *v* 溃烂

festive *adj* 节日

festivity *n* 节日

fetid *adj* 恶臭

fetus *n* 胎儿

feud *n* 宿怨

fever *n* 发烧

feverish *adj* 发烧

few *adj* 少数

fewer *adj* 更少

fiancé *n* 未婚夫

fiber *n* 纤维

fickle *adj* 变幻无常

fiction *n* 小说

fictitious *adj* 虚构

fiddle *n* 欺诈，小提琴

fidelity *n* 保真度

field *n* 场，田地

fierce *adj* 激烈

fiery *adj* 火热

fifteen *adj* 十五

fifth *adj* 第五

fifty *adj* 五十

fifty-fifty *adv* 对半

fig *n* 无花果，一点儿

fight *iv* 打斗

fight *n* 战斗

fighter *n* 战斗者，战斗机

figure *n* 数字，身材

figure out *v* 想出，理解，明白

file *v* 提交档案

file *n* 档案

fill *v* 填补

filling *n* 装填

film *n* 电影

filter *n* 滤波器

filter *v* 过滤

filth *n* 污物

filthy *adj* 污秽

fin *n* 鱼翅

final *adj* 最后

finalize *v* 把（计划，稿件等）最后定下来，定案

finance *v* 贷款

financial *adj* 金融

find *iv* 找到

find out *v* 找出

fine *n* 罚款

fine *v* 罚款

fine *adv* 美妙

fine *adj* 好

fine print *n* 小字

finger *n* 手指

fingernail *n* 指甲

fingerprint *n* 指纹

fingertip *n* 指尖

finish *v* 完成

Finland *n* 芬兰

Finnish *adj* 芬兰的

fire *v* 开火

fire *n* 火

firearm *n* 枪械

firecracker *n* 爆竹

firefighter *n* 消防队员

fireman *n* 消防员

fireplace *n* 壁炉

firewood *n* 柴火

fireworks *n* 烟花

firm *adj* 坚定

firm *n* 公司

firmness *n* 坚定性

first *adj* 第一

fish *n* 鱼

fisherman *n* 渔夫

fishy *adj* （味道或气味）象鱼的，可疑的

fist *n* 拳头

fit *n* 一阵

fit *v* 适合

fitness *n* 健身

fitting *adj* 适合的

five *adj* 五

fix *v* 修理

fjord *n* 峡湾

flag *n* 旗

flagpole *n* 旗杆

flamboyant *adj* 浮夸

flame *n* 火焰

flammable *adj* 易燃

flank *n* 侧翼

flare *n* 火光

flare-up *n* 燃起

flash *n* 闪光

flashlight *n* 手电筒

flashy *adj* 华丽

flat *n* 公寓

flat *adj* 平

flatten *v* 压平

flatter *v* 谄媚

flattery *n* 奉承，谄媚的举动

flaunt *v* 标榜

flavor *n* 风味

flaw *n* 瑕疵

flawless *adj* 无瑕疵

flea *n* 跳蚤

flee *iv* 逃亡

fleece *n* 羊毛·一次剪得的羊毛，羊毛状物

fleet *n* 舰队

fleeting *adj* 暂短

flesh *n* 骨肉

flex *v* 弯曲，伸缩

flexible *adj* 灵活

flicker v 闪烁
flier n 飞行者，传单
flight n 飞行，航班
flimsy adj 脆弱
flip v 倒
flirt v 调情
float v 浮
flock n 群
flog v 鞭打
flood v 发洪水
floodgate n 闸门
flooding n 溢流，淹没
floodlight n 泛光灯
floor n 地板
flop n 拍击声
floss n 丝棉，丝线
flour n 面粉
flourish v 蓬勃发展
flow v 流
flow n 流
flower n 花
flowerpot n 花盆
flu n 流感
fluctuate v 波动，涨落
fluently adv 流利
fluid n 流体
flunk v 不及格
flush v 冲水
flute n 长笛
flutter v 颤振
fly iv 飞
fly n 苍蝇

foam n 泡沫
focus n 焦点
focus on v 以...为焦点，集中于
foe n 仇敌
fog n 雾
foggy adj 多雾的
foil v 阻止
fold v 叠
folder n 文件夹
folks n 乡亲
folksy adj 亲切
follow v 跟从
follower n 追随者
folly n 蠢事
fond adj 喜欢
fondle v 爱抚
fondness n 喜欢
food n 食品
foodstuff n 食品
fool v 愚弄
fool adj 傻子，笨蛋
foolproof adj 极简单
foot n 脚
football n 足球
footnote n 脚注
footprint n 足迹
footstep n 脚步
footwear n 鞋类
for pre 为
forbid iv 禁止
force n 武力，暴力，力量
force v 强迫

forceful *adj* 有力

forcibly *adv* 强行

forecast *iv* 预测

forefront *n* 前列

foreground *n* （图画，景物等的）前景，最突出的地位

forehead *n* 前额

foreign *adj* 外国的

foreigner *n* 外国人

foreman *n* 工头

foremost *adj* 首要

foresee *iv* 预见

foreshadow *v* 预示

foresight *n* 远见

forest *n* 森林

foretaste *n* 预见

foretell *v* 预知

forever *adv* 永远

forewarn *v* 预警

foreword *n* 前言

forfeit *v* 弃权

forge *v* 伪造

forgery *n* 伪造

forget *v* 忘记

forgivable *adj* 可以原谅

forgive *v* 原谅

forgiveness *n* 宽恕

fork *n* 叉

form *n* 形式，表格

formal *adj* 正式的

formality *n* 正式

formalize *v* 正规化

formally *adv* 正式地

format *n* 格式

formation *n* 形成

former *adj* 前

formerly *adv* 原

formidable *adj* 强大

formula *n* 公式

forsake *iv* 抛弃

fort *n* 炮台

forthcoming *adj* 即将到来的

forthright *adj* 直率的（地），直截了当的

fortify *v* 坚定

fortitude *n* 坚忍不拔

fortress *n* 堡垒

fortunate *adj* 幸运

fortune *n* 财富

forty *adj* 四十

forward *adv* 前进

fossil *n* 化石

foster *v* 收养，培养，促进

foul *adj* 犯规

foundation *n* 基础，基金会

founder *n* 创始人

foundry *n* 铸造，铸造车间

fountain *n* 喷泉

four *adj* 四

fourteen *adj* 十四

fourth *adj* 第四

fox *n* 狐狸

foxy *adj* 狡猾

fraction *n* 分数

F

F

fracture _n_ 裂缝，裂痕，折断

fragile _adj_ 脆弱

fragment _n_ 片段

fragrance _n_ 香水

fragrant _adj_ 芬芳的

frail _adj_ 虚弱

frailty _n_ 脆弱

frame _n_ 框架

frame _v_ 框，陷害

framework _n_ 框架

France _n_ 法国

franchise _n_ 特许经销权，
  选举权，特权

frank _adj_ 坦率

frankly _adv_ 坦白地

frankness _n_ 坦率

frantic _adj_ 疯狂

fraternal _adj_ 互助

fraternity _n_ 全体同行，同人，
  男大学生联谊会

fraud _n_ 诈骗

fraudulent _adj_ 欺诈

freckle _n_ 雀斑

freckled _adj_ 有雀斑

free _v_ 释放

free _adj_ 免费

freedom _n_ 自由

freeway _n_ 高速公路

freeze _iv_ 冻结

freezer _n_ 冷冻机

freezing _adj_ 冻结

freight _n_ 货运

French _adj_ 法国的

frenetic _adj_ 狂热

frenzied _adj_ 疯狂的，狂暴的

frenzy _n_ 疯狂

frequency _n_ 频率

frequent _adj_ 频繁

frequent _v_ 时常发生的，频繁的

fresh _adj_ 新鲜

freshen _v_ 变得新鲜

freshness _n_ 新鲜

friar _n_ 男修道士

friction _n_ 摩擦

Friday _n_ 星期五

fried _adj_ 油炸

friend _n_ 朋友

friendship _n_ 友谊

fries _n_ 薯条

frigate _n_ 护航舰，大型驱逐舰

fright _n_ 恐惧

frighten _v_ 吓唬

frightening _adj_ 可怕

frigid _adj_ 寒冷

fringe _n_ 边缘

frivolous _adj_ 轻佻

frog _n_ 青蛙

from _pre_ 从

front _n_ 前面

front _adj_ 前面的

frontage _n_ 正面

frontier _n_ 边界，边境

frost _n_ 霜冻

frostbite _n_ 冻伤

frostbitten *adj* 冻伤的
frosty *adj* 冷淡的
frown *v* 皱眉
frozen *adj* 冻结
frugal *adj* 俭朴
frugality *n* 节俭
fruit *n* 水果
fruitful *adj* 多产的，富有成效的
fruity *adj* 果味的
frustrate *v* 挫败
frustration *n* 沮丧
fry *v* 油炸
frying pan *n* 煎锅
fuel *n* 燃料
fuel *v* 加燃料（油），刺激
fugitive *n* 逃亡者
fulfill *v* 完成
fulfillment *n* 履行，实现，完成
full *adj* 满满的，饱的
fully *adv* 充分
fumes *n* 油烟
fumigate *v* 熏
fun *n* 有趣
function *n* 功能
fund *n* 基金
fund *v* 给...拨款
fundamental *adj* 基本的
funds *n* 基金
funeral *n* 葬礼
fungus *n* 真菌
funny *adj* 搞笑
fur *n* 皮草

furious *adj* 愤怒
furiously *adv* 愤怒地
furnace *n* 熔炉
furnish *v* 装备
furnishings *n* 设备，陈设品
furniture *n* 家具
furor *n* 狂怒
furrow *n* 犁沟
furry *adj* 毛茸茸
further *adv* 进一步
furthermore *adv* 此外
fury *n* 愤怒
fuse *n* 保险丝
fusion *n* 联合，合并
fuss *n* 小题大做
fussy *adj* 挑剔
futile *adj* 徒劳
futility *n* 徒劳
future *n* 未来
fuzzy *adj* 模糊

F
G

G

gadget *n* 小工具
gag *n* 箝口物，笑话，恶作剧
gag *v* 塞住口部，遏制言论
gage *v* 测量
gain *v* 获得

G

gain *n* 获得，收益

gal *n* 加仑

galaxy *n* 银河

gale *n* 烈风

gall bladder *n* 浩大

gallant *adj* 胆囊

gallery *n* 画廊

gallon *n* 加仑

gallop *v* 疾驰，飞奔

gallows *n* 绞架

galvanize *v* 电镀，激励

gamble *v* 赌

game *n* 游戏

gang *n* 帮会

gangrene *n* 坏疽

gangster *n* 匪徒

gap *n* 差距

garage *n* 车库

garbage *n* 垃圾

garden *n* 花园

gardener *n* 园丁

gargle *v* 漱口

garland *n* 花环，奖品

garlic *n* 大蒜

garment *n* 服装

garnish *v* 装饰

garnish *v* 装饰

garrison *n* 驻军

garrulous *adj* 伶牙俐齿

garter *n* 袜带

gas *n* 燃气

gash *n* 伤口

gasoline *n* 汽油

gasp *v* 喘气

gastric *adj* 胃的

gate *n* 门

gather *v* 聚会

gathering *n* 聚会

gauge *v* 测量

gauze *n* 沙布，薄纱

gaze *v* 凝视

gear *n* 齿轮，车档

geese *n* 鹅

gem *n* 宝石

gender *n* 性别

gene *n* 基因

general *n* 一般

generalize *v* 一概而论

generate *v* 产生

generation *n* 一代人（或产品），产生

generator *n* 发电机

generic *adj* 通用

generosity *n* 慷慨

genetic *adj* 遗传

genial *adj* 温暖

genius *n* 天才

genocide *n* 种族灭绝

genteel *adj* 上流社会的

gentle *adj* 温柔

gentleman *n* 绅士

gentleness *n* 温柔

genuflect *v* 屈膝，跪拜

genuine *adj* 真实的，真正的

geography *n* 地理学

geology *n* 地质学

geometry *n* 几何

germ *n* 毒菌，胚芽

German *adj* 德国的

Germany *n* 德国

germinate *v* 发芽

gerund *n* 动名词

gestation *n* 妊娠

gesticulate *v* 做手势表达

gesture *n* 姿势

get *iv* 获得

get along *v* 相处

get away *v* 脱身

get back *v* 取回

get by *v* 通过

get down *v* 下来，写下，趴下

get down to *v* 开始，着手

get in *v* 进

get off *v* 下车

get out *v* 出去

get over *v* 渡过

get together *v* 相聚

get up *v* 起床

geyser *n* 喷泉

ghastly *adj* 阴森，可怕

ghost *n* 鬼

giant *n* 巨人

gift *n* 礼品，才能

gifted *adj* 有才能的

gigantic *adj* 巨型

giggle *v* 嘻笑

gimmick *n* 聪明之举

ginger *n* 生姜

gingerly *adv* 小心谨慎地

giraffe *n* 长颈鹿

girl *n* 女孩

girlfriend *n* 女友

give *iv* 给予

give away *v* 赠送

give back *v* 给回

give in *v* 让步

give out *v* 让出

give up *v* 放弃

glacier *n* 冰川

glad *adj* 高兴

gladiator *n* 角斗士

glamorous *adj* 璀璨

glance *n* 一瞥

glance *n* 一瞥

gland *n* 腺

glare *n* 眩光

glass *n* 玻璃

glasses *n* 眼镜

glassware *n* 玻璃器皿

gleam *n* 微光

gleam *v* 照耀

glide *v* 滑翔

glimmer *n* 微光

glimpse *n* 一瞥

glimpse *v* 闪亮，闪烁

glitter *v* 闪烁

globe *n* 地球

globule *n* 小球，小珠，水珠

G

G

gloom n 忧愁
gloomy adj 灰暗
glorify v 赞美
glorious adj 光荣
glory n 荣耀
gloss n 光泽
glossary n 词汇
glossy adj 亮泽
glove n 手套
glow v 焕发
glucose n 葡萄糖
glue n 胶水
glue v 胶粘
glut n 供过于求，过量
glutton n 暴饮暴食者
gnaw v 啃
go iv 去
go ahead v 继续
go away v 走开
go back v 回去
go down v 下来
go in v 参加
go on v 继续
go out v 出去
go over v 复习
go through v 经历
go under v 失败
go up v 上升
goad v 刺激，激励
goal n 目标
goalkeeper n 守门员
goat n 山羊

gobble v 吞并
God n 上帝
goddess n 女神
godless adj 无神论
goggles n 护目镜
gold n 黄金
golden adj 金（黄）色的，
　金的，金制的
good adj 好
good-looking adj 好看的
goodness n 善
goods n 商品
goodwill n 友好，亲善，信誉
goof v 闲混，犯错误，做蠢事
goof n 愚蠢的人，愚蠢的错误
goose n 鹅
gorge n 峡谷
gorgeous adj 华丽
gorilla n 大猩猩
gory adj 血淋淋
gospel n 福音
gossip v 说闲话
gossip n 闲话
gout n 痛风
govern v 统治，治理，管理
government n 政府
governor n 总督，州长
gown n 袍子
grab v 抓
grace n 宽限期，优雅
graceful adj 优雅的
gracious adj 殷勤

grade *n* 等级，成绩

gradual *adj* 循序渐进

graduate *v* 毕业

graduation *n* 毕业

graft *v* 嫁接，移植，<美>贪污

graft *n* 移植，嫁接，贪污

grain *n* 粮食

gram *n* 克

grammar *n* 语法

grand *adj* 宏伟

grandchild *n* 祖孙

granddad *n* 爷爷，外公

grandfather *n* 爷爷，外公

grandmother *n* 奶奶，祖母

grandparents *n* 祖父母

grandson *n* 孙子，外孙

grandstand *n* 看台

granite *n* 花岗岩

granny *n* 奶奶

grant *v* 赠款，授予

grant *n* 赠款

grape *n* 葡萄

grapefruit *n* 柚子，柚子树

grapevine *n* 葡萄

graphic *adj* 图解

grasp *n* 把握

grasp *v* 把握

grass *n* 草

grassroots *adj* 基层

grateful *adj* 感谢

gratify *v* 满足

gratifying *adj* 可喜的，令人满足的

gratitude *n* 感谢

gratuity *n* 酬金

grave *adj* 严重

grave *n* 坟墓

gravel *n* 砾石

gravely *adv* 严重

gravestone *n* 墓碑

graveyard *n* 墓园

gravitate *v* 受吸引，下沉，重力吸引

gravity *n* 重力

gravy *n* 肉汁，轻易得来的钱

gray *adj* 灰色的

grayish *adj* 灰色的，灰白的，阴沉的

graze *v* 吃草

graze *n* 吃草

grease *v* 润滑

grease *n* 润滑脂，油腻

greasy *adj* 油腻

great *adj* 大的，伟大的，好极的

greatness *n* 伟大

Greece *n* 希腊

greed *n* 贪婪

greedy *adj* 贪心

Greek *adj* 希腊的

green *adj* 绿色

green bean *n* 绿豆

greenhouse *n* 温室

Greenland *n* 格陵兰

greet *v* 迎接

greetings *n* 问候

G

gregarious *adj* 群居

grenade *n* 手榴弹

greyhound *n* 长腿猎狗

grief *n* 悲痛

grievance *n* 委屈

grieve *v* 伤心

grill *v* 烧烤

grill *n* 烧烤

grim *adj* 严峻

grimace *n* 鬼脸

grime *n* 污秽物

grind *iv* 磨碎

grip *v* 抓

grip *n* 抓

gripe *n* 牢骚

grisly *adj* 恐怖

groan *v* 呻吟

groan *n* 呻吟

groceries *n* 杂货

groin *n* 腹股沟

groom *n* 新郎

groove *n* 槽

gross *adj* 总的，显著的，粗俗的

grossly *adv* 非常，很，下流地

grotesque *adj* 怪诞

grotto *n* 洞穴

grouch *v* 不满

grouchy *adj* 不满的

ground *n* 地面

ground floor *n* 一楼，地面层

groundless *adj* 无根据

groundwork *n* 地基

group *n* 小组

grow *iv* 成长

grow up *v* 长大

growl *v* 咆哮

grown-up *n* 成人

growth *n* 增长

grudge *n* 不满，怨恨，妒嫉

grudgingly *adv* 吝惜地

grueling *adj* 伤脑筋

gruesome *adj* 令人毛骨悚然

grumble *v* 发牢骚

grumpy *adj* 脾气坏

guarantee *v* 保证

guarantee *n* 保证

guarantor *n* 担保人

guard *n* 后卫

guardian *n* 监护人

guerrilla *n* 游击队

guess *v* 猜

guess *n* 猜

guest *n* 客人

guidance *n* 指导

guide *v* 指导

guide *n* 指南

guidebook *n* 指南

guidelines *n* 指导方针，准则

guild *n* 行会，同业公会

guile *n* 欺骗

guillotine *n* 断头台

guilt *n* 罪恶感

guilty *adj* 内疚的，有罪的

guise *n* 假装

guitar *n* 吉他
gulf *n* 海湾
gull *n* 海鸥
gullible *adj* 轻信
gulp *v* 一大口
gulp *n* 一大口
gulp down *v* 一大口下来
gum *n* 口香糖
gun *n* 枪
gun down *v* 开枪打伤，枪杀
gunfire *n* 枪声
gunman *n* 枪手
gunpowder *n* 火药
gunshot *n* 枪弹
gust *n* 阵风
gusto *n* 爱好，兴致勃勃
gusty *adj* 强劲
gut *n* 肠
guts *n* 胆量
gutter *n* 排水沟
guy *n* 家伙
guzzle *v* 痛饮
gymnasium *n* 健身房
gynecology *n* 妇科
gypsy *n* 吉普赛人

H

habit *n* 习惯
habitable *adj* 可居住
habitual *adj* 惯性
hack *v* 黑客入侵
haggle *v* 讨价还价
hail *n* 冰雹
hail *v* 下冰雹
hair *n* 头发
hairbrush *n* 毛刷
haircut *n* 理发
hairdo *n* 发型，发式
hairdresser *n* 美发师
hairpiece *n* 假发，假眉毛
hairy *adj* 多毛的
half *n* 一半
half *adj* 一半
hall *n* 大厅
hallucinate *v* 幻觉
hallway *n* 走道
halt *v* 停止
halve *v* 对分
ham *n* 火腿
hamburger *n* 汉堡包
hamlet *n* 村庄
hammer *n* 锤
hammock *n* 吊床
hand *n* 手
hand down *v* 把…传下去
hand in *v* 交给

G
H

hand out v 发给
hand over v 移交
handbag n 手袋
handbook n 手册
handcuff v 上手拷
handcuffs n 手铐
handful n 一小撮
handgun n 手枪
handicap n （身体或智力的）缺陷，障碍
handkerchief n 手帕
handle v 处理
handle n 门把
handmade adj 手工制作
handout n 施舍
handrail n 扶手
handshake n 握手
handsome adj 英俊
handwriting n 书写
handy adj 得心应手，手巧的
hang iv 悬挂，吊，吊死
hang around v 流连
hang on v 坚持
hang up v 挂断电话
hanger n 心烦
hang-up n 吊架
happen v 发生
happening n 发生
happiness n 幸福
happy adj 快乐
harass v 骚扰
harassment n 骚扰

harbor n 海港，港口
hard adj 硬，困难的
harden v 磨砺
hardly adv 几乎不
hardness n 硬度
hardship n 困难
hardware n 硬件
hardwood n 硬木
hardy adj 强壮
hare n 野兔
harm v 伤害，损害
harm n 伤害，损害
harmful adj 有害
harmless adj 无害
harmonize v 协调
harmony n 和谐
harp n 竖琴
harpoon n 鱼叉
harrowing adj 痛苦的
harsh adj 苛刻
harshly adv 严厉
harshness n 苛刻
harvest n 丰收
harvest v 丰收
hashish n 大麻
hassle v 烦扰
hassle n 困难，争吵
haste n 匆匆
hasten v 催促
hastily adv 匆匆
hasty adj 仓促
hat n 帽子

hatchet *n* 斧头

hate *v* 恨

hateful *adj* 可恨

hatred *n* 仇恨

haughty *adj* 傲慢

haul *v* 拖拉

haunt *v* 常出没于，使苦恼，萦绕

have *iv* 有

have to *v* 必须

haven *n* 避风港

havoc *n* 肆虐

hawk *n* 鹰

hay *n* 干草

haystack *n* 干草堆

hazard *n* 危险

hazardous *adj* 危险的

haze *n* 阴霾

hazelnut *n* 榛子

hazy *adj* 朦胧

he *pro* 他

head *n* 头部

head for *v* 出发

headache *n* 头痛

heading *n* 标题

head-on *adv* 迎头，迎面

headphones *n* 耳机

headquarters *n* 总部

headway *n* 进展

heal *v* 愈合

healer *n* 愈疗者

health *n* 健康

healthy *adj* 健康

heap *n* 堆

heap *v* 堆

hear *iv* 听到

hearing *n* 听证会

hearsay *n* 传闻

hearse *n* 灵车

heart *n* 心脏

heartbeat *n* 心跳

heartburn *n* 胃（心）灼热，心痛

hearten *v* 鼓舞

heartfelt *adj* 衷心

hearth *n* 壁炉边

heartless *adj* 无情

hearty *adj* 热诚

heat *v* 加热

heat *n* 热气

heat wave *n* 热浪

heater *n* 加热器

heathen *n* 异教徒

heating *n* 加热，供暖

heatstroke *n* 中暑

heaven *n* 天堂

heavenly *adj* 天堂的

heaviness *n* 沉重

heavy *adj* 重的，大量的，严重的

heckle *v* 质问

hectic *adj* 忙碌

heed *v* 倾听

heel *n* 足跟

H

height *n* 身高

heighten *v* 提高

heinous *adj* 可憎的，十恶不赦的

heir *n* 继承人

heiress *n* 女继承人

heist *n* 偷窃

helicopter *n* 直升机

hell *n* 地狱

hello *e* 你好

helm *n* 掌舵，控制

helmet *n* 头盔

help *v* 帮助

help *n* 帮助

helper *n* 帮手

helpful *adj* 有帮助

helpless *adj* 无助的，无依靠的

hem *n* 下摆

hemisphere *n* 半球

hemorrhage *n* 出血，溢血

hen *n* 母鸡

hence *adv* 因此

henchman *n* 亲信，心腹

her *adj* 她

herald *v* 欢迎

herald *n* 使者

herb *n* 药草

here *adv* 这里

hereafter *adv* 此后

hereby *adv* 特此

hereditary *adj* 遗传性的，可继承的

heresy *n* 异端

heretic *adj* 异端的，异教的

heritage *n* 遗产

hermetic *adj* 密封的，炼金术的

hermit *n* 隐士

hernia *n* 疝气

hero *n* 英雄

heroic *adj* 英雄的，英勇的，崇高的

heroin *n* 海洛因

heroism *n* 英雄主义

hers *pro* 她的

herself *pro* 她自己

hesitant *adj* 迟疑的，犹豫不定的

hesitate *v* 犹豫

hesitation *n* 犹豫

heyday *n* 全盛时期，青春期

hiccup *n* 打嗝

hidden *adj* 隐藏的，秘密的

hide *iv* 隐藏

hideaway *n* 隐居地

hideous *adj* 极其丑陋的，难看的

hierarchy *n* 等级

high *adj* 高的

highlight *n* 最精彩的部分

highly *adv* 高度地

Highness *n* 殿下

highway *n* 高速公路

hijack *v* 劫持（尤指劫机）

hijack *n* 劫持（尤指劫机）

hijacker *n* 劫机犯

hike *v* 徒步旅行

hike *n* 徒步旅行

hilarious *adj* 搞笑

hill *n* 山

hillside *n* 山坡

hilltop *n* 小山顶

hilly *adj* 多小山

hilt *n* 柄，刀把，剑柄

hinder *v* 阻碍

hindrance *n* 障碍

hindsight *n* 事后分析

hinge *v* 铰链

hinge *n* 铰链

hint *n* 暗示

hint *v* 暗示

hip *n* 髋关节

hire *v* 雇佣

his *adj* 他的

his *pro* 他的

Hispanic *adj* 西班牙裔

hiss *v* 发嘘声

historian *n* 历史学家

history *n* 历史

hit *n* 一击，击中

hit *iv* 打，击，击中

hit back *v* 还击

hitch *n* 免费搭（车旅行），系住

hitch up *v* 拴住

hitchhike *n* 搭车旅行

hitherto *adv* 至此

hive *n* 蜂巢

hoard *v* 囤积

hoarse *adj* 嘶哑

hoax *n* 骗局

hobby *n* 嗜好

hog *n* 猪

hoist *v* 升起，升高，举起

hoist *n* 起重机，升高

hold *iv* 拿，保持，掌握

hold back *v* 隐瞒

hold on to *v* 坚持

hold out *v* 给予

hold up *v* 阻止

holdup *n* 持枪抢劫，停下

hole *n* 洞

holiday *n* 假日

holiness *n* 神圣

Holland *n* 荷兰

hollow *adj* 空的

holocaust *n* 大屠杀

holy *adj* 神圣的

homage *n* 尊敬，敬意，崇敬

home *n* 家

homeland *n* 家园

homeless *adj* 无家可归

homely *adj* 家常的，平凡的，相貌平庸的

homemade *adj* 自制的，本国制的

homesick *adj* 想家

hometown *n* 故乡

homework *n* 功课

homicide n 谋杀
homily n 讲道
honest adj 诚实的
honesty n 诚实
honey n 蜂蜜，甜心
honeymoon n 蜜月
honk v 按喇叭
honor n 荣誉
hood n 风帽，（排风）罩，车盖
hoodlum n 流氓
hoof n 蹄
hook n 钩子
hooligan n 流氓
hop v 跳跃，单脚跳
hope n 希望
hopeful adj 有希望的，怀有希望的
hopefully adv 但愿
hopeless adj 绝望的，没有希望的
horizon n 地平线
horizontal adj 水平的
hormone n 激素
horn n 喇叭
horrendous adj 可怕的，令人惊惧的
horrible adj 可怕的
horrify v 恐惧
horror n 惊恐
horse n 马
hose n 胶管

hospital n 医院
hospitality n 好客
hospitalize v 住院
host n 主人，主持人
hostage n 人质
hostess n 女主持人
hostile adj 敌对的，敌意的
hostility n 敌意
hot adj 热
hotel n 酒店
hound n 猎犬
hour n 小时
hourly adv 每小时
house n 房屋，公司，（H-）议院
household n 家居
housekeeper n 管家
housewife n 家庭主妇
housework n 家务
hover v 翱翔
how adv 如何
however c 然而
howl v 嗥
howl n 嗥声
hub n 枢纽
huddle v 蜷缩
hug v 拥抱
hug n 拥抱
huge adj 巨大
hull n 船体
hum v 哼曲子，发嗡嗡声
human adj 人类的

human being *n* 人类
humanities *n* 人文
humankind *n* 人类
humble *adj* 谦逊的，卑贱的
humbly *adv* 恭顺地，谦卑地
humid *adj* 潮湿的
humidity *n* 湿度
humiliate *v* 羞辱
humility *n* 谦卑
humor *n* 幽默
humorous *adj* 幽默的，诙谐的
hump *n* 驼峰
hunch *n* 直觉
hunchback *n* 驼背
hunched *adj* 驼背的
hundred *adj* 一百
hundredth *adj* 第一百
hunger *n* 饥饿
hungry *adj* 饥饿的，感到饿的
hunt *v* 狩猎
hunter *n* 猎人
hunting *n* 狩猎
hurdle *n* 跳栏，栏架
hurl *v* 投掷
hurricane *n* 飓风
hurriedly *adv* 仓促
hurry *v* 加快
hurry up *v* 加快
hurt *iv* 伤害
hurt *adj* 伤害，痛苦
hurtful *adj* 造成损害的，有害的
husband *n* 丈夫

hush *n* （使）安静下来，安静，寂静
hush up *v* 静寂下来
husky *adj* 多壳
hustle *n* 忙碌
hut *n* 小屋
hydraulic *adj* 水力的
hydrogen *n* 氢气
hyena *n* 鬣狗
hygiene *n* 卫生学
hymn *n* 圣歌
hyphen *n* 连字号
hypnosis *n* 催眠状态，催眠
hypnotize *v* 施催眠术
hypocrisy *n* 伪善
hypocrite *adj* 伪君子
hypothesis *n* 假说
hysteria *n* 癔症
hysterical *adj* 歇斯底里

H
I

I *pro* 我
ice *n* 冰
ice cream *n* 冰淇淋
ice cube *n* 冰块
ice skate *v* 滑冰
iceberg *n* 冰山

icebox n 冰箱
ice-cold adj 冰冷的
icon n 图标
icy adj 冰冷的
idea n 主意
ideal adj 理想的，想象的
identical adj 相同
identify v 认出，鉴定
identity n 身份
ideology n 意识形态
idiom n 成语
idiot n 白痴
idiotic adj 白痴
idle adj 懒散的，空闲的，无用的
idol n 偶像
idolatry n 偶像崇拜
if c 如果
ignite v 点燃
ignorance n 无知
ignorant adj 无知的
ignore v 忽视
ill adj 生病
illegal adj 非法的
illegible adj 难以辨认
illegitimate adj 违法的，私生的
illicit adj 不合法的
illiterate adj 文盲
illness n 疾病
illogical adj 不合逻辑的，不合常理的
illuminate v 照亮

illusion n 幻象
illustrate v 说明
illustration n 说明，例证，图解
illustrious adj 杰出的
image n 形象
imagination n 想象力
imagine v 想象
imbalance n 失衡
imitate v 模仿
imitation n 仿制
immaculate adj 无瑕的
immature adj 不成熟的
immaturity n 不成熟
immediately adv 立即
immense adj 巨大的
immensity n 巨大
immerse v 沉浸
immersion n 沉浸
immigrant n 移民
immigrate v 移民
immigration n 移民
imminent adj 即将发生的，临近的
immobile adj 固定的
immobilize v 固定
immoral adj 不道德的
immorality n 不道德
immortal adj 不朽的，永远的
immortality n 永生
immune adj 免疫的
immunity n 免疫力
immunize v 免疫接种

immutable *adj* 不变的

impact *n* 影响

impact *v* 影响

impair *v* 损害

impartial *adj* 公正的，公平的

impatience *n* 不耐烦

impatient *adj* 不耐烦的，急躁的

impeccable *adj* 无瑕疵的

impediment *n* 妨碍，阻碍物

impending *adj* 将发生的

imperfection *n* 美中不足

imperial *adj* 帝国的，皇家的

imperialism *n* 帝国主义

impersonal *adj* 客观的

impertinence *n* 俏皮

impertinent *adj* 无礼的，不相干的

impetuous *adj* 冲动的

implacable *adj* 难平息的

implant *v* 植入

implement *v* 落实

implicate *v* 牵连

implication *n* 蕴涵

implicit *adj* 含蓄的

implore *v* 恳请

imply *v* 暗示

impolite *adj* 不礼貌的，粗鲁的

import *v* 进口

importance *n* 重要性

importation *n* 进口

impose *v* 施加

imposing *adj* 印象深的

imposition *n* 强加

impossibility *n* 不可能

impossible *adj* 不可能的

impotent *adj* 无能的

impound *v* 扣押

impoverished *adj* 贫穷的，虚弱的

impractical *adj* 不现实的，不实用的

imprecise *adj* 不精确的

impress *v* 打动

impressive *adj* 印象深的

imprison *v* 监禁

improbable *adj* 不大可能的，不像会发生的

impromptu *adv* 即兴

improper *adj* 不恰当的，不正确的

improve *v* 改善

improvement *n* 改善

improvise *v* 即兴创作

impulse *n* 冲动

impulsive *adj* 推进的，冲动的

impunity *n* 不受惩罚

impure *adj* 不纯的

in *pre* 在里面

in depth *adv* 深入

inability *n* 无能

inaccessible *adj* 达不到的，难接近的

inaccurate *adj* 不准确的

inadequate *adj* 不足的

inadmissible *adj* 不能承认的，不能接受的，不能允许的

inappropriate *adj* 不适宜的

inasmuch as *c* 因为

inaugurate *v* 投产

inauguration *n* 就职

incalculable *n* 不可数的，极大的

incapable *adj* 无能的

incapacitate *v* 丧失

incarcerate *v* 禁闭

incense *n* 香火

incentive *n* 奖励

inception *n* 成立

incessant *adj* 不停的，连续不断的

inch *n* 英寸

incident *n* 事件

incidentally *adv* 顺便

incision *n* 切口

incite *v* 煽动

incitement *n* 煽动

inclination *n* 倾角

incline *v* 倾斜

include *v* 包括

inclusive *adv* 包含的

incoherent *adj* 不连贯的

income *n* 收入

incoming *adj* 正来临的，新任的

incompatible *adj* 不相容

incompetence *n* 无能

incompetent *adj* 无能的

incomplete *adj* 不完全的

inconsistent *adj* 不一致的

incontinence *n* 无节制

inconvenient *adj* 不方便的

incorporate *v* 纳入

incorrect *adj* 不正确的

incorrigible *adj* 不可救药的

increase *v* 增加

increase *n* 增加

increasing *adj* 增加的

incredible *adj* 难以置信的

increment *n* 增量

incriminate *v* 牵连

incur *v* 招致

incurable *adj* 无药可救的

indecency *n* 猥亵

indecision *n* 优柔寡断

indecisive *adj* 不明确的，犹豫不定的

indeed *adv* 的确

indefinite *adj* 无限期的，不明确的

indemnify *v* 赔偿

indemnity *n* 赔偿

independence *n* 独立

independent *adj* 独立的

index *n* 指数

indicate *v* 显示

indication *n* 迹象

indict *v* 起诉

indifference *n* 冷漠

indifferent *adj* 冷漠的

indigent *adj* 贫穷的，贫困的

indigestion *n* 消化不良

indirect *adj* 间接的

indiscreet *adj* 轻率的

indiscretion *n* 口误

indispensable *adj* 必不可少的，必需的

indisposed *adj* 不愿意的，身体不适的

indisputable *adj* 无可争辩的

indivisible *adj* 不可分割的

indoctrinate *v* 灌输

indoor *adv* 室内

induce *v* 诱使

indulge *v* 沉迷

indulgent *adj* 放纵的

industrious *adj* 勤劳的

industry *n* 工业

ineffective *adj* 无效的

inefficient *adj* 低效的

inept *adj* 无能的

inequality *n* 不平等

inevitable *adj* 无可避免的

inexcusable *adj* 不可原谅的

inexpensive *adj* 廉价的

inexperienced *adj* 经验不足的

inexplicable *adj* 无法解释的，难理解的

infallible *adj* 绝不会错的，绝对不可靠的

infamous *adj* 臭名昭著的

infancy *n* 婴儿期

infant *n* 婴儿

infantry *n* 步兵

infect *v* 感染

infection *n* 感染

infectious *adj* 传染的

infer *v* 推断

inferior *adj* 下等的

infertile *adj* 不孕的

infested *adj* 蝗灾的

infidelity *n* 不忠

infiltrate *v* 渗透

infiltration *n* 渗透

infinite *adj* 无限的

infirmary *n* 疗养院

inflammation *n* 炎症

inflate *v* 膨胀

inflation *n* 通货膨胀

inflexible *adj* 不可弯曲的，不可变更的

inflict *v* 造成

influence *n* 影响力

influential *adj* 有影响的

influenza *n* 流感

influx *n* 涌入

inform *v* 通知

informal *adj* 非正式的

informality *n* 非正式

informant *n* 线人

information *n* 资讯

informer *n* 举报人

infraction *n* 违背

infrequent *adj* 少有的

infuriate v 惹怒

infusion n 注入

ingenuity n 机巧

ingest v 咽下，吞下

ingot n 钢锭

ingrained adj 根深蒂固的

ingratiate v 讨好

ingratitude n 忘恩负义

ingredient n 成分

inhabit v 居住

inhabitable adj 可居住的

inhabitant n 居民

inhale v 吸

inherit v 继承

inheritance n 继承

inhibit v 抑制

inhuman adj 不人道的

initial adj 开始的，最初的

initially adv 起初

initials n 缩写

initiate v 启动

initiative n 倡议

inject v 注入

injection n 注射，注射物

injure v 受伤

injurious adj 有害的

injury n 伤

injustice n 不公正

ink n 油墨

inkling n 暗示，细微的迹象

inlaid adj 镶嵌的

inland adv 内陆

inland adj 内陆的

in-laws n 姻亲

inmate n 犯人

inn n 客栈

innate adj 天生的，固有的，天赋的

inner adj 内在的

innocence n 无辜

innocent adj 无辜的

innovation n 创新

innuendo n 影射

innumerable adj 无数的

input n 输入

inquest n 审讯

inquire v 查询

inquiry n 询问

inquisition n 侦查

insane adj 疯狂的

insanity n 疯狂

insatiable adj 贪心的

inscription n 题词

insect n 昆虫

insecurity n 不安全

insensitive adj 麻木的

inseparable adj 密不可分的

insert v 插入

insertion n 插入

inside adj 内

inside pre 在里面

inside out adv 从里到外

insignificant adj 微不足道的

insincere adj 虚伪的

insincerity *n* 伪善

insinuate *v* 影射

insinuation *v* 影射

insipid *adj* 平淡的

insist *v* 坚持

insistence *n* 坚持

insolent *adj* 傲慢的

insoluble *adj* 不溶性的

insomnia *n* 失眠

inspect *v* 检查

inspection *n* 检查

inspector *n* 检查员，监察员

inspiration *n* 灵感，鼓舞人心的人（或事物）

inspire *v* 鼓舞，激起，给...以灵感

instability *n* 不稳定

install *v* 安装

installation *n* 安装

installment *n* 分期付款

instance *n* 例子

instant *n* 立即的，紧急的

instantly *adv* 即刻

instead *adv* 反而

instigate *v* 煽动

instill *v* 灌输

instinct *n* 本能

institute *v* 学会，研究所

institution *n* 机构，学院

instruct *v* 指示

instructor *n* 指导员

insufficient *adj* 不足的

insulate *v* 绝缘

insulation *n* 绝缘体

insult *v* 侮辱

insult *n* 侮辱

insurance *n* 保险

insure *v* 投保

insurgency *n* 叛乱

insurrection *n* 暴动

intact *adj* 完好无损的

intake *n* 进水闸

integrate *v* 集成

integration *n* 一体化

integrity *n* 诚信

intelligent *adj* 聪明的

intend *v* 打算

intense *adj* 强烈的，紧张的，认真的

intensify *v* 加大

intensity *n* 强度

intensive *adj* 密集的

intention *n* 意向

intercede *v* 交涉

intercept *v* 拦截

intercession *n* 干涉

interchange *v* 互换

interchange *n* 互换

interest *n* 利息，兴趣

interested *adj* 有兴趣的

interesting *adj* 有趣的

interfere *v* 干涉

interference *n* 干扰

interior *adj* 内部的

interlude n 插曲
intermediary n 中介
intern v 实习生
interpret v 解释，翻译
interpretation n 释义，翻译
interpreter n 传译员
interrogate v 审问
interrupt v 中断
interruption n 中断
intersect v 相交
intertwine v 交织
interval n 间隔，间距
intervene v 介入
intervention n 干预
interview n 访谈
intestine n 肠子
intimacy n 亲密度
intimate adj 亲密的
intimidate v 恐吓
intolerable adj 无法忍受的
intolerance n 不宽容
intoxicated adj 陶醉的
intravenous adj 静脉内的
intrepid adj 强悍的
intricate adj 错综复杂的
intrigue n 阴谋
intriguing adj 吸引人的，有趣的
intrinsic adj 内在的
introduce v 介绍
introduction n 导言，介绍
introvert adj 内向的
intrude v 入侵

intruder n 入侵者
intrusion n 入侵
intuition n 直觉
inundate v 淹没
invade v 入侵
invader n 侵略者
invalid n 无效的，站不住脚的
invalidate v 作废
invaluable adj 无价的
invasion n 入侵
invent v 发明
invention n 发明
inventory n 库存
invest v 投资
investigate v 调查
investigation n 调查
investment n 投资
investor n 投资者
invincible adj 战无不胜的
invisible adj 无形的
invitation n 邀请
invite v 邀请
invoice n 发票
invoke v 引用
involve v 涉及
involved v 参与
involvement n 参与
inward adj 内部的
inwards adv 在内
iodine n 碘
irate adj 发怒的
Ireland n 爱尔兰

Irish *adj* 爱尔兰的
iron *n* 铁
iron *v* 僵硬的
ironic *adj* 讽刺的
irony *n* 讽刺
irrational *adj* 不合理的
irrefutable *adj* 无可辩驳的
irregular *adj* 不规则的
irrelevant *adj* 不相干的
irreparable *adj* 不可补救的
irresistible *adj* 不可抗拒的
irrespective *adj* 不考虑的，不顾及的
irreversible *adj* 不可逆转的
irrevocable *adj* 一成不变的
irrigate *v* 灌水
irrigation *n* 灌溉
irritate *v* 触怒
irritating *adj* 令人厌烦的
Islamic *adj* 伊斯兰的
island *n* 岛屿
isle *n* 小岛
isolate *v* 孤立
isolation *n* 隔离
issue *n* 问题
Italian *adj* 意大利的
italics *adj* 楷体字
Italy *n* 意大利
itch *v* 痒
itchiness *n* 发痒
item *n* 项目
itemize *v* 分项

itinerary *n* 行程
ivory *n* 象牙

J

jackal *n* 豺
jacket *n* 夹克
jackpot *n* 中奖
jaguar *n* 捷豹
jail *n* 坐牢
jail *v* 坐牢
jailer *n* 狱警
jam *n* 果酱
janitor *n* 校工
January *n* 一月
Japan *n* 日本
Japanese *adj* 日语
jar *n* 瓦罐
jasmine *n* 茉莉花
jaw *n* 下颌的
jealous *adj* 嫉妒的
jealousy *n* 嫉妒
jeans *n* 牛仔
jeopardize *v* 危害
jerk *n* 反射，混蛋
jerk *adj* 反射的
jersey *n* 新泽西
Jew *n* 犹太人

jewel n 宝石
jeweler n 珠宝商
jewelry store n 珠宝店
Jewish adj 犹太的
jigsaw n 拼图
job n 工作
jobless adj 失业的
join v 加入
joint n 联合
jointly adv 联合
joke n 笑话
joke v 开玩笑
jokingly adv 说笑
jolly adj 快活的
jolt v 动荡
jolt n 动荡
journal n 杂志，期刊，日报
journalist n 记者
journey n 征途
jovial adj 快活的
joy n 喜悦
joyful adj 欢乐的
joyfully adv 快乐地
jubilant adj 欢快
Judaism n 犹太教
judge n 法官，裁判
judgment n 判断
judicious adj 明智的
jug n 水罐
juggler n 变戏法者
juice n 果汁
juicy adj 多汁的

July n 七月
jump v 跳
jump n 跳
jumpy adj 跳动的
junction n 路口
June n 六月
jungle n 密林
junior adj 初级的，小辈的
junk n 垃圾
jury n 陪审团
just adj 刚
justice n 司法
justify v 辩解
justly adv 公正地，正当地
juvenile n 少年
juvenile adj 少年的

K

kangaroo n 袋鼠
karate n 空手道
keep iv 保持
keep on v 继续
keep up v 跟上
keg n 小桶
kennel n 狗窝
kettle n 水壶
key n 关键，钥匙

key ring *n* 钥匙扣
keyboard *n* 键盘
kick *v* 踢
kickback *n* 回扣
kickoff *n* 开球
kid *n* 孩子
kidnap *v* 绑票
kidnapper *n* 绑匪
kidnapping *n* 绑架
kidney *n* 肾脏
kidney bean *n* 菜豆
kill *v* 杀
killer *n* 杀手
killing *n* 杀害
kilogram *n* 公斤
kilometer *n* 公里
kilowatt *n* 千瓦
kind *adj* 好心的
kindle *v* 点燃
kindly *adv* 好心地
kindness *n* 好心
king *n* 国王
kingdom *n* 王国
kinship *n* 亲情
kiosk *n* 小亭
kiss *v* 吻
kiss *n* 吻
kitchen *n* 厨房
kite *n* 风筝
kitten *n* 小猫
knee *n* 膝关节
kneecap *n* 髌骨

kneel *iv* 下跪
knife *n* 刀
knight *n* 骑士
knit *v* 针织
knob *n* 旋钮
knock *n* 敲
knock *v* 敲
knot *n* 结
know *iv* 知道
know-how *n* 实践知识，技术秘诀，诀窍
knowingly *adv* 狡黠地，机警地
knowledge *n* 知识

K
L

L

lab *n* 实验室
label *n* 标签
labor *n* 劳动
laborer *n* 劳动者
labyrinth *n* 迷宫
lace *n* 花边
lack *v* 缺乏
lack *n* 缺乏
lad *n* 小伙子
ladder *n* 阶梯
laden *adj* 装载的
lady *n* 夫人
ladylike *adj* 淑女般的

lagoon n 盐水湖

lake n 湖

lamb n 羊肉

lame adj 跛脚的，松散的

lament v 悲叹

lament n 悲叹

lamp n 灯

lamppost n 灯柱

lampshade n 灯罩

land n 土地

land v 着地

landfill n 填埋场

landing n 登陆

landlady n 女房东

landlocked adj 内陆的

landlord n 房东

landscape n 景观

lane n 车道

language n 语言

languish v 衰弱

lantern n 灯笼

lap n 膝部

lapse n 流逝

lapse v 流逝

larceny n 偷窃

lard n 猪油

large adj 大的，大型的

larynx n 喉

laser n 激光

lash n 鞭子

lash v 鞭打

lash out v 抨击

last v 持续

last adj 过去的

last name n 姓氏

last night adv 昨晚

lasting adj 持久

lastly adv 最后

latch n 门闩

late adv 晚

lately adv 近来

later adv 后来

later adj 后来的

lateral adj 侧向

latest adj 最新的

lather n 泡沫

latitude n 纬度

latter adj 后者

laugh v 笑

laugh n 笑

laughable adj 可笑的

laughing stock n 笑柄

laughter n 笑声

launch n 发射

launch v 发射

laundry n 洗衣

lavatory n 卫生间

lavish adj 奢华

lavish v 奢华

law n 法

law-abiding adj 守法的

lawful adj 合法的

lawmaker n 立发者

lawn n 草坪

lawsuit *n* 官司
lawyer *n* 律师
lax *adj* 懒散的，松弛的
laxative *adj* 泻的
lay *n* 位置
lay *iv* 躺
lay off *v* 裁员
layer *n* 层
layman *n* 门外汉
lay-out *n* 版面设计
laziness *n* 懒
lazy *adj* 懒惰的
lead *iv* 领导
lead *n* 领导，铅
leaded *adj* 含铅
leader *n* 领导人
leadership *n* 领导
leading *adj* 领先的，主要的
leaf *n* 叶
leaflet *n* 传单
league *n* 同盟
leak *v* 泄漏
leak *n* 泄漏
leakage *n* 泄漏
lean *adj* 弱的
lean *iv* 倾斜
lean back *v* 往后靠
lean on *v* 靠在
leaning *n* 靠
leap *iv* 飞跃
leap *n* 飞跃
leap year *n* 闰年

learn *iv* 学习
learned *adj* 博学的
learner *n* 学习者
learning *n* 学习
lease *v* 租赁
lease *n* 租赁
leash *n* 皮带
least *adj* 至少
leather *n* 皮革
leave *iv* 离开
leave out *v* 省去，不考虑，遗漏
lectern *n* 讲台
lecture *n* 演讲
ledger *n* 总帐
leech *n* 水蛭
leftovers *n* 剩菜
leg *n* 腿
legacy *n* 遗产
legal *adj* 法律的
legality *n* 合法性
legalize *v* 合法化
legend *n* 传奇
legible *adj* 易读的
legion *n* 军团
legislate *v* 立法
legislation *n* 立法
legislature *n* 立法机关
legitimate *adj* 合法的
leisure *n* 休闲
lemon *n* 柠檬
lemonade *n* 柠檬水

L

lend *iv* 借出

length *n* 长度

lengthen *v* 拉长

lengthy *adj* 长的

leniency *n* 从宽处理

lenient *adj* 宽大的，仁慈的

lens *n* 晶状体

Lent *n* 4天宗教礼拜

lentil *n* 扁豆

leopard *n* 豹

leper *n* 麻疯病患者

leprosy *n* 麻风病

less *adj* 少的

lessee *n* 承租人

lessen *v* 淡化

lesser *adj* 较少的

lesson *n* 教训，课程

lessor *n* 出租人

let *iv* 让

let down *v* 辜负

let go *v* 放手

let in *v* 让

let out *v* 让

lethal *adj* 致命的

letter *n* 信，字

lettuce *n* 生菜

leukemia *n* 白血病

level *v* 平衡的

level *n* 级

lever *n* 杠杆

leverage *n* 杠杆作用

levy *v* 征收

lewd *adj* 淫的

liability *n* 法律责任

liable *adj* 承担责任的

liaison *n* 联络

liar *adj* 说谎者

libel *n* 诽谤

liberate *v* 解放

liberation *n* 解放

liberty *n* 自由

librarian *n* 馆员

library *n* 图书馆

lice *n* 虱子

license *n* 许可

license *v* 授予许可

lick *v* 舔

lid *n* 盖子

lie *iv* 躺

lie *v* 说谎

lie *n* 谎言

lieu *n* 代替

lieutenant *n* 中尉

life *n* 生活，生命

lifeguard *n* 救生员

lifeless *adj* 死的

lifestyle *n* 生活方式

lifetime *adj* 一生

lift *v* 升

lift off *v* 发射

lift-off *n* 发射

ligament *n* 韧带

light *iv* 打火

light *adj* 轻的

light n 光
lighter n 打火机
lighthouse n 灯塔
lighting n 照明
lightly adv 轻微
lightning n 闪电
lightweight n 轻量级
likable adj 若人喜欢的
like pre 像
like v 喜欢
likelihood n 可能性
likely adv 可能的
likeness n 相像
likewise adv 同样
liking n 喜欢
limb n 肢体
lime n 石灰
limestone n 石灰石
limit n 极限
limit v 限制
limitation n 极限
limp v 跛行
limp n 跛行
linchpin n 主轴
line n 线
line up v 排队
linen n 亚麻布
linger v 徘徊
lingerie n 内衣
lingering adj 拖延的，依依不
　舍的
lining n 衬里

link v 链接
link n 链接
lion n 狮子
lioness n 母狮子
lip n 唇
liqueur n 烈酒
liquid n 液体
liquidate v 清算
liquidation n 清算
liquor n 酒
list v 列
list n 名单
listen v 听
listener n 听众
litany n 祈祷
liter n 升
liter n 公升
literal adj 照字面的，原义的
literally adv 从字面上
literate adj 有文化的
literature n 文学
litigate v 打官司
litigation n 诉讼
litter n 废弃物
little adj 小的
little bit n 一点点
little by little adv 一点点
liturgy n 礼拜仪式
live adj 现场的
live v 活
live off v 存活
live up v 实现

livelihood *n* 生计
lively *adj* 活泼的
liver *n* 肝
livestock *n* 家畜
livid *adj* 苍白
living room *n* 客厅
lizard *n* 蜥蜴
load *v* 负载
load *n* 负载
loaded *adj* 满载的
loaf *n* 面包
loan *v* 贷款
loan *n* 贷款
loathe *v* 讨厌
loathing *n* 厌恶
lobby *n* 大堂
lobby *v* 游说
lobster *n* 龙虾
local *adj* 当地的
localize *v* 本地化
locate *v* 寻回，位于
located *adj* 位于
location *n* 地点
lock *v* 锁
lock *n* 锁，（头发的）一缕，船闸
lock up *v* 锁上，锁起来
locker room *n* 更衣室
locksmith *n* 锁匠
locust *n* 蝗虫
lodge *v* 投诉，住
lodging *n* 住宿

lofty *adj* 崇高的
log *n* 日志
log *v* 逻辑
log in *v* 登录
log off *v* 注销
logic *n* 有逻辑的
logical *adj* 腰部
loin *n* 游荡
loiter *v* 寂寞
loneliness *n* 寂寞
lonely *adv* 孤家寡人
loner *adj* 寂寞的
lonesome *adj* 长
long *adj* 渴望
long for *v* 向往
longing *n* 经度
longitude *n* 耐久
long-standing *adj* 长期存在的，长时间的
long-term *adj* 长期的
look *n* 看
look *v* 看
look after *v* 照顾
look at *v* 看
look down *v* 瞧不起
look for *v* 寻找
look forward *v* 期待
look into *v* 查看
look out *v* 当心
look over *v* 查看
look through *v* 浏览
looking glass *n* 镜子

looks *n* 长相

loom *n* 织机

loom *v* 织

loophole *n* 漏洞

loose *v* 放松

loose *adj* 松散的

loosen *v* 放松

loot *v* 战利

loot *n* 战利品

lord *n* 主

lordship *n* 贵族权力，阁下

lose *iv* 输，失去

loser *n* 输家

loss *n* 损失

lot *adv* 很多

lotion *n* 洗剂

lots *adj* 很多

lottery *n* 彩票

loud *adj* 大声的

loudly *adv* 响亮地

loudspeaker *n* 扬声器

lounge *n* 休息室

louse *n* 虱子

lousy *adj* 糟糕的

lovable *adj* 可爱的

love *v* 爱

love *n* 爱

lovely *adj* 可爱的

lover *n* 情人

loving *adj* 充满爱的

low *adj* 低的

lower *adj* 更低的

low-key *adj* 卑贱的

lowly *adj* 低调的

loyal *adj* 忠诚的

loyalty *n* 忠诚

lubricate *v* 润滑

lubrication *n* 润滑

lucid *adj* 清楚的

luck *n* 运气

lucky *adj* 幸运的

lucrative *adj* 利润丰厚的

ludicrous *adj* 可笑的

luggage *n* 行李

lukewarm *adj* 温热

lull *n* 暂时平息

lumber *n* 木材

luminous *adj* 光亮的

lump *n* 小方块，（肿）块

lump sum *n* 总价

lump together *v* 把放在一起

lunacy *n* 精神错乱

lunatic *adj* 疯子的

lunch *n* 午餐

lung *n* 肺

lure *v* 诱惑

lurid *adj* 刺眼的

lurk *v* 隐藏

lush *adj* 茂密的

lust *v* 有情欲

lust *n* 渴望

lustful *adj* 性欲的

luxurious *adj* 豪华的

luxury *n* 奢侈品

L

lynch v 私刑处死
lynx n 猞猁
lyrics n 歌词

M

machine n 机器
machine gun n 机枪
mad adj 疯狂的，大怒
madam n 女士
madden v 大怒
madly adv 疯狂的
madman n 疯子
madness n 疯狂
magazine n 杂志
magic n 魔术
magical adj 神奇的
magician n 魔术师
magistrate n 行政官
magnet n 磁铁
magnetic adj 磁性的
magnetism n 磁性，吸引力
magnificent adj 宏伟的
magnify v 放大
magnitude n 震级
mahogany n 桃花心木
maid n 女仆
maiden n 少女
mail v 邮寄

mail n 邮件
mailbox n 信箱
mailman n 邮递员
maim v 致残
main adj 主要的
mainland n 大陆
mainly adv 主要
maintain v 保持
maintenance n 维修
majestic adj 雄伟的，壮观的
majesty n 陛下
major n 专业
major adj 主要的
major in v 主修
majority n 多数
make n 制作
make iv 做
make up v 组成
make up for v 弥补
maker n 制造商
makeup n 化妆品，组成
malaria n 疟疾
male n 男性
malevolent adj 恶意的
malfunction v 出故障
malfunction n 故障
malice n 恶毒
malign v 中伤
malignancy n 敌意
malignant adj 敌意的
mall n 商城
malnutrition n 营养不良

malpractice v 营私舞弊

mammal n 哺乳动物

mammoth n 声势浩大

man n 男子

manage v 管理

manageable adj 可管理的，可处理的

management n 管理

manager n 经理

mandate n 命令

mandatory adj 必须的

maneuver n 机动

manger n 槽，牛槽

mangle v 轧

manhandle v 人工推动

manhunt n 追捕

maniac adj 发狂的，癫狂的，疯狂的

manifest v 表明，证明，使显现

manipulate v 操控

mankind n 人类

manliness n 勇敢

manly adj 男子汉的

manner n 方式

mannerism n 动作

manners n 礼仪

manpower n 人力

mansion n 豪宅

manslaughter n 过失杀人（罪）

manual n 手册

manual adj 手动的

manufacture v 制造

manure n 肥料

manuscript n 手稿

many adj 许多

map n 地图

marble n 大理石

march v 游行

march n 游行

March n 三月

mare n 母马

margin n 边际，利润

marginal adj 少量的

marinate v 用卤汁泡

marine adj 海洋的

marital adj 婚姻的

mark n 标志

mark v 作标记

mark down v 扣分

marker n 指示器，指向标，标识

market n 市场

marksman n 射手

marmalade n 果酱

marriage n 婚姻

married adj 已婚的

marrow n 骨髓

marry v 结婚

Mars n 火星

marshal n 元帅

martyr n 烈士

martyrdom n 殉道

marvel n 奇迹

M

marvelous *adj* 精彩的

Marxist *adj* 马克思主义者

masculine *adj* 男性的，男子的，男子气的

mash *v* 挤压

mask *n* 面具

masochism *n* 受虐狂

mason *n* 泥工

masquerade *v* 伪装

mass *n* 堆，大量[pl.]群众

massacre *n* 屠杀

massage *n* 按摩

massage *v* 按摩

masseur *n* 男按摩师

masseuse *n* 女按摩师

massive *adj* 大量的

mast *n* 桅杆

master *n* 硕士，老师，主人

master *v* 掌握

mastermind *n* 主谋

mastermind *v* 主谋

masterpiece *n* 杰作

mastery *n* 精通

mat *n* 垫子

match *n* 比赛，对手，火柴

match *v* 配

mate *n* 配偶，伙伴

material *n* 材料

materialism *n* 唯物主义

maternal *adj* 产妇的

maternity *n* 分娩

math *n* 数学

matriculate *v* 报名入学

matrimony *n* 婚姻

matter *n* 事

mattress *n* 床垫

mature *adj* 成熟的

maturity *n* 成熟

maul *v* 殴打

maxim *n* 格言

maximum *adj* 最高（大）的，顶点的

May *n* 五月

may *iv* 可以做

may-be *adv* 也许

mayhem *n* 打斗

mayor *n* 市长

maze *n* 迷宫

meadow *n* 草甸

meager *adj* 很薄的

meal *n* 餐

mean *iv* 表示

mean *adj* 刻薄的

meaning *n* 含义

meaningful *adj* 有意义的

meaningless *adj* 无意义的

meanness *n* 刻薄

means *n* 手段

meantime *adv* 与此同时

meanwhile *adv* 与此同时

measles *n* 麻疹

measure *v* 测量

measurement *n* 测量

meat *n* 肉类

meatball n 肉丸

mechanic n 机工

mechanism n 机械装置，机制，机理

mechanize v 机械化

medal n 勋章

medallion n 奖章

meddle v 干涉

mediate v 调解

mediator n 调解员

medication n 服药

medicinal adj 药用的

medicine n 医药

medieval adj 中世纪的

mediocre adj 平庸的

mediocrity n 平庸

meditate v 打坐

meditation n 打坐

medium adj 中等的

meek adj 温顺的

meekness n 温顺

meet iv 满足，见面

meeting n 会议

melancholy n 愁绪

mellow adj 慵懒的

mellow v 放松

melodic adj 旋律优美的，旋律的

melody n 旋律

melon n 甜瓜

melt v 熔

member n 会员

membership n 成员

membrane n 膜

memento n 纪念品

memo n 备忘录

memoirs n 回忆录

memorable adj 难忘的

memorize v 背诵

memory n 记忆

men n 男

menace n 威胁

mend v 修复

meningitis n 脑膜炎

menopause n 更年期

menstruation n 月经

mental adj 精神的

mentality n 精神

mentally adv 精神上

mention v 提到

mention n 提到

menu n 菜单

merchandise n 商品

merchant n 商家

merciful adj 慈悲

merciless adj 无情的

mercury n 汞

mercy n 慈悲

merely adv 只

merge v 合并

merger n 合并

merit n 值得

merit v 值得

mermaid n 美人鱼

M

M

merry *adj* 愉快的
mesh *n* 滤网
mesmerize *v* 施以催眠术，迷住
mess *n* 一团糟
mess around *v* 玩弄
mess up *v* 弄糟
message *n* 信息
messenger *n* 信使
Messiah *n* 救世主
messy *adj* 凌乱的
metal *n* 金属
metallic *adj* 金属的
metaphor *n* 隐喻
meteor *n* 流星
meter *n* 米
method *n* 方法
methodical *adj* 有条不紊
meticulous *adj* 细致的
metric *adj* 公制的
metropolis *n* 大都会
Mexican *adj* 墨西哥的
mice *n* 小鼠
microbe *n* 微生物
microphone *n* 麦克风
microscope *n* 显微镜
microwave *n* 微波炉
midair *n* 半空
midday *n* 中午
middle *n* 中间
middleman *n* 中间人
midget *n* 侏儒
midnight *n* 午夜

midsummer *n* 盛夏
midwife *n* 接生婆
mighty *adj* 强大的
migraine *n* 偏头痛
migrant *n* 移民
migrate *v* 迁移
mild *adj* 温和的，温柔的
mildew *n* 霉
mile *n* 英里
mileage *n* 里程
milestone *n* 里程碑
militant *adj* 好战的
milk *n* 牛奶
milky *adj* 乳状的
mill *n* 磨房
millennium *n* 千年
milligram *n* 毫克
millimeter *n* 毫米
million *n* 万
millionaire *adj* 百万富翁，
  大富翁
mime *v* 模仿
mince *v* 剁碎
mincemeat *n* 碎肉
mind *v* 介意
mind *n* 思想
mind-boggling *adj* 让人难以置
  信
mindful *adj* 留心的，不忘的
mindless *adj* 无意识的
mine *n* 矿井
mine *v* 挖矿

mine *pro* 我的

minefield *n* 布雷区

miner *n* 矿工

mineral *n* 矿产

mingle *v* 混合

miniature *n* 缩影

minimize *v* 尽量减少

minimum *n* 最少

miniskirt *n* 迷你裙

minister *n* 部长

minister *v* 照顾，给予帮助

ministry *n* 部

minor *adj* 轻微的，未成年人的

minority *n* 少数民族

mint *n* 薄荷

mint *v* 铸造

minus *adj* 减去的

minute *n* 一分钟

miracle *n* 奇迹

miraculous *adj* 奇迹般的

mirage *n* 幻影

mirror *n* 镜子

misbehave *v* 行为无礼貌，行为不端

miscalculate *v* 算错

miscarriage *n* 流产

miscarry *v* 流产

mischief *n* 作怪

mischievous *adj* 恶作剧的

misconduct *n* 失当行为

misconstrue *v* 误解

misdemeanor *n* 轻罪

miser *n* 守财奴

miserable *adj* 凄惨的

misery *n* 苦难

misfit *adj* 错位的

misfortune *n* 不幸

misgiving *n* 忧虑

misguided *adj* 误入歧途的

misinterpret *v* 误解

misjudge *v* 错估

mislead *v* 误导

misleading *adj* 误导的

mismanage *v* 管理不当

misplace *v* 错位

misprint *n* 打印错误

miss *v* 想念

miss *n* 小姐

missile *n* 导弹

missing *adj* 失踪的

mission *n* 使命

missionary *n* 传教

mist *n* 薄雾

mistake *iv* 犯错误

mistake *n* 错误

mistaken *adj* 犯错的，错误的

mister *n* 先生

mistreat *v* 虐待

mistreatment *n* 虐待

mistress *n* 情妇

mistrust *n* 不信任

mistrust *v* 不信任

misty *adj* 薄雾的

misunderstand *v* 误会

M

misuse n 滥用
mitigate v 减轻
mix v 混合
mixed-up adj 混杂的
mixer n 搅拌机
mixture n 混合，混合剂
mix-up n 混合
moan v 呻吟
moan n 呻吟
mob v 挤压
mob n 暴徒
mobile adj 移动的
mobilize v 调动
mobster n 流氓
mock v 嘲弄
mockery n 嘲弄
mode n 模式
model n 模型，模特
moderate adj 中度的
moderation n 中庸
modern adj 现代的
modernize v 现代化
modest adj 谦虚
modesty n 谦虚
modify v 修改
module n 模块
moisten v 滋润
moisture n 水分
molar n 槽牙
mold v 制作模具
mold n 模式，模子，模型
mold adj 制模，发霉

moldy adj 霉变的
mole n 痣
molecule n 分子
molest v 骚扰
mom n 妈妈
moment n 时刻
momentarily adv 瞬间
momentous adj 重大的
monarch n 君主
monarchy n 君主立宪制
monastery n 修道院
monastic adj 寺院的
Monday n 星期一
money n 钱
money order n 汇票
monitor v 监视，监督，监听
monk n 和尚
monkey n 猴
monogamy n 一夫一妻
monologue n 独白
monopolize v 垄断
monopoly n 垄断，专卖，垄断物
（商品）
monotonous adj 单调的
monotony n 单调
monster n 怪物
monstrous adj 巨大的
month n 月
monthly adv 每月的，每月一次的
monument n 纪念碑
monumental adj 纪念碑的，不朽
的

mood *n* 心情
moody *adj* 情绪化的
moon *n* 月亮
moor *v* 停泊
mop *v* 擦洗
moral *adj* 有道德的
moral *n* 道德
morality *n* 道德
more *adj* 更多
moreover *adv* 此外
morning *n* 上午
moron *adj* 愚蠢的
morphine *n* 吗啡
morsel *n* 少量
mortal *adj* 凡人的
mortality *n* 致命性，死亡率
mortar *n* 砂浆
mortgage *n* 按揭
mortification *n* 节制
mortify *v* 节制
mortuary *n* 太平间
mosaic *n* 马赛克
mosque *n* 清真寺
mosquito *n* 蚊子
moss *n* 青苔
most *adj* 最多的
mostly *adv* 大多
motel *n* 汽车旅馆
moth *n* 蛾
mother *n* 母亲
motherhood *n* 母性
mother-in-law *n* 岳母，婆婆

motion *n* 议案，动感
motionless *adj* 不动的
motivate *v* 激励
motive *n* 动机
motor *n* 发动机，电动机
motorcycle *n* 摩托车
motto *n* 座右铭
mount *n* 登
mount *v* 登上，镶住
mountain *n* 山
mountainous *adj* 多山的
mourn *v* 哀悼
mourning *n* 哀悼
mouse *n* 鼠，鼠标
mouth *n* 口
move *n* 运动
move *v* 移动
move back *v* 回迁
move forward *v* 向前
move out *v* 迁出
move up *v* 向上，升职
movement *n* 运动
movie *n* 电影
mow *v* 割
much *adv* 很多
mucus *n* 粘液
mud *n* 泥
muddle *n* 混乱，糊涂
muddy *adj* 泥泞的
muffle *v* 裹住
muffler *n* 消声器
mug *n* 杯

M

mug v 持枪抢劫

mugging n 持枪抢劫

mule n 骡子

multiple adj 复合的，多重的，多种多样的

multiplication n 乘法

multiply v 乘以

multitude n 许多

mumble v 嘟囔

mummy n 木乃伊

mumps n 腮腺炎

munch v 咀嚼

munitions n 弹药

murder n 谋杀

murderer n 杀人犯

murky adj 灰暗的

murmur v 小声说（话），小声抱怨

murmur n 私语

muscle n 肌肉

museum n 博物馆

mushroom n 蘑菇

music n 音乐

musician n 音乐家

Muslim adj 穆斯林的

must iv 要

mustache n 短须

mustard n 芥末

muster v 集合，鼓起

mutate v 变种

mute adj 缄默的，哑的，不发音的

mutilate v 致残

mutiny n 反叛

mutually adv 相互

muzzle v 堵嘴

muzzle n 枪口

my adj 我的

myopic adj 近视的

myself pro 我自己

mysterious adj 神秘的

mystery n 谜

mystic adj 神秘的

mystify v 神化

myth n 神话

N

nag v 啰嗦

nagging adj 啰嗦的

nail n 指甲

naive adj 天真的

naked adj 赤裸的

name n 姓名

namely adv 即

nanny n 保姆

nap n 午睡

napkin n 餐巾

narcotic n 麻醉

narrate v 叙说

M
N

narrow *adj* 狭窄（隘）的，勉强的

narrowly *adv* 勉强地，严密地

nasty *adj* 讨厌的

nation *n* 国家

national *adj* 全国的

nationality *n* 国籍

nationalize *v* 国有化

native *adj* 本国的，本土的，当地的

natural *adj* 自然的

naturally *adv* 自然地

nature *n* 性质，自然

naughty *adj* 顽皮的

nausea *n* 恶心

nave *n* 殿

navel *n* 肚脐

navigate *v* 浏览

navigation *n* 导航

navy *n* 海军

navy blue *adj* 深蓝色（的）

near *pre* 近

nearby *adj* 附近的

nearly *adv* 几乎

nearsighted *adj* 近视的

neat *adj* 整齐的

neatly *adv* 整齐

necessary *adj* 必要的

necessitate *v* 需要

necessity *n* 必要性

neck *n* 颈部

necklace *n* 项链

necktie *n* 领带

need *v* 需要

need *n* 需要

needle *n* 针

needless *adj* 多余的

needy *adj* 贫困，需要的

negative *adj* 否定的，消极的

neglect *v* 忽视

neglect *n* 忽视

negligence *n* 疏忽

negligent *adj* 疏忽的

negotiate *v* 谈判

negotiation *n* 谈判

neighbor *n* 邻居

neighborhood *n* 邻里

neither *adj* 既不

neither *adv* 也不

nephew *n* 侄子

nerve *n* 神经

nervous *adj* 神经紧张的，神经系统的

nest *n* 巢

net *n* 净

Netherlands *n* 荷兰

network *n* 网络

neurotic *adj* 神经质的

neutral *adj* 中立的，不偏不倚的

neutralize *v* 中立

never *adv* 从未

nevertheless *adv* 然而

new *adj* 新的

newborn *n* 新生儿

N

newcomer *n* 新人

newly *adv* 新近地，重新地

newlywed *adj* 新婚

news *n* 新闻

newscast *n* 新闻

newsletter *n* 新闻简报

newspaper *n* 报纸

newsstand *n* 报摊

next *adj* 接下的

next door *adj* 隔壁

nibble *v* 蚕食

nice *adj* 好的，可爱的，友好的

nicely *adv* 好

nickel *n* 镍，十美分

nickname *n* 昵称

nicotine *n* 尼古丁

niece *n* 侄女

night *n* 夜

nightfall *n* 入夜

nightgown *n* 女睡袍

nightingale *n* 夜莺

nightmare *n* 梦魇

nine *adj* 九

nineteen *adj* 十九

ninety *adj* 九十

ninth *adj* 第九

nip *n* 咬

nip *v* 咬

nipple *n* 乳头

nitpicking *adj* 挑剔的，吹毛求疵的

nitrogen *n* 氮

no one *pro* 没有人

nobility *n* 贵族

noble *adj* 高尚的，宏伟的，贵族的

nobleman *adj* 贵族

nobody *pro* 没有人，无名

nocturnal *adj* 夜的

nod *v* 点头

noise *n* 噪音

noisily *adv* 喧哗

noisy *adj* 嘈杂的，喧闹的

nominate *v* 提名

none *pre* 无

nonetheless *c* 尽管如此

nonsense *n* 胡说八道

nonsmoker *n* 不吸烟者

nonstop *adv* 马不停蹄

noon *n* 中午

noose *n* 陷阱

nor *c* 也不

norm *n* 准则

normal *adj* 正常的，平常的，正规的

normalize *v* 正常化

normally *adv* 通常

north *n* 北

northeast *n* 东北

northern *adj* 北部的

northerner *adj* 北方人

Norway *n* 挪威

Norwegian *adj* 挪威的

nose *n* 鼻子

nosedive *adv* 急转直下

nostalgia *n* 怀旧

nostril *n* 鼻孔

nosy *adj* 好管闲事的，爱追问的

not *adv* 不

notable *adj* 值得注意的，著名的

notably *adv* 显着

notary *n* 公证

notation *n* 乐谱

note *v* 注

notebook *n* 笔记本

noteworthy *adj* 值得注意的

nothing *n* 无关

notice *v* 注意

notice *n* 公告

noticeable *adj* 显而易见的

notification *n* 通知

notify *v* 通知

notion *n* 概念

notorious *adj* 臭名昭著的，声名狼藉的

noun *n* 名词

nourish *v* 滋养

nourishment *n* 养料

novel *n* 小说

novelist *n* 小说家

novelty *n* 新奇事物，新奇（感）

November *n* 十一月

novice *n* 新手

now *adv* 现在

nowadays *adv* 当今

nowhere *adv* 无处

noxious *adj* 有毒的

nozzle *n* 喷嘴

nuance *n* 细微差别

nuclear *adj* 核子的，核能的

nude *adj* 裸体的

nudism *n* 裸体主义

nudist *n* 裸体主义者

nudity *n* 裸体

nuisance *n* 讨厌

null *adj* 无效的

nullify *v* 使无效，废除

numb *adj* 麻木的

number *n* 数字，号码

numbness *n* 麻木，愚蠢

numerous *adj* 无数的

nun *n* 尼姑

nurse *n* 护士

nurse *v* 护理

nursery *n* 苗圃，托儿所

nurture *v* 培育

nut *n* 螺母，坚果

nutrition *n* 坚果壳

nutritious *adj* 营养的

nut-shell *adv* 胡桃壳

nutty *adj* 有坚果的，古怪的

N

O

oak n 橡树

oar n 桨

oasis n 绿洲

oath n 宣誓

oatmeal n 燕麦片

obedience n 服从

obedient adj 服从的

obese adj 肥胖的

obey v 服从

object v 反对，提出 ... 作为反对的理由

object n 对象，物

objection n 反对

objective n 客观的，不带偏见的

obligate v 强制

obligation n 义务

obligatory adj 强制的

oblige v 迫使

obliged adj 义不容辞的，感激的

oblique adj 倾斜的

obliterate v 抹杀

oblivion n 湮没

oblivious adj 忘却的

oblong adj 长方形的

obnoxious adj 厌恶的

obscene adj 色情的

obscenity n 淫秽

obscure adj 难解的，不著名的，微暗的

obscurity n 朦胧

observation n 观察，评论

observatory n 天文台，气象台，了望台

observe v 观察

obsess v 迷恋

obsession n 痴迷

obsolete adj 已过时

obstacle n 障碍

obstinacy n 一意孤行

obstinate adj 顽固的

obstruct v 阻塞，堵塞，阻碍

obstruction n 阻碍

obtain v 获得

obvious adj 显而易见的

obviously adv 显然

occasion n 场合

occasionally adv 偶尔

occult adj 不可思议的，神秘的

occupant n 居住者

occupation n 占据，职业

occupy v 占据

occur v 发生

occurrence n 发生

ocean n 海洋

October n 十月

octopus n 章鱼

odd adj 奇数，奇怪的

oddity n 奇妙

odds n 可能性

odious adj 臭色的

odometer n 里程表

odor *n* 气味

odyssey *n* 冒险旅行

of *pre* 的

off *adv* 下，不准的

offend *v* 触犯

offense *n* 进攻

offensive *adj* 进攻的

offer *v* 提供

offer *n* 提供

offering *n* 提供

office *n* 办公室

officer *n* 办公员

official *adj* 正式的，官方的，公务上的

officiate *v* 担任

offset *v* 抵销

offspring *n* 后代

off-the-record *adj* 私下承认的

often *adv* 常常

oil *n* 石油

ointment *n* 软膏

okay *adv* 还好，可以

old *adj* 老

old age *n* 晚年

old-fashioned *adj* 老式的，过时的

olive *n* 橄榄树

Olympics *n* 奥运

omelet *n* 煎蛋

omen *n* 前兆

ominous *adj* 不祥的

omission *n* 遗漏

omit *v* 略去

on *pre* 在上面，关于

once *adv* 一旦，一次

once *c* 一旦

one *adj* 一

oneself *pre* 自己

ongoing *adj* 持续的

onion *n* 洋葱

onlooker *n* 旁观者

only *adv* 只

onset *n* 起始

onslaught *n* 冲击

onwards *adv* 往前

opaque *adj* 不透明的

open *v* 打开

open *adj* 公开的

open up *v* 开放

opening *n* 开幕

open-minded *adj* 开明的

openness *n* 公开性

opera *n* 歌剧

operate *v* 经营

operation *n* 操作

opinion *n* 意见

opinionated *adj* 固执己见

opium *n* 鸦片

opponent *n* 对手

opportune *adj* 合时宜的

opportunity *n* 机会

oppose *v* 反对

opposite *adj* 相反的

opposite *adv* 相反

opposite *n* 相反

opposition *n* 反对

oppress *v* 欺压

oppression *n* 压迫

opt for *v* 选择

optical *adj* 光学的

optician *n* 配镜师

optimism *n* 乐观

optimistic *adj* 乐观的

option *n* 选项

optional *adj* 可以任选的，非强制的

opulence *n* 富裕

or *c* 或

oracle *n* 神谕

orally *adv* 口头地

orange *n* 橙色，橙子

orangutan *n* 猩猩

orbit *n* 轨道

orchard *n* 果园

orchestra *n* 乐团

ordain *v* 规定

ordeal *n* 磨难

order *n* 命令

ordinarily *adv* 通常

ordinary *adj* 普通的

ordination *n* 整理

ore *n* 矿石

organ *n* 器官

organism *n* 有机体

organist *n* 风琴师

organization *n* 组织

organize *v* 组织

orient *n* 东方

oriental *adj* 东方的

orientation *n* 方向

oriented *adj* 面向

origin *n* 原产地

original *adj* 原始的

originally *adv* 原本

originate *v* 源于

ornament *n* 饰品

ornamental *adj* 装饰的

orphan *n* 孤儿

orphanage *n* 孤儿院

orthodox *adj* 东正教

ostentatious *adj* 浮华的

ostrich *n* 鸵鸟

other *adj* 其他

otherwise *adv* 否则

otter *n* 水獭

ought to *iv* 应该

ounce *n* 盎司

our *adj* 我们的

ours *pro* 我们的

ourselves *pro* 我们自己

oust *v* 驱逐

out *adv* 外面

outbreak *n* 爆发

outburst *n* 爆发

outcast *adj* 抛弃的

outcome *n* 结果

outcry *n* 喊叫

outdated *adj* 已过时

outdo _v_ 胜过

outdoor _adv_ 户外的，野外的，露天的

outdoors _adv_ 户外

outer _adj_ 外面（表）的，远离中心的

outfit _n_ 服装

outgoing _adj_ 外向的

outgrow _v_ 不敷支

outing _n_ 郊游

outlast _v_ 禁止

outlaw _v_ 经久

outlet _n_ 插座，出口

outline _n_ 纲要

outline _v_ 写纲要

outlive _v_ 活得长

outlook _n_ 展望

outmoded _adj_ 老式的

outnumber _v_ 多于

outpatient _n_ 门诊病人

outperform _v_ 超越

outpouring _n_ 流露

output _n_ 输出

outrage _n_ 愤怒

outrageous _adj_ 极无礼的

outright _adj_ 彻底的

outrun _v_ 逃脱

outset _n_ 最初

outshine _v_ 胜过

outside _adv_ 外面

outsider _n_ 局外人

outskirts _n_ 郊区

outspoken _adj_ 敢言的

outstanding _adj_ 优秀的

outstretched _adj_ 向外伸展

outward _adj_ 向外

outweigh _v_ 胜过

oval _adj_ 椭圆形的

ovary _n_ [植]子房，[解]卵巢

ovation _n_ 热烈的欢迎

oven _n_ 烘箱

over _pre_ 超过

overall _adv_ 总体

overbearing _adj_ 骄傲自大的

overboard _adv_ 过火，向船外

overcast _adj_ 阴天的

overcharge _v_ 过高索价

overcoat _n_ 大衣

overcome _v_ 克服

overcrowded _adj_ 过度拥挤的

overdo _v_ 过分做

overdone _adj_ 太过份的

overdose _n_ 过量

overdue _adj_ 逾期的

overestimate _v_ 高估

overflow _v_ 溢流

overhaul _v_ 检修

overlap _v_ 重叠

overlook _v_ 忽视

overnight _adv_ 隔夜

overpower _v_ 压倒

overrate _v_ 过份高估

override _v_ 凌驾

overrule _v_ 否决

O

overrun v 超支

overseas adv 海外

oversee v 监督

overshadow v 掩盖

oversight n 疏忽，照料

overstate v 夸大

overstep v 超出

overtake v 追上

overthrow v 推翻

overthrow n 推翻

overtime adv 加班

overturn v 推翻

overview n 概况

overweight adj 超重的

overwhelm v 压倒

owe v 欠

owing to adv 由于

owl n 猫头鹰

own v 拥有

own adj 自己的

owner n 主人

ownership n 所有权

ox n 牛

oxen n 黄牛

oxygen n 氧气

oyster n 牡蛎

P

pace v 按节奏走

pace n 节奏

pacify v 安抚

pack v 打包

package n 包裹

pact n 协议

pad v 垫

padding n 填料

paddle v 划桨

padlock n 挂锁

pagan adj 异教的，异教徒的

page n 页

pail n 桶

pain n 疼痛

painful adj 痛苦的

painkiller n 止痛药

painless adj 无痛的，不痛的

paint v 涂画

paint n 涂料

paintbrush n 画笔

painter n 画家

painting n 画

pair n 一双

pajamas n 睡衣

pal n 伙伴

palace n 宫殿

palate n 上颚

pale adj 苍白的

paleness n 苍白

O
P

palm n 棕榈，手掌
palpable adj 可触知的
paltry adj 琐碎的
pamper v 纵容
pamphlet n 小册子
pan n 平底锅
pancreas n 胰腺
pander v 迎合
pang n 剧痛
panic n 恐慌
panorama n 全景
panther n 豹
pantry n 茶水
pants n 裤
pantyhose n 连裤袜
papacy n 罗马教皇的职位
（权力、任期）
paper n 文件，纸
paperclip n 回形针
paperwork n 文件
parable n 寓言
parachute n 降落伞
parade n 巡游
paradise n 天堂
paradox n 矛盾
paragraph n 段
parakeet n 长尾小鹦鹉
parallel n 并行
paralysis n 瘫痪
paralyze v 瘫痪
parameters n 参数
paramount adj 极为重要的，
至高无上的

paranoid adj 偏执的
parasite n 寄生虫
paratrooper n 伞兵
parcel n 包裹
parcel post n 包裹单
parch v 烘
parchment n 羊皮纸
pardon v 原谅
pardon n 原谅
parenthesis n 插入语
parents n 家长
parish n 教区
parishioner n 教区居民
parity n 平价
park v 停泊
park n 公园
parking n 停车，停车场
parliament n 议会
parochial adj 狭隘的
parrot n 鹦鹉
parsley n 香菜
parsnip n 防风草
part v 分开
part n 部分
partial adj 部分的
partially adv 部分地
participate v 参加
participation n 参与
participle n 分词
particle n 粒子
particular adj 尤其
particularly adv 尤其

P

parting n 临别

partisan n 党派

partition n 分割

partly adv 部分

partner n 合作伙伴

partnership n 伙伴关系

partridge n 鹧鸪

party n 党，派队

pass n 通过，通行证

pass v 通过

pass around v 传开

pass away v 过世

pass out v 分发，昏过去

passage n 通道

passenger n 乘客

passer-by n 路人

passion n 激情

passionate adj 激情的

passive adj 被动的，消极的

passport n 护照

password n 密码

past adj 过去的

paste v 糊，贴

paste n 浆糊，膏

pasteurize v 杀菌

pastime n 消遣

pastor n 牧师

pastoral adj 田园生活的，
宁静的

pastry n 糕饼

pasture n 牧草

pat n 轻拍

patch v 补丁

patch n 补丁

patent n 专利

patent adj 专利的，显著的

paternity n 父系，父系后裔

path n 路径

pathetic adj 可怜的

patience n 耐心

patient adj 有耐心的

patio n 露台

patriarch n 族长

patrimony n 世袭

patriot n 爱国者

patriotic adj 爱国的

patrol n 巡逻

patron n 赞助人

patronage n 光顾

patronize v 光顾

pattern n 样式

pavement n 路面

pavilion n 亭

paw n 熊掌

pawn v 典当

pawnbroker n 当押商

pay n 薪酬

pay iv 付钱

pay back v 回馈，回击

pay off v 偿清

pay slip n 工资单

payable adj 应付的，支付的

paycheck n 薪资

payee n 收款人

payment n 付款

payroll n 发薪

pea n 豌豆

peace n 和平

peaceful adj 和平的

peach n 桃

peacock n 孔雀

peak n 高峰

peanut n 花生

pear n 梨

pearl n 珍珠

peasant n 农民

pebble n 卵石

peck v 啄

peck n 啄

peculiar adj 奇怪的，特有的

pedagogy n 教育学

pedal n 踏板

pedantic adj 迂腐的，卖弄学问的

pedestrian n 行人

peel v 去皮

peel n 果皮

peep v 偷看

peer n 同行

pelican n 鹈鹕

pellet n 药丸

pen n 钢笔

penalize v 惩罚

penalty n 罚款

penance n 忏悔

penchant n 爱好

pencil n 铅笔

pendant n 吊坠

pending adj 待定的，迫近的

pendulum n 钟摆

penetrate v 渗透

penguin n 企鹅

penicillin n 青霉素

peninsula n 半岛

penitent n 忏悔

penniless adj 身无分文的

penny n 便士，分

pension n 退休金

pentagon n 五角大楼

pent-up adj 幽闭的，被压抑的

people n 人

pepper n 辣椒

per pre 每

perceive v 察觉

percent adv 百分比

percentage n 百分比

perception n 感知（能力），觉察（力），观念

perennial adj 常年的，多年的

perfect adj 完美的，完全的

perfection n 完美

perforate v 穿孔

perforation n 穿孔

perform v 演出

performance n 绩效，演出

perfume n 香水

perhaps adv 或许

peril n 危亡

P

perilous *adj* 危险的

perimeter *n* 周长

period *n* 周期

perish *v* 消灭

perishable *adj* 易腐烂的，会枯萎的

perjury *n* 伪证罪

permanent *adj* 永久的

permeate *v* 渗入

permission *n* 许可

permit *v* 允许

pernicious *adj* 有害的

perpetrate *v* 犯罪

persecute *v* 迫害

persevere *v* 坚持

persist *v* 坚持

persistence *n* 毅力

persistent *adj* 坚持不懈的

person *n* 人

personal *adj* 个人的

personality *n* 个性

personify *v* 拟人化

personnel *n* [总称]人员，员工，人事部门

perspective *n* 视角，观点

perspiration *n* 汗水，流汗

perspire *v* 出汗

persuade *v* 说服

persuasion *n* 说服力

persuasive *adj* 说服力的

pertain *v* 属于

pertinent *adj* 有关系的，相关的

perturb *v* 烦扰

perverse *adj* 反常的

pervert *v* 贪赃枉法

pervert *adj* 变态的

pessimism *n* 悲观

pessimistic *adj* 悲观的

pest *n* 虫害

pester *v* 使烦恼

pesticide *n* 农药

pet *n* 宠物

petal *n* 花瓣

petite *adj* 迷你的

petition *n* 请愿书

petrified *adj* 石化的

petroleum *n* 石油

pettiness *n* 微小

petty *adj* 微小的，零用的

pew *n* 座位

phantom *n* 幽灵

pharmacist *n* 药剂师

pharmacy *n* 药剂，药剂店

phase *n* 阶段

pheasant *n* 野鸡

phenomenon *n* 现象

philosopher *n* 哲学家

philosophy *n* 哲学

phobia *n* 恐怖症

phone *n* 电话

phone *v* 打电话

phony *adj* 假的，伪造的

phosphorus *n* 磷

photo *n* 照片

P

photocopy *n* 影印

photograph *v* 拍照

photographer *n* 摄影师

photography *n* 摄影

phrase *n* 短语

physically *adj* 按照自然规律，身体上地

physician *n* 医师

physics *n* 物理学

pianist *n* 钢琴家

piano *n* 钢琴

pick *v* 接，摘

pick up *v* 拿起

pickpocket *n* 扒手

pickup *n* 搭便车

picture *n* 图片

picture *v* 想像

picturesque *adj* 风景如画的

pie *n* 馅饼

piece *n* 作品，件

piecemeal *adv* 零碎的

pier *n* 码头

pierce *v* 刺穿

piercing *n* 刺耳

piety *n* 虔诚

pig *n* 猪

pigeon *n* 乳鸽

piggy bank *n* 储蓄罐

pile *v* 堆积

pile *n* 堆

pile up *v* 堆积

pilfer *v* 窃取

pilgrim *n* 朝圣者

pilgrimage *n* 朝圣

pill *n* 丸

pillage *v* 掠夺

pillar *n* 支柱

pillow *n* 枕头

pillowcase *n* 枕套

pilot *n* 试点，飞行员

pimple *n* 丘疹

pin *n* 针

pincers *n* 钳子

pinch *v* 夹

pinch *n* 夹子

pine *n* 松树

pineapple *n* 菠萝

pink *adj* 粉红的

pinpoint *v* 指出

pint *n* 品脱

pioneer *n* 先锋

pious *adj* 虔诚的

pipe *n* 管子，烟斗，管乐器

pipeline *n* 管道

piracy *n* 盗版

pirate *n* 海盗

pistol *n* 手枪

pit *n* 坑

pitch-black *adj* 漆黑的，极黑的

pitchfork *n* 干草叉

pitfall *n* 陷阱

pitiful *adj* 可怜的

pity *n* 可惜

placard *n* 标语牌

P

placate v 安抚

place n 地方

placid adj 平和的

plague n 鼠疫

plain n 平原

plain adj 清晰的，简单的，坦率的

plainly adv 平坦地，简单地

plaintiff n 原告

plan v 计划

plan n 计划

plane n 飞机

planet n 星球

plant v 种植

plant n 植物

plaster n 膏药

plaster v 涂膏药

plastic n 塑料

plate n 板，碟子

plateau n 高原

platform n 平台

platinum n 白金

platoon n 排

plausible adj 振振有词的

play v 玩

play n 戏剧

player n 玩家，播放器

playful adj 好玩的

playground n 游乐场

plea n 认罪

plead v 恳求

pleasant adj 宜人的

please v 取悦

pleasing adj 使人愉快的，合意的

pleasure n 乐趣

pleat n 褶

pleated adj 折叠的

pledge v 承诺

pledge n 承诺

plentiful adj 丰富的，充足的，大量的

plenty n 大量

pliable adj 柔韧的

pliers n 钳子

plot v 阴谋

plot n 阴谋

plow v 犁

ploy n 伎俩

pluck v 采摘

plug v 插

plug n 插头

plum n 梅子

plumber n 水管工

plumbing n 配管

plummet v 骤降

plump adj 饱满的

plunder v 掠夺

plunge v 倾没

plunge n 倾没

plural n 复数

plus adv 另加

plush adj 毛绒的

plutonium n 钚

pneumonia *n* 肺炎

pocket *n* 口袋

poem *n* 诗

poet *n* 诗人

poetry *n* 诗歌

poignant *adj* 尖锐的

point *n* 点

point *v* 指点

pointed *adj* 针对的

pointless *adj* 无意义的

poise *n* 世故

poison *v* 下毒

poison *n* 毒药

poisoning *n* 中毒

poisonous *adj* 有毒的

Poland *n* 波兰

polar *adj* 极地的

pole *n* 极点

police *n* 警察

policeman *n* 警察

policy *n* 政策

Polish *adj* 波兰的

polish *n* 完美

polish *v* 擦亮

polite *adj* 有礼貌的

politeness *n* 礼貌

politician *n* 政治家

politics *n* 政治

poll *n* 民意测验[pl.]大选

pollen *n* 花粉

pollute *v* 污染

pollution *n* 污染

polygamist *adj* 多配偶的

polygamy *n* 一夫多妻制

pomegranate *n* 石榴

pomposity *n* 浮华

pond *n* 池塘

ponder *v* 想

pontiff *n* 教宗

pool *n* 池

pool *v* 共用，汇集

poor *n* 穷人

poorly *adv* 很差

popcorn *n* 爆米花

Pope *n* 教宗

poppy *n* 鸦片

popular *adj* 流行的

popularize *v* 普及

populate *v* 填充

population *n* 人口

porcelain *n* 瓷器

porch *n* 门廊

porcupine *n* 豪猪

pore *n* 孔隙

pork *n* 猪肉

porous *adj* 多孔的

port *n* 港口

portable *adj* 便携式的

portent *n* 预兆

porter *n* 搬运工

portion *n* 部分

portrait *n* 画像

portray *v* 描绘

Portugal *n* 葡萄牙

P

Portuguese *adj* 葡萄牙的

pose *v* 摆姿势

pose *n* 姿势

posh *adj* 毫华的

position *n* 立场，职位

positive *adj* 正面，乐观的

possess *v* 占有，拥有

possession *n* 财产

possibility *n* 可能性

possible *adj* 可能的

post *n* 邮政

post office *n* 邮费

postage *n* 明信片

postcard *n* 海报

poster *n* 海报，装饰画，急行旅人

posterity *n* 邮差

postman *n* 邮戳

postmark *n* 邮政局

postpone *v* 推迟

postponement *n* 推迟

pot *n* 火锅，罐

potato *n* 马铃薯

potent *adj*（药等）效力大的，威力大的

potential *adj* 有潜力的

pothole *n* 坑洞

poultry *n* 家禽

pound *v* 重击

pound *n* 英镑，磅

pour *v* 倾倒

poverty *n* 贫困

powder *n* 粉

power *n* 电力，力量

powerful *adj* 强大的

powerless *adj* 无能为力的

practical *adj* 实用的

practice *v* 练习

practice *v* 执业

practicing *adj* 实践的

pragmatist *adj* 实用主义者

prairie *n* 大草原

praise *v* 表扬

praise *n* 好评

praiseworthy *adj* 值得称道的

prank *n* 恶作剧

prawn *n* 对虾

pray *v* 祈祷

prayer *n* 祈祷

preach *v* 说教

preacher *n* 布道者

preaching *n* 说教

preamble *n* 序言

precarious *adj* 岌岌可危的

precaution *n* 防范

precede *v* 在之前

precedent *n* 先例

preceding *adj* 在前面的

precept *n* 道德箴言，规则，训诫

precious *adj* 珍贵的

precipice *n* 悬崖

precipitate *v* 沉淀

precise *adj* 精确的

precision n 精密
precocious adj 早熟的
precursor n 前驱
predecessor n 前任
predicament n 困境
predict v 预测
prediction n 预测
predilection n 偏好
predisposed adj 预设的
predominate v 占主导地位
preempt v 抢占
prefabricate v 预制
preface n 前言
prefer v 更喜欢
preference n 偏好
prefix n 前缀
pregnancy n 怀孕
pregnant adj 怀孕的，妊娠的
prehistoric adj 史前的
prejudice n 偏见，成见
preliminary adj 预备的，初步的
prelude n 前奏
premature adj 早产的
premeditate v 预谋
premeditation n 预谋
premier adj 首要的
premise n 前提
premises n 房地
premonition n 预感
preoccupation n 全神贯注
preoccupy v 专注
preparation n 准备

prepare v 准备
preposition n 介词
prerequisite n 先决条件
prerogative n 特权
prescribe v 开处方，规定
prescription n 处方
presence n 驻留
present adj 目前的
present v 代表
presentation n 陈述
preserve v 保存
preside v 主持
presidency n 总统的职务
president n 主席
press n 新闻
press v 按
pressing adj 迫切的
pressure v 施压
pressure n 压力
prestige n 威望
presume v 假定
presumption n 推定
presuppose v 假定
presupposition n 预设
pretend v 假装
pretense n 幌子
pretension n 资格
pretty adj 漂亮的
prevail v 战胜
prevalent adj 流行的，普遍的
prevent v 防止
prevention n 预防

preventive *adj* 预防的
preview *n* 预览
previous *adj* 以前的，先于的
previously *adv* 此前
prey *n* 猎物
price *n* 价格
pricey *adj* 高价的
prick *v* 刺
pride *n* 骄傲
priest *n* 牧师
priestess *n* 祭司
priesthood *n* 神职人员
primacy *n* 首要
primarily *adv* 主要
prime *adj* 首要的
primitive *adj* 原始的
prince *n* 王子
princess *n* 公主
principal *adj* 主要的
principle *n* 原则
print *v* 打印
print *n* 打印本
printer *n* 打印机
printing *n* 印刷
prior *adj* 事先的
priority *n* 优先
prism *n* 棱镜
prison *n* 监狱
prisoner *n* 囚犯
privacy *n* 隐私
private *adj* 私人的
privilege *n* 特权

prize *n* 奖
probability *n* 概率
probable *adj* 可能的
probe *v* 探查
probing *n* 试探
problem *n* 问题
problematic *adj* 有问题的
procedure *n* 程序
proceed *v* 进行
proceedings *n* 行动，诉讼
proceeds *n* 收益
process *v* 进行
process *n* 过程
procession *n* 游行
proclaim *v* 宣告
proclamation *n* 宣言，公布
procrastinate *v* 延迟
procreate *v* 生育
procure *v* 采购
prod *v* 刺
prodigious *adj* 巨大的
prodigy *n* 奇迹
produce *v* 生产
produce *n* 生产
product *n* 产品
production *n* 生产
productive *adj* 多产的，富饶的
profane *adj* 亵渎的
profess *v* 公开宣称
profession *n* 专业
professional *adj* 专业的
professor *n* 教授

proficiency *n* 精通
proficient *adj* 精通的
profile *n* 简介
profit *v* 盈利
profit *n* 利润
profitable *adj* 有利的
profound *adj* 深刻的
program *n* 节目，项目
programmer *n* 程序员
progress *v* 进展
progress *n* 进展
progressive *adj* 渐进式的
prohibit *v* 禁止
prohibition *n* 禁止
project *v* 计划，预计，设计
project *n* 项目
projectile *n* 弹丸
prologue *n* 序幕
prolong *v* 延长
promenade *n* 长廊
prominent *adj* 突出的
promiscuous *adj* 滥交的，
　杂乱的
promise *n* 诺言
promote *v* 推广
promotion *n* 推广，升职
prompt *adj* 迅速的
prone *adj* 倾向的
pronoun *n* 代词
pronounce *v* 宣判，发音
proof *n* 证明
propaganda *n* 宣传

propagate *v* 宣传
propel *v* 推进
propensity *n* 倾向
proper *adj* 适当的
properly *adv* 妥善地
property *n* 财产
prophecy *n* 预言
prophet *n* 先知
proportion *n* 比例
proposal *n* 建议
propose *v* 提建议，求婚
proposition *n* 命题，提议
prose *n* 散文
prosecute *v* 检控
prosecutor *n* 检察官
prospect *n* 展望
prosper *v* 蓬勃发展
prosperity *n* 繁荣
prosperous *adj* 繁荣的
prostate *n* 前列腺
prostrate *adj* 卧倒的，拜倒的，
　瓦解的
protect *v* 保护
protection *n* 保护
protein *n* 蛋白质
protest *v* 抗议
protest *n* 抗议
protocol *n* 协议
prototype *n* 原型
protract *v* 延长
protracted *adj* 延长的
protrude *v* 凸

proud *adj* 骄傲的，自豪的

proudly *adv* 自豪地

prove *v* 证明

proven *adj* 证实的

proverb *n* 谚语

provide *v* 提供

providence *n* 上帝

providing that *c* 前提是

province *n* 省

provision *n* 提供

provisional *adj* 临时的

provocation *n* 挑衅

provoke *v* 挑衅

prow *n* 飞机前部

prowl *v* 四处觅食

prowler *n* 徘徊

proximity *n* 接近

proxy *n* 代理

prudence *n* 谨慎

prudent *adj* 谨慎的

prune *v* 修剪

prune *n* 修剪

prurient *adj* 淫荡的

pseudonym *n* 笔名

psychiatrist *n* 精神科医师

psychiatry *n* 精神病学

psychic *adj* 心理的

psychology *n* 心理学

psychopath *n* 精神变态者

puberty *n* 青春期

public *adj* 公众的，公共的

publication *n* 出版

publicity *n* 宣传

publicly *adv* 公开地

publish *v* 出版

publisher *n* 出版社

pudding *n* 布丁

puerile *adj* 幼稚的

puff *v* 吹嘘

puffy *adj* 浮肿的，膨胀的

pull *v* 拉

pull ahead *v* 提前

pull down *v* 拉下

pull out *v* 退出

pulley *n* 滑轮

pulp *n* 纸浆

pulpit *n* 讲坛

pulsate *v* 搏动

pulse *n* 脉冲

pulverize *v* 粉碎

pump *v*（用泵）抽（水），抽吸

pump *n* 泵

pumpkin *n* 南瓜

punch *v* 拳打

punch *n* 拳打

punctual *adj* 准时的

puncture *n* 刺

punish *v* 惩罚

punishable *adj* 该罚的，可罚的

punishment *n* 处罚

pupil *n* 瞳孔，学生

puppet *n* 木偶

puppy *n* 小狗

purchase *v* 购买

purchase *n* 购买

pure *adj* 纯的

puree *n* 纯汁浓汤

purgatory *n* 炼狱

purge *n* 清除

purge *v* 清除

purification *n* 净化

purify *v* 净化

purity *n* 纯度

purple *adj* 紫色的

purpose *n* 目的

purposely *adv* 故意地

purse *n* 钱包

pursue *v* 追求

pursuit *n* 追求

pus *n* 脓

push *v* 推

pushy *adj* 固执己见的，莽撞的，强求的

put *iv* 放

put aside *v* 放在一边

put away *v* 移去

put off *v* 推迟

put out *v* 救

put up *v* 忍受

put up with *v* 忍耐

putrid *adj* 腐臭的

puzzle *n* 字迷

puzzling *adj* 令人费解的

pyramid *n* 金字塔

python *n* 巨蟒

quagmire *n* 泥潭

quail *n* 鹌鹑

quake *v* 震动

qualify *v* 有资格

quality *n* 质量

qualm *n* 疑虑

quandary *n* 困惑

quantity *n* 数量

quarrel *v* 吵架

quarrel *n* 吵架

quarrelsome *adj* 喜欢争吵的，好争论的

quarry *n* 采石场，猎物

quarter *n* 季度，四分之一

quarterly *adj* 每季的

quarters *n* 处所

quash *v* 废除

queen *n* 女王

queer *adj* 奇怪的

quell *v* 平息

quench *v* 解渴

quest *n* 搜寻

question *v* 提问

question *n* 问题

questionable *adj* 可疑的，不可靠的

questionnaire *n* 问卷

queue *n* 队列

quick *adj* 快速的

P
Q

quicken v 加快
quickly adv 快速地
quicksand n 流沙
quiet adj 安静的
quietness n 安静
quilt n 棉被
quit iv 戒
quite adv 非常
quiver v 颤抖
quiz v 提问答
quotation n 报价
quote v 报价
quotient n 商数

rabbi n 犹太教教士
rabbit n 兔子
rabies n 狂犬病
raccoon n 浣熊
race v 赛跑
race n 种族
racism n 种族主义
racist adj 种族主义者
racket n 球拍
racketeering n 敲诈
radar n 雷达
radiation n 辐射

radiator n 暖气片，散热器
radical adj 根本的
radio n 收音机
radish n 萝卜
radius n 半径
raffle n 抽奖
raft n 木筏
rag n 旧布
rage n 愤怒
ragged adj 褴褛的
raid n 袭击
raid v 袭击
raider n 入侵者
rail n 路轨
railroad n 铁路
rain n 雨
rain v 下雨
rainbow n 彩虹
raincoat n 雨衣
rainfall n 降雨量
rainy adj 多雨的
raise v 上升，增高
raise v 上升，培养
raisin n 葡萄干
rake n 犁耙
rally n 集会
ram n 公羊
ram v 强行
ramification n 分枝
ramp n 舷梯
rampage v 狂暴行为
rampant adj 繁茂的

ranch *n* 农场

rancor *n* 仇恨

randomly *adv* 任意地，随机地

range *n* 范围

rank *n* 等级

rank *v* 排名

ransack *v* 彻底搜索

ransom *v* 赎金

rape *v* 强奸

rape *n* 强奸

rapid *adj* 迅速的

rapist *n* 强奸犯

rapport *n* 融洽的关系

rare *adj* 稀有的，珍奇的

rarely *adv* 很少地

rascal *n* 淘气鬼，流氓

rash *v* 生疹

rash *n* 疹

raspberry *n* 莓

rat *n* 鼠

rate *n* 率

rather *adv* 宁可

ratification *n* 批准

ratify *v* 批准

ratio *n* 比率

ration *v* 定量

ration *n* 定量

rational *adj* 合理的

rationalize *v* 合理化

rattle *v* 吵闹

ravage *v* 毁坏，破坏，掠夺

ravage *n* 破坏

rave *v* 吹捧

raven *n* 掠夺

ravine *n* 山沟

raw *adj* 未加工的，生的

ray *n* 光

raze *v* 忘却

razor *n* 剃刀

reach *v* 达到，伸手，达成

reach *n* 伸手可及的距离

react *v* 起反应

reaction *n* 反应

read *iv* 读

reader *n* 读者

readiness *n* 准备就绪，愿意

reading *n* 读物

ready *adj* 准备好

real *adj* 真实的

realism *n* 现实主义

reality *n* 现实

realize *v* 体会到

really *adv* 真正地

realm *n* 领土

realty *n* 不动产

reap *v* 收割

reappear *v* 再现

rear *v* 后退

rear *n* 后方

rear *adj* 后方的

reason *v* 推论

reason *n* 原因

reasonable *adj* 合理的

reasoning *n* 推理

R

reassure v 再保证
rebate n 折扣
rebel v 反叛
rebel n 反叛分子，反对者
rebellion n 叛乱
rebirth n 重生
rebound v 反弹
rebuff v 拒绝
rebuff n 拒绝
rebuild v 改建，重建
rebuke v 谴责
rebuke n 谴责
rebut v 反驳
recall v 回忆
recant v 撤回
recap v 重述要点
recapture v 夺回
recede v 后退
receipt n 收据
receive v 收到
recent adj 最近的
reception n 招待会
receptionist n 招待员
receptive adj 接收能力强的，
　能迅速接受的
recess n 停止
recession n 后退，经济衰退
recharge v 再充电
recipe n 食谱
reciprocal adj 相互的
recital n 吟诵
recite v 背诵

reckless adj 鲁莽的
reckon v 总计
reckon on v 总计
reclaim v 开垦
recline v 斜倚
recluse n 隐居者
recognition n 公认
recognize v 认出
recollect v 回忆
recollection n 回忆，记忆力，
　记忆
recommend v 推荐
recompense v 报偿
recompense n 报偿，回礼，
　赔偿
reconcile v 和解
reconsider v 反思
reconstruct v 重建
record v 记录
record n 纪录
recorder n 记录员，记录器
recording n 录音
recount n 重新计数
recoup v 收回
recourse v 依赖
recourse n 依赖
recover v 恢复
recovery n 恢复
recreate v 再创造
recreation n 休闲
recruit v 招募
recruit n 新兵，新成员

R

recruitment *n* 招募
rectangle *n* 长方形
rectangular *adj* 长方形的
rectify *v* 矫正
rector *n* 神父
rectum *n* 直肠
recuperate *v* 恢复
recur *v* 复发
recurrence *n* 再现
recycle *v* 回收利用（废物等）
red *adj* 红色的
red tape *n* 繁文缛节
redden *v* 变红
redeem *v* 赎回
redemption *n* 收兑
red-hot *adj* 炽热的
redo *v* 重做
redouble *v* 加倍
redress *v* 赔偿
reduce *v* 减少
redundant *adj* 被解雇的，多余
　的，过剩的
reed *n* 芦苇
reef *n* 礁石
reel *n* 卷轴
reelect *v* 重选
reenactment *n* 再制定
reentry *n* 再进入
refer to *v* 参考
referee *n* 裁判员，推荐人，
　仲裁者
reference *n* 参考

referendum *n* 公民投票
refill *v* 替换，加满
refinance *v* 重新贷款
refine *v* 提炼
refinery *n* 精炼厂
reflect *v* 反映，反射
reflection *n* 反射
reflexive *adj* 反射性的，
　折转的，自反的
reform *v* 改革
reform *n* 改革
refrain *v* 禁止
refresh *v* 刷新
refreshing *adj* 清新的
refreshment *n* 茶点
refrigerate *v* 冷藏
refuel *v* 加油
refuge *n* 避难所
refugee *n* 难民
refund *v* 退款
refund *n* 退款
refurbish *v* 再制造
refusal *n* 拒绝
refuse *v* 拒绝
refuse *n* 拒绝
refute *v* 反驳
regain *v* 收回，恢复
regal *adj* 豪华的
regard *v* 尊敬
regarding *pre* 关于
regardless *adv* 不管怎么样
regards *n* 问候

R

regeneration n 再生

regent n 董事

regime n 政权

regiment n 军团

region n 区域

regional adj 区域的

register v 注册

registration n 注册

regret v 后悔

regret n 遗憾

regrettable adj 遗憾的

regularity n 规律性

regularly adv 时常

regulate v 调控

regulation n 规章，规则

rehabilitate v 恢复原状

rehearsal n 排练

rehearse v 排练

reign v 执政

reign n 王朝

reimburse v 偿还

reimbursement n 退款

rein v 勒马

rein n 马勒

reindeer n 驯鹿

reinforce v 加强

reinforcements n 增强

reiterate v 重申

reject v 拒绝

rejection n 拒绝

rejoice v 使高兴

rejoin v 使再结合，再加入，再回答

rejuvenate v 充满活力

relapse n 复发

related adj 相关

relationship n 关系

relative adj 相对的

relative n 亲戚

relax v 放松

relax n 减轻，放松

relaxing adj 放松的

relay v 中转

release v 发行，释放

relegate v 转移

relent v 变温和

relentless adj 不懈的

relevant adj 相关的

reliable adj 可靠的

reliance n 信赖

relic n 遗物

relief n 轻松，宽慰，缓解（除）

relieve v 解除

religion n 宗教

religious adj 宗教的

relinquish v 放弃

relish v 获得快乐

relive v 再体验

relocate v 调迁

relocation n 拆迁

reluctant adj 勉强的

reluctantly adv 勉强地

rely on v 依靠

remain v 保持

remainder n 剩余物，其余的人
remaining adj 残余的
remains n 剩余的
remake v 重制
remark v 评论
remark n 评论
remarkable adj 卓越的
remarry v 再婚
remedy v 补救
remedy n 补救
remember v 记住
remembrance n 记忆
remind v 提醒
reminder n 提示
remission n 宽恕
remit v 汇寄
remittance n 汇寄
remnant n 残余
remodel v 改造
remorse n 后悔
remorseful adj 后悔的
remote adj 遥远的
removal n 撤除
remove v 去除
remunerate v 酬赏
renew v 更新
renewal n 更新
renounce v 放弃
renovate v 更新
renovation n 整修
renowned adj 有名的，有声誉的

rent v 租
rent n 租费
reorganize v 整顿
repair v 修理
reparation n 赔偿
repatriate v 遣返回国
repay v 回报
repayment n 偿还
repeal v 撤销
repeal n 撤销
repeat v 重复
repel v 排斥
repent v 悔悟
repentance n 悔悟
repetition n 重复
replace v 替换
replacement n 替换
replay n 重赛
replenish v 重新补充
replete adj 充满的
replica n 复制品
replicate v 复制
reply v 回复
reply n 回复
report v 报道
report n 报告
reportedly adv 据报道
reporter n 记者
repose v 歇息
repose n 歇息
represent v 现，表示，描绘，代表

R

repress v 抑制

repression n 抑制

reprieve n 缓刑

reprint v 重印

reprint n 印本

reprisal n 报复

reproach v 责备

reproach n 责备

reproduce v 再生产

reproduction n 再生产

reptile n 爬行动物

republic n 共和国，共和党

repudiate v 否定

repugnant adj 讨厌的，违反的

repulse v 击退

repulse n 击退

repulsive adj 厌恶的

reputation n 名誉

reputedly adv 据说，根据风评

request v 请求

request n 请求

require v 要求

requirement n 要求

rescue v 营救，救援

rescue n 抢救

research v 研究

research n 研究

resemblance n 相似

resemble v 类似

resent v 对…表示忿恨，怨恨

resentment n 怨气

reservation n 保留，定位子

reserve v 保留，定位子

reservoir n 水库

reside v 居住

residence n 住处，住宅，居住

residue n 残滓

resign v 辞职

resignation n 辞职

resilient adj 韧性的

resist v 抵（反）抗，抵制

resistance n 反抗，抵制，抵抗力（性）

resolute adj 刚毅的

resolution n 决议，计划

resolve v 解决

resort v 求助（或凭借）（对象），采用（的办法）

resounding adj 回响的

resource n 资源

respect v 尊敬

respect n 尊敬

respectful adj 尊敬的

respective adj 各自的

respiration n 呼吸作用

respite n 暂时的缓和，缓刑

respond v 反应

response n 反应

responsibility n 责任

responsible adj 有责任的

responsive adj 应答的，回答的，响应的

rest v 休息

rest n 休息

rest room *n* 洗手间

restaurant *n* 餐厅

restful *adj* 宁静的

restitution *n* 归还，赔偿

restless *adj* 不安定的

restoration *n* 恢复

restore *v* 恢复

restrain *v* 阻止，控制，抑制

restraint *n* 抑制，限制，克制

restrict *v* 禁止

result *n* 结果

resume *v* 重新开始

resumption *n* 重新开始

resurface *v* 重铺路面，重新露面

resurrection *n* 复活

resuscitate *v* 复苏

retain *v* 保留

retaliate *v* 报复

retaliation *n* 报复

retarded *adj* 智力迟钝的，智力发育迟缓的

retention *n* 保留

retire *v* 退休

retirement *n* 退休

retract *v* 缩回

retreat *v* 撤退

retreat *n* 撤退

retrieval *n* 取回，补偿

retrieve *v* 重新得到，收回，挽回

retroactive *adj* 再生的，反馈的

return *v* 回归

return *n* 回归

reunion *n* 团聚

reveal *v* 显露

revealing *adj* 有启迪作用的，透露内情的

revel *v* 狂欢作乐，陶醉

revelation *n* 显露，启示

revenge *v* 复仇

revenge *n* 复仇

revenue *n* 收入

reverence *n* 尊重

reversal *n* 逆转

reverse *n* 反面，逆境

reversible *adj* 可逆转的

revert *v* 恢复

review *v* 回顾

review *n* 回顾，复习

revise *v* 修改

revision *n* 修订

revive *v* 使重生，恢复精神

revoke *v* 撤销，取消，废除

revolt *v* 反叛

revolt *n* 反叛

revolting *adj* 反抗的

revolve *v* 旋转

revolver *v* 左轮手枪

revue *n* 时事讽刺剧

revulsion *n* 突变

reward *v* 奖励

reward *n* 奖品

rewarding *adj* 有报酬的，有益的，值得的

R

rheumatism n 风湿病
rhinoceros n 犀牛
rhyme n 押韵
rhythm n 节奏
rib n 肋骨
ribbon n 丝带
rice n 米饭
rich adj 富有的
rid of iv 摆脱
riddle n 谜语
ride iv 骑（马），乘（车）
ridge n 脊，山脊，垄
ridicule v 嘲笑
ridicule n 嘲笑
ridiculous adj 可笑的
rifle n 步枪
rift n 裂口
right adv 右边
right adj 正确的
right n 权利
rigid adj 正直的
rigor n 严厉
rim n 外缘
ring iv 摇铃，打电话
ring n 圆环，戒指
ringleader n 罪魁，头目
rinse v 冲洗
riot v 暴乱
riot n 暴乱
rip v 裂开
rip apart v 分裂
rip off v 偷窃

ripe adj 成熟
ripen v 成熟
ripple n 波纹
rise iv 上升
risk v 冒险
risk n 风险
risky adj 有风险的
rite n 宗教礼拜式
rival n 对手
rivalry n 竞争
river n 河
rivet v 吸引（注意力）
riveting adj 非常精彩的
road n 道路
roam v 漫游
roar v 咆哮
roar n 吼声
roast v 烘烤
roast n 烤熟的肉
rob v 抢夺
robber n 强盗
robbery n 抢劫
robe n 长袍
robust adj 健壮的
rock n 石头
rocket n 火箭
rocky adj 多石的
rod n 杆，棒
rodent n 啮齿类动物（如鼠等）
roll v 卷，滚
romance n 言情

roof n 屋顶
room n 房间
roomy adj 宽敞的
rooster n 公鸡
root n 根
rope n 绳索
rosary n （天主教的）玫瑰经，玫瑰经经文书
rose n 玫瑰花
rosy adj 玫瑰色
rot v 腐烂
rot n 腐烂
rotate v 转动
rotation n 转动
rotten adj 腐烂的
rough adj 粗糙的，艰难的
round adj 圆的
roundup n 召集
rouse v 唤醒
rousing adj 唤醒的，鼓舞的
route n 路线，路程
routine n 惯例
row v 排列
row n 列
rowdy adj 吵闹的，粗暴的
royal adj 王室的，皇家的
royalty n 皇族
rub v 磨擦
rubber n 橡胶
rubbish n 垃圾
rubble n 瓦砾
ruby n 红宝石

rudder n 船舵，领导者
rude adj 粗鲁的，不礼貌的
rudeness n 粗鲁
rudimentary adj 基本的
rug n 地毯
ruin v 毁坏
ruin n 废墟
rule v 统治，裁决
rule n 规则，惯例，统治
ruler n 直尺
rum n 朗姆酒
rumble v 发隆隆声
rumble n 隆隆声
rumor n 传闻，谣言
run iv 运行，跑
run away v 逃跑
run into v 碰到
run out v 用完
run over v 在...上驶过，碾过
run up v 积欠（账款、债务等）
runner n 跑步者
runway n 跑道，时装舞台
rupture n 破裂
rupture v 破裂
rural adj 农村的
ruse n 诡计，计策
rush v 冲
Russia n 俄罗斯
Russian adj 俄罗斯的
rust v 生锈
rust n 铁锈
rustic adj 乡村的，粗野的

R

rust-proof *adj* 防锈

rusty *adj* 生锈的

ruthless *adj* 无情

rye *n* 黑麦

S

sabotage *v* 阴谋破坏，蓄意破坏

sabotage *n* 阴谋破坏，蓄意破坏

sack *v* 解雇，洗劫

sack *n* 麻袋[the～]解雇，洗劫

sacrament *n* 圣礼

sacred *adj* 神圣的

sacrifice *n* 牺牲

sacrilege *n* 盗窃圣物（如从教堂盗窃），亵渎（神物、神灵）罪

sad *adj* 伤心

sadden *v* 使伤心

saddle *n* 马鞍

sadist *n* 性虐待狂者，虐待狂者

sadness *n* 悲伤

safe *adj* 安全

safeguard *n* 维护

safety *n* 安全

sail *v* 启航

sail *n* 启航

sailboat *n* 帆船

sailor *n* 水兵

saint *n* 圣人

salad *n* 沙拉

salary *n* 薪金

sale *n* 出售

sale slip *n* 售货单

salesman *n* 推销员

saliva *n* 唾液

salmon *n* 鲑鱼

saloon *n* 轿车

salt *n* 盐

salty *adj* 太咸

salvage *v* 打捞

salvation *n* 救赎

same *adj* 一样的

sample *n* 样本

sanctify *v* 圣化

sanction *v* 制裁

sanction *n* 制裁

sanctity *n* 神圣，圣洁，尊严

sanctuary *n* 圣所

sand *n* 沙

sandal *n* 凉鞋

sandpaper *n* 砂纸

sandwich *n* 三明治

sane *adj* 神志正常的，清醒的

sanity *n* 理智

sap *n* 树液，汁液，<俚>易上当的人

sap *v* 耗尽**

sapphire n 青玉

sarcasm n 讽刺

sarcastic adj 讽刺的

sardine n 沙丁鱼

satanic adj 邪恶的

satellite n 卫星

satire n 讽刺，讽刺作品

satisfaction n 满意

satisfactory adj 满意的

satisfy v 使满意，符合（要求等）

saturate v 饱和

Saturday n 星期六

sauce n 调味汁，佐料

saucepan n 平底锅

saucer n 茶碟

sausage n 香肠

savage adj 野蛮的

savagery n 野蛮

save v 拯救

savings n 储蓄

savior n 救世主

savor v 品尝，欣赏

saw iv 看到，锯

saw n 锯子

say iv 说

saying n 说法

scaffolding n 脚手架

scald v 烫伤

scale v 标度

scale n 规模

scalp n 头皮

scam n 骗局

scan v 细看，审视，扫描

scandal n 丑闻

scandalize v 丑闻化

scapegoat n 替罪羊

scar n 伤痕

scarce adj 稀缺的

scarcely adv 几乎没有

scarcity n 稀缺

scare v 吓唬

scare n 吓唬

scare away v 吓走

scarf n 丝巾

scary adj 可怕的

scatter v 消散

scenario n 剧情说明书，剧本

scene n 现场

scenery n 风景

scenic adj 景色的

scent n 嗅觉

schedule v 定时间

schedule n 附表，时间计划

scheme n 计划，方案，阴谋

schism n 分裂

scholar n 学者

scholarship n 奖学金

school n 学校

science n 科学

scientific adj 科学的

scientist n 科学家

scissors n 剪刀

scoff v 嘲笑

S

scold *v* 骂

scolding *n* 骂

scooter *n* 踏板车，小型摩托车

scope *n* 范围

scorch *v* 烧焦

score *n* 评分

score *v* 得（分），刻痕于

scorn *v* 轻蔑，鄙视

scornful *n* 轻蔑的

scorpion *n* 蝎子

scoundrel *n* 歹徒

scour *v* 冲刷

scourge *n* 灾祸

scout *n* 童军

scramble *v* 爬行，搅拌

scrambled *adj* 密码形式的

scrap *n* 小块

scrap *v* 处理

scrape *v* 刮

scratch *v* 打草稿

scratch *n* 抓痕，草稿

scream *v* 尖叫

scream *n* 尖叫

screech *v* 尖哭

screen *n* 屏幕

screen *v* 检验

screw *v* 用螺钉固定，拧紧

screw *n* 螺钉，滥交

screwdriver *n* 螺丝刀

scribble *v* 草写

script *n* 剧本

scroll *n* 卷轴，纸卷，画卷

scrub *v* 磨砂

scruples *n* 顾忌

scrupulous *adj* 一丝不苟

scrutiny *n* 审议

scuffle *n* 扭打

sculptor *n* 雕塑家

sculpture *n* 雕塑

sea *n* 海

seafood *n* 海鲜

seagull *n* 海鸥

seal *v* 印章，封锁

seal *n* 印章

seal off *v* 封锁

seam *n* 缝隙

seamless *adj* 无缝的

seamstress *n* 裁缝

search *v* 搜索

search *n* 搜索，寻找

seashore *n* 海滨

seasick *adj* 晕船的

seaside *adj* 海边的

season *n* 季节

seasonal *adj* 季节性的

seasoning *n* 调味品

seat *n* 座椅

seated *adj* 坐下

secede *v* 脱离

secluded *adj* 僻静的

seclusion *n* 隐居

second *n* 第二

secondary *adj* 中级的

secrecy *n* 秘密，隐私

secret _n_ 秘密
secretary _n_ 秘书
secretly _adv_ 秘密地
sect _n_ 学派
section _n_ 部分
sector _n_ 部门
secure _v_ 使安全，获得
secure _adj_ 安全的，牢靠的
security _n_ 安全，保障，抵押品
sedate _v_ 使沉着
sedation _n_ 镇静
seduce _v_ 诱惑
seduction _n_ 诱惑
see _iv_ 见
seed _n_ 种子
seedless _adj_ 无籽
seedy _adj_ 多种子
seek _iv_ 寻求
seem _v_ 看来
see-through _adj_ 看穿
segment _n_ 部分
segregate _v_ 分隔
segregation _n_ 隔离
seize _v_ 抓住，捉住，夺取
seizure _n_ 扣押
seldom _adv_ 很少地
select _v_ 选择
selection _n_ 选择
self-conscious _adj_ 自觉的，忸怩的
self-esteem _n_ 自尊
self-evident _adj_ 不言自明的

self-interest _n_ 自利原则，自身利益
selfish _adj_ 自私的
selfishness _n_ 自私
self-respect _n_ 自尊
sell _iv_ 出售
seller _n_ 卖家
sellout _n_ 出卖
semblance _n_ 假象
semester _n_ 学期
seminary _n_ 修道院
senate _n_ 参议院
senator _n_ 参议员
send _iv_ 发送
sender _n_ 发送人
senile _adj_ 年老的
senior _adj_ 高级的，老年的
seniority _n_ 长辈
sensation _n_ 感觉
sense _v_ 感觉
sense _n_ 感觉，意义
senseless _adj_ 无意义
sensible _adj_ 易察觉
sensitive _adj_ 敏感的
sensual _adj_ 感官的
sentence _v_ 判决
sentence _n_ 句，判决
sentiment _n_ 情绪
sentimental _adj_ 感伤的
sentry _n_ 哨兵
separate _v_ 隔离
separate _adj_ 单独的

S

separation n 分离

September n 九月

sequel n 续集

sequence n 连续，一连串，次序

serenade n 小夜曲

serene adj 宁静的

serenity n 宁静

sergeant n 军士

series n 系列

serious adj 严重的，认真的

seriousness n 严重性，认真

sermon n 布道

serpent n 蛇

serum n 血清

servant n 仆人

serve v 服务

service n 服务

service v 服务

session n 会议，部分

set n 一套

set iv 设定，设置

set about v 开始，着手

set off v 出发，启程，激起

set out v 动身，起程，开始

set up up 成立

setback n 挫折

setting n 环境，背景，布景

settle v 定居

settle down v 安顿下来

settle for v 定居为

settlement n 解决，协议，居留地

settler n 定居者

setup n 设定

seven adj 七

seventeen adj 十七

seventh adj 第七

seventy adj 七十

sever v 断绝

several adj 几个

severance n 切断

severe adj 严重的，严厉的

severity n 严重性

sew v 缝纫

sewage n 污水

sewer n 下水道

sewing n 缝纫

sex n 性别

sexuality n 性欲

shabby adj 破旧

shack n 棚子

shackle n 铁链

shade n 荫，阴凉处

shadow n 影子

shady adj 有黑幕的，遮荫的

shake iv 摇

shaken adj 动摇的

shaky adj 摇摇欲坠

shallow adj 浅

sham n 以为

shambles n 摇晃不稳

shame v 羞耻，可惜

shame n 使丢脸，使羞愧

shameful adj 可耻的

shameless *adj* 无耻的

shape *v* 塑造，定形

shape *n* 形状，形式，身材

share *v* 分享

share *n* 分享，份

shareholder *n* 股东

shark *n* 鲨鱼

sharp *adj* 锋利的

sharpen *v* 削尖

sharpener *n* 磨削器

shatter *v* 粉碎

shattering *adj* 震惊的，累人的

shave *v* 剃

she *pro* 她

shear *iv* 剪

shed *iv* 避免，脱

sheep *n* 羊

sheets *n* 床单

shelf *n* 架子，搁板

shell *n* 壳

shellfish *n* 贝，甲壳类动物

shelter *v* 避难

shelter *n* 避难所

shelves *n* 架子

shepherd *n* 牧羊人

sherry *n* 雪利酒

shield *v* 保护

shield *n* 盾牌

shift *n* 移动，轮班

shift *v* 移动

shine *iv* 照耀

shiny *adj* 闪亮的

ship *n* 船舶

shipment *n* 装运

shipwreck *n* 沉船

shipyard *n* 船厂

shirk *v* 推卸

shirt *n* 衬衫

shiver *v* 颤栗

shiver *n* 颤栗

shock *v* 使震惊

shock *n* 震惊

shocking *adj* 令人震惊的，可怕的

shoddy *adj* 伪劣

shoe *n* 鞋

shoe polish *n* 擦鞋膏

shoe store *n* 鞋店

shoelace *n* 鞋带

shoot *iv* 射击

shoot down *v* 击落

shop *v* 逛街

shop *n* 商店

shoplifting *n* 入店行窃

shopping *n* 购物

shore *n* 岸上

short *adj* 短，矮

shortage *n* 短缺

shortcoming *n* 缺点

shortcut *n* 捷径

shorten *v* 缩短

shorthand *n* 速记

short-lived *adj* 短命的，短暂的

shortly *adv* 不久

S

shorts n 短裤

shortsighted adj 短见

shot n 注射，发射，拍摄

shotgun n 鸟枪

shoulder n 肩

shout v 喊

shout n 喊

shouting n 高喊

shove v 推

shove n 推

shovel n 铲子

show iv 展示

show off v 炫耀

show up v 出现

showdown n 摊牌，最后的决战

shower n 淋浴

shrapnel n 弹片

shred v 撕成碎片

shred n 碎片

shrewd adj 精明

shriek v 尖叫

shriek n 尖叫声

shrimp n 虾

shrine n 圣地，圣坛

shrink iv 收缩

shroud n 寿衣

shrouded adj 寿衣

shrub n 灌木

shrug v 耸肩

shudder n 战栗，震颤

shudder v 战栗，震颤

shuffle v 拖曳

shun v 避开

shut iv 关闭

shut off v 关闭

shut up v 闭嘴

shuttle v 穿梭

shy adj 害羞的

shyness n 害羞

sick adj 有病的

sicken v 厌恶

sickening adj 令人作呕

sickle n 镰刀

sickness n 疾病

side n 边

sideburns n 双鬓

sidestep v 回避

sidewalk n 人行道

sideways adv 斜向一边

siege n 围困

siege v 围困

sift v 筛，过滤，详审

sigh n 叹息

sigh v 叹息

sight n 视线

sightseeing v 观光

sign v 登记，签名

sign n 标记，符号

signal n 信号

signature n 签字

significance n 意义

significant adj 相当数量的，意义重大的

signify v 标志着

S

silence *n* 沉默
silence *v* 沉默
silent *adj* 沉默的
silhouette *n* 剪影
silk *n* 丝绸
silly *adj* 傻的，糊涂的
silver *n* 白银
silver plated *adj* 白银的
silversmith *n* 白银加工师
silverware *n* 银器
similar *adj* 类似
similarity *n* 相似
simmer *v* 低温煮
simple *adj* 简单的
simplicity *n* 简单
simplify *v* 简化
simply *adv* 简单地
simulate *v* 模拟
simultaneous *adj* 同声传译，
　同时
sin *v* 有罪孽
sin *n* 罪孽
since *c* 因为
since *pre* 自从
since then *adv* 从那时起
sincere *adj* 真诚
sincerity *n* 诚意
sinful *adj* 罪孽深重
sing *iv* 唱
singer *n* 歌手
single *n* 单程票，单人房间，
　单身者

single *adj* 单一的
singlehanded *adj* 一手
single-minded *adj* 下定决心的
singular *adj* 奇异的
sinister *n* 险恶
sink *iv* 下沉
sink in *v* 下沉
sinner *n* 罪人
sip *v* 小口地喝
sip *n* 一口饮料
sir *n* 先生
siren *n* 警报器
sirloin *n* 牛腩
sissy *adj* 胆小的
sister *n* 妹妹
sister-in-law *n* 嫂子，弟媳
sit *iv* 坐
site *n* 网站，地点
sitting *n* 就餐时段，供人画像或
　拍照期间
situated *adj* 坐落
situation *n* 情况
six *adj* 六
sixteen *adj* 十六
sixth *adj* 第六
sixty *adj* 六十
sizable *adj* 相当大的
size *n* 大小
size up *v* 估计，判断
skate *v* 溜冰
skate *n* 溜冰
skeleton *n* 骨架

S

skeptic *adj* 怀疑者，怀疑论者
skeptic *adj* 怀疑的，有疑问的
sketch *v* 素描
sketch *n* 素描
sketchy *adj* 粗略的
ski *v* 滑雪
skill *n* 技巧
skillful *adj* 灵巧的，娴熟的
skim *v* 脱皮
skin *v* 划破
skin *n* 皮肤
skinny *adj* 皮的，皮包骨头的
skip *v* 跳过
skip *n* 跳过
skirmish *n* 小冲突
skirt *n* 裙子
skull *n* 头骨
sky *n* 天空
skylight *n* 天窗
skyscraper *n* 摩天楼
slab *n* 平板
slack *adj* 松驰的
slacken *v* 放松
slacks *n* 休闲裤
slam *v* 大满贯
slander *n* 诽谤
slanted *adj* 倾斜的
slap *n* 侮辱，掴，拍击声
slap *v* 侮辱，拍击，惩罚
slash *n* 深砍
slash *v* 深砍
slate *n* 板岩

slaughter *v* 屠宰
slaughter *n* 屠宰
slave *n* 奴隶
slavery *n* 奴役
slay *iv* 斩
sleazy *adj* 单薄的
sleep *iv* 睡
sleep *n* 睡眠
sleeve *n* 袖子
sleeveless *adj* 无袖的
sleigh *n* 雪橇
slender *adj* 苗条的
slice *v* 切
slice *n* 切片
slide *iv* 滑到一边
slightly *adv* 稍微
slim *adj* 苗条的
slip *v* 滑动
slip *n* 滑动
slipper *n* 拖鞋
slippery *adj* 滑的
slit *iv* 裂缝
slob *adj* 懒汉，粗俗汉，笨蛋
slogan *n* 口号
slope *n* 斜坡
sloppy *adj* 肥大的，潦草的，
草率的
slot *n* 插槽
slow *adj* 慢的
slow down *v* 放缓
slow motion *n* 慢动作
slowly *adv* 慢慢地

S

sluggish *adj* 呆滞的

slum *n* 贫民窟

slump *v* 暴跌

slump *n* 不景气，暴跌

slur *v* 诋毁

sly *adj* 狡猾的

smack *n* 击响

smack *v* 击响

small *adj* 小的

small print *n* 小字

smallpox *n* 天花

smart *adj* 聪明的

smash *v* 粉碎

smear *n* 污迹

smear *v* 涂片

smell *iv* 闻

smelly *adj* 发臭的

smile *v* 微笑

smile *n* 微笑

smith *n* 匠

smoke *v* 吸烟，以烟熏

smoked *adj* 熏的

smoker *n* 吸烟者

smoking gun *n* 烟雾弹

smooth *v* 使顺利

smooth *adj* 顺利的

smoothly *adv* 顺利地

smoothness *n* 光滑

smother *v* 扼杀

smuggler *n* 走私贩

snail *n* 蜗牛

snake *n* 蛇

snapshot *n* 快照

snare *v* 圈套

snare *n* 圈套

snatch *v* 抓举

sneak *v* 告密，溜进

sneeze *v* 打喷嚏

sneeze *n* 喷嚏

sniff *v* 嗅，嗤之以鼻

sniper *n* 狙击手

snitch *v* 打小报告

snooze *v* 打盹

snore *v* 打鼾

snore *n* 打鼾声

snow *v* 下雪

snow *n* 雪

snowfall *n* 降雪

snowflake *n* 雪花

snub *v* 冷落，斥责，止住

snub *n* 怠慢，冷落

soak *v* 浸泡

soak in *v* 泡在

soak up *v* 浸透

soar *v* 飙升

sob *v* 呜咽

sob *n* 呜咽

sober *adj* 清醒

so-called *adj* 所谓的

sociable *adj* 好交际的，友好的

socialism *n* 社会主义

socialist *adj* 社会主义的

socialize *v* 社交

society *n* 社会

S

sock *n* 袜子

sod *n* 草皮

soda *n* 纯碱

sofa *n* 沙发

soft *adj* 软的

soften *v* 软化

softly *adv* 温柔的

softness *n* 软

soggy *adj* 潮湿的

soil *v* 施肥

soil *n* 土壤

soiled *adj* 施过肥的

solace *n* 安慰

solar *adj* 太阳能的

solder *v* 焊料

soldier *n* 士兵

sold-out *adj* 全部预售完的，满座的

sole *n* 唯一

sole *adj* 唯一

solely *adv* 独自地，单独地，完全

solemn *adj* 庄严的

solicit *v* 征求

solid *adj* 固的

solidarity *n* 声援

solitary *adj* 孤独的

solitude *n* 孤独

soluble *adj* 可溶的

solution *n* 解决方案

solve *v* 解决

solvent *adj* 溶剂的

somber *adj* 低沉的

some *adj* 一些

somebody *pro* 某人

someday *adv* 某一天

somehow *adv* 有点，以某种方法

someone *pro* 某人

something *pro* 东西

sometimes *adv* 有时

someway *adv* 某种方法

somewhat *adv* 有点

son *n* 儿子

song *n* 唱歌

son-in-law *n* 女婿

soon *adv* 不久

soothe *v* 抚慰

sorcerer *n* 魔法师

sorcery *n* 巫术

sore *n* 痛

sore *adj* 痛的

sorrow *n* 悲哀

sorrowful *adj* 伤感的

sorry *adj* 抱歉的

sort *n* 排序

sort out *v* 整理，弄清楚

soul *n* 灵魂

sound *n* 声音

sound *v* 听起来

sound out *v* 试探

soup *n* 汤

sour *adj* 酸溜溜的

source *n* 资源

south *n* 南

S

southbound *adv* 南面

southeast *n* 东南

southern *adj* 南部的

southerner *n* 南方人

southwest *n* 西南

souvenir *n* 纪念品

sovereign *adj* 至高无上的，有独立主权的

sovereignty *n* 主权

soviet *adj* 前苏联的

sow *iv* 种

spa *n* 温泉

space *n* 空间

space out *v* 开小差

spacious *adj* 宽敞的

spade *n* 铁锹

Spain *n* 西班牙

span *v* 跨过

span *n* 跨度

Spaniard *n* 西班牙人

Spanish *adj* 西班牙的

spank *v* 打

spanking *n* 责打

spare *v* 抽出，饶恕

spare *adj* 备用的

spare part *n* 零部件

sparingly *adv* 节俭地，保守地

spark *n* 星火

spark off *v* 击火花

spark plug *n* 火花塞

sparkle *v* 闪闪发光

sparrow *n* 麻雀

sparse *adj* 稀少的

spasm *n* 痉挛

speak *iv* 说

speaker *n* 发言人，音响

spear *n* 矛

spearhead *v* 当领导

special *adj* 特别的

specialize *v* 专攻

specialty *n* 专科

species *n* 物种

specific *adj* 具体的

specimen *n* 标本

speck *n* 斑点

spectacle *n* 眼镜

spectator *n* 观众，旁观者

speculate *v* 猜测

speculation *n* 投机

speech *n* 讲话

speechless *adj* 无言以对的

speed *iv* 超速

speed *n* 高速

speedily *adv* 迅速

speedy *adj* 迅速的

spell *iv* 咒，拼写

spell *n* 咒语

spelling *n* 拼写

spend *iv* 用（钱），花（时间等）

spending *n* 开销，消费

sperm *n* 精子

sphere *n* 球

spice *n* 香料

S

spicy *adj* 辣的

spider *n* 蜘蛛

spider web *n* 蜘蛛网

spill *iv* 溢漏

spill *n* 溢漏

spin *iv* 自旋

spine *n* 脊柱

spineless *adj* 无脊柱的

spinster *n* 未婚女人，老处女

spirit *n* 精神

spiritual *adj* 精神的

spit *iv* 吐痰

spite *n* 尽管

spiteful *adj* 恶意的，怀恨的

splash *v* 溅，泼

splendid *adj* 极好的，壮丽的，辉煌的

splendor *n* 异彩

splint *n* 夹板

splinter *n* 分裂

splinter *v* 分裂

split *n* 分裂

split *iv* 分裂

split up *v* 分裂

spoil *v* 溺爱

spoils *n* 赃物

sponge *n* 海绵

sponsor *n* 赞助商

spontaneity *n* 自发性

spontaneous *adj* 自发的，自然的

spooky *adj* 惊悚的

spool *n* 阀芯

spoon *n* 勺子

spoonful *n* 一勺

sporadic *adj* 零星的

sport *n* 体育

sportsman *n* 运动员

sporty *adj* 运动的

spot *v* 看见

spot *n* 斑点，点

spotless *adj* 一尘不染的

spotlight *n* 聚光灯

spouse *n* 配偶

sprain *v* 扭伤

sprawl *v* 扩张

spray *v* 喷

spread *iv* 蔓延

spring *iv* 喷泉

spring *n* 春天，喷泉

springboard *n* 跳板

sprinkle *v* 洒，撒

sprout *v* 萌发

spruce up *v* 打扫

spur *v* 激励，鞭策

spur *n* 刺激（物），激励

spy *v* 监视

spy *n* 间谍

squalid *adj* 肮脏的

squander *v* 挥霍

square *adj* 方的

square *n* 广场

squash *v* 压

squeak *v* 发吱吱声

squeaky *adj* 吱吱声的
squeamish *adj* 恶心的
squeeze *v* 挤压
squeeze in *v* 挤进
squeeze up *v* 挤压
squid *n* 鱿鱼
squirrel *n* 松鼠
stab *v* 刺戳
stab *n* 刺戳
stability *n* 稳定
stable *adj* 稳定的，沉稳的
stable *n* 马厩
stack *v* 堆
stack *n* 堆
staff *n* 工作人员
stage *n* 阶段，舞台
stage *v* 上演，举办
stagger *v* 摇摆
staggering *adj* 摇摆的
stagnant *adj* 停滞的
stagnate *v* 停滞
stagnation *n* 停滞
stain *v* 污点
stain *n* 污点
stair *n* 楼梯
staircase *n* 楼梯
stairs *n* 楼梯
stake *n* 桩，利害关系，股份
stake *v* 打赌
stale *adj* 陈旧的
stalemate *n* 僵局
stalk *v* 查找

stalk *n* 查找
stall *n* 档
stall *v* 档
stammer *v* 口吃
stamp *v* 盖邮戳
stamp *n* 邮票
stamp out *v* 杜绝
stampede *n* 踩踏
stand *iv* 站立
stand *n* 台，摊，立场
stand for *v* 主张，代表
stand out *v* 突出
stand up *v* 起立
standard *n* 标准
standardize *v* 规范
standing *n* 站立
standpoint *n* 立场
standstill *adj* 停顿
staple *v* 订书
staple *n* 主食
stapler *n* 订书机
star *n* 明星，星星
starch *n* 淀粉
starchy *adj* 淀粉的
stare *v* 盯
stark *adj* 荒凉的，严酷的
start *v* 开始
start *n* 开始
startle *v* 惊吓
startled *adj* 震惊的，受惊吓的
starvation *n* 饥饿
starve *v* 挨饿

S

state n 国家，州，状态

state v 声明

statement n 声明

station n 站

stationary adj 固定的，静止不动的

stationery n 文具

statistic n 统计

statue n 雕像

status n 地位

statute n 成文法，法令，法规

staunch adj 刚烈的

stay v 暂住，保持，延缓

stay n 逗留，延缓

steady adj 稳重的，持续的

steak n 牛排

steal iv 窃取

stealthy adj 秘密的

steam n 蒸汽

steel n 钢

steep adj 陡峭的

stem n 干，词根

stem v 起源于（from）

stench n 恶臭

step n 步

step down v 下台

step out v 出去

step up v 加快，加速

stepbrother n 继兄弟

step-by-step adv 按部就班

stepdaughter n 继女

stepfather n 继父

stepladder n 阶梯

stepmother n 继母

stepsister n 继姐妹

stepson n 继子

sterile adj 不育的

sterilize v 消毒

stern n 船尾

stern adj 严厉的

sternly adv 严厉地

stew n 大杂烩

stewardess n 空中小姐

stick v 拈着

stick iv 坚持

stick around v 逗留

stick out v 突出

stick to v 坚持

sticker n 贴纸，标签

sticky adj 粘的，粘性的

stiff adj 刚性的

stiffen v 变硬

stiffness n 硬度

stifle v 扼杀

stifling adj 令人窒息的

still adj 静止的，不动的

still adv 依然

stimulant n 兴奋剂

stimulate v 刺激

stimulus n 刺激

sting iv 蜇

sting n 蜇

stinging adj 刺痛的

stingy adj 吝啬的，菲薄的

stink *iv* 发臭
stink *n* 发臭
stinking *adj* 臭的
stipulate *v* 规定
stir *v* 搅拌
stir up *v* 挑起
stitch *v* 针
stitch *n* 针
stock *v* 存储
stock *n* 股票，存储
stocking *n* 长袜
stockpile *n* 储存
stockroom *n* 储藏室
stoic *adj* 坚忍克己的，禁欲的
stomach *n* 胃
stone *n* 石头
stone *v* 投石头
stool *n* 大便
stop *v* 停止
stop *n* 停止，站
stop by *v* 路过
stop over *v* 停留
storage *n* 存储
store *v* 存储
store *n* 商店
stork *n* 鹳
storm *n* 风暴
stormy *adj* 风暴的
story *n* 故事，楼层
stove *n* 炉灶
straight *adj* 直的，坦率的
straighten out *v* 整顿

strain *v* 应变
strain *n* 应变
strained *adj* 紧张
strainer *n* 滤网
strait *n* 海峡
stranded *adj* 搁浅的，进退两难的
strange *adj* 奇怪的，奇异的
stranger *n* 陌生人
strangle *v* 扼杀
strap *n* 肩带
strategy *n* 策略
straw *n* 稻草
strawberry *n* 草莓
stray *adj* 迷路的
stray *v* 迷路
stream *n* 流
street *n* 街
streetcar *n* 街车
streetlight *n* 路灯
strength *n* 实力，力量，强度
strengthen *v* 加强
strenuous *adj* 艰苦的
stress *n* 压力
stressful *adj* 有压力的
stretch *n* 舒展
stretch *v* 舒展
stretcher *n* 担架
strict *adj* 严格的
stride *iv* 大步
strife *n* 内乱
strike *n* 罢工

S

strike *iv* 罢工
strike back *v* 反击
strike out *v* 剔除
strike up *v* 罢工
striking *n* 显著的，惹人注目的
string *n* 串，线
stringent *adj* 严厉的，令人信服的
strip *n* 条，带状物
strip *v* 脱光衣服，剥夺
stripe *n* 条纹
striped *adj* 条纹的
strive *iv* 力争
stroke *n* 中风
stroll *v* 漫步
strong *adj* 强壮的，牢固的，坚强的
structure *n* 结构
struggle *v* 斗争
struggle *n* 斗争
stub *n* 票根
stubborn *adj* 顽固的
student *n* 学生
study *v* 学习
stuff *n* 东西
stuff *v* 塞东西
stuffing *n* 馅
stuffy *adj* 室闷的
stumble *v* 蹒跚
stun *v* 震惊
stunning *adj* 惊人的
stupendous *adj* 巨大的，大得惊人的

stupid *adj* 笨的
stupidity *n* 愚蠢
sturdy *adj* 坚固的
stutter *v* 口吃
style *n* 风格
subdue *v* 制服，使顺从，征服
subdued *adj* 被征服的，屈从的
subject *v* 使服从，使隶属
subject *n* 主题
sublime *adj* 壮美的
submerge *v* 下潜
submissive *adj* 服从的
submit *v* 提交
subpoena *v* 传票
subpoena *n* 传票
subscribe *v* 订阅
subscription *n* 订阅
subsequent *adj* 随后的
subsidiary *adj* 辅助的，附设的
subsidize *v* 补贴
subsidy *n* 补贴
subsist *v* 维持生活，生存
substance *n* 物质
substandard *adj* 标准以下的，不合规格的
substantial *adj* 大量的，坚固的，实质的
substitute *v* 替代
substitute *n* 替代
subtitle *n* 副标题，字幕
subtle *adj* 微妙的
subtract *v* 减

subtraction *n* 减法
suburb *n* 郊区
subway *n* 地铁
succeed *v* 成功
success *n* 成功
successful *adj* 成功的
successor *n* 继任者
succulent *adj* 多汁的
succumb *v* 屈服
such *adj* 这类
suck *v* 吮
sucker *adj* 傻瓜，吸盘，吸管
sudden *adj* 突然的
suddenly *adv* 突然地
sue *v* 控告
suffer *v* 受苦
suffer from *v* 遭受
suffering *n* 痛苦
sufficient *adj* 充足的
suffocate *v* 窒息
sugar *n* 糖
suggest *v* 建议
suggestion *n* 建议
suggestive *adj* 暗示的，启发的
suicide *n* 自杀
suit *n* 西装
suitable *adj* 适合的
suitcase *n* 手提箱
sulfur *n* 硫（磺）
sullen *adj* 不高兴的
sum *n* 总和
sum up *v* 总结

summarize *v* 总结
summary *n* 摘要
summer *n* 夏天
summit *n* 峰顶，最高级会议
summon *v* 传召
sumptuous *adj* 丰盛的
sun *n* 太阳
sun block *n* 滤光剂，防晒乳
sunburn *n* 晒伤
Sunday *n* 周日
sundown *n* 日落
sunglasses *n* 墨镜
sunken *adj* 沉没的
sunny *adj* 晴天的
sunrise *n* 日出
sunset *n* 夕阳
superb *adj* 极好的，高质量的
superfluous *adj* 过剩的
superior *adj* 上级的，较高的
superiority *n* 优势
supermarket *n* 超市
superpower *n* 超级大国
supersede *v* 取代
superstition *n* 迷信
supervise *v* 监督
supervision *n* 监督
supper *n* 晚饭
supple *adj* 柔软的
supplier *n* 供应商
supplies *n* 用品
supply *v* 供应
support *v* 支持

S

supporter *n* 支持者
suppose *v* 料想，以为，假定
supposing *c* 假设
supposition *n* 假设
suppress *v* 压制
supremacy *n* 霸权
supreme *adj* 最高的
surcharge *n* 附加费
sure *adj* 肯定
surely *adv* 肯定
surf *v* 冲浪
surface *n* 表面
surge *n* 浪涌
surgeon *n* 外科医生
surgical *adv* 外科的
surname *n* 姓
surpass *v* 超越
surplus *n* 剩余
surprise *v* 惊喜
surprise *n* 惊奇，令人惊奇的事物
surrender *v* 投降
surrender *n* 投降
surround *v* 环绕
surroundings *n* 周围
surveillance *n* 监察
survey *n* 调查
survival *n* 生存
survive *v* 生存
survivor *n* 生还者
susceptible *adj* 易受影响的
suspect *v* 推测，怀疑

suspect *n* 疑犯
suspend *v* 暂停
suspenders *n* 吊杆
suspense *n* 悬疑
suspension *n* 暂停，暂时剥夺，悬浮液
suspicion *n* 猜疑
suspicious *adj* 猜疑的，可疑的
sustain *v* 维持
sustenance *n* 寄托
swallow *n* 海燕
swamp *n* 沼泽
swamped *adj* 陷入沼泽的
swan *n* 天鹅
swap *v* 交换
swap *n* 交换
swarm *n* 群
sway *v* 摆动
swear *iv* 宣誓
sweat *n* 汗水
sweat *v* 出汗
sweater *n* 毛衣
Sweden *n* 瑞典
Swedish *adj* 瑞典的
sweep *iv* 打扫
sweet *adj* 甜的
sweeten *v* 使变甜
sweetheart *n* 爱人，情人
sweetness *n* 甜
sweets *n* 甜食
swell *iv* 胀大
swelling *n* 肿胀

S

swift *adj* 迅速的
swim *iv* 游泳
swimmer *n* 游泳者
swimming *n* 游泳
swindle *v* 骗局
swindle *n* 骗局
swindler *n* 骗子
swing *iv* 摆动
swing *n* 摆动
Swiss *adj* 瑞士的
switch *v* 开关，换动
switch *n* 开关，换动
switch off *v* 关掉
switch on *v* 打开
Switzerland *n* 瑞士
swivel *v* 转体
swollen *adj* 肿胀的
sword *n* 剑
swordfish *n* 箭鱼
syllable *n* 音节
symbol *n* 符号
symbolic *adj* 象征的
symmetry *n* 对称性
sympathize *v* 同情
sympathy *n* 同情
symphony *n* 交响曲
symptom *n* 症状
synagogue *n* 犹太教堂
synchronize *v* 同步
synod *n* 主教
synonym *n* 别名
synthesis *n* 合成

syphilis *n* 梅毒
syringe *n* 注射器
syrup *n* 糖浆
system *n* 系统
systematic *adj* 系统的，分类的，体系的

T

table *n* 表，桌子
tablecloth *n* 桌布
tablespoon *n* 汤匙
tablet *n* 药片，碑，牌
tack *n* 大头钉
tackle *v* 解决
tact *n* 机智
tactful *adj* 机智的，老练的
tactical *adj* 战术上的，足智多谋的
tactics *n* 策略，战术
tag *n* 标签
tail *n* 尾巴
tail *v* 跟踪
tailor *n* 裁缝
tainted *adj* 污点的，感染的
take *iv* 采取，带，拿
take apart *v* 分开
take away *v* 拿走

S
T

take back v 收回
take in v 接受，吸收
take off v 出发
take out v 带…出去，除掉
take over v 接管
tale n 故事
talent n 人才
talk v 交谈
talkative adj 健谈
tall adj 高大的
tame v 温顺的，乏味的
tangent n 正切
tangerine n 桔子
tangible adj 有形
tangle n 纠纷
tank n 坦克
tanned adj 古铜色的
tantamount to adj 同等
tantrum n 勃然大怒
tap n 轻拍，自来水
tap into v 深入了解
tape n 磁带
tape recorder n 录音机
tapestry n 挂毯
tar n 焦油
tarantula n 狼蛛
tardy adv 迟缓的
target n 目标
tariff n 关税
tarnish v 玷污
tart n 蛋塔杯模，妓女
tartar n 齿垢

task n 任务
taste v 品尝
taste n 品味
tasteful adj 有滋味的，好吃的
tasteless adj 无味的
tasty adj 美味的
tavern n 酒馆
tax n 税
tea n 茶叶
teach iv 教
teacher n 教师
team n 团队
teapot n 茶壶
tear iv 流泪，撕
tear n 泪
tearful adj 含泪的，悲伤的
tease v 捉弄
teaspoon n 茶匙
technical adj 技术的
technicality n 技术性
technician n 技术员
technique n 技巧
technology n 科技
tedious adj 乏味的，繁琐的
tedium n 单调
teenager n 少年
teeth n 牙齿
telegram n 电报
telepathy n 感应
telephone n 电话
telescope n 望远镜
televise v 直播

television *n* 电视

tell *iv* 告诉

teller *n* 出纳员

telling *adj* 有效的，有力的

temper *n* 脾气

temperature *n* 温度

tempest *n* 暴风雨

temple *n* 庙

temporary *adj* 临时的

tempt *v* 诱惑

temptation *n* 诱惑

tempting *adj* 引诱人的，吸引人的

ten *adj* 十

tenacity *n* 固执

tenant *n* 房客

tendency *n* 趋势

tender *adj* 柔软的，温柔的

tenderness *n* 柔软，温柔

tennis *n* 网球

tenor *n* 男高音

tense *adj* 紧张的

tension *n* 紧张

tent *n* 帐篷

tentacle *n* 触手

tentative *adj* 暂定的

tenth *n* 第十

tenuous *adj* 脆弱的，稀薄的

tepid *adj* 温热的

term *n* 任期，学期

terminate *v* 终止

terminology *n* 术语，术语学

termite *n* 白蚁

terms *n* 条款

terrace *n* 阳台

terrain *n* 地形

terrestrial *adj* 陆地的，天线的

terrible *adj* 可怕的

terrific *adj* 可怕的，极好的

terrify *v* 恐吓

terrifying *adj* 可怕的

territory *n* 领土

terror *n* 恐怖

terrorism *n* 恐怖主义

terrorist *n* 恐怖主义者

terrorize *v* 恐吓

terse *adj* 简洁的

test *v* 测试

test *n* 测试

testament *n* 全书

testify *v* 作证

testimony *n* 证词

text *n* 文本

textbook *n* 教科书

texture *n* 质地，组织，结构

thank *v* 感谢

thankful *adj* 感激的

thanks *n* 谢谢

that *adj* 那

thaw *v* 解冻

thaw *n* 解冻

theater *n* 影剧院

theft *n* 盗窃

theme *n* 主题

themselves *pro* 他们自己
then *adv* 然后
theologian *n* 神学家
theology *n* 神学
theory *n* 理论
therapy *n* 疗法
there *adv* 那里
therefore *adv* 因此
thermometer *n* 温度计
thermostat *n* 恒温器
these *adj* 这些
thesis *n* 论文
they *pro* 他们
thick *adj* 厚的，粗的，浓的
thicken *v* 变厚
thickness *n* 厚度
thief *n* 小偷
thigh *n* 大腿
thin *adj* 薄的
thing *n* 物
think *iv* 想
thinly *adv* 薄地
third *adj* 第三
thirst *v* 渴望，口渴
thirsty *adj* 干渴的
thirteen *adj* 十三
thirty *adj* 三十
this *adj* 这
thorn *n* 刺
thorny *adj* 棘手的
thorough *adj* 彻底的
those *adj* 那些

though *c* 虽然
thought *n* 想法
thoughtful *adj* 周到的
thousand *adj* 一千
thread *v* 穿针
thread *n* 螺纹，针线
threat *n* 威胁
threaten *v* 威胁
three *adj* 三
thresh *v* 打谷
threshold *n* 门槛，门口，起始点
thrifty *adj* 节俭的
thrill *v* 兴奋
thrill *n* 兴奋
thrive *v* 兴旺
throat *n* 喉咙
throb *n* 跳动
throb *v* 跳动
thrombosis *n* 血栓症
throne *n* 王座
throng *n* 人群
through *pre* 通过
throw *iv* 投掷
throw away *v* 扔掉
throw up *v* 呕吐，产生（想法）
thug *n* 暴徒
thumb *n* 拇指
thumbtack *n* 大头钉
thunder *n* 打雷
thunderbolt *n* 雷电，霹雳

thunderstorm *n* 雷阵雨

Thursday *n* 星期四

thus *adv* 因此

thwart *v* 挫败

thyroid *n* 甲状腺

tickle *v* 抓痒

tickle *n* 痒

ticklish *adj* 痒

tidal wave *n* 潮汐波，浪潮

tide *n* 浪潮

tidy *adj* 整洁的

tie *v* 约束，捆绑，打结

tie *n* 束缚，领带，绳，不分胜负

tiger *n* 老虎

tight *adj* 紧的

tighten *v* 收紧

tile *n* 瓷砖

till *adv* 直到

till *v* 直到

tilt *v* 倾斜

timber *n* 木材

time *n* 时间

time *v* 记时

timeless *adj* 永恒

timely *adj* 及时的

times *n* 倍

timetable *n* 时间表

timid *adj* 胆小的

timidity *n* 胆怯

tin *n* 锡，罐头

tiny *adj* 小小的

tip *n* 秘诀，小费

tiptoe *n* 脚尖

tired *adj* 累的

tiredness *n* 困倦

tireless *adj* 不知疲倦的

tiresome *adj* 劳累的

tissue *n* 组织，纸巾

title *n* 标题

to *pre* 至

toad *n* 蟾蜍

toast *v* 致祝酒辞，烤面包

toast *n* 致祝酒辞，烤面包

toaster *n* 烤面包机，烤面包的人，祝酒人

tobacco *n* 烟草

today *adv* 今天

toddler *n* 小孩

toe *n* 脚趾

toenail *n* 趾甲

together *adv* 连同一起

toil *v* 辛苦从事

toilet *n* 厕所

token *n* 令牌，象征

tolerable *adj* 可容忍的

tolerance *n* 宽容

tolerate *v* 容忍

toll *n* 收费

toll *v* 收费

tomato *n* 番茄

tomb *n* 墓

tombstone *n* 墓碑

tomorrow *adv* 明天

T

ton *n* 吨
tone *n* 声调
tongs *n* 钳子
tongue *n* 舌
tonic *n* 补品
tonight *adv* 今晚
tonsil *n* 扁桃体
too *adv* 太，也
tool *n* 工具
tooth *n* 牙齿
toothache *n* 牙痛
toothpick *n* 牙签
top *n* 顶部
topic *n* 话题
topple *v* 推翻
torch *n* 火炬
torment *v* 折磨
torment *n* 折磨
torrent *n* 洪流
torrid *adj* 炎热的
torso *n* 躯干
tortoise *n* 草龟
torture *v* 折磨
torture *n* 折磨
toss *v* 抛
total *adj* 总计的
totalitarian *adj* 极权主义的
totality *n* 总体
touch *n* 触摸
touch *v* 触摸
touch on *v* 接触
touch up *v* 触摸起来

touching *adj* 感人的
tough *adj* 困难的，坚强的
toughen *v* 增韧
tour *n* 游览
tourism *n* 旅游业
tourist *n* 旅游者
tournament *n* 比赛，锦标赛
tow *v* 拖曳
tow truck *n* 拖车
towards *pre* 向
towel *n* 毛巾
tower *n* 塔
towering *adj* 耸立的
town *n* 镇
town hall *n* 市政厅
toxic *adj* 有毒的
toxin *n* 毒素
toy *n* 玩具
trace *v* 跟踪
track *n* 田径
track *v* 跟踪
traction *n* 牵引
tractor *n* 拖拉机
trade *n* 贸易
trade *v* 贸易
trademark *n* 商标
trader *n* 贸易商
tradition *n* 传统
traffic *n* 交通（量），（非法）交易
traffic *v* （非法）交易
tragedy *n* 悲剧

tragic *adj* 悲惨的
trail *v* 跟着
trail *n* 步道
trailer *n* 挂车，短片
train *n* 火车
train *v* 训练
trainee *n* 学员，接受培训人员
trainer *n* 教练
training *n* 培训
trait *n* 特征
traitor *n* 叛徒，卖国贼
trajectory *n* 轨迹
tram *n* 电车
trample *v* 践踏
trance *n* 昏迷
tranquility *n* 安宁
transaction *n* 交易
transcend *v* 超越
transcribe *v* 抄写
transfer *v* 转让
transfer *n* 转让
transform *v* 转换，改变，改造
transformation *n* 转型
transfusion *n* 输血
transient *adj* 瞬变的
transit *n* 运输
transition *n* 过渡
translate *v* 翻译
translator *n* 译者
transmit *v* 传输
transparent *adj* 透明的
transplant *v* 移植

transport *v* 运输
trap *n* 陷阱
trash *n* 垃圾
trash can *n* 垃圾桶
traumatic *adj* 外伤性
traumatize *v* 创伤
travel *v* 旅行
traveler *n* 旅行者
tray *n* 托盘
treacherous *adj* 奸诈的
treachery *n* 奸诈
tread *iv* 踩
treason *n* 叛国
treasure *n* 金银财宝，财富，珍品
treasurer *n* 财务官
treat *v* 对待
treat *n* 款待，宴飨
treatment *n* 治疗
treaty *n* 条约
tree *n* 树
tremble *v* 颤栗
tremendous *adj* 巨大的
tremor *n* 震颤
trench *n* 战壕
trend *n* 趋势
trendy *adj* 新潮的
trespass *v* 擅闯
trial *n* 审判
triangle *n* 三角
tribe *n* 部落
tribulation *n* 磨难

tribunal n 法庭
tribute n 致敬
trick v 捉弄
trick n 伎俩
trickle v 涓流
tricky adj 棘手的，有伎俩的
trigger v 触发
trigger n 触发
trim v 修剪
trimester n 孕期
trimmings n 配菜
trip n 行程
trip v 行程
triple adj 三倍的，三联的
tripod n 三脚架
triumph n 凯旋
triumphant adj 胜利的，
　得意扬扬的
trivial adj 琐碎的，不重要的
trivialize v 轻描淡写
trolley n 小车
troop n 部队
trophy n 奖杯
tropic n 北回归线
tropical adj 热带的
trouble n 麻烦
trouble v 惹麻烦
troublesome adj 麻烦的
trousers n 长裤
trout n 鳟鱼
truce n 休战
truck n 卡车

trucker n 卡车司机
trumped-up adj 捏造的
trumpet n 喇叭
trunk n 树干，车后箱
trust v 信任
trust n 信托，信任
truth n 真相
truthful adj 如实的
try v 尝试
tub n 浴盆
tuberculosis n 肺结核
Tuesday n 星期二
tuition n 学费
tulip n 郁金香
tumble v 摔
tummy n 肚子
tumor n 肿瘤
tumult n 风暴
tumultuous adj 乱哄哄的，
　喧哗的
tuna n 金枪鱼
tune n 调
tune v 调好
tune up v 定调
tunic n 长袍
tunnel n 隧道
turbine n 涡轮
turbulence n 湍流
turf n 草坪
Turk adj 土耳其的
Turkey n 土耳其
turmoil adj 动乱的

turn *n* 轮，转
turn *v* 转
turn back *v* 回头
turn down *v* 拒绝
turn in *v* 交
turn off *v* 关掉
turn on *v* 打开
turn out *v* 结果是，出现
turn over *v* 移交
turn up *v* 出现，调大
turret *n* 塔楼
turtle *n* 龟
tusk *n* （象）长牙
tutor *n* 家教
tweezers *n* 镊子
twelfth *adj* 第十二
twelve *adj* 十二
twentieth *adj* 第二十
twenty *adj* 二十
twice *adv* 两次
twilight *n* 曙光
twin *n* 双胞胎
twinkle *v* 眨眼
twist *v* 转弯
twist *n* 转弯
twisted *adj* 扭曲的
twister *n* 捻线机
two *adj* 二
tycoon *n* 大亨
type *n* 类型，种类
type *v* 打字
typical *adj* 典型的

tyranny *n* 暴政
tyrant *n* 暴君，专横的人

ugliness *n* 丑陋
ugly *adj* 丑陋的
ulcer *n* 溃疡
ultimate *adj* 最后的
ultimatum *n* 最后通牒
ultrasound *n* 超声波
umbrella *n* 伞
umpire *n* 裁判员，仲裁人
unable *adj* 不能的，无能为力的
unanimity *n* 全体一致
unarmed *adj* 非武装的，手无寸铁的
unassuming *adj* 不摆架子
unattached *adj* 独立的
unavoidable *adj* 难免的
unaware *adj* 未察觉的
unbearable *adj* 无法忍受的
unbeatable *adj* 打不败的
unbelievable *adj* 难以相信的
unbiased *adj* 公正的
unbroken *adj* 完整的
unbutton *v* 解扣
uncertain *adj* 不确定的

uncle *n* 叔叔，伯父

uncomfortable *adj* 不舒服的

uncommon *adj* 非常的，非凡的

unconscious *adj* 失去知觉的，无意的

uncover *v* 揭露

undecided *adj* 未确定的

undeniable *adj* 不容置疑的

under *pre* 在下面

undercover *adj* 暗中进行的

underdog *n* 处劣势方

undergo *v* 接受

underground *adj* 地下的

underlie *v* 构成…的基础（或起因），引起

underline *v* 强调

underlying *adj* 下属，手下

undermine *v* 破坏

underneath *pre* 在下面

underpass *n* 地下过道

understand *v* 理解

understandable *adj* 可以理解的

understanding *adj* 善解人意的

undertake *v* 承担

underwear *n* 内衣

underwrite *v* 承保，写在……下面

undeserved *adj* 不该受的

undesirable *adj* 令人不悦的，讨厌的

undisputed *adj* 毫无疑问的

undo *v* 解开

undoubtedly *adv* 无容置疑地

undress *v* 脱衣

undue *adj* 过度地

unearth *v* 发掘

uneasiness *n* 拘束

uneasy *adj* 心神不安的

uneducated *adj* 无知的

unemployed *adj* 失业的

unemployment *n* 失业

unending *adj* 无止境的

unequal *adj* 不同等的

unequivocal *adj* 毫不含糊的

uneven *adj* 参差不齐的

uneventful *adj* 无重大事件的，平凡的

unexpected *adj* 意想不到的

unfailing *adj* 经久不衰的

unfair *adj* 不合理的

unfairly *adv* 不合理地

unfairness *n* 不合理性

unfaithful *adj* 不忠实的，不贞洁的，不准确的

unfamiliar *adj* 不熟悉的

unfasten *v* 解开

unfavorable *adj* 不适宜的，不利的

unfit *adj* 不合适的

unfold *v* 展开

unforeseen *adj* 未预见到的

unforgettable *adj* 难忘的

unfounded *adj* 无事实根据的

unfriendly *adj* 不友好的

unfurnished *adj* 未完成的

ungrateful *adj* 令人厌恶的

unhappiness *n* 不幸，不悦

unhappy *adj* 不愉快的

unharmed *adj* 未受伤的

unhealthy *adj* 不健康

unheard-of *adj* 前所未闻的

unhurt *adj* 没有受害的

unification *n* 统一

uniform *n* 制服

uniformity *n* 均一

unify *v* 统一

unilateral *adj* 单边的

union *n* 联合

unique *adj* 独特的

unit *n* 单位，单元

unite *v* 团结

unity *n* 团结

universal *adj* 普遍的

universe *n* 宇宙

university *n* 大学

unjust *adj* 不公道的

unjustified *adj* 不正当的

unknown *adj* 未知的

unlawful *adj* 不合法的

unleaded *adj* 无铅的，不含铅的

unleash *v* 解开

unless *c* 除非

unlike *adj* 不同的

unlikely *adj* 不太可能的

unlimited *adj* 无限的

unload *v* 卸载

unlock *v* 开锁

unlucky *adj* 不幸的

unmarried *adj* 未婚的

unmask *v* 撕下面具

unmistakable *adj* 准确无误的

unnecessary *adj* 没必要的

unnoticed *adj* 未被察觉的

unoccupied *adj* 空闲的，没人住的

unofficially *adv* 非官方地

unpack *v* 打开

unpleasant *adj* 令人不快的

unplug *v* 拔去塞子

unpopular *adj* 不受欢迎的

unpredictable *adj* 变化莫测的

unprofitable *adj* 无利润的

unprotected *adj* 无保护的

unravel *v* 解开

unreal *adj* 虚幻的

unrealistic *adj* 不切实际的

unreasonable *adj* 不合情理的

unrelated *adj* 无关的

unreliable *adj* 不可靠的

unrest *n* 不安，动荡

unsafe *adj* 不安全的

unselfish *adj* 无私的

unspeakable *adj* 难以说出口的

unstable *adj* 不稳定的

unsteady *adj* 不平稳的

unsuccessful *adj* 不成功的

unsuitable *adj* 不合适的

unsuspecting *adj* 信任的

U

unthinkable *adj* 难以想象的
untie *v* 解开
until *pre* 直到
untimely *adj* 不适时的
untouchable *adj* 达不到的
untrue *adj* 不真实的
unusual *adj* 异常的
unveil *v* 揭幕
unwillingly *adv* 不愿意地
unwind *v* 解开，松开
unwise *adj* 不明智的
unwrap *v* 打开
upbringing *n* 养育
upcoming *adj* 即将来临的
update *v* 更新
upgrade *v* 升级
upheaval *n* 大变动
uphill *adv* 上升
uphold *v* 维护
upholstery *n* 室内装饰品
upkeep *n* 保养
upon *pre* 在
upper *adj* 上部的
upright *adj* 挺直的，正值的
uprising *n* 起义
uproar *n* 骚乱
uproot *v* 连根拔起
upset *v* 翻倒
upside-down *adv* 颠倒地
upstairs *adv* 在楼上
uptight *adj* 紧张的
up-to-date *adj* 最新的

upturn *n* 向上
upwards *adv* 朝上地
urban *adj* 城市的
urge *n* 敦促
urge *v* 敦促
urgency *n* 紧急
urgent *adj* 紧急的
urinate *v* 小便
urine *n* 尿
urn *n* 缸
us *pre* 我们
usage *n* 用法
use *v* 使用
use *n* 使用
used to *adj* 过去常常
useful *adj* 有用的
usefulness *n* 有用性
useless *adj* 无用的
user *n* 用户，使用者
usher *n* 带位者
usual *adj* 平常的
usurp *v* 强占
utensil *n* 器物
uterus *n* 子宫体
utilize *v* 使用，利用
utmost *adj* 最大的
utter *v* 发出（声音），说

V

vacancy *n* 空位
vacant *adj* 空的
vacate *v* 空出
vacation *n* 假期
vaccinate *v* 接种
vaccine *n* 疫苗
vacillate *v* 犹豫
vagrant *n* 流浪者
vague *adj* 隐晦的，模糊的
vain *adj* 自负的
vainly *adv* 自负地
valiant *adj* 雄豪的
valid *adj* 有效的
validate *v* 确认
validity *n* 有效性
valley *n* 山谷，溪谷
valuable *adj* 珍贵的
value *n* 价值，价值观
valve *n* 阀门
vampire *n* 吸血鬼
van *n* 搬运车
vandal *n* 艺术品破坏者
vandalism *n* 故意破坏
vandalize *v* 破坏
vanguard *n* 先锋
vanish *v* 消失
vanity *n* 虚荣
vanquish *v* 征服
vaporize *v* 汽化

variable *adj* 易变的
varied *adj* 各种各样的
variety *n* 品种
various *adj* 各种各样的
varnish *v* 油漆
varnish *n* 油漆
vary *v* 变化
vase *n* 花瓶
vast *adj* 浩大的
veal *n* 小牛肉
veer *v* 转向
vegetable *v* 蔬菜
vegetarian *v* 素食主义者
vegetation *n* 植被
vehicle *n* 车辆
veil *n* 面纱
vein *n* 静脉
velocity *n* 速度
velvet *n* 天鹅绒
venerate *v* 崇敬
vengeance *n* 复仇
venison *n* 鹿肉
venom *n* 毒液
vent *n* 出气孔
ventilate *v* 通风
ventilation *n* 通风
venture *v* 冒险，敢于
venture *n* 冒险（事业），风险
verb *n* 动词
verbally *adv* 口头上地
verbatim *adv* 逐字地
verdict *n* 定案

verge *n* 边缘
verification *n* 证明
verify *v* 核实
versatile *adj* 多才多艺的
verse *n* 诗歌
versed *adj* 熟练的
version *n* 版本
versus *pre* 对，比
vertebra *n* 椎骨
very *adv* 非常
vessel *n* 船
vest *n* 背心
vestige *n* 痕迹
veteran *n* 退伍军人
veterinarian *n* 兽医
veto *v* 否决
viaduct *n* 桥梁
vibrant *adj* 充满活力的
vibrate *v* 振动
vibration *n* 振动
vice *n* 缺点，弱点
vicinity *n* 近处
vicious *adj* 狠毒的
victim *n* 受害者
victimize *v* 欺骗
victor *n* 胜者
victorious *adj* 胜利的
victory *n* 胜利
view *n* 看法，视野
view *v* 看
viewpoint *n* 观点
vigil *n* 守夜

village *n* 村庄
villager *n* 村民
villain *n* 恶棍
vindicate *v* 辩护
vindictive *adj* 恶意的
vine *n* 藤
vinegar *n* 醋
vineyard *n* 葡萄园
violate *v* 违犯
violence *n* 暴力
violent *adj* 暴力的
violet *n* 紫罗兰色
violin *n* 小提琴
violinist *n* 小提琴手
viper *n* 蛇蝎
virgin *n* 处女
virginity *n* 处女身
virile *adj* 男性的
virility *n* 性能力
virtually *adv* 实际上，事实上
virtue *n* 美德，德行，优点
virtuous *adj* 贞洁的
virulent *adj* 有剧毒的
virus *n* 病毒
visibility *n* 可见性
visible *adj* 看得见的
vision *n* 视觉
visit *n* 参观，访问
visit *v* 参观，访问
visitor *n* 访客
visual *adj* 视觉的
visualize *v* 形象化

V

vital *adj* 重要的

vitality *n* 生命力

vitamin *n* 维生素

vivacious *adj* 活泼的

vivid *adj* 生动的

vocabulary *n* 词汇量

vocation *n* 职业

vogue *n* 流行，风行，时髦

voice *n* 声音

void *adj* 无效的

volatile *adj* 挥发性

volcano *n* 火山

volleyball *n* 排球

voltage *n* 电压

volume *n* 容量，音量

volunteer *n* 志愿者

vomit *v* 呕吐

vomit *n* 呕吐物

vote *v* 表决

vote *n* 投票

voting *n* 投票

vouch for *v* 为担保

voucher *n* 凭单，收据

vow *v* 发誓

vowel *n* 元音

voyage *v* 远航

voyager *n* 航海者

vulgar *adj* 粗俗的

vulgarity *n* 粗俗

vulnerable *adj* 脆弱的

vulture *n* 秃鹰，兀鹰

wafer *n* 薄酥饼

wag *v* 摇摆

wage *n* 薪水

wagon *n* 无盖货车

wail *v* 嚎啕

wail *n* 嚎啕声

waist *n* 腰部

wait *v* 等待

waiter *n* 服务员

waiting *n* 等待

waitress *n* 女服务员

waive *v* 放弃，不坚持

wake up *iv* 醒来

walk *v* 步行

walk *n* 散步

walkout *n* 罢工

wall *n* 墙壁

wallet *n* 钱包

walnut *n* 核桃

walrus *n* 海象

waltz *n* 华尔兹

wander *v* 漫步

wanderer *n* 流浪汉

wane *v* 减少

want *v* 要

war *n* 战争

ward *n* 病区

warden *n* 监察员，监狱长

wardrobe *n* 衣橱

warehouse n 仓库
warfare n 战争
warm adj 温暖的
warm up v 热身
warmth n 温暖
warn v 警告
warning n 警告
warp v 弯曲
warped adj 弯曲的
warrant v 保证
warrant n 保证
warranty n 保单
warrior n 战士
warship n 军舰
wart n 疣
wary adj 机警的
wash v 洗涤
washable adj 可洗的，洗得掉的
wasp n 黄蜂
waste v 浪费
waste n 废物
waste basket n 废物篮
wasteful adj 浪费的
watch n 手表，监视，看守
watch v 看
watch out v 当心
watchful adj 注意的
watchmaker n 制表者
water n 水
water v 浇水
water down v 冲淡
water heater n 热水器

waterfall n 瀑布
watermelon n 西瓜
waterproof adj 水密的
watershed n 分水岭，重大事件
watertight adj 水密的
watery adj 含水的
watt n 瓦特
wave n 波浪
waver v 减弱，踌躇，摇摆
wavy adj 波浪的
wax n 蜡
way n 方式 道路
way in n 入口
way out n 出口
we pro 我们
weak adj 软弱的
weaken v 减弱
weakness n 弱点
wealth n 财富
wealthy adj 富有的
weapon n 武器
wear n 穿戴
wear iv 穿
wear down v 用尽
wear out v 穿旧，用尽
weary adj 疲倦的
weather n 天气
weave iv 织
web n 网，网络
web site n 网站
wed iv 结婚
wedding n 婚礼

wedge *n* 楔子

Wednesday *n* 星期三

weed *n* 锄杂草

weed *v* 杂草

week *n* 星期

weekday *adj* 周一到周五

weekend *n* 周末

weekly *adv* 每周

weep *iv* 啜泣

weigh *v* 称重

weight *n* 重量

weird *adj* 古怪的

welcome *v* 欢迎

welcome *n* 欢迎

weld *v* 焊接

welder *n* 焊工

welfare *n* 福利

well *n* 井

well-known *adj* 有名的

well-to-do *adj* 富有的

west *n* 西方

westbound *adv* 向西

western *adj* 西方的，西部的

westerner *adj* 西方人

wet *adj* 湿的

whale *n* 鲸鱼

wharf *n* 码头

what *adj* 什么

whatever *adj* 无论什么

wheat *n* 麦子

wheel *n* 轮子

wheelbarrow *n* 独轮车

wheelchair *n* 轮椅

wheeze *v* 喘息

when *c* 当...的时候

whenever *adv* 每当

where *adv* 在哪里

whereabouts *n* 下落，落脚处

whereas *c* 而

whereupon *c* 接下来

wherever *c* 无论在哪

whether *c* 是否

which *adj* 哪个

while *c* 当时

whim *n* 异想天开

whine *v* 呜咽

whip *v* 鞭打

whip *n* 鞭子

whirl *v* 旋转

whirlpool *n* 旋涡

whiskers *n* 颊须

whisper *v* 耳语

whisper *n* 耳语

whistle *v* 吹口哨

whistle *n* 口哨

white *adj* 白色的

whiten *v* 漂白

whittle *v* 削（木头），削减

who *pro* 谁

whoever *pro* 无论谁

whole *adj* 整个的

wholehearted *adj* 真心实意的

wholesale *n* 批发

wholesome *adj* 有益健康的，有益身心健康的

whom *pro* 谁

why *adv* 为什么

wicked *adj* 邪恶的

wickedness *n* 邪恶

wide *adj* 宽的，广泛的

widely *adv* 广泛地

widen *v* 加宽，扩展

widespread *adj* 普遍的

widow *n* 寡妇

widower *n* 鳏夫

width *n* 宽度

wield *v* 挥动

wife *n* 妻子

wig *n* 假发

wiggle *v* 扭动

wild *adj* 野生的，荒凉的，狂热的

wild boar *n* 野公猪

wilderness *n* 原野

wildlife *n* 野生物

will *n* 意志，遗言

willfully *adv* 任性的，故意的

willing *adj* 愿意的

willingly *adv* 愿意地

willingness *n* 自愿

willow *n* 杨柳

wily *adj* 男性生殖器官

wimp *adj* 软弱无力

win *iv* 赢

win back *v* 赢取

wind *n* 风，气息

wind *iv* 绕，缠

wind up *v* 结束

winding *adj* 绕

windmill *n* 风车

window *n* 窗口

windpipe *n* 气管

windshield *n* 挡风玻璃

windy *adj* 风大的

wine *n* 酒

winery *n* 酿酒厂

wing *n* 翅膀

wink *n* 挤眼

wink *v* 挤眼

winner *n* 优胜者

winter *n* 冬天

wipe *v* 抹

wipe out *v* 擦掉，擦净，彻底摧毁

wire *n* 导线

wireless *adj* 无线的

wisdom *n* 智慧

wise *adj* 明智的

wish *v* 愿望

wish *n* 愿望

wit *n* 机智

witch *n* 巫婆

witchcraft *n* 巫术

with *pre* 和

withdraw *v* 收回，撤消，撤退

withdrawal *n* 取回，提款，撤退

withdrawn *adj* 隐退的，离群的

wither *v* 枯萎

W

withhold *iv* 扣压
within *pre* 在之内
without *pre* 除外，没有
withstand *v* 承受
witness *n* 目击证人
witty *adj* 机智的
wives *n* 妻子
wizard *n* 巫师
wobble *v* 摆动
woes *n* 悲哀
wolf *n* 狼
woman *n* 女人
womb *n* 子宫
women *n* 女人
wonder *v* 猜想
wonder *n* 奇迹
wonderful *adj* 极好的，惊人的
wood *n* 木头
wooden *adj* 木的
wool *n* 羊毛
woolen *adj* 羊毛的
word *n* 词
wording *n* 措辞
work *n* 工作
work *v* 工作
work out *v* 解决，健身
workable *adj* 可行的
workbook *n* 作业簿
worker *n* 工作者
workshop *n* 车间，作坊，研讨会
world *n* 世界

worldly *adj* 世间的
worldwide *adj* 全世界的
worm *n* 蠕虫
worn-out *adj* 破旧的
worrisome *adj* 令人烦恼
worry *v* 担心
worry *n* 忧虑
worse *adj* 更坏（的），更差（的），更糟（的）
worsen *v* 恶化
worship *n* 崇拜
worst *adj* 最坏的
worth *adj* 有价值的
worthless *adj* 不值得的
worthwhile *adj* 值得的
worthy *adj* 值得的
would-be *adj* 想成为
wound *n* 伤口
wound *v* 受伤
woven *adj* 编织的
wrap *v* 套
wrap up *v* 包裹，完成
wrapping *n* 包裹
wrath *n* 愤怒
wreath *n* 花圈
wreck *v* 毁坏，使遇难
wreckage *n* 失事（船等），残骸
wrench *n* 板钳
wrestle *v* 格斗
wrestler *n* 摔跤手
wrestling *n* 摔跤

wretched *adj* 难受的，可怜的
wring *iv* 绞
wrinkle *v* 打皱
wrinkle *n* 皱纹
wrist *n* 手腕
write *iv* 写
write down *v* 记下，记录
writer *n* 作家
writhe *v* 翻滚，扭动
writing *n* 著作，作品
written *adj* 书面的
wrong *adj* 错误的

X-mas *n* 圣诞节
X-ray *n* X-射线

yacht *n* 游艇
yam *n* 薯类
yard *n* 后院，码
yarn *n* 毛线
yawn *n* 哈欠
yawn *v* 打哈欠
year *n* 年
yearly *adv* 每年的，一年一度的
yearn *v* 渴望，切盼
yeast *n* 酵母
yell *v* 叫喊
yellow *adj* 黄色
yes *adv* 是
yesterday *adv* 昨天
yet *c* 还未
yield *v* 屈服，产生
yield *n* 出产量，让行
yoke *n* 轭
yolk *n* 卵黄质
you *pro* 你
young *adj* 年轻的
youngster *n* 年轻人
your *adj* 你的
yours *pro* 你的
yourself *pro* 你自己
youth *n* 青年时期
youthful *adj* 青春的

Z

zap *v* 击溃，射杀
zeal *n* 热忱
zealous *adj* 热心的，热衷的
zebra *n* 斑马
zero *n* 零

zest *n* 热心
zinc *n* 锌
zip code *n* 邮政编码
zipper *n* 拉链
zone *n* 区域
zoo *n* 动物园
zoology *n* 动物学

Z

Chinese-English

Bilingual Dictionaries, Inc.

Abbreviations

a - article - 冠词
adj - adjective - 形容词
adv - adverb - 副词
c - conjunction - 连词
e - exclamation - 惊叹号
n - noun - 名词
pre - preposition - 介词
pro - pronoun - 代词
v - verb - 动词

A

ā lā bó de 阿拉伯的 *adj* Arabic
ā sī pǐ lín 阿司匹林 *n* aspirin
āi dào 哀悼 *n* condolences, mourning
āi dào 哀悼 *v* mourn
āi qiú 哀求 *v* entreat
ái è 挨饿 *v* starve
ái zhèng 癌症 *n* cancer
ái zhèng de 癌症的 *adj* cancerous
ǎi 矮 *adj* short
ǎi zi 矮子 *n* dwarf
ài 爱 *v* love
ài 爱 *n* love
ài de 爱的 *adj* affectionate
ài ěr lán 爱尔兰 *n* Ireland
ài ěr lán de 爱尔兰的 *adj* Irish
ài fǔ 爱抚 *n* caress
ài fǔ 爱抚 *v* caress, fondle
ài guó de 爱国的 *adj* patriotic
ài guó zhě 爱国者 *n* patriot
ài hào 爱好 *adj* fancy
ài hào 爱好 *n* gusto, penchant
ài mù 爱慕 *n* adoration
ài mù 爱慕 *v* adore
ài ren 爱人 *n* sweetheart
ài zhǐ huī tā rén de 爱指挥他人的 *adj* bossy
ài zhuī wèn de 爱追问的 *adj* nosy
ài mèi de 暧昧的 *adj* ambiguous
ài mèi guān xì 暧昧关系 *n* affair
ān dùn xià lái 安顿下来 *v* settle down
ān fǔ 安抚 *v* appease, conciliate, pacify, placate
ān fǔ de 安抚的 *adj* conciliatory
ān jìng 安静 *v* hush
ān jìng 安静 *n* quietness
ān jìng de 安静的 *adj* quiet
ān níng 安宁 *n* tranquility
ān pái 安排 *v* arrange, install
ān pái 安排 *n* arrangement
ān quán 安全 *adj* safe
ān quán 安全 *n* safety, security
ān quán de 安全的 *adj* secure
ān wèi 安慰 *v* console
ān wèi 安慰 *n* solace
ān zhuāng 安装 *v* install
ān zhuāng 安装 *n* installation
ān 氨 *n* ammonia
ān chún 鹌鹑 *n* quail
àn shàng 岸上 *n* shore
àn 按 *v* press
àn bù jiù bān 按部就班 *adv* step-by-step
àn jiē 按揭 *n* mortgage
àn jié zòu zǒu 按节奏走 *v* pace
àn lǎ ba 按喇叭 *v* honk
àn mó 按摩 *n* massage
àn mó 按摩 *v* massage
àn niǔ 按钮 *n* button
àn zhào zì rán guī lǜ 按照自然规律 *adj* physically
àn jiàn 案件 *n* case
àn lì 案例 *n* case
àn dàn 暗淡 *adj* dismal
àn shā 暗杀 *v* assassinate
àn shā 暗杀 *n* assassination

àn shì 暗示 *n* allusion, hint, inkling

àn shì 暗示 *v* connote, hint, imply

àn shì de 暗示的 *adj* suggestive

àn zhǐ 暗指 *n* allusion

àn zhōng de 暗中的 *adj* clandestine

àn zhōng jìn xíng de 暗中进行的 *adj* undercover

àn zì xiào 暗自笑 *v* chuckle

āng zāng de 肮脏的 *adj* dirty, squalid

áng guì de 昂贵的 *adj* costly, expensive

áng guì de 昂贵地 *adv* dearly

àng sī 盎司 *n* ounce

āo dào 凹道 *n* draw

āo hén 凹痕 *n* dent

áo xiáng 翱翔 *v* hover

ào màn 傲慢 *n* arrogance

ào màn 傲慢 *adj* haughty

ào màn de 傲慢的 *adj* arrogant, insolent

ào yùn 奥运 *n* Olympics

ào nǎo 懊恼 *n* chagrin

B

bā 八 *adj* eight

bā shí 八十 *adj* eighty

bā yuè 八月 *n* August

pá shǒu 扒手 *n* pickpocket

bá qù sāi zi 拔去塞子 *v* unplug

bá hù de 跋扈的 *adj* bossy

bǎ （jì huà ） 把（计划） *v* finalize

bǎ ……hū lái huàn qù 把……呼来唤去 *v* boss around

bǎ ……kòu jǐn 把……扣紧 *v* buckle up

bǎ ……lián xiǎng zài yī qǐ 把……联想在一起 *v* associate

bǎ ……shāo chéng tàn huī 把……烧成炭灰 *v* char

bǎ …chuán xià qù 把…传下去 *v* hand down

bǎ fàng zài yī qǐ 把放在一起 *v* lump together

bǎ wò 把握 *n* grasp

bǎ wò 把握 *v* grasp

bǎ zi 靶子 *n* butt

bà ba 爸爸 *n* dad

bà gōng 罢工 *n* strike, walkout

bà gōng 罢工 *iv* strike, strike up

bà miǎn 罢免 *v* depose

bà quán 霸权 *n* supremacy

bái chī 白痴 *n* idiot

bái chī 白痴 *adj* idiotic

bái jīn 白金 *n* platinum

bái lán dì 白兰地 *n* brandy

bái nèi zhàng 白内障 *n* cataract

bái sè de 白色的 *adj* white

bái xuè bìng 白血病 *n* leukemia

bái yǐ 白蚁 *n* termite

bái yín 白银 *n* silver

bái yín de 白银的 *adj* silver plated

bái yín jiā gōng shī 白银加工师 *n* silversmith

bǎi fēn bǐ 百分比 *adv* percent

bǎi fēn bǐ 百分比 *n* percentage

bǎi kē quán shū 百科全书 *n* encyclopedia

bǎi nián jì niàn 百年纪念 *n* centenary

bǎi wàn fù wēng 百万富翁 *adj* millionaire

bǎi shù 柏树 *n* cypress

bǎi dòng 摆动 *v* sway, wobble, swing

bǎi dòng 摆动 *n* swing

bǎi tuō 摆脱 *iv* rid of

bǎi zī shì 摆姿势 *v* pose

bài huài 败坏 *v* defile

bài huài ...de míng shēng 败坏…的名声 *v* discredit

bài dǎo de 拜倒的 *adj* prostrate

bài fǎng 拜访 *v* call on

bān 班 *n* class

bān jī 班机 *n* airliner

bān diǎn 斑点 *n* speck, spot

bān mǎ 斑马 *n* zebra

bān yùn 搬运 *v* carry, convey

bān yùn chē 搬运车 *n* van

bān yùn gōng 搬运工 *n* porter

bǎn 板 *n* board, plate

bǎn lì 板栗 *n* chestnut

bǎn qián 板钳 *n* wrench

bǎn qiú 板球 *n* cricket

bǎn yán 板岩 *n* slate

bǎn běn 版本 *n* edition, version

bǎn miàn shè jì 版面设计 *n* layout

bǎn quán 版权 *n* copyright

bàn fǎ 办法 *n* approach

bàn gōng shì 办公室 *n* office

bàn gōng yuán 办公员 *n* officer

bàn shì yuán 办事员 *n* clerk

bàn dǎo 半岛 *n* peninsula

bàn jìng 半径 *n* radius

bàn kāi de 半开的 *adj* ajar

bàn kōng 半空 *n* midair

bàn qiú 半球 *n* hemisphere

bàn shēn xiàng 半身像 *n* bust

bàn xìn bàn yí de 半信半疑的 *adj* dubious

bàn láng 伴郎 *n* best man

bàn lǚ guān xì 伴侣关系 *n* companionship

bàn niáng 伴娘 *n* bridesmaid

bàn suí zhe 伴随着 *v* accompany

bāng huì 帮会 *n* gang

bāng shǒu 帮手 *n* helper

bāng xiōng 帮凶 *n* accomplice

bāng zhù 帮助 *v* help

bāng zhù 帮助 *n* help

bǎng fěi 绑匪 *n* kidnapper

bǎng jià 绑架 *n* kidnapping

bǎng piào 绑票 *v* kidnap

páng guāng 膀胱 *n* bladder

bàng 棒 *n* rod

bàng qiú 棒球 *n* baseball

bàng 磅 *n* pound

bāo 包 *n* bundle

bāo guǒ 包裹 *n* package, parcel; wrapping

bāo guǒ 包裹 *v* wrap up

bāo guǒ dān 包裹单 *n* parcel post

bāo hán 包含 *v* comprise, encompass

bāo hán de 包含的 *adv* inclusive
bāo han 包涵 *v* cover
bāo kuò 包括 *v* include
bāo wéi 包围 *v* circle, embrace, encircle, envelop
bǎo bèi 宝贝 *n* baby
bǎo shí 宝石 *n* gem, jewel
bǎo de 饱的 *adj* full
bǎo hé 饱和 *v* saturate
bǎo mǎn de 饱满的 *adj* plump
bǎo cáng 保藏 *v* conserve
bǎo chí 保持 *n* conservation
bǎo chí 保持 *iv* hold, keep, maintain, remain, stay, reserve, retain
bǎo cún 保存 *n* conservation
bǎo cún 保存 *v* conserve, preserve
bǎo dān 保单 *n* warranty
bǎo hù 保护 *v* protect, shield
bǎo hù 保护 *n* protection
bǎo liú 保留 *n* reservation, retention
bǎo mǔ 保姆 *n* nanny
bǎo shì 保释 *n* bail
bǎo shì chū lái 保释出来 *v* bail out
bǎo shǒu de 保守的 *adj* conservative
bǎo shǒu de 保守地 *adv* sparingly
bǎo wèi 保卫 *v* champion
bǎo xiǎn 保险 *n* insurance
bǎo xiǎn gàng 保险杠 *n* bumper
bǎo xiǎn sī 保险丝 *n* fuse
bǎo yǎng 保养 *n* upkeep

bǎo zhàng 保障 *n* security
bǎo zhēn dù 保真度 *n* fidelity
bǎo zhèng 保证 *n* assurance, guarantee, warrant
bǎo zhèng 保证 *v* assure, guarantee, warrant
bǎo lěi 堡垒 *n* fortress
bào cháng 报偿 *v* recompense
bào cháng 报偿 *n* recompense
bào chóu 报仇 *v* avenge
bào dào 报到 *v* check in
bào dào 报道 *v* report
bào fù 报复 *n* reprisal, retaliation
bào fù 报复 *v* retaliate
bào gào 报告 *n* report
bào jià 报价 *n* quotation
bào jià 报价 *v* quote
bào míng 报名 *v* enroll
bào míng 报名 *n* enrollment
bào míng rù xué 报名入学 *v* matriculate
bào tān 报摊 *n* newsstand
bào xiǎo 报晓 *v* crow
bào zhǐ 报纸 *n* newspaper
bào qiàn de 抱歉的 *adj* sorry
bào yuàn 抱怨 *v* complain
bào 豹 *n* leopard, panther
bào diē 暴跌 *v* slump
bào diē 暴跌 *n* slump
bào dòng 暴动 *n* insurrection
bào fēng xuě 暴风雪 *n* blizzard
bào fēng yǔ 暴风雨 *n* tempest
bào jūn 暴君 *n* despot, tyrant
bào lì 暴力 *n* force, violence
bào lì de 暴力的 *adj* violent

bào lù zài wài de 暴露在外的 *adj* exposed

bào luàn 暴乱 *n* commotion, riot

bào luàn 暴乱 *v* riot

bào nüè de 暴虐的 *adj* despotic

bào tú 暴徒 *n* mob, thug

bào xíng 暴行 *n* atrocity, barbarism

bào yǐn bào shí zhě 暴饮暴食者 *n* glutton

bào zhèng 暴政 *n* tyranny

bào fā 爆发 *v* erupt

bào fā 爆发 *n* outbreak, outburst

bào liè 爆裂 *n* blowout

bào liè 爆裂 *v* crack

bào mǐ huā 爆米花 *n* popcorn

bào zhà 爆炸 *n* blast, explosion

bào zhà 爆炸 *iv* blow up, burst, explode

bào zhà（shēng） 爆炸（声）*n* detonation

bào zhú 爆竹 *n* firecracker

bēi jiàn de 卑贱的 *adj* humble, low-key

bēi liè de 卑劣的 *adj* despicable

bēi 杯 *n* chalice, cup, mug

bēi bāo 背包 *n* backpack

bēi āi 悲哀 *n* sorrow, woes

bēi cǎn de 悲惨的 *adj* cruel, deplorable, tragic

bēi guān 悲观 *n* pessimism

bēi guān de 悲观的 *adj* pessimistic

bēi jù 悲剧 *n* tragedy

bēi shāng 悲伤 *n* sadness

bēi shāng de 悲伤的 *adj* tearful

bēi tàn 悲叹 *v* lament

bēi tàn 悲叹 *n* lament

bēi tòng 悲痛 *n* grief

bēi 碑 *n* tablet

běi 北 *n* north

běi bù de 北部的 *adj* northern

běi fāng rén 北方人 *adj* northerner

běi huí guī xiàn 北回归线 *n* tropic

běi jí 北极 *adj* arctic

bèi 贝 *n* shellfish

bèi léi mào 贝雷帽 *n* beret

bèi fèn 备份 *n* backup

bèi wàng lù 备忘录 *n* memo

bèi yòng de 备用的 *adj* spare

bèi bù 背部 *n* back

bèi jǐng 背景 *n* background, context, setting

bèi pàn 背叛 *n* betrayal, defection

bèi pàn 背叛 *v* defect

bèi shū 背书 *n* endorsement

bèi sòng 背诵 *v* memorize, recite

bèi xīn 背心 *n* vest

bèi 倍 *n* times

bèi bāo wéi de lǐng tǔ 被包围的领土 *n* enclave

bèi bō duó de 被剥夺的 *adj* deprived

bèi dǎ bài de 被打败的 *adj* beaten

bèi dān ge 被耽搁 *v* bog down

bèi dòng de 被动的 *adj* passive

bèi fēn jiě 被分解 *v* decompose

bèi gào 被告 *n* defendant

bèi jiàn tà de 被践踏的 *adj* downtrodden

B

bèi jiě gù de 被解雇的 *adj* redundant

bèi kòng fàn zuì de rén 被控犯罪的人 *n* culprit

bèi pāo qì de rén 被抛弃的人 *n* castaway

bèi qiáng zhì de 被强制的 *adj* compulsory

bèi shù fù de 被束缚的 *adj* bound

bèi yā yì de 被压抑的 *adj* pent-up

bèi yā zhì de 被压制的 *adj* downtrodden

bèi zhēng fú de 被征服的 *adj* subdued

bèi zhù fú de 被祝福的 *adj* blessed

běn dì huà 本地化 *v* localize

běn guó de 本国的 *adj* native

běn guó zhì de 本国制的 *adj* homemade

běn néng 本能 *n* instinct

běn tǔ de 本土的 *adj* native

běn zhì 本质 *n* essence

bèn dàn 笨蛋 *adj* fool, slob

bèn de 笨的 *adj* stupid

bèn zhòng de 笨重的 *adj* bulky

bèn zhuō de 笨拙的 *adj* awkward, clumsy

bèn zhuō de xiū bǔ 笨拙地修补 *v* botch

bēng kuì 崩溃 *n* breakdown, collapse

bēng kuì 崩溃 *v* collapse, crumble

bēng dài 绷带 *n* bandage

bèng 泵 *n* pump

bī zǒu 逼走 *v* drive away

bí kǒng 鼻孔 *n* nostril

bí zi 鼻子 *n* nose

bǐ 比 *pre* versus

bǐ jiào 比较 *v* compare

bǐ jiào 比较 *n* comparison

bǐ jiào de 比较的 *adj* comparative

bǐ lì shí 比利时 *n* Belgium

bǐ lì shí de 比利时的 *adj* Belgian

bǐ lì 比例 *n* proportion

bǐ lǜ 比率 *n* ratio

bǐ sài 比赛 *n* match, tournament

bǐ sài xiàng mù 比赛项目 *n* event

bǐ jì běn 笔记本 *n* notebook

bǐ míng 笔名 *n* pseudonym

bǐ zhí de 笔直的 *adj* erect

bǐ shì 鄙视 *v* despise, scorn

bǐ shì 鄙视 *n* disdain

bì bù kě shǎo de 必不可少的 *adj* indispensable

bì rán de 必然的 *adj* consequent

bì xū 必须 *v* have to

bì xū de 必须的 *adj* mandatory

bì xū de 必需的 *adj* indispensable

bì yào de 必要的 *adj* necessary

bì yào xìng 必要性 *n* necessity

bì yè 毕业 *v* graduate

bì yè 毕业 *n* graduation

bì zuǐ 闭嘴 *v* shut up

bì hù suǒ 庇护所 *n* asylum

bì xià 陛下 *n* majesty

bì chú 壁橱 *n* closet

bì lěi 壁垒 *n* bulwark

bì lú 壁炉 *n* fireplace

bì lú biān 壁炉边 *n* hearth

bì fēng gǎng 避风港 *n* haven

bì kāi 避开 *n* avoidance
bì kāi 避开 *v* shun
bì miǎn 避免 *v* avert, avoid, fend off, shed
bì miǎn 避免 *n* avoidance
bì nàn 避难 *v* shelter
bì nàn suǒ 避难所 *n* refuge, shelter
biān 边 *n* side
biān jì 边际 *n* margin
biān jiè 边界 *n* boundary, frontier
biān jiè xiàn 边界线 *n* borderline
biān jìng 边境 *n* border, frontier
biān yuán 边缘 *n* brim, brink, edge, fringe, verge
biān chéng fǎ diǎn 编成法典 *v* codify
biān duì 编队 *n* array
biān jí 编辑 *v* edit
biān mǎ 编码 *v* codify
biān nián shǐ 编年史 *n* chronicle
biān xiě 编写 *v* compile
biān zhī de 编织的 *adj* woven
biān fú 蝙蝠 *n* bat
biān cè 鞭策 *v* spur
biān dǎ 鞭打 *v* flog, lash, whip
biān zi 鞭子 *n* lash, whip
biǎn dī 贬低 *v* belittle, debase, demean
biǎn sǔn de 贬损的 *adj* derogatory
biǎn zhí 贬值 *v* depreciate, devalue
biǎn zhí 贬值 *n* devaluation
biǎn dòu 扁豆 *n* lentil
biǎn táo tǐ 扁桃体 *n* tonsil
biàn lì 便利 *v* facilitate

biàn lì shè shī 便利设施 *n* amenities
biàn mì 便秘 *n* constipation
biàn shì 便士 *n* penny
biàn xié shì de 便携式的 *adj* portable
pián yi huò 便宜货 *n* bargain
biàn àn 变暗 *v* darken
biàn bó 变薄 *v* attenuate
biàn de xīn xiān 变得新鲜 *v* freshen
biàn hóng 变红 *v* redden
biàn hòu 变厚 *v* thicken
biàn huà 变化 *v* vary
biàn huà mò cè de 变化莫测的 *adj* unpredictable
biàn huài 变坏 *v* degenerate
biàn huàn wú cháng 变幻无常 *adj* fickle
biàn shǎo 变少 *v* diminish
biàn tài de 变态的 *adj* pervert
biàn wēn hé 变温和 *v* relent
biàn xì fǎ zhě 变戏法者 *n* juggler
biàn xiǎo 变小 *v* attenuate, diminish
biàn xíng 变形 *v* deform
biàn yìng 变硬 *v* stiffen
biàn zhì 变质 *v* curdle
biàn zhǒng 变种 *v* mutate
biàn hù 辩护 *v* defend, vindicate
biàn hù zhě 辩护者 *n* defender
biàn jiě 辩解 *n* allegation
biàn jiě 辩解 *v* allege, justify
biàn lùn 辩论 *v* debate
biàn lùn 辩论 *n* debate

biàn zi 辫子 *n* braid
biāo bǎng 标榜 *v* flaunt
biāo běn 标本 *n* specimen
biāo dù 标度 *v* scale
biāo jì 标记 *n* sign
biāo qiān 标签 *n* label, sticker, tag
biāo zhì 标识 *n* marker
biāo tí 标题 *n* heading, title
biāo yǔ 标语 *n* catchword
biāo yǔ pái 标语牌 *n* placard
biāo zhì 标志 *n* mark
biāo zhì zhe 标志着 *v* signify
biāo zhǔn 标准 *n* criterion, standard
biāo zhǔn yǐ xià de 标准以下的 *adj* substandard
biāo shēng 飙升 *v* soar
biǎo 表 *n* table
biǎo dá 表达 *n* articulation, expression
biǎo gé 表格 *n* form
biǎo jué 表决 *v* vote
biǎo miàn 表面 *n* surface
biǎo miàn lóng qǐ 表面隆起 *n* bump
biǎo míng 表明 *v* manifest
biǎo shì 表示 *v* denote, mean, represent
biǎo shì tóng yì de 表示同意的 *adj* affirmative
biǎo xiàn 表现 *v* behave
biǎo xiōng dì zǐ mèi 表兄弟姊妹 *n* cousin
biǎo yáng 表扬 *v* commend, praise

biǎo yáng 表扬 *n* commendation
bié chù 别处 *adv* elsewhere
bié de 别的 *adj* another
bié míng 别名 *n* synonym
bìn gǔ 髌骨 *n* kneecap
bīng 冰 *n* ice
bīng báo 冰雹 *n* hail
bīng chuān 冰川 *n* glacier
bīng kuài 冰块 *n* ice cube
bīng lěng de 冰冷的 *adj* ice-cold, icy
bīng qí lín 冰淇淋 *n* ice cream
bīng shān 冰山 *n* iceberg
bīng xiāng 冰箱 *n* icebox
bīng gōng chǎng 兵工厂 *n* arsenal
bīng yíng 兵营 *n* camp
bǐng 柄 *n* hilt
bǐng gān 饼干 *n* biscuit
bìng cún 并存 *v* coexist
bìng fā de 并发的 *adj* concurrent
bìng fā zhèng 并发症 *n* complication
bìng liè 并列 *adv* abreast
bìng liè de 并列的 *adj* collateral
bìng pái 并排 *adv* abreast
bìng qiě 并且 *c* and
bìng tūn 并吞 *n* annexation
bìng xíng 并行 *n* parallel
bìng xíng de 并行的 *adj* collateral
bìng 病 *n* ailment
bìng dú 病毒 *n* virus
bìng qū 病区 *n* ward
bō hào 拨号 *n* dial
bō hào 拨号 *v* dial
bō hào yīn 拨号音 *n* dial tone

bō dòng 波动 *v* fluctuate
bō jí 波及 *v* embroil
bō lán 波兰 *n* Poland
bō lán de 波兰的 *adj* Polish
bō làng 波浪 *n* wave
bō làng de 波浪的 *adj* wavy
bō wén 波纹 *n* ripple
bō li 玻璃 *n* glass
bō li qì mǐn 玻璃器皿 *n* glassware
bō duó 剥夺 *n* deprivation
bō duó 剥夺 *v* deprive, strip
bō duó jì chéng quán 剥夺继承权 *v* disinherit
bō xuē 剥削 *v* exploit
bō luó 菠萝 *n* pineapple
bō fàng qì 播放器 *n* player
bō sòng 播送 *v* broadcast
bō sòng 播送 *n* broadcast
bō yīn yuán 播音员 *n* announcer
bó fù 伯父 *n* uncle
bó jué fū rén 伯爵夫人 *n* countess
bó chuán 驳船 *n* barge
bó rán dà nù 勃然大怒 *n* tantrum
bó lǎn huì 博览会 *n* fair
bó shì 博士 *n* doctor
bó wù guǎn 博物馆 *n* museum
bó xué de 博学的 *adj* learned
bó dòng 搏动 *v* pulsate
bó de 薄的 *adj* attenuating, thin
bó de 薄地 *adv* thinly
bò hé 薄荷 *n* mint
báo shā 薄纱 *n* gauze
báo sū bǐng 薄酥饼 *n* wafer
bó wù 薄雾 *n* mist

bó wù de 薄雾的 *adj* misty
bǒ jiǎo de 跛脚的 *adj* lame
bǒ xíng 跛行 *v* limp
bǒ xíng 跛行 *n* limp
bǔ cháng 补偿 *v* atone, compensate, expiate
bǔ cháng 补偿 *n* atonement, compensation, expiation, retrieval
bǔ dīng 补丁 *v* patch
bǔ dīng 补丁 *n* patch
bǔ jiù 补救 *v* remedy
bǔ jiù 补救 *n* remedy
bǔ pǐn 补品 *n* tonic
bǔ tiē 补贴 *n* allowance, subsidy
bǔ tiē 补贴 *v* subsidize
bǔ zú wù 补足物 *n* complement
bǔ rǔ dòng wù 哺乳动物 *n* mammal
bǔ huò 捕获 *v* capture
bǔ huò 捕获 *n* capture
bù 不 *adv* not
bù ān 不安 *n* discomfort, unrest
bù ān dìng de 不安定的 *adj* restless
bù ān quán 不安全 *n* insecurity
bù ān quán de 不安全的 *adj* unsafe
bù bǎi jià zi 不摆架子 *adj* unassuming
bù biàn de 不变的 *adj* immutable
bù cè de shì 不测的事 *n* eventuality
bù chéng gōng de 不成功的 *adj* unsuccessful

B

bù chéng shú 不成熟 *n*
immaturity

bù chéng shú de 不成熟的 *adj*
immature

bù chéng shí 不诚实 *adj* dishonest

bù chéng shí 不诚实 *n* dishonesty

bù chún de 不纯的 *adj* impure

bù dà kě néng de 不大可能的 *adj*
improbable

bù dài piān jiàn de 不带偏见的 *n*
objective

bù dào dé 不道德 *n* immorality

bù dào dé de 不道德的 *adj*
amoral, immoral

bù tiáo hé de 不调和的 *adj*
discordant

bù dòng chǎn 不动产 *n* realty

bù dòng de 不动的 *adj*
motionless, still

bù fā yīn de 不发音的 *adj* mute

bù fǎ xíng wéi 不法行为 *n*
dishonesty

bù fāng biàn de 不方便的 *adj*
inconvenient

bù fēn shèng fù 不分胜负 *n* tie

bù fū zhī 不敷支 *v* outgrow

bù fú cóng 不服从 *n* disobedience

bù fú cóng de 不服从的 *adj*
disobedient

bù gāi shòu de 不该受的 *adj*
undeserved

bù gāo xìng 不高兴 *n* displeasure

bù gāo xìng de 不高兴的 *adj*
sullen

bù gōng dào de 不公道的 *adj*
unjust

bù gōng zhèng 不公正 *n* injustice

bù gù jí de 不顾及的 *adj*
irrespective

bù guǎn zěn me yàng 不管怎么
样 *adv* regardless

bù guǎn zěn yàng 不管怎样 *pro*
anyhow

bù guāng cǎi de 不光彩的 *adj*
dishonorable

bù guī zé de 不规则的 *adj*
irregular

bù hán qiān de 不含铅的 *adj*
unleaded

bù hé cháng lǐ de 不合常理的 *adj*
illogical

bù hé fǎ de 不合法的 *adj* illicit,
unlawful

bù hé guī gé de 不合规格的 *adj*
substandard

bù hé lǐ de 不合理的 *adj* irrational,
unfair

bù hé lǐ de 不合理地 *adv* unfairly

bù hé lǐ xìng 不合理性 *n*
unfairness

bù hé luó jí de 不合逻辑的 *adj*
illogical

bù hé qíng lǐ de 不合情理的 *adj*
unreasonable

bù hé shì de 不合适的 *adj* unfit,
unsuitable

bù hé 不和 *n* discord

bù hé xié de 不和谐的 *adj*
dissonant

bù jí gé 不及格 *v* flunk

bù jiān chí 不坚持 *v* waive

bù jiàn kāng 不健康 *adj* unhealthy
bù jìn de 不尽的 *adj* endless
bù jīng què de 不精确的 *adj* imprecise
bù jǐng qì 不景气 *n* depression, slump
bù jìng 不敬 *n* disrespect
bù jìng de 不敬的 *adj* disrespectful
bù jiǔ 不久 *adv* shortly, soon
bù kǎo lǜ 不考虑 *v* leave out
bù kǎo lǜ de 不考虑的 *adj* irrespective
bù kě biàn gēng de 不可变更的 *adj* inflexible
bù kě bǔ jiù de 不可补救的 *adj* irreparable
bù kě fēn gē de 不可分割的 *adj* indivisible
bù kě jiù yào de 不可救药的 *adj* incorrigible
bù kě kàng jù de 不可抗拒的 *adj* irresistible
bù kě kào de 不可靠的 *adj* questionable, unreliable
bù kě néng 不可能 *n* impossibility
bù kě néng de 不可能的 *adj* impossible
bù kě nì zhuǎn de 不可逆转的 *adj* irreversible
bù kě shǔ de 不可数的 *n* incalculable
bù kě sī yì de 不可思议的 *adj* occult
bù kě wān qū de 不可弯曲的 *adj* inflexible

bù kě yuán liàng de 不可原谅的 *adj* inexcusable
bù kě zhī lùn zhě 不可知论者 *n* agnostic
bù kuài 不快 *n* displeasure
bù kuān róng 不宽容 *n* intolerance
bù lǐ mào de 不礼貌的 *adj* impolite, rude
bù lǐ huì 不理会 *v* disregard
bù lì 不利 *n* disadvantage
bù lì de 不利的 *adj* adverse, detrimental, unfavorable
bù lì tiáo jiàn 不利条件 *n* disadvantage
bù lián guàn de 不连贯的 *adj* incoherent
bù lǚ xíng yì wù 不履行义务 *n* defection
bù mǎn 不满 *adj* discontent
bù mǎn 不满 *v* grouch
bù mǎn 不满 *n* grudge
bù mǎn de 不满的 *adj* grouchy
bù mǎn yì 不满意 *adj* dissatisfied
bù máo de 不毛的 *adj* arid
bù míng què de 不明确的 *adj* indecisive, indefinite
bù míng zhì de 不明智的 *adj* unwise
bù nài fán 不耐烦 *n* impatience
bù nài fán de 不耐烦的 *adj* impatient
bù néng chéng rèn de 不能承认的 *adj* inadmissible
bù néng de 不能的 *adj* unable

B

bù néng jiē shòu de 不能接受的
adj inadmissible

bù néng yǔn xǔ de 不能允许的
adj inadmissible

bù piān bù yǐ de 不偏不倚的 *adj*
neutral

bù píng děng 不平等 *n* inequality

bù píng wěn de 不平稳的 *adj*
unsteady

bù qià dàng de 不恰当的 *adj*
improper

bù qiè shí jì de 不切实际的 *adj*
unrealistic

bù què dìng de 不确定的 *adj*
uncertain

bù rén dào de 不人道的 *adj*
inhuman

bù róng zhì yí de 不容置疑的 *adj*
undeniable

bù róng xìng de 不溶性的 *adj*
insoluble

bù shí yòng de 不实用的 *adj*
impractical

bù shì 不适 *n* discomfort

bù shì shí de 不适时的 *adj*
untimely

bù shì yí de 不适宜的 *adj*
inappropriate, unfavorable

bù shòu chéng fá 不受惩罚 *n*
impunity

bù shòu huān yíng de 不受欢迎
的 *adj* unpopular

bù shū fu de 不舒服的 *adj*
uncomfortable

bù shú xī de 不熟悉的 *adj*
unfamiliar

bù tài kě néng de 不太可能的 *adj*
unlikely

bù tǎn shuài de 不坦率的 *adj*
devious

bù tíng de 不停的 *adj* incessant

bù tíng de 不停地 *adv* ceaselessly

bù tóng 不同 *n* disparity

bù tóng de 不同的 *adj* different,
distinct, unlike

bù tóng děng de 不同等的 *adj*
unequal

bù tóng yì 不同意 *v* disagree

bù tóng yì de 不同意的 *adj*
dissident

bù tóng yú 不同于 *v* differ

bù tòng de 不痛的 *adj* painless

bù tòu míng de 不透明的 *adj*
opaque

bù tòu qì de 不透气的 *adj* airtight

bù tuán jié 不团结 *n* disunity

bù wán quán de 不完全的 *adj*
incomplete

bù wàng de 不忘的 *adj* mindful

bù wěn dìng 不稳定 *n* instability

bù wěn dìng de 不稳定的 *adj*
unstable

bù xī yān zhě 不吸烟者 *n*
nonsmoker

bù xiàn shí de 不现实的 *adj*
impractical

bù xiāng gān de 不相干的 *adj*
extraneous, impertinent,
irrelevant

bù xiāng róng 不相容 *adj*
incompatible

bù xiāng sì 不相似 *adj* dissimilar

bù xiāng xìn 不相信 *n* disbelief

bù xiáng de 不祥的 *adj* ominous

bù xiàng huì fā shēng de 不像会发生的 *adj* improbable

bù xié tiáo de 不协调的 *adj* dissonant

bù xiè de 不懈的 *adj* relentless

bù xìn rèn 不信任 *n* distrust, mistrust

bù xìn rèn 不信任 *v* distrust, mistrust

bù xìn rèn de 不信任的 *adj* distrustful

bù xìng 不幸 *n* distress, misfortune, unhappiness

bù xìng de 不幸的 *adj* unlucky

bù xiǔ de 不朽的 *adj* immortal, monumental

bù yán zì míng de 不言自明的 *adj* self-evident

bù yī zhì 不一致 *n* disagreement

bù yī zhì de 不一致的 *adj* discordant, inconsistent

bù yǒu hǎo de 不友好的 *adj* unfriendly

bù yú kuài de 不愉快的 *adj* disagreeable, unhappy

bù yù de 不育的 *adj* sterile

bù yuàn yì de 不愿意的 *adj* indisposed

bù yuàn yì de 不愿意地 *adv* unwillingly

bù yuè 不悦 *n* unhappiness

bù yuè de 不悦的 *adj* disgruntled

bù yùn de 不孕的 *adj* infertile

bù zài bào huàn xiǎng de 不再抱幻想的 *adj* disenchanted

bù zài zháo mí de 不再着迷的 *adj* disenchanted

bù zài chǎng 不在场 *n* absence

bù zài chǎng 不在场 *adj* absent

bù zàn chéng 不赞成 *n* disapproval

bù zàn chéng 不赞成 *v* disapprove

bù zhēn jié de 不贞洁的 *adj* unfaithful

bù zhēn shí de 不真实的 *adj* untrue

bù zhèng dāng de 不正当的 *adj* unjustified

bù zhèng què de 不正确的 *adj* improper, incorrect

bù zhī pí juàn de 不知疲倦的 *adj* tireless

bù zhí dé de 不值得的 *adj* worthless

bù zhōng 不忠 *n* disloyalty, infidelity

bù zhōng de 不忠的 *adj* disloyal

bù zhōng shí de 不忠实的 *adj* unfaithful

bù zhòng yào de 不重要的 *adj* trivial

bù zhù míng de 不著名的 *adj* obscure

bù zhǔn de 不准的 *adv* off

bù zhǔn què de 不准确的 *adj* inaccurate, unfaithful

bù zú 不足 *n* deficiency

B
C

bù zú de 不足的 *adj* deficient, inadequate, insufficient
bù 布 *n* cloth
bù dào 布道 *n* sermon
bù dào zhě 布道者 *n* preacher
bù dīng 布丁 *n* pudding
bù jǐng 布景 *n* setting
bù léi qū 布雷区 *n* minefield
bù 步 *n* step
bù bīng 步兵 *n* infantry
bù dào 步道 *n* trail
bù qiāng 步枪 *n* rifle
bù xíng 步行 *v* walk
bù 钚 *n* plutonium
bù 部 *n* ministry
bù zhǎng 部长 *n* minister
bù duì 部队 *n* troop
bù fen 部分 *n* part, portion, section, segment, session
bù fen 部分 *adv* partly
bù fen de 部分的 *adj* partial
bù fen de 部分地 *adv* partially
bù luò 部落 *n* tribe
bù mén 部门 *n* department, division, sector
bù shǔ 部署 *v* deploy
bù shǔ 部署 *n* deployment
bù jì 簿记 *n* bookkeeping

C

cā chú qì 擦除器 *n* eraser
cā diào 擦掉 *v* wipe out
cā jìng 擦净 *v* wipe out
cā liàng 擦亮 *v* brush up, polish
cā shāng 擦伤 *n* bruise
cā xǐ 擦洗 *v* mop
cā xié gāo 擦鞋膏 *n* shoe polish
cāi 猜 *v* guess
cāi 猜 *n* guess
cāi cè 猜测 *v* speculate
cāi xiǎng 猜想 *n* conjecture
cāi xiǎng 猜想 *v* wonder
cāi yí 猜疑 *n* suspicion
cāi yí de 猜疑的 *adj* suspicious
cái néng 才能 *n* aptitude, capacity, gift
cái liào 材料 *n* material
cái chǎn 财产 *n* possession, property
cái fù 财富 *n* fortune, treasure, wealth
cái wù guān 财务官 *n* treasurer
cái wù 财物 *n* belongings
cái feng 裁缝 *n* seamstress, tailor
cái jiǎn 裁剪 *n* clipping, cut
cái jué 裁决 *v* rule
cái jūn 裁军 *v* disarm
cái jūn 裁军 *n* disarmament
cái pàn 裁判 *n* judge
cái pàn yuán 裁判员 *n* referee, umpire
cái yuán 裁员 *v* lay off

cǎi gòu 采购 *v* procure
cǎi qǔ 采取 *v* adopt, take
cǎi qǔ 采取 *n* adoption
cǎi shí chǎng 采石场 *n* quarry
cǎi yòng （de bàn fǎ）采用（的办法）*v* resort
cǎi yòng de 采用的 *adj* adoptive
cǎi zhāi 采摘 *v* pluck
cǎi hóng 彩虹 *n* rainbow
cǎi piào 彩票 *n* lottery
cǎi 踩 *iv* tread
cǎi tà 踩踏 *n* stampede
cài 菜 *n* dish
cài dān 菜单 *n* menu
cài dòu 菜豆 *n* kidney bean
cài huā 菜花 *n* cauliflower
cēn cī bù qí de 参差不齐的 *adj* uneven
cān guān 参观 *n* visit
cān guān 参观 *v* visit
cān jiā 参加 *v* attend, go in, participate
cān jiā huó dòng 参加活动 *v* campaign
cān kǎo 参考 *v* refer to
cān kǎo 参考 *n* reference
cān sài de rén （wù）参赛的人（物）*n* entry
cān sài zhě 参赛者 *n* contestant
cān shù 参数 *n* parameters
cān yì yuán 参议员 *n* senator
cān yì yuàn 参议院 *n* senate
cān yù 参与 *n* engagement, involvement, participation
cān yù 参与 *v* involved

cān 餐 *n* meal
cān jīn 餐巾 *n* napkin
cān jù 餐具 *n* cutlery
cān tīng 餐厅 *n* canteen, restaurant
cán bào de 残暴的 *adj* atrocious
cán fèi 残废 *adj* disabled
cán hái 残骸 *n* wreckage
cán jí 残疾 *n* disability
cán kù 残酷 *n* cruelty
cán kù de 残酷的 *adj* cruel
cán kù duì dài 残酷对待 *v* brutalize
cán rěn de 残忍的 *adj* brutal
cán rěn de 残忍的 *n* brutality
cán yú 残余 *n* remnant
cán yú de 残余的 *adj* remaining
cán zǐ 残滓 *n* residue
cán shí 蚕食 *v* nibble
cán kuì de 惭愧的 *adj* ashamed
càn làn de 灿烂的 *adj* brilliant
cāng cù 仓促 *adj* hasty
cāng cù 仓促 *adv* hurriedly
cāng kù 仓库 *n* depot, warehouse
cāng bái 苍白 *adj* livid
cāng bái 苍白 *n* paleness
cāng bái de 苍白的 *adj* pale
cāng yíng 苍蝇 *n* fly
cáng shēn chù 藏身处 *n* burrow
cāo kòng 操控 *v* manipulate
cāo zuò 操作 *n* operation
cáo zá de 嘈杂的 *adj* noisy
cáo 槽 *n* groove, manager
cáo yá 槽牙 *n* molar
cǎo 草 *n* grass

căo àn 草案 *n* draft

căo diàn 草甸 *n* meadow

căo găo 草稿 *n* scratch

căo guī 草龟 *n* tortoise

căo shuài de 草率的 *adj* sloppy

căo méi 草莓 *n* strawberry

căo pí 草皮 *n* sod

căo píng 草坪 *n* lawn, turf

căo xiě 草写 *v* scribble

cè xiàng 侧向 *adj* lateral

cè yì 侧翼 *n* flank

cè suŏ 厕所 *n* toilet

cè liáng 测量 *v* gage, gauge, measure

cè shì 测试 *v* test

cè shì 测试 *n* test

cè luè 策略 *n* strategy, tactics

céng 层 *n* layer

chā 叉 *n* fork

chā 插 *v* plug

chā cáo 插槽 *n* slot

chā qǔ 插曲 *n* episode, interlude

chā rù 插入 *v* insert

chā rù 插入 *n* insertion

chā rù yǔ 插入语 *n* parenthesis

chā tóu 插头 *n* plug

chā zuò 插座 *n* outlet

chá kàn 查看 *v* look into, look over

chá míng 查明 *v* ascertain, detect

chá xún 查询 *v* inquire

chá zhăo 查找 *v* stalk

chá zhăo 查找 *n* stalk

chá chí 茶匙 *n* teaspoon

chá diăn 茶点 *n* refreshment

chá dié 茶碟 *n* saucer

chá hú 茶壶 *n* teapot

chá shuĭ 茶水 *n* pantry

chá yè 茶叶 *n* tea

chá jué 察觉 *v* detect, perceive

chá jué chū 察觉出 *v* discern

chā bié 差别 *n* difference, distinction, discrepancy, disparity

chā cuò 差错 *n* error

chā jù 差距 *n* gap

chāi shì 差事 *n* errand

chāi chú 拆除 *n* demolition

chāi chú 拆除 *v* dismantle

chāi huĭ 拆毁 *v* demolish

chāi qiān 拆迁 *n* relocation

chāi xiè 拆卸 *v* detach

chái huo 柴火 *n* firewood

chái 豺 *n* jackal

chān jiă 掺假 *v* adulterate

chān zá 掺杂 *v* adulterate

chán 缠 *iv* wind

chán chán zuò shēng 潺潺作声 *v* babble

chán chú 蟾蜍 *n* toad

chăn fù de 产妇的 *adj* maternal

chăn pĭn 产品 *n* product

chăn shēng 产生 *iv* arise, generate, yield

chăn shēng 产生 *n* generation

chăn shēng (xiăng fă) 产生（想法）*v* throw up

chăn mèi 谄媚 *v* flatter

chăn mèi de jŭ dòng 谄媚的举动 *n* flattery

chǎn zi 铲子 *n* shovel

chàn huǐ 忏悔 *n* penance, penitent

chàn huǐ shì 忏悔室 *n* confessional

chàn huǐ zhě 忏悔者 *n* confessor

chàn dǒu 颤抖 *v* quiver

zhàn lì 颤栗 *v* shiver, tremble

zhàn lì 颤栗 *n* shiver

chàn zhèn 颤振 *v* flutter

zhǎng 长 *adj* lonesome

zhǎng bèi 长辈 *n* elder, seniority

zhǎng chū zhī tiáo 长出枝条 *v* branch out

zhǎng dà 长大 *v* grow up

cháng de 长的 *adj* lengthy

cháng dèng 长凳 *n* bench

cháng dí 长笛 *n* flute

cháng dù 长度 *n* length

cháng fāng xíng 长方形 *n* rectangle

cháng fāng xíng de 长方形的 *adj* oblong, rectangular

zhǎng guān 长官 *n* chief

cháng jǐng lù 长颈鹿 *n* giraffe

cháng kù 长裤 *n* trousers

cháng láng 长廊 *n* promenade

cháng páo 长袍 *n* robe, tunic

cháng qī cún zài de 长期存在的 *adj* long-standing

cháng qī de 长期的 *adj* long-term

cháng shā fā 长沙发 *n* couch

cháng shí jiān de 长时间的 *adj* long-standing

cháng tuǐ liè gǒu 长腿猎狗 *n* greyhound

cháng wà 长袜 *n* stocking

cháng wěi xiǎo yīng wǔ 长尾小鹦鹉 *n* parakeet

zhǎng xiàng 长相 *n* looks

cháng cháng 肠 *n* bowels, gut

cháng zi 肠子 *n* intestine

cháng shì 尝试 *n* effort, endeavor

cháng shì 尝试 *v* endeavor, try

cháng huán 偿还 *v* reimburse

cháng huán 偿还 *n* repayment

cháng qīng 偿清 *v* pay off

cháng cháng 常常 *adv* often

cháng chū mò yú 常出没于 *v* haunt

cháng guī de 常规的 *adj* conventional

cháng nián de 常年的 *adj* perennial

chǎng 场 *n* field

chǎng hé 场合 *n* occasion

chàng yì 倡议 *n* initiative

chàng 唱 *iv* sing

chàng gē 唱歌 *n* song

chāo xiě 抄写 *v* transcribe

chāo chū 超出 *v* overstep

chāo guò 超过 *v* exceed

chāo guò 超过 *pre* over

chāo jí dà guó 超级大国 *n* superpower

chāo shēng bō 超声波 *n* ultrasound

chāo shì 超市 *n* supermarket

chāo sù 超速 *iv* speed

chāo yuè 超越 *adv* beyond

chāo yuè 超越 *v* excel, outperform, surpass, transcend

chāo yuè 超越 *n* excess

chāo zhī 超支 *v* overrun

chāo zhòng de 超重的 *adj* overweight

cháo 巢 *n* nest

cháo shàng de 朝上地 *adv* upwards

cháo shèng 朝圣 *n* pilgrimage

cháo shèng zhě 朝圣者 *n* pilgrim

cháo xiǎn jì 朝鲜蓟 *n* artichoke

cháo nòng 嘲弄 *v* mock

cháo nòng 嘲弄 *n* mockery

cháo xiào 嘲笑 *v* deride, ridicule, scoff

cháo xiào 嘲笑 *n* ridicule

cháo shī de 潮湿的 *adj* damp, humid, soggy

cháo xī bō 潮汐波 *n* tidal wave

chǎo jià 吵架 *v* quarrel

chǎo jià 吵架 *n* quarrel

chǎo nào 吵闹 *v* rattle

chǎo nào de 吵闹的 *adj* rowdy

chē dàng 车档 *n* gear

chē dào 车道 *n* driveway, lane

chē gài 车盖 *n* hood

chē hòu xiāng 车后箱 *n* trunk

chē jiān 车间 *n* workshop

chē kù 车库 *n* garage

chē liàng 车辆 *n* vehicle

chē zhóu 车轴 *n* axle

chè dǐ cuī huǐ 彻底摧毁 *v* wipe out

chè dǐ de 彻底的 *adj* outright, thorough

chè dǐ sōu suǒ 彻底搜索 *v* ransack

chè chú 撤除 *n* removal

chè huí 撤回 *v* recant

chè tuì 撤退 *v* retreat, withdraw

chè tuì 撤退 *n* retreat, withdrawal

chè xiāo 撤消 *v* withdraw

chè xiāo 撤销 *v* repeal, revoke

chè xiāo 撤销 *n* repeal

chén 尘 *n* dirt

chén chuán 沉船 *n* shipwreck

chén diàn 沉淀 *v* precipitate

chén jìn 沉浸 *v* immerse

chén jìn 沉浸 *n* immersion

chén mò de 沉没的 *adj* sunken

chén mí 沉迷 *v* indulge

chén mò 沉默 *n* silence

chén mò 沉默 *v* silence

chén mò de 沉默的 *adj* silent

chén mò guǎ yán 沉默寡言 *adj* dumb

chén sī 沉思 *v* contemplate

chén wěn de 沉稳的 *adj* stable

chén zhòng 沉重 *n* heaviness

chén zhòng de 沉重的 *adj* burdensome

chén zhuó de 沉着的 *adj* composed

chén fǔ 陈腐 *n* banality

chén jiù de 陈旧的 *adj* antiquated, stale

chén shè pǐn 陈设品 *n* furnishings

chén shù 陈述 *n* presentation

chèn lǐ 衬里 *n* lining

chèn shān 衬衫 *n* shirt

chēng hū 称呼 *v* address

chēng zàn 称赞 *v* acclaim, commend

chēng zàn 称赞 _n_ commendation

chēng zàn de 称赞的 _adj_
  complimentary

chēng zhòng 称重 _v_ weigh

chéng běn 成本 _n_ cost

chéng zhǎng 成长 _iv_ grow

chéng fèn 成分 _n_ component,
  element, ingredient

chéng gōng 成功 _v_ succeed

chéng gōng 成功 _n_ success

chéng gōng de 成功的 _adj_
  successful

chéng jì 成绩 _n_ grade

chéng jiàn 成见 _n_ prejudice

chéng jiù 成就 _n_ accomplishment,
  attainment

chéng lì 成立 _n_ inception

chéng lì 成立 _up_ set up

chéng pī shā sǐ 成批杀死 _v_
  decimate

chéng qún 成群 _v_ cluster

chéng rén 成人 _n_ adult, grown-up

chéng shú 成熟 _n_ maturity

chéng shú 成熟 _adj_ ripe

chéng shú 成熟 _v_ ripen

chéng shú de 成熟的 _adj_ mature

chéng tuán 成团 _v_ agglomerate

chéng wéi 成为 _iv_ become

chéng wéi pào yǐng 成为泡影 _v_
  fall through

chéng wén fǎ 成文法 _n_ statute

chéng wèn tí de 成问题的 _adj_
  debatable

chéng yǔ 成语 _n_ idiom

chéng yuán 成员 _n_ membership

chéng bǎo 承保 _v_ underwrite

chéng dān 承担 _v_ undertake

chéng dān zé rèn de 承担责任的
  adj liable

chéng nuò 承诺 _v_ pledge

chéng nuò 承诺 _n_ pledge

chéng rèn 承认 _v_ acknowledge,
  admit

chéng rèn 承认 _n_ admission

chéng shòu 承受 _v_ withstand

chéng zū rén 承租人 _n_ lessee

chéng kěn de 诚恳的 _adj_ cordial

chéng shí 诚实 _n_ honesty

chéng shí de 诚实的 _adj_ honest

chéng xìn 诚信 _n_ integrity

chéng yì 诚意 _n_ sincerity

chéng bǎo 城堡 _n_ castle

chéng shì 城市 _n_ city

chéng shì de 城市的 _adj_ urban

chéng （**chē**）乘（车）_iv_ ride

chéng fǎ 乘法 _n_ multiplication

chéng kè 乘客 _n_ passenger

chéng yǐ 乘以 _v_ multiply

chéng fá 惩罚 _v_ chastise, penalize,
  punish, slap

chéng fá 惩罚 _n_ chastisement

chéng dù 程度 _n_ degree, extent

chéng xù 程序 _n_ procedure

chéng xù yuán 程序员 _n_
  programmer

chéng qīng 澄清 _n_ clarification

chéng qīng 澄清 _v_ clarify, clear

chéng sè 橙色 _n_ orange

chéng zi 橙子 _n_ orange

chī 吃 _iv_ eat

chī cǎo 吃草 *v* graze

chī cǎo 吃草 *n* graze

chī fàn de kè rén 吃饭的客人 *n* diner

chī tóng lèi de dòng wù 吃同类的动物 *n* cannibal

chī wǎn fàn 吃晚饭 *v* dine

chī zhī yǐ bí 嗤之以鼻 *v* sniff

chī mí 痴迷 *n* obsession

chí 池 *n* pool

chí táng 池塘 *n* pond

chí dùn de 迟钝的 *adj* dumb

chí huǎn de 迟缓的 *adv* tardy

chí lái de 迟来的 *adj* belated

chí yí de 迟疑的 *adj* hesitant

chí jiǔ 持久 *adj* lasting

chí qiāng qiǎng jié 持枪抢劫 *n* holdup, mugging

chí qiāng qiǎng jié 持枪抢劫 *v* mug

chí xù 持续 *v* last

chí xù de 持续的 *adj* constant, ongoing, steady

chí xù de 持续地 *adv* ceaselessly

chí yǒu rén 持有人 *n* bearer

chí cùn 尺寸 *n* dimension

chǐ gòu 齿垢 *n* tartar

chǐ lún 齿轮 *n* gear

chǐ rǔ 耻辱 *n* disgrace, dishonor

chǐ rǔ 耻辱 *v* disgrace

chì zé 斥责 *v* snub

chì dào 赤道 *n* equator

chì jiǎo 赤脚 *adj* barefoot

chì luǒ de 赤裸的 *adj* naked

chì zì 赤字 *n* deficit

chì rè de 炽热的 *adj* red-hot

chì bǎng 翅膀 *n* wing

chōng diàn 充电 *v* charge

chōng fèn 充分 *adv* fully

chōng mǎn 充满 *v* abound

chōng mǎn ài de 充满爱的 *adj* loving

chōng mǎn de 充满的 *adj* replete

chōng mǎn huó lì 充满活力 *v* rejuvenate

chōng mǎn huó lì de 充满活力的 *adj* vibrant

chōng zú 充足 *n* abundance

chōng zú de 充足的 *adj* adequate, ample, plentiful, sufficient

chōng 冲 *v* rush

chōng dàn 冲淡 *v* dilute, water down, clash

chōng dòng 冲动 *n* impulse

chōng dòng de 冲动的 *adj* impetuous, impulsive

chōng fēng 冲锋 *n* charge

chōng jī 冲击 *n* concussion, onslaught

chōng làng 冲浪 *v* surf

chōng shuā 冲刷 *v* scour

chōng shuǐ 冲水 *v* flush

chōng tū 冲突 *n* clash, conflict, discord

chōng tū 冲突 *v* conflict

chōng tū de 冲突的 *adj* conflicting

chōng xǐ 冲洗 *v* rinse

chóng hài 虫害 *n* pest

chóng dié 重叠 *v* overlap

chóng fù 重复 *v* duplicate, repeat

chóng fù 重复 *n* duplication, repetition

chóng hūn 重婚 *n* bigamy

chóng jiàn 重建 *v* rebuild, reconstruct

chóng pù lù miàn 重铺路面 *v* resurface

chóng sài 重赛 *n* replay

chóng shēn 重申 *v* reiterate

chóng shēng 重生 *n* rebirth

chóng shù yào diǎn 重述要点 *v* recap

chóng xīn 重新 *adv* afresh, anew

chóng xīn bǔ chōng 重新补充 *v* replenish

chóng xīn dài kuǎn 重新贷款 *v* refinance

chóng xīn dé dào 重新得到 *v* retrieve

chóng xīn de 重新地 *adv* newly

chóng xīn jì shù 重新计数 *n* recount

chóng xīn kāi shǐ 重新开始 *v* resume

chóng xīn kāi shǐ 重新开始 *n* resumption

chóng xīn lòu miàn 重新露面 *v* resurface

chóng xīn shěn chá 重新审查 *v* double-check

chóng xuǎn 重选 *v* reelect

chóng yìn 重印 *v* reprint

chóng zhì 重制 *v* remake

chóng zuò 重做 *v* redo

chóng bài 崇拜 *n* adoration, worship

chóng bài 崇拜 *v* adore

chóng bài zhě 崇拜者 *n* admirer

chóng gāo de 崇高的 *adj* heroic, lofty

chóng jìng 崇敬 *n* homage

chóng jìng 崇敬 *v* venerate

chǒng wù 宠物 *n* pet

chōu chū 抽出 *v* spare

chōu jiǎng 抽奖 *n* raffle

chōu qiān 抽签 *n* draw

chōu tì 抽屉 *n* drawer

chōu xī 抽吸 *v* pump

chōu xiàng de 抽象的 *adj* abstract

chóu dí 仇敌 *n* foe

chóu hèn 仇恨 *n* hatred, rancor

chóu xù 愁绪 *n* melancholy

chóu jīn 酬金 *n* gratuity

chóu shǎng 酬赏 *v* remunerate

chóu chú 踌躇 *v* waver

chǒu huà 丑化 *v* deface

chǒu lòu 丑陋 *n* ugliness

chǒu lòu de 丑陋的 *adj* ugly

chǒu wén 丑闻 *n* scandal

chǒu wén huà 丑闻化 *v* scandalize

chòu chóng 臭虫 *n* bug

chòu de 臭的 *adj* stinking

chòu míng zhāo zhù de 臭名昭著的 *adj* infamous, notorious

chòu sè de 臭色的 *adj* odious

chū bǎn 出版 *n* publication

chū bǎn 出版 *v* publish

chū bǎn shè 出版社 *n* publisher

chū chǎn liàng 出产量 *n* yield

chū dòng 出动 *v* call out

C

chū fā 出发 *n* departure

chū fā 出发 *v* head for, set off, take off

chū gù zhàng 出故障 *v* malfunction

chū guó 出国 *adv* abroad

chū hǎi kǒu 出海口 *n* estuary

chū hàn 出汗 *v* perspire, sweat

chū jià 出价 *n* bid

chū jià 出价 *iv* bid

chū jìng 出境 *n* exit

chū kǒu 出口 *v* export

chū kǒu 出口 *n* outlet, way out

chū lai 出来 *v* come out

chū mài 出卖 *v* betray, double-cross

chū mài 出卖 *n* sellout

chū nà yuán 出纳员 *n* cashier, teller

chū qì kǒng 出气孔 *n* vent

chū qu 出去 *v* get out, go out, step out

chū shēng 出生 *v* be born

chū shēng 出生 *n* birth

chū shēng 出生 *adj* born

chū shòu 出售 *n* sale

chū shòu 出售 *iv* sell

chū xí 出席 *v* attend

chū xí 出席 *n* attendance

chū xiàn 出现 *n* Advent

chū xiàn 出现 *v* appear, arise, come up, emerge, show up, turn out, turn up

chū xiě 出血 *n* bleeding, hemorrhage

chū zū chē 出租车 *n* cab

chū zū rén 出租人 *n* lessor

chū bù de 初步的 *adj* preliminary

chū cì jìn rù shè jiāo jiè 初次进入社交界 *n* debut

chū jí de 初级的 *adj* elementary, junior

chū xué zhě 初学者 *n* beginner

chú ……yǐ wài 除……以外 *pre* barring

chú chòu jì 除臭剂 *n* deodorant

chú diào 除掉 *v* take out

chú diào ……de léi guǎn 除掉……的雷管 *v* defuse

chú fēi 除非 *c* unless

chú le 除了 *adv* aside from

chú le 除了 *pre* except

chú shuāng 除霜 *v* defrost

chú wài 除外 *pre* without

chú fáng 厨房 *n* kitchen

chú shī 厨师 *n* chef, cook

chú zá cǎo 锄杂草 *n* weed

chú jú 雏菊 *n* daisy

chú guì 橱柜 *n* cupboard

chǔ cáng jià 储藏架 *n* cabinet

chǔ cáng shì 储藏室 *n* stockroom

chǔ cún 储存 *n* stockpile

chǔ xù 储蓄 *n* savings

chǔ xù guàn 储蓄罐 *n* piggy bank

chǔ fá 处罚 *n* punishment

chǔ fāng 处方 *n* prescription

chǔ lǐ 处理 *v* address, deal, handle, scrap

chǔ liè shì fāng 处劣势方 *n* underdog

chǔ nǚ 处女 *n* virgin
chǔ nǚ shēn 处女身 *n* virginity
chù suǒ 处所 *n* quarters
chǔ xíng 处刑 *v* condemn
chǔ zhì 处置 *n* disposal
chǔ zhì 处置 *v* dispose
chù diàn 触电 *v* electrocute
chù fā 触发 *v* trigger
chù fā 触发 *n* trigger
chù fàn 触犯 *v* offend
chù mō 触摸 *n* touch
chù mō 触摸 *v* touch
chù mō qǐ lái 触摸起来 *v* touch up
chù nù 触怒 *v* irritate
chù shǒu 触手 *n* tentacle
chuò qì 啜泣 *iv* weep
chuān 穿 *iv* wear
chuān dài 穿戴 *n* wear
chuān jiù 穿旧 *v* wear out
chuān kǒng 穿孔 *v* perforate
chuān kǒng 穿孔 *n* perforation
chuān suō 穿梭 *v* shuttle
chuān yī 穿衣 *v* clothe
chuān yuè 穿越 *pre* across
chuān zhēn 穿针 *v* thread
chuán bō 传播 *v* diffuse, disseminate
chuán dá 传达 *v* convey
chuán dān 传单 *n* flier, leaflet
chuán dǎo 传导 *v* conduct
chuán dào zhě 传道者 *n* apostle
zhuàn jì 传记 *n* biography
chuán jiào 传教 *n* missionary
chuán kāi 传开 *v* pass around

chuán piào 传票 *v* subpoena
chuán piào 传票 *n* subpoena
chuán qí 传奇 *n* legend
chuán rǎn de 传染的 *adj* infectious
chuán rǎn xìng de 传染性的 *adj* contagious
chuán shū 传输 *v* transmit
chuán tǒng 传统 *n* tradition
chuán wén 传闻 *n* hearsay, rumor
chuán yì yuán 传译员 *n* interpreter
chuán zhào 传召 *v* summon
chuán 船 *n* boat, vessel
chuán bó 船舶 *n* ship
chuán zhǎng 船长 *n* captain
chuán chǎng 船厂 *n* shipyard
chuán duò 船舵 *n* rudder
chuán máo 船锚 *n* anchor
chuán tǐ 船体 *n* hull
chuán wěi 船尾 *n* stern
chuán wù 船坞 *n* dock
chuán zhá 船闸 *n* lock
chuǎn qì 喘气 *v* gasp
chuǎn xī 喘息 *v* wheeze
chuàn 串 *n* bunch, cluster, string
chuàn lián 串联 *n* cascade
chuāng kǒu 窗口 *n* window
chuāng lián 窗帘 *n* curtain
chuáng 床 *n* bed
chuáng dān 床单 *n* bedspread, sheets
chuáng diàn 床垫 *n* mattress
chuáng zhào 床罩 *n* bedspread
chuǎng rù 闯入 *v* break in, burst into

C

chuāng shāng 创伤 *v* traumatize
chuàng shǐ rén 创始人 *n* founder
chuàng xīn 创新 *n* innovation
chuàng yì de 创意的 *adj* creative
chuàng zào 创造 *n* creation
chuàng zào lì 创造力 *n* creativity
chuàng zào wù 创造物 *n* creature
chuàng zào zhě 创造者 *n* creator
chuī 吹 *iv* blow
chuī kǒu shào 吹口哨 *v* whistle
chuī máo qiú cī de 吹毛求疵的 *adj* nitpicking
chuī pěng 吹捧 *v* rave
chuī xī 吹熄 *iv* blow out
chuī xū 吹嘘 *v* brag
chuī xū 吹嘘 *n* puff
chuí tóu sàng qì 垂头丧气 *adj* downcast
chuí xián 垂涎 *v* covet
chuí 锤 *n* hammer
chūn tiān 春天 *n* spring
chún de 纯的 *adj* pure
chún dù 纯度 *n* purity
chún jiǎn 纯碱 *n* soda
chún zhī nóng tāng 纯汁浓汤 *n* puree
chún 唇 *n* lip
chǔn shì 蠢事 *n* folly
chuò xué 辍学 *n* drop
chuò xué 辍学 *v* drop, drop out
cí 词 *n* word
cí gēn 词根 *n* stem
cí huì 词汇 *n* glossary
cí huì liàng 词汇量 *n* vocabulary
cí wěi biàn huà 词尾变化 *n* declension

cí qì 瓷器 *n* porcelain
cí zhuān 瓷砖 *n* tile
cí bēi 慈悲 *adj* merciful
cí bēi 慈悲 *n* mercy
cí shàn 慈善 *n* charity
cí shàn de 慈善的 *adj* charitable
cí tuì 辞退 *v* dismiss
cí zhí 辞职 *v* resign
cí zhí 辞职 *n* resignation
cí dài 磁带 *n* tape
cí pán 磁盘 *n* disk
cí tiě 磁铁 *n* magnet
cí xìng 磁性 *n* magnetism
cí xìng de 磁性的 *adj* magnetic
cí xìng dòng wù 雌性动物 *n* female
cǐ hòu 此后 *adv* hereafter
cǐ qián 此前 *adv* previously
cǐ wài 此外 *pre* besides
cǐ wài 此外 *adv* furthermore, moreover
cì xù 次序 *n* sequence
cì 刺 *v* prick, prod
cì 刺 *n* puncture, thorn
cì chuān 刺穿 *v* pierce
cì chuō 刺戳 *v* stab
cì chuō 刺戳 *n* stab
cì dāo 刺刀 *n* bayonet
cì ěr 刺耳 *n* piercing
cì jī 刺激 *v* fuel, goad, stimulate
cì jī 刺激 *n* stimulus
cì jī (wù) 刺激（物）*n* spur
cì kè 刺客 *n* assassin
cì tòng de 刺痛的 *adj* stinging
cì xiù 刺绣 *v* embroider

cì xiù 刺绣 *n* embroidery
cì yǎn de 刺眼的 *adj* lurid
cóng 从 *pre* from
cóng kuān chǔ lǐ 从宽处理 *n* leniency
cóng lǐ dào wài 从里到外 *adv* inside out
cóng nà shí qǐ 从那时起 *adv* since then
cóng shì 从事 *v* engage
cóng wèi 从未 *adv* never
cóng yuǎn fāng 从远方 *adv* afar
cóng zì miàn shàng 从字面上 *adv* literally
cōng cōng 匆匆 *n* haste
cōng cōng 匆匆 *adv* hastily
cōng míng de 聪明的 *adj* bright, clever, intelligent, smart
cōng míng zhī jǔ 聪明之举 *n* gimmick
cóng 丛 *n* cluster
cóng shēng 丛生 *v* cluster
cū bào de 粗暴的 *adj* rowdy
cū bèn 粗笨 *n* clumsiness
cū cāo de 粗糙的 *adj* coarse, crude, rough
cū de 粗的 *adj* thick
cū lǔ 粗鲁 *n* rudeness
cū lǔ de 粗鲁的 *adj* crass, impolite, rude
cū lüè de 粗略的 *adj* sketchy
cū sú 粗俗 *n* vulgarity
cū sú de 粗俗的 *adj* gross, vulgar
cū sú hàn 粗俗汉 *adj* slob
cū xīn de 粗心的 *adj* careless
cū xīn de 粗心的 *n* carelessness

cū yě de 粗野的 *adj* rustic
cù jìn 促进 *v* boost, foster
cù jìn 促进 *n* boost
cù cù 醋 *n* vinegar
cuī cù 催促 *v* hasten
cuī mián 催眠 *n* hypnosis
cuī mián zhuàng tài 催眠状态 *n* hypnosis
cuī qíng de 催情的 *adj* aphrodisiac
cuī huǐ 摧毁 *v* destroy
cuǐ càn 璀璨 *adj* glamorous
cuì de 脆的 *adj* crisp, crispy
cuì ruò 脆弱 *adj* flimsy, fragile
cuì ruò 脆弱 *n* frailty
cuì ruò de 脆弱的 *adj* brittle, tenuous, vulnerable
cūn mín 村民 *n* villager
cūn shè 村舍 *n* cottage
cūn zhuāng 村庄 *n* hamlet, village
cún chǔ 存储 *v* stock, store
cún chǔ 存储 *n* stock, storage
cún huó 存活 *v* live off
cún huò 存货 *n* backlog
cún kuǎn 存款 *n* deposit
cún zài 存在 *iv* be, exist
cún zài 存在 *n* being, existence
cuò bài 挫败 *v* confound, frustrate, thwart
cuò shāng 挫伤 *v* bruise
cuò zhé 挫折 *v* discouragement
cuò zhé 挫折 *n* setback
cuò cí 措辞 *n* wording
cuò gū 错估 *v* misjudge
cuò jué 错觉 *n* delusion
cuò wèi 错位 *v* dislocate, misplace

cuò wèi de 错位的 *adj* misfit

cuò wù 错误 *n* fault, mistake

cuò wù de 错误的 *adj* erroneous, faulty, mistaken, wrong

cuò zōng fù zá de 错综复杂的 *adj* intricate

D

dā biàn chē 搭便车 *n* pickup

dā chē lǚ xíng 搭车旅行 *n* hitchhike

dá bù dào de 达不到的 *adj* inaccessible, untouchable

dá chéng 达成 *v* reach

dá dào 达到 *v* achieve, attain, reach

dá dào 达到 *n* attainment

dá dào gāo cháo 达到高潮 *v* culminate

dá yú jí diǎn 达于极点 *v* culminate

dá àn 答案 *n* answer

dǎ 打 *iv* beat, hit, spank

dǎ 打 *n* beating

dǎ bài 打败 *n* beating

dǎ bài 打败 *v* defeat

dǎ bāo 打包 *v* pack

dǎ bù bài de 打不败的 *adj* unbeatable

dǎ cǎo gǎo 打草稿 *v* scratch

dǎ diàn huà 打电话 *v* phone, ring

dǎ dòng 打动 *v* impress

dǎ dòu 打斗 *iv* fight

dǎ dòu 打斗 *n* mayhem

dǎ dǔ 打赌 *iv* bet, stake

dǎ dǔ 打赌 *n* bet

dǎ duàn 打断 *v* break in

dǎ dǔn 打盹 *v* snooze

dǎ gé 打嗝 *v* belch, burp

dǎ gé 打嗝 *n* belch, burp, hiccup

dǎ gǔ 打谷 *v* thresh

dǎ guān sī 打官司 *v* litigate

dǎ hā qiàn 打哈欠 *v* yawn

dǎ hān 打鼾 *v* snore

dǎ hān shēng 打鼾声 *n* snore

dǎ huǒ 打火 *iv* light

dǎ huǒ jī 打火机 *n* lighter

dǎ jī 打击 *iv* beat, blow

dǎ jī 打击 *n* blow

dǎ jià 打架 *n* brawl

dǎ jiǎo 打搅 *v* bother

dǎ jié 打结 *v* tie

dǎ kāi 打开 *v* open, switch on, turn on, unpack, unwrap

dǎ kē shuì 打瞌睡 *v* doze

dǎ lāo 打捞 *v* salvage

dǎ léi 打雷 *n* thunder

dǎ pēn tì 打喷嚏 *v* sneeze

dǎ pò 打破 *iv* break

dǎ rǎo 打扰 *v* disturb

dǎ sǎo 打扫 *v* spruce up, sweep

dǎ shàng ěr hào 打上耳号 *v* earmark

dǎ suàn 打算 *v* intend

dǎ suì 打碎 *v* break up

dǎ xiǎo bào gào 打小报告 *v* snitch

dǎ yìn 打印 *v* print

dǎ yìn běn 打印本 *n* print

dǎ yìn cuò wù 打印错误 *n* misprint

dǎ yìn jī 打印机 *n* printer

dǎ zhé 打折 *v* discount

dǎ zhòu 打皱 *v* wrinkle

dǎ zì 打字 *v* type

dǎ zuò 打坐 *v* meditate

dǎ zuò 打坐 *n* meditation

dà bà 大坝 *n* dam

dà bái cài 大白菜 *n* cabbage

dà bāo 大包 *n* bale

dà biàn 大便 *n* stool

dà biàn dòng 大变动 *n* upheaval

dà biāo tí 大标题 *n* banner

dà bǎi zi 大伯子 *n* brother-in-law

dà bù 大步 *iv* stride

dà cǎo yuán 大草原 *n* prairie

dà chén 大臣 *n* chancellor

dà cuò 大错 *n* blunder

dà dǎn 大胆 *n* audacity, boldness; dare

dà dǎn de 大胆的 *adj* audacious, bold, daring

dà dào 大道 *n* avenue

dà dé jīng rén de 大得惊人的 *adj* stupendous

dà de 大的 *adj* big, great, large

dà dòng xué 大洞穴 *n* cavern

dà dū huì 大都会 *n* metropolis

dà duō 大多 *adv* mostly

dà fǎ guān 大法官 *n* chancellor

dà fāng de 大方的 *adj* decent

dà fēng xuě 大风雪 *n* blizzard

dà fù wēng 大富翁 *adj* millionaire

dà gài 大概 *adv* about

dà hēng 大亨 *n* tycoon

dà huì 大会 *n* assembly, convention

dà huò 大祸 *n* catastrophe, disaster

dà jiào 大叫 *n* cry, crying

dà jiào táng 大教堂 *n* cathedral

dà kuài 大块 *n* block, chunk

dà kǔn 大捆 *n* bale

dà lǐ shí 大理石 *n* marble

dà liàng 大量 *n* plenty

dà liàng qún zhòng 大量[pl.]群众 *n* mass

dà liàng de 大量的 *adj* heavy, massive, plentiful, substantial

dà liàng huǐ miè 大量毁灭 *v* decimate

dà lù 大陆 *n* continent, mainland

dà lù de 大陆的 *adj* continental

dà má 大麻 *n* hashish

dà mài 大麦 *n* barley

dà mǎn guàn 大满贯 *v* slam

dà nǎo 大脑 *n* brain

dà nǎo de 大脑的 *adj* cerebral

dà nù 大怒 *adj* mad

dà nù 大怒 *v* madden

dà pào 大炮 *n* artillery, cannon

dà pī 大批 *n* bulk

dà pī de lí qù 大批的离去 *n* exodus

dà pù bù 大瀑布 *n* cataract

dà qì 大气 *n* atmosphere

dà qì de 大气的 *adj* atmospheric

dà shè 大赦 *n* amnesty

dà shēng de 大声的 *adj* loud

dà shēng de 大声地 *adv* aloud

dà shēng hū hǎn 大声呼喊 *v* cry out

dà shēng jiào huan 大声叫唤 *v* call out

dà shǐ 大使 *n* ambassador

dà shǐ guǎn 大使馆 *n* embassy

dà shì 大事 *n* event

dà shù zhī 大树枝 *n* bough

dà suàn 大蒜 *n* garlic

dà táng 大堂 *n* lobby

dà tīng 大厅 *n* hall

dà tóu dīng 大头钉 *n* tack, thumbtack

dà tú shā 大屠杀 *n* carnage, holocaust

dà tuǐ 大腿 *n* thigh

dà shà 大厦 *n* edifice

dà xiàng 大象 *n* elephant

dà xiǎo 大小 *n* bulk, size

dà xiě zì mǔ 大写字母 *n* capital letter

dà xīng xing 大猩猩 *n* gorilla

dà xíng de 大型的 *adj* large

dà xíng qū zhú jiàn 大型驱逐舰 *n* frigate

dà xué 大学 *n* university

dà yī 大衣 *n* coat, overcoat

dà yuán shí 大圆石 *n* boulder

dà yuē 大约 *pro* around

dà yuē de 大约的 *adj* approximate

dà zá huì 大杂烩 *n* stew

dà zāi nàn 大灾难 *n* catastrophe

dà zhǔ jiào 大主教 *n* archbishop

dà zhǔ jiào guǎn qū 大主教管区 *n* diocese

dāi zhì de 呆滞的 *adj* sluggish

dǎi tú 歹徒 *n* scoundrel

dài biǎo 代表 *adv* behalf（on）

dài biǎo 代表 *n* delegate

dài biǎo 代表 *v* epitomize, present, represent, stand for

dài biǎo tuán 代表团 *n* delegation

dài cí 代词 *n* pronoun

dài lǐ 代理 *n* agency, proxy

dài lǐ rén 代理人 *n* agent

dài mǎ 代码 *n* code

dài shù 代数 *n* algebra

dài tì 代替 *n* lieu

dài 带 *iv* bring, take

dài ...chū qù 带...出去 *v* take out

dài huí 带回 *v* bring back

dài kòu 带扣 *n* buckle

dài wèi zhě 带位者 *n* usher

dài nián xìng de 带粘性的 *adj* adhesive

dài zhuàng wù 带状物 *n* strip

dài zi 带子 *n* belt

dài dìng de 待定的 *adj* pending

dài hū de 怠忽的 *adj* delinquent

dài màn 怠慢 *n* snub

dài kuǎn 贷款 *v* finance, loan

dài kuǎn 贷款 *n* loan

dài 袋 *n* bag

dài shǔ 袋鼠 *n* kangaroo

dài zhuàng de 袋状的 *adj* baggy

dài bǔ 逮捕 *v* apprehend, arrest

dài bǔ 逮捕 *n* arrest

dān mài 丹麦 *n* Denmark

dān biān de 单边的 *adj* unilateral

dān bó de 单薄的 *adj* sleazy

dān chéng piào 单程票 *n* single

dān diào 单调 *n* monotony, tedium

dān diào de 单调的 *adj* monotonous

dān dú de 单独的 *adj* alone, separate

dān dú de 单独地 *adv* solely

dān huáng guǎn 单簧管 *n* clarinet

dān jiǎo tiào 单脚跳 *v* hop

dān rén fáng jiān 单人房间 *n* single

dān shēn hàn 单身汉 *n* bachelor

dān shēn zhě 单身者 *n* single

dān wèi 单位 *n* unit

dān yī de 单一的 *adj* single

dān yuán 单元 *n* unit

dān bǎo rén 担保人 *n* guarantor

dān jià 担架 *n* stretcher

dān rèn 担任 *v* officiate

dān xīn 担心 *n* concern

dān xīn 担心 *v* worry

dān xīn de 担心的 *adj* apprehensive

dǎn gù chún 胆固醇 *n* cholesterol

dǎn liàng 胆量 *n* guts

dǎn náng 胆囊 *adj* gallant

dǎn qiè 胆怯 *n* cowardice, timidity

dǎn qiè de 胆怯的 *adv* cowardly

dǎn xiǎo de 胆小的 *adj* sissy, timid

dǎn zhī 胆汁 *n* bile

dàn shì 但是 *c* but

dàn yuàn 但愿 *adv* hopefully

tán chū 弹出 *v* eject

dàn jìng 弹径 *n* caliber

dàn mù 弹幕 *n* barrage

dàn piàn 弹片 *n* shrapnel

tán tiào 弹跳 *v* bounce

tán tiào 弹跳 *n* bounce

dàn wán 弹丸 *n* projectile

dàn yào 弹药 *n* ammunition, munitions

dàn yào tǒng 弹药筒 *n* cartridge

dàn chū 淡出 *v* fade

dàn huà 淡化 *v* lessen

dàn bái zhì 蛋白质 *n* protein

dàn gāo 蛋糕 *n* cake

dàn nǎi shā sī 蛋奶沙司 *n* custard

dàn qīng 蛋清 *n* egg white

dàn tǎ bēi mú 蛋塔杯模 *n* tart

dàn 氮 *n* nitrogen

dāng …de shí hou 当…的时候 *c* when

dāng dài de 当代的 *adj* contemporary

dāng dì de 当地的 *adj* local, native

dāng jīn 当今 *adv* nowadays

dāng lǐng dǎo 当领导 *v* spearhead

dāng qián de 当前的 *adj* current

dāng rán de 当然的 *adj* consequent

dāng shí 当时 *c* while

dāng xīn 当心 *v* look out, watch out

dàng yā shāng 当押商 *n* pawnbroker

dǎng fēng bō lí 挡风玻璃 *n* windshield

dǎng ní bǎn 挡泥板 *n* fender

dǎng 党 *n* party

dǎng pài 党派 *n* clan, partisan

dàng 档 *n* stall

dàng 档 *v* stall

dàng àn 档案 *n* archive, file

dāo 刀 *n* cutlery, knife

dāo bà 刀把 *n* hilt

dāo jù 刀具 *n* cutter, cyanide

dāo piàn 刀片 *n* blade

dǎo dàn 导弹 *n* missile

dǎo háng 导航 *n* navigation

dǎo tǐ 导体 *n* conductor

dǎo xiàn 导线 *n* wire

dǎo yán 导言 *n* introduction

dǎo yǎn 导演 *n* director

dǎo yóu 导游 *n* courier

dǎo yǔ 岛屿 *n* island

dǎo 倒 *v* flip

dào jì shí 倒计时 *n* countdown

dǎo tā 倒塌 *v* come down

dǎo xià 倒下 *v* fall down

dào dá 到达 *n* arrival

dào dá 到达 *v* arrive

dào jué dǐng 到绝顶 *v* culminate

dào lái 到来 *n* Advent

dào qī 到期 *adj* due

dào qī 到期 *v* expire

dào 盗 *v* burglarize

dào bǎn 盗版 *n* piracy

dào qiè 盗窃 *n* burglary, theft

dào qiè shèng wù （rú cóng jiào táng dào qiè） 盗窃圣物（如从教堂盗窃） *n* sacrilege

dào yòng 盗用 *v* embezzle

dào dé 道德 *n* ethics, moral, morality

dào dé zhēn yán 道德箴言 *n* precept

dào lù 道路 *n* road

dào qiàn 道歉 *v* apologize

dào qiàn 道歉 *n* apology

dào cǎo 稻草 *n* straw

dé （fēn） 得（分） *v* score

dé tǐ 得体 *n* decency

dé tǐ de 得体的 *adj* decent

dé xīn yìng shǒu 得心应手 *adj* handy

dé yì yáng yáng de 得意扬扬的 *adj* triumphant

dé zì 得自 *v* derive

dé guó 德国 *n* Germany

dé guó de 德国的 *adj* German

dé xíng 德行 *n* virtue

de 的 *pre* of

dēng 灯 *n* lamp

dēng huǒ guǎn zhì 灯火管制 *n* blackout

dēng lóng 灯笼 *n* lantern

dēng pào 灯泡 *n* bulb

dēng tǎ 灯塔 *n* beacon, lighthouse

dēng zhào 灯罩 *n* lampshade

dēng zhù 灯柱 *n* lamppost

dēng 登 *n* mount

dēng jī 登机 *v* board

dēng jì 登记 *v* check in, sign

dēng lù 登陆 *n* landing

dēng lù 登录 *v* log in

dēng shàng 登上 *v* mount

D

děng dài 等待 *v* await, wait
děng dài 等待 *n* waiting
děng gāo xiàn 等高线 *n* contour
děng jí 等级 *n* grade, hierarchy, rank
děng jí zhì dù 等级制度 *n* caste
děng tóng 等同 *v* equate
dī chén de 低沉的 *adj* somber
dī de 低的 *adj* low
dī diào de 低调的 *adj* lowly
dī liè de 低劣的 *adj* appalling
dī mí 低迷 *adj* downturn
dī wēn zhǔ 低温煮 *v* simmer
dī xiào de 低效的 *adj* inefficient
dī fang 提防 *v* beware
dī fang 堤防 *n* dike
dī guàn 滴灌 *v* drip
dī guàn 滴灌 *n* drip
dí què 的确 *adv* indeed
dí duì de 敌对的 *adj* hostile
dí rén 敌人 *n* enemy
dí yì 敌意 *n* animosity, hostility, malignancy
dí yì de 敌意的 *adj* hostile, malignant
dǐ huǐ 诋毁 *v* slur
dǐ bù 底部 *n* bottom
dǐ（fǎn）kàng 抵（反）抗 *v* resist
dǐ kàng lì（xìng） 抵抗力（性）*n* resistance
dǐ xiāo 抵消 *v* counteract
dǐ xiāo 抵销 *v* offset
dǐ yā pǐn 抵押品 *n* security
dǐ zhì 抵制 *v* boycott, resist

dǐ zhì 抵制 *n* resistance
dì bǎn 地板 *n* floor
dì chǎn 地产 *n* estate
dì diǎn 地点 *n* location, site
dì fāng 地方 *n* place
dì jī 地基 *n* groundwork
dì jiào 地窖 *n* cellar
dì láo 地牢 *n* dungeon
dì lǐ xué 地理学 *n* geography
dì miàn 地面 *n* ground
dì miàn céng 地面层 *n* ground floor
dì píng xiàn 地平线 *n* horizon
dì qiú 地球 *n* earth, globe
dì qū 地区 *n* area
dì tǎn 地毯 *n* carpet, rug
dì tiě 地铁 *n* subway
dì tú 地图 *n* map
dì wèi 地位 *n* status
dì xià de 地下的 *adj* underground
dì xià diāo bǎo 地下碉堡 *n* bunker
dì xià guò dào 地下过道 *n* underpass
dì xià mù xué 地下墓穴 *n* catacomb
dì xià shì 地下室 *n* basement
dì xíng 地形 *n* terrain
dì yù 地狱 *n* hell
dì zhèn 地震 *n* earthquake
dì zhǐ 地址 *n* address
dì zhì xué 地质学 *n* geology
dì xí 弟媳 *n* sister-in-law
dì guó 帝国 *n* empire
dì guó de 帝国的 *adj* imperial

D

dì guó zhǔ yì 帝国主义 *n* imperialism

dì bā 第八 *adj* eighth

dì èr 第二 *n* second

dì èr shí 第二十 *adj* twentieth

dì jiǔ 第九 *adj* ninth

dì liù 第六 *adj* sixth

dì qī 第七 *adj* seventh

dì sān 第三 *adj* third

dì shí 第十 *n* tenth

dì shí èr 第十二 *adj* twelfth

dì shí yī 第十一 *adj* eleventh

dì sì 第四 *adj* fourth

dì wǔ 第五 *adj* fifth

dì yī 第一 *adj* first

dì yī bǎi 第一百 *adj* hundredth

diān bǒ de 颠簸的 *adj* bumpy

diān dǎo de 颠倒地 *adv* upside-down

diān kuáng de 癫狂的 *adj* maniac

diān xián bìng 癫痫病 *n* epilepsy

diǎn dàng 典当 *v* pawn

diǎn lǐ 典礼 *n* ceremony

diǎn xíng de 典型的 *adj* characteristic, typical

diǎn 点 *n* dot, point, spot

diǎn jī 点击 *v* click

diǎn rán 点燃 *v* ignite, kindle

diǎn tóu 点头 *v* nod

diǎn 碘 *n* iodine

diàn bào 电报 *n* telegram

diàn chē 电车 *n* tram

diàn chí 电池 *n* battery

diàn de 电的 *adj* electric

diàn dòng de 电动的 *adj* electric

diàn dòng jī 电动机 *n* motor

diàn dù 电镀 *v* galvanize

diàn gōng 电工 *n* electrician

diàn hè 电荷 *n* charge

diàn huà 电话 *n* phone, telephone

diàn lǎn 电缆 *n* cable

diàn lù 电路 *n* circuit

diàn qì huà 电气化 *v* electrify

diàn shì 电视 *n* television

diàn tī 电梯 *n* elevator

diàn yā 电压 *n* voltage

diàn yǐng 电影 *n* film, movie

diàn yǐng yuàn 电影院 *n* cinema

diàn zǐ 电子 *adj* electronic

diàn 垫 *v* pad

diàn zi 垫子 *n* cushion, mat

diàn rǔ 玷辱 *v* desecrate

diàn wū 玷污 *v* blemish, tarnish

diàn fěn 淀粉 *n* starch

diàn fěn de 淀粉的 *adj* starchy

diàn 殿 *n* nave

diàn xià 殿下 *n* Highness

diāo kè 雕刻 *v* carve, engrave

diāo kè 雕刻 *n* engraving

diāo sù 雕塑 *n* sculpture

diāo sù jiā 雕塑家 *n* sculptor

diāo xiàng 雕像 *n* statue

diào 吊 *iv* hang

diào chuáng 吊床 *n* hammock

diào gān 吊杆 *n* suspenders

diào jià 吊架 *n* hang-up

diào sǐ 吊死 *iv* hang

diào zhuì 吊坠 *n* pendant

diào 调 *n* tune

diào chá 调查 *v* investigate

diào chá 调查 *n* investigation, survey

diào dòng 调动 *v* arouse, mobilize

dié dié bù xiū 喋喋不休 *v* babble

dié dié 叠 *v* fold

dié zi 碟子 *n* dish, plate

dīng 盯 *v* stare

dìng láo 钉牢 *v* clinch

dǐng bù 顶部 *n* crest, top

dǐng diǎn 顶点 *n* apex

dǐng diǎn de 顶点的 *adj* maximum

dìng hūn 订婚 *v* engage

dìng hūn 订婚 *n* engagement

dìng hūn le de 订婚了的 *adj* engaged

dìng shū 订书 *v* staple

dìng shū jī 订书机 *n* stapler

dìng yuē 订约 *v* contract

dìng yuè 订阅 *v* subscribe

dìng yuè 订阅 *n* subscription

dìng àn 定案 *v* finalize

dìng àn 定案 *n* verdict

dìng diào 定调 *v* tune up

dìng jū 定居 *v* settle

dìng jū wéi 定居为 *v* settle for

dìng jū zhě 定居者 *n* settler

dìng liàng 定量 *v* ration

dìng liàng 定量 *n* ration

dìng shí jiān 定时间 *v* schedule

dìng wèi zi 定位子 *n* reservation

dìng wèi zi 定位子 *v* reserve

dìng xíng 定形 *v* shape

dìng yì 定义 *v* define

dìng yì 定义 *n* definition

dìng zuì 定罪 *v* convict

dìng zuò de 定做的 *adj* custom-made

dōng běi 东北 *n* northeast

dōng fāng 东方 *n* east; orient

dōng fāng de 东方的 *adj* eastern; oriental

dōng fāng rén 东方人 *n* easterner

dōng miàn 东面 *adj* eastbound

dōng nán 东南 *n* southeast

dōng xī 东西 *pro* something

dōng xī 东西 *n* stuff

dōng zhèng jiào 东正教 *adj* orthodox

dōng tiān 冬天 *n* winter

dǒng shì 董事 *n* regent

dǒng shì huì 董事会 *n* board

dòng cí 动词 *n* verb

dòng dàng 动荡 *v* jolt

dòng dàng 动荡 *n* jolt, unrest

dòng gǎn 动感 *n* motion

dòng huà 动画 *n* animation

dòng jī 动机 *n* motive

dòng luàn de 动乱的 *adj* turmoil

dòng mài 动脉 *n* artery

dòng míng cí 动名词 *n* gerund

dòng shēn 动身 *v* set out

dòng tài de 动态的 *adj* dynamic

dòng wù 动物 *n* animal, creature

dòng wù xué 动物学 *n* zoology

dòng wù yuán 动物园 *n* zoo

dòng yáo de 动摇的 *adj* shaken

dòng yī dòng 动一动 *v* budge

dòng zuò 动作 *n* mannerism

dòng jié 冻结 *iv* freeze

D

dòng jié 冻结 *adj* freezing, frozen

dòng shāng 冻伤 *n* frostbite

dòng shāng de 冻伤的 *adj* frostbitten

dòng 洞 *n* cave, hole

dòng shì 洞室 *n* cavity

dòng xué 洞穴 *n* burrow, grotto

dòu niú 斗牛 *n* bull fight

dòu niú shì 斗牛士 *n* bull fighter

dǒu peng 斗篷 *n* cloak

dòu zhēng 斗争 *v* struggle

dòu zhēng 斗争 *n* struggle

dǒu qiào de 陡峭的 *adj* steep

dòu 豆 *n* bean

dòu hào 逗号 *n* comma

dòu lè 逗乐 *v* amuse

dòu liú 逗留 *n* stay

dòu liú 逗留 *v* stick around

dū nang 嘟囔 *v* mumble

dú jūn 毒菌 *n* germ

dú pǐn 毒品 *n* dope

dú sù 毒素 *n* toxin

dú yào 毒药 *n* poison

dú yè 毒液 *n* venom

dú 读 *iv* read

dú wù 读物 *n* reading

dú zhě 读者 *n* reader

dú bái 独白 *n* monologue

dú cái de 独裁的 *adj* dictatorial

dú cái zhě 独裁者 *n* dictator

dú cái zhǔ yì zhě de 独裁主义者的 *adj* authoritarian

dú lì 独立 *n* independence

dú lì de 独立的 *adj* independent, unattached

dú lún chē 独轮车 *n* wheelbarrow

dú mù zhōu 独木舟 *n* canoe

dú shēn 独身 *n* celibacy

dú shēn de 独身的 *adj* celibate

dú tè de 独特的 *adj* unique

dú zì de 独自地 *adv* solely

dǔ sè 堵塞 *v* obstruct

dǔ zuǐ 堵嘴 *v* muzzle

dǔ 赌 *v* gamble

dǔ chǎng 赌场 *n* casino

dù jí 妒嫉 *n* grudge

dù jué 杜绝 *v* stamp out

dù zhuàn 杜撰 *v* fabricate

dù pí 肚皮 *n* belly

dù qí 肚脐 *n* belly button, navel

dù zi 肚子 *n* tummy

dù shu 度数 *n* degree

dù chuán 渡船 *n* ferry

dù guò 渡过 *v* get over

dù kǒu 渡口 *n* crossing, ferry

duān zhuāng dé tǐ 端庄得体 *n* decorum

duǎn 短 *adj* short

duǎn hào 短号 *n* cornet

duǎn jiàn 短见 *adj* shortsighted

duǎn jiàn 短剑 *n* dagger

duǎn kù 短裤 *n* shorts

duǎn mìng de 短命的 *adj* short-lived

duǎn nèi kù 短内裤 *n* briefs

duǎn piān 短片 *n* trailer

duǎn quē 短缺 *n* shortage

duǎn wěn è 短吻鳄 *n* alligator

duǎn xū 短须 *n* mustache

duǎn yǔ 短语 *n* phrase

duǎn zàn 短暂 *n* brevity

duǎn zàn de 短暂的 *adj* brief, short-lived

duàn 段 *n* paragraph

duàn diàn 断电 *n* blackout

duàn diào de 断掉的 *adj* broken

duàn jiāo tū rán tíng zhǐ 断交突然停止 *v* break off

duàn jué 断绝 *v* sever

duàn kāi 断开 *v* disconnect

duàn tóu tái 断头台 *n* guillotine

duàn yán 断言 *n* allegation, assertion

duàn yán 断言 *v* allege, assert

duī 堆 *n* heap, mass, pile

duī 堆 *v* heap, stack

duī féi 堆肥 *n* compost

duī jī 堆积 *v* pile, pile up

duì zhǎng 队长 *n* captain

duì liè 队列 *n* queue

duì 对 *pre* versus

duì ...biǎo shì fèn hèn 对…表示愤恨 *v* resent

duì bàn 对半 *adv* fifty-fifty

duì bǐ 对比 *v* contrast

duì bǐ 对比 *n* contrast

duì chèn xìng 对称性 *n* symmetry

duì dài 对待 *v* treat

duì fāng 对方 *adj* each other

duì fēn 对分 *v* halve

duì huà 对话 *n* dialogue

duì jiǎo xiàn de 对角线的 *adj* diagonal

duì kàng 对抗 *v* confront

duì kàng 对抗 *n* confrontation

duì qí 对齐 *n* alignment

duì shǒu 对手 *n* adversary, match, opponent, rival

duì xiā 对虾 *n* prawn

duì xiàng 对象 *n* object

duì zhì 对峙 *n* confrontation

duì zhǔn 对准 *v* direct

dūn 吨 *n* ton

dūn cù 敦促 *n* urge

dūn cù 敦促 *v* urge

dūn fú 蹲伏 *v* crouch

tún jī 囤积 *v* hoard

dùn pái 盾牌 *n* shield

dùn de 钝的 *adj* blunt

dùn dù 钝度 *n* bluntness

duō cái duō yì de 多才多艺的 *adj* versatile

duō cǎi de 多彩的 *adj* colorful

duō chǎn de 多产的 *adj* fruitful, productive

duō huī chén 多灰尘 *adj* dusty

duō ké 多壳 *adj* husky

duō kǒng de 多孔的 *adj* porous

duō máo de 多毛的 *adj* hairy

duō nián de 多年的 *adj* perennial

duō pèi ǒu de 多配偶的 *adj* polygamist

duō shān de 多山的 *adj* mountainous

duō shí de 多石的 *adj* rocky

duō shù 多数 *n* majority

duō wù de 多雾的 *adj* foggy

duō xiǎo shān 多小山 *adj* hilly

duō yàng 多样 *adj* diverse

duō yàng huà 多样化 *v* diversify

D

duō yàng xìng 多样性 *n* diversity

duō yú 多于 *v* outnumber

duō yú de 多余的 *adj* needless, redundant

duō yǔ de 多雨的 *adj* rainy

duō yún de 多云的 *adj* cloudy

duō zhī de 多汁的 *adj* juicy, succulent

duō zhǒng duō yàng de 多种多样的 *adj* multiple

duō zhǒng zi 多种子 *adj* seedy

duō chóng de 多重的 *adj* multiple

duó huí 夺回 *v* recapture

duó qǔ 夺取 *v* seize

duò 剁 *v* chop

duò 剁 *n* chop

duò suì 剁碎 *v* mince

duò luò 堕落 *v* degenerate

duò luò 堕落 *n* degradation, depravity

duò luò de 堕落的 *adj* degenerate

E

é luó sī 俄罗斯 *n* Russia

é luó sī de 俄罗斯的 *adj* Russian

é 鹅 *n* geese, goose

é luǎn shí 鹅卵石 *n* cobblestone

é 蛾 *n* moth

é wài de 额外的 *adj* additional

é wài de 额外的 *adv* extra

è yùn 厄运 *n* doom

è shā 扼杀 *v* smother, stifle, strangle

è 轭 *n* yoke

è bà 恶霸 *adj* bully

è chòu 恶臭 *adj* fetid

è chòu 恶臭 *n* stench

è dú 恶毒 *n* malice

è dú de 恶毒的 *adj* diabolical

è gùn 恶棍 *n* villain

è huà 恶化 *n* aggravation, deterioration

è huà 恶化 *v* compound, deteriorate, worsen

è liè de 恶劣地 *adv* badly

è mó 恶魔 *n* demon

è xí 恶习 *n* depravity

ě xīn 恶心 *n* nausea

ě xīn de 恶心的 *adj* squeamish

è yì de 恶意的 *adj* malevolent, spiteful, vindictive

è zuò jù 恶作剧 *n* escapade, gag, prank

è zuò jù de 恶作剧的 *adj* mischievous

è zhì yán lùn 遏制言论 *v* gag

è yú 鳄鱼 *n* crocodile

ēn huì 恩惠 *n* bounty

ēn rén 恩人 *n* benefactor

ér tóng 儿童 *n* child, children

ér xí 儿媳 *n* daughter-in-law

ér zi 儿子 *n* son

ér 而 *c* whereas

ér qiě 而且 *pre* besides

ěr duo 耳朵 *n* ear

ěr huán 耳环 *n* earring

ěr jī 耳机 *n* earphones, headphones

ěr là 耳蜡 *n* earwax

ěr tòng 耳痛 *n* earache

ěr yǔ 耳语 *v* whisper

ěr yǔ 耳语 *n* whisper

èr 二 *adj* two

èr shí 二十 *adj* twenty

èr yuè 二月 *n* February

F

fā biǎo 发表 *v* deliver

fā biǎo yǎn shuō 发表演说 *v* address

fā chòu 发臭 *iv* stink

fā chòu 发臭 *n* stink

fā chòu de 发臭的 *adj* smelly

fā chū 发出 *v* emanate

fā chū（shēng yīn） 发出（声音）*v* utter

fā chū wēng wēng shēng 发出嗡嗡声 *v* buzz

fā diàn jī 发电机 *n* generator

fā dòng jī 发动机 *n* engine, motor

fā fēng shì de 发疯似的 *adj* cranky

fā gā zhī gā zhī shēng de 发嘎吱嘎吱声的 *adj* crunchy

fā gěi 发给 *v* hand out

fā hóng shuǐ 发洪水 *v* flood

fā hūn 发昏 *v* daze

fā jiào 发酵 *v* ferment

fā jiào 发酵 *n* ferment

fā jué 发掘 *v* unearth

fā kuáng de 发狂的 *adj* maniac

fā láo sāo 发牢骚 *v* grumble

fā liàng de 发亮的 *adv* alight

fā gē zhī shēng 发咯吱声 *v* creak

fā lóng lóng shēng 发隆隆声 *v* rumble

fā méi 发霉 *adj* mold

fā míng 发明 *v* devise, invent

fā míng 发明 *n* invention

fā nù de 发怒的 *adj* irate

fā piào 发票 *n* invoice

fā qiú dé fēn 发球得分 *n* ace

fā shāo 发烧 *n* fever

fā shāo 发烧 *adj* feverish

fā shè 发射 *n* launch, lift off; shot

fā shè 发射 *v* launch, lift off

fā shēng 发生 *v* come about, happen, occur

fā shēng 发生 *n* happening, occurrence

fà shì 发式 *n* hairdo

fā shì 发誓 *v* vow

fā sòng 发送 *iv* send

fā sòng de huò wù 发送的货物 *n* delivery

fā sòng rén 发送人 *n* sender

fā wēng wēng shēng 发嗡嗡声 *v* hum

fā xiàn 发现 *v* discover

fā xiàn 发现 *n* discovery

fā xīn 发薪 *n* payroll

F

fā xíng 发行 *v* release
fā xū shēng 发嘘声 *v* hiss
fā yá 发芽 *v* germinate
fā yán rén 发言人 *n* speaker
fā yǎng 发痒 *n* itchiness
fā yīn 发音 *v* articulate, pronounce
fā zhǎn 发展 *n* development
fā zhī zhī shēng 发吱吱声 *v* squeak
fā zhí zhào gěi 发执照给 *v* charter
fá wèi de 乏味的 *v* tame
fá wèi de 乏味的 *adj* tedious
fá kuǎn 罚款 *n* fine, penalty
fá kuǎn 罚款 *v* fine
fá mén 阀门 *n* valve
fá xīn 阀芯 *n* spool
fǎ 法 *n* law
fǎ guān 法官 *n* judge
fǎ guī 法规 *n* statute
fǎ guó 法国 *n* France
fǎ guó de 法国的 *adj* French
fǎ jǐng 法警 *n* bailiff
fǎ lìng 法令 *n* decree, statute
fǎ lǜ de 法律的 *adj* legal
fǎ lǜ zé rèn 法律责任 *n* liability
fǎ shì cháng gùn miàn bāo 法式长棍面包 *n* baguette
fǎ tíng 法庭 *n* tribunal
fǎ yī 法衣 *n* cassock
fǎ yuàn 法院 *n* court, courthouse
fà xíng 发型 *n* hairdo
fān bù 帆布 *n* canvas
fān chuán 帆船 *n* sailboat
fān qié 番茄 *n* tomato

fān dǎo 翻倒 *v* upset
fān gǔn 翻滚 *v* writhe
fān liǎng bèi 翻两倍 *v* double
fān yì 翻译 *v* interpret, translate
fān yì 翻译 *n* interpretation
fán rén de 凡人的 *adj* mortal
fán nǎo 烦恼 *n* care
fán rǎo 烦扰 *v* annoy, hassle, perturb
fán rǎo de 烦扰的 *adj* distraught
fán rén de 烦人的 *adj* annoying
fán mào de 繁茂的 *adj* rampant
fán róng 繁荣 *v* boom
fán róng 繁荣 *n* prosperity
fán róng de 繁荣的 *adj* prosperous
fán suǒ de 繁琐的 *adj* tedious
fán wén rù jié 繁文缛节 *n* red tape
fán zhí 繁殖 *iv* breed
fǎn bó 反驳 *v* contradict, counter, rebut, refute
fǎn cháng 反常 *adj* abnormal
fǎn cháng de 反常的 *adj* perverse
fǎn cháng xìng 反常性 *n* abnormality
fǎn chōng 反冲 *n* backlash
fǎn tán 反弹 *v* rebound
fǎn duì 反对 *pre* against
fǎn duì 反对 *n* aversion, objection, opposition
fǎn duì 反对 *v* counter, object, oppose
fǎn duì de 反对的 *adj* averse
fǎn duì zhě 反对者 *n* rebel
fǎn ér 反而 *adv* instead

fǎn gǎn 反感 *n* allergy, antipathy, disgust

fǎn gǎn de 反感的 *adj* allergic

fǎn jī 反击 *v* strike back

fǎn kàng 反抗 *v* defy

fǎn kàng 反抗 *n* resistance

fǎn kàng de 反抗的 *adj* defiant, revolting

fǎn kuì 反馈 *n* feedback

fǎn kuì de 反馈的 *adj* retroactive

fǎn miàn 反面 *n* reverse

fǎn pàn 反叛 *n* mutiny, revolt

fǎn pàn 反叛 *v* rebel, revolt

fǎn pàn fèn zǐ 反叛分子 *n* rebel

fǎn shè 反射 *n* jerk, reflection

fǎn shè 反射 *v* reflect

fǎn shè de 反射的 *adj* jerk

fǎn shè xìng de 反射性的 *adj* reflexive

fǎn sī 反思 *v* reconsider

fǎn yìng 反应 *n* reaction, response

fǎn yìng 反应 *v* respond

fǎn yìng 反映 *v* reflect

fǎn zhèng 反证 *v* disprove

fàn cuò 犯错 *v* err

fàn cuò de 犯错的 *adj* mistaken

fàn cuò wù 犯错误 *v* goof, mistake

fàn guī 犯规 *adj* foul

fàn rén 犯人 *n* inmate

fàn zuì 犯罪 *v* commit, perpetrate

fàn zuì 犯罪 *n* crime

fàn zuì de 犯罪的 *adj* criminal

fàn guāng dēng 泛光灯 *n* floodlight

fàn tīng 饭厅 *n* dining room

fàn wéi 范围 *n* extent, range, scope

fāng àn 方案 *n* scheme

fāng biàn 方便 *n* convenience

fāng biàn de 方便的 *adj* convenient

fāng chéng 方程 *n* equation

fāng de 方的 *adj* square

fāng fǎ 方法 *n* method

fāng miàn 方面 *n* aspect, dimension, facet

fāng shì 方式 *n* manner

fāng shì dào lù 方式 道路 *n* way

fāng xiàng 方向 *n* direction, orientation

fāng yán 方言 *n* dialect

fāng zhàng 方丈 *n* abbot

fāng zhōu 方舟 *n* ark

fāng xiāng de 芳香的 *adj* aromatic

fáng bō dī 防波堤 *n* bulwark

fáng fàn 防范 *n* precaution

fáng fēng cǎo 防风草 *n* parsnip

fáng fǔ jì 防腐剂 *n* conserve

fáng hù 防护 *v* defend

fáng shài rǔ 防晒乳 *n* sun block

fáng shǒu 防守 *n* defense

fáng wèi 防卫 *v* defend, fend

fáng wèi quān 防卫圈 *n* cordon

fáng wèi zhě 防卫者 *n* defender

fáng xiù 防锈 *adj* rust-proof

fáng zhǐ 防止 *v* prevent

fáng ài 妨碍 *n* impediment

fáng dì 房地 *n* premises

fáng dōng 房东 *n* landlord

F

F

fáng jiān 房间 *n* chamber, room
fáng kè 房客 *n* tenant
fáng wū 房屋 *n* house
fǎng zhì 仿制 *n* imitation
fǎng zhì pǐn 仿制品 *n* dummy
fǎng kè 访客 *n* visitor
fǎng tán 访谈 *n* interview
fǎng wèn 访问 *n* visit
fǎng wèn 访问 *v* visit
fàng 放 *iv* put
fàng dà 放大 *v* amplify, enlarge, magnify
fàng dà qì 放大器 *n* amplifier
fàng dàng de 放荡的 *adj* dissolute
fàng diàn 放电 *v* discharge
fàng diàn 放电 *n* discharge
fàng huǎn 放缓 *v* slow down
fàng qì 放气 *v* deflate
fàng qì 放弃 *v* abandon, back down, break away, give up, relinquish, renounce, waive
fàng qì 放弃 *n* abandonment
fàng qì de shì /wù 放弃的事/物 *n* abandonment
fàng shè xìng chén jiàng [wù] 放射性沉降[物] *n* fallout
fàng shǒu 放手 *v* let go
fàng sōng 放松 *v* loose, loosen, mellow, relax, slacken
fàng sōng 放松 *n* relax
fàng sōng de 放松的 *adj* relaxing
fàng xià 放下 *v* drop, drop off
fàng zài yī biān 放在一边 *v* put aside
fàng zhú 放逐 *v* banish

fàng zhú 放逐 *n* banishment
fàng zòng de 放纵的 *adj* indulgent
fēi 飞 *iv* fly
fēi bēn 飞奔 *v* gallop
fēi biāo 飞镖 *n* dart
fēi dì 飞地 *n* enclave
fēi jī 飞机 *n* aircraft, airplane, plane
fēi jī pǎo dào 飞机跑道 *n* airstrip
fēi jī qián bù 飞机前部 *n* prow
fēi xíng 飞行 *n* flight
fēi xíng yuán 飞行员 *n* aviator, pilot
fēi xíng zhě 飞行者 *n* flier
fēi yuè 飞跃 *iv* leap
fēi yuè 飞跃 *n* leap
fēi cháng 非常 *adv* exceedingly, grossly, quite, very
fēi cháng de 非常的 *adj* uncommon
fēi cháng jīng cǎi de 非常精彩的 *adj* riveting
fēi fǎ de 非法的 *adj* illegal
（fēi fǎ）jiāo yì （非法）交易 *v* traffic
（fēi fǎ）jiāo yì （非法）交易 *n* traffic
fēi fán de 非凡的 *adj* uncommon
fēi fán de lǐng dǎo lì 非凡的领导力 *n* charisma
fēi guān fāng de 非官方地 *adv* unofficially
fēi nàn 非难 *n* condemnation
fēi qiáng zhì de 非强制的 *adj* optional

fēi wǔ zhuāng de 非武装的 *adj* unarmed

fēi yù qī de shōu huò 非预期的 收获 *n* fallout

fēi zhèng shì 非正式 *n* informality

fēi zhèng shì de 非正式的 *adj* informal

fěi bó de 菲薄的 *adj* stingy

féi dà de 肥大的 *adj* sloppy

féi liào 肥料 *n* manure

féi nì 肥腻 *adj* fatty

féi pàng de 肥胖的 *adj* corpulent, obese

féi wò 肥沃 *adj* fertile

fěi tú 匪徒 *n* gangster

fěi bàng 诽谤 *n* calumny, libel, slander

fěi bàng 诽谤 *v* denigrate

fèi jiào 吠叫 *v* bark

fèi shēng 吠声 *n* bark

fèi chú 废除 *v* abolish, abrogate, nullify, quash, revoke

fèi chù 废黜 *v* depose

fèi qì pái fàng 废气排放 *n* emission

fèi qì 废弃 *n* disuse

fèi qì wù 废弃物 *n* litter

fèi wù 废物 *n* waste

fèi wù lán 废物篮 *n* waste basket

fèi xū 废墟 *n* ruin

fèi zhǐ 废止 *v* annul

fèi zhǐ 废止 *n* annulment

fèi 肺 *n* lung

fèi jié hé 肺结核 *n* tuberculosis

fèi yán 肺炎 *n* pneumonia

fèi jiě de 费解的 *adj* convoluted

fèi yong 费用 *n* charge, expense, fee

fēn 分 *n* cent, penny

fèn bù qīng fāng xiàng huò mù biāo de 分不清方向或目标的 *adj* disoriented

fēn bù 分布 *n* distribution

fēn cí 分词 *n* participle

fēn fā 分发 *v* dispense, distribute, pass out

fēn fā 分发 *n* distribution

fēn gē 分割 *n* partition

fēn gé 分隔 *v* segregate

fēn jiě 分解 *v* decompose

fēn kāi 分开 *adv* apart

fēn kāi 分开 *v* divide, part, take apart

fēn lèi 分类 *n* assortment

fēn lèi 分类 *v* classify

fēn lèi de 分类的 *adj* systematic

fēn lí 分离 *adv* apart

fēn lí 分离 *n* separation

fēn liè 分裂 *v* break up, rip apart, splinter, split up, split

fēn liè 分裂 *n* schism, splinter, split

fēn liú 分流 *v* divert

fēn miǎn 分娩 *n* maternity

fēn mǔ 分母 *n* denominator

fēn pài 分派 *v* assign, dispatch

fēn pài 分派 *n* assignment

fēn pèi 分配 *v* allocate, allot, deal, dispense

fēn pèi 分配 *n* allotment, dispensation, distribution

fēn qī cháng huán 分期偿还 v amortize

fēn qī fù kuǎn 分期付款 n down payment, installment

fèn shǒu 分手 v break up

fēn shù 分数 n fraction

fēn shuǐ lǐng 分水岭 n watershed

fēn xī 分析 n analysis

fēn xī 分析 v analyze

fēn xiǎng 分享 v share

fēn xiǎng 分享 n share

fēn xiàng 分项 v itemize

fēn xīn 分心 v distract

fēn xīn 分心 n distraction

fēn zhī jī gòu 分支机构 n branch office

fēn zhī 分枝 n ramification

fēn zǐ 分子 n molecule

fēn fāng de 芬芳的 adj balmy, fragrant

fēn lán 芬兰 n Finland

fēn lán de 芬兰的 adj Finnish

fén mù 坟墓 n grave

fěn 粉 n powder

fěn bǐ 粉笔 n chalk

fěn hóng de 粉红的 adj pink

fěn suì 粉碎 v pulverize, shatter, smash

fèn 份 n share

fèn é 份额 n allotment

fèn nù 愤怒 n anger, fury, outrage, rage, wrath

fèn nù 愤怒 adj furious

fèn nù de 愤怒的 adj angry

fèn nù de 愤怒地 adv furiously

fèn shì jí sú de 愤世嫉俗的 adj cynic

fēng fù 丰富 n abundance

fēng fù 丰富 v enrich

fēng fù de 丰富的 adj abundant, plentiful

fēng shèng de 丰盛的 adj sumptuous

fēng shōu 丰收 n harvest

fēng shōu 丰收 v harvest

fēng 风 n wind

fēng bào 风暴 n storm, tumult

fēng bào de 风暴的 adj stormy

fēng chē 风车 n windmill

fēng dà de 风大的 adj windy

fēng dù 风度 n demeanor

fēng gé 风格 n style

fēng jǐng 风景 n scenery

fēng jǐng rú huà de 风景如画的 adj picturesque

fēng mào 风帽 n hood

fēng qín shī 风琴师 n organist

fēng shàn 风扇 n fan

fēng shī bìng 风湿病 n rheumatism

fēng wèi 风味 n flavor

fēng xiǎn 风险 n risk, venture

fēng xíng 风行 n vogue

fēng zheng 风筝 n kite

fēng miàn 封面 n cover

fēng suǒ 封锁 v bar, seal, blockade, cordon off, seal off

fēng suǒ 封锁 n blockade, blockage

fēng kuáng 疯狂 n craziness, frenzy, insanity, madness

fēng kuáng 疯狂 *adj* frantic

fēng kuáng de 疯狂的 *adj* crazy, demented, frenzied, insane, mad, manic

fēng kuáng de 疯狂的 *adv* madly

fēng zi 疯子 *n* madman

fēng zi de 疯子的 *adj* lunatic

fēng dǐng 峰顶 *n* summit

fēng huǒ 烽火 *n* beacon

fēng lì 锋利 *adj* edgy

fēng lì de 锋利的 *adj* sharp

fēng cháo 蜂巢 *n* hive

fēng mì 蜂蜜 *n* honey

fēng míng qì 蜂鸣器 *n* buzzer

fēng xiāng 蜂箱 *n* beehive

féng bǔ 缝补 *v* darn

féng rèn 缝纫 *v* sew

féng rèn 缝纫 *n* sewing

fèng xì 缝隙 *n* seam

fěng cì 讽刺 *n* irony, sarcasm, satire

fěng cì de 讽刺的 *adj* ironic, sarcastic

fěng cì huà 讽刺画 *n* caricature

fěng cì zuò pǐn 讽刺作品 *n* satire

fèng cheng 奉承 *n* adulation, flattery

fèng xiàn 奉献 *v* consecrate

fèng xiàn 奉献 *n* consecration, dedication, devotion

fǒu dìng 否定 *v* repudiate

fǒu dìng de 否定的 *adj* negative

fǒu jué 否决 *v* overrule, veto

fǒu rèn 否认 *n* denial

fǒu rèn 否认 *v* deny, disclaim, disown

fǒu zé 否则 *adv* else, otherwise

fū fù 夫妇 *n* couple

fū rén 夫人 *n* lady

fū liào 敷料 *n* dressing

fú jī 伏击 *v* ambush

fú shǒu 扶手 *n* handrail

fú shǒu yǐ 扶手椅 *n* armchair

fú cóng 服从 *n* compliance, obedience

fú cóng 服从 *v* obey

fú cóng de 服从的 *adj* compliant, obedient, submissive

fú shì 服饰 *n* costume

fú shuǐ tǔ 服水土 *v* acclimatize

fú tiē de 服贴的 *adj* amenable

fú wù 服务 *v* serve, service

fú wù 服务 *n* service

fú wù tái 服务台 *n* desk

fú wù yuán 服务员 *n* attendant, waiter

fú yào 服药 *n* medication

fú zhuāng 服装 *n* apparel, clothing, garment, outfit

fú zhuāng yuán 服装员 *n* dresser

fú lǔ 俘虏 *n* captive

fú 浮 *v* float

fú biāo 浮标 *n* buoy

fú huá 浮华 *n* pomposity

fú huá de 浮华的 *adj* dashing, ostentatious

fú kuā 浮夸 *adj* flamboyant

fú zhǒng de 浮肿的 *adj* puffy

fú hào 符号 *n* sign, symbol

fú hé 符合 *v* conform, correspond

fú hé （yāo qiú děng） 符合 （要求等） *v* satisfy

F

fú hé shí shàng de 符合时尚的 *adj* fashionable

fú lì 福利 *n* welfare

fú yīn 福音 *n* gospel

fú shè 辐射 *n* radiation

fǔ wèi 抚慰 *v* soothe

fǔ 斧 *n* ax

fǔ tóu 斧头 *n* chopper, hatchet

fǔ dǎo 辅导 *v* coach

fǔ yīn 辅音 *n* consonant

fǔ zhù de 辅助的 *adj* auxiliary, subsidiary

fǔ bài 腐败 *v* corrupt

fǔ bài 腐败 *n* corruption

fǔ bài de 腐败的 *adj* corrupt

fǔ chòu de 腐臭的 *adj* putrid

fǔ làn 腐烂 *v* decay, rot

fǔ làn 腐烂 *n* decay, rot

fǔ làn de 腐烂的 *adj* rotten

fǔ shí 腐蚀 *v* corrode

fǔ xiǔ 腐朽 *v* decay

fǔ xiǔ 腐朽 *n* decay

fù qīn 父亲 *n* father

fù quán 父权 *n* fatherhood

fù xì 父系 *n* paternity

fù xì hòu yì 父系后裔 *n* paternity

fù kuǎn 付款 *n* payment

fù qián 付钱 *iv* pay

fù kē 妇科 *n* gynecology

fù dān 负担 *n* burden

fù dān 负担 *v* burden

fù dān de qǐ 负担得起 *v* afford

fù dān de qǐ de 负担得起的 *adj* affordable

fù zài 负载 *v* load

fù zài 负载 *n* load

fù biǎo 附表 *n* schedule

fù jì 附寄 *v* enclose

fù jiā 附加 *n* annexation

fù jiā de 附加的 *adj* additional

fù jiā fèi 附加费 *n* surcharge

fù jiā wù 附加物 *n* annexation

fù jiàn 附件 *n* annex, attachment

fù jìn de 附近的 *adj* nearby

fù lù 附录 *n* appendix

fù shàng 附上 *v* affix, attach

fù shàng de 附上的 *adj* attached

fù shè de 附设的 *adj* subsidiary

fù shǔ 附属 *n* affiliation

fù shǔ de 附属的 *adj* collateral

fù shǔ wù 附属物 *n* annex

fù chóu 复仇 *v* revenge

fù chóu 复仇 *n* revenge, vengeance

fù fā 复发 *v* recur

fù fā 复发 *n* relapse

fù hé de 复合的 *adj* multiple

fù hé 复核 *v* double-check

fù huó 复活 *n* resurrection

fù huó jié 复活节 *n* Easter

fù shù 复数 *n* plural

fù sū 复苏 *v* resuscitate

fù xí 复习 *v* go over

fù xí 复习 *n* review

fù yìn 复印 *v* duplicate

fù yìn jī 复印机 *n* copier

fù yuán 复原 *n* comeback

fù zá 复杂 *n* complication

fù zá de 复杂的 *adj* complex

fù zá huà 复杂化 *v* complicate

fù zá xìng 复杂性 _n_ complexity

fù zhì 复制 _v_ copy, duplicate, replicate

fù zhì 复制 _n_ copy, duplication

fù zhì pǐn 复制品 _n_ replica

fù běn 副本 _n_ counterpart

fù biāo tí 副标题 _n_ subtitle

fù chǎn wù 副产物 _n_ by-product

fù cí 副词 _n_ adverb

fù zhǔ jì 副主祭 _n_ deacon

fù ráo de 富饶的 _adj_ productive

fù yǒu chéng xiào de 富有成效的 _adj_ fruitful

fù yǒu de 富有的 _adj_ rich, wealthy, well-to-do

fù yú 富于 _v_ abound

fù yù 富裕 _n_ affluence, opulence

fù yù de 富裕的 _adj_ affluent

fù yǔ shēng mìng 赋予生命 _v_ animate

fù bù 腹部 _n_ abdomen

fù gǔ gōu 腹股沟 _n_ groin

fù xiè 腹泻 _n_ diarrhea

fù gài fàn wéi 覆盖范围 _n_ coverage

G

gāi fá de 该罚的 _adj_ punishable

gǎi biàn 改变 _v_ alter, change, transform

gǎi biàn 改变 _n_ alteration, change

gǎi gé 改革 _n_ reform

gǎi gé yùn dòng 改革运动 _n_ crusade

gǎi gé zhě 改革者 _n_ crusader

gǎi jiàn 改建 _v_ rebuild

gǎi shàn 改善 _v_ improve

gǎi shàn 改善 _n_ improvement

gǎi zào 改造 _v_ remodel, transform, reform

gǎi zōng zhě 改宗者 _n_ convert

gài yóu chuō 盖邮戳 _v_ stamp

gài zhù 盖住 _v_ cover

gài zi 盖子 _n_ cover, lid

gài kuàng 概况 _n_ overview

gài kuò de 概括地 _adv_ broadly

gài lǜ 概率 _n_ probability

gài niàn 概念 _n_ concept, conception, notion

gàn 干 _n_ stem

gān bēi 干杯 _n_ cheers

gān cǎo 干草 _n_ hay

gān cǎo chā 干草叉 _n_ pitchfork

gān cǎo duī 干草堆 _n_ haystack

gān de 干的 _adj_ dry

gān jìng de 干净的 _adj_ clean

gān kě de 干渴的 _adj_ thirsty

gān rǎo 干扰 _n_ disturbance, interference

gān shè 干涉 _n_ intercession

gān shè 干涉 _v_ interfere, meddle

gān xǐ 干洗 _v_ dry-clean

gān yù 干预 _n_ intervention

gān zào de 干燥的 _adj_ arid

gān 杆 _n_ rod

gān 肝 _n_ liver

gǎn shàng 赶上 _v_ catch up

F
G

gǎn yán de 敢言的 *adj* outspoken

gǎn yú 敢于 *v* dare, venture

gǎn dào è de 感到饿的 *adj* hungry

gǎn dào jí dù tòng kǔ 感到极度痛苦 *v* agonize

gǎn guān de 感官的 *adj* sensual

gǎn jī 感激 *v* appreciate

gǎn jī 感激 *n* appreciation

gǎn jī de 感激的 *adj* obliged, thankful

gǎn jué 感觉 *iv* feel, sense

gǎn jué 感觉 *n* feeling, sensation, sense

gǎn qíng 感情 *n* feelings

gǎn rǎn 感染 *v* infect

gǎn rǎn 感染 *n* infection

gǎn rǎn de 感染的 *adj* tainted

gǎn rén de 感人的 *adj* touching

gǎn shāng de 感伤的 *adj* sentimental

gǎn xiè 感谢 *adj* grateful

gǎn xiè 感谢 *n* gratitude

gǎn xiè 感谢 *v* thank

gǎn yìng 感应 *n* telepathy

gǎn zhī (néng lì) 感知（能力）*n* perception

gǎn lǎn shù 橄榄树 *n* olive

gāng 刚 *adj* just

gāng liè de 刚烈的 *adj* staunch

gāng xìng de 刚性的 *adj* stiff

gāng yì de 刚毅的 *adj* resolute

gǎng tíng 岗亭 *n* booth

gāng yào 纲要 *n* compendium, outline

gāng 缸 *n* cylinder, urn

gāng 钢 *n* steel

gāng bǐ 钢笔 *n* pen

gāng dìng 钢锭 *n* ingot

gāng qín 钢琴 *n* piano

gāng qín jiā 钢琴家 *n* pianist

gǎng kǒu 港口 *n* harbor, port

gàng gǎn 杠杆 *n* lever

gàng gǎn zuò yòng 杠杆作用 *n* leverage

gāo cháo 高潮 *n* climax

gāo dà de 高大的 *adj* tall

gāo de 高的 *adj* high

gāo dù 高度 *n* altitude, elevation

gāo dù de 高度地 *adv* highly

gāo fēng 高峰 *n* peak

gāo gū 高估 *v* overestimate

gāo guān 高官 *n* dignitary

gāo hǎn 高喊 *n* shouting

gāo jí de 高级的 *adj* senior

gāo jià de 高价的 *adj* pricey

gāo sēng 高僧 *n* dignitary

gāo shàng 高尚 *n* elevation

gāo shàng de 高尚的 *adj* noble

gāo shǒu 高手 *n* ace

gāo sù 高速 *n* speed

gāo sù gōng lù 高速公路 *n* freeway, highway

gāo xiào lǜ 高效率 *adj* efficient

gāo xìng 高兴 *adj* glad

gāo yuán 高原 *n* plateau

gāo zhì liàng de 高质量的 *adj* superb

gāo 膏 *n* paste

gāo yào 膏药 *n* plaster

gāo bǐng 糕饼 *n* pastry

gǎo luàn 搞乱 *v* confuse

gǎo xiào 搞笑 *adj* funny, hilarious

（**gǎo jiàn děng**）**zuì hòu dìng xià lái** （稿件等）最后定下来 *v* finalize

gào bié 告别 *n* farewell

gào jí de 告急的 *adj* alarming

gào jiě shì 告解室 *n* confessional

gào jiè 告诫 *v* admonish

gào jiè 告诫 *n* admonition

gào mì 告密 *v* sneak

gào su 告诉 *iv* tell

gē 割 *v* mow

gē bāo pí 割包皮 *v* circumcise

gē bāo pí 割包皮 *n* circumcision

gē lǐ 割礼 *n* circumcision

gē yīn dì 割阴蒂 *v* circumcise

gē bǎn 搁板 *n* shelf

gē qiǎn de 搁浅的 *adj* stranded

gē cí 歌词 *n* lyrics

gē jù 歌剧 *n* opera

gē shǒu 歌手 *n* singer

gé lóu 阁楼 *n* attic

gé xià 阁下 *n* lordship

gé biàn huà 格变化 *n* declension

gé dòu 格斗 *v* wrestle

gé líng lán 格陵兰 *n* Greenland

gé shì 格式 *n* format

gé yán 格言 *n* maxim

gé lí 蛤蜊 *n* clam

gé bì 隔壁 *adj* next door

gé jiān 隔间 *n* compartment

gé lí 隔离 *n* isolation, segregation

gé lí 隔离 *v* separate

gé yè 隔夜 *adv* overnight

gè rén de 个人的 *adj* corporal, personal

gè xìng 个性 *n* personality

gè 各 *adv* apiece

gè shì gè yàng de dā pèi 各式各样的搭配 *n* assortment

gè zhǒng gè yàng de 各种各样的 *adj* assorted, varied, various

gè zì de 各自的 *adj* respective

gěi …bō kuǎn 给…拨款 *v* fund

gěi …rǎn sè 给…染色 *v* dye

gěi …yǐ líng gǎn 给…以灵感 *v* inspire

gěi huí 给回 *v* give back

gěi mǒu rén chī huò dǎ xīng fèn jì 给某人吃或打兴奋剂 *v* dope

gēn 根 *n* root

gēn běn de 根本的 *adj* essential, radical

gēn chú 根除 *v* eradicate

gēn jù 根据 *pre* according to

gēn jù fēng píng 根据风评 *adv* reputedly

gēn shēn dì gù 根深蒂固 *adj* entrenched

gēn shēn dì gù de 根深蒂固的 *adj* ingrained

gēn cóng 跟从 *v* follow

gēn shàng 跟上 *v* keep up

gēn zhe 跟着 *v* trail

gēn zōng 跟踪 *v* tail, trace, track

gēng nián qī 更年期 *n* menopause

gēng xīn 更新 *v* renew, renovate, update

gēng xīn 更新 *n* renewal

G

G

gēng yī shì 更衣室 *n* locker room

gēng zhèng 更正 *n* correction

gēng zhòng 耕种 *n* cultivation, culture

gēng zuò 耕作 *v* cultivate

gēng zuò 耕作 *n* cultivation, farming

gèng 更 *c* even more

gèng chà（de） 更差（的）*adj* worse

gèng dī de 更低的 *adj* lower

gèng duō 更多 *adj* more

gèng hǎo de 更好的 *adj* better

gèng huài（de） 更坏（的）*adj* worse

gèng shǎo 更少 *adj* fewer

gèng xǐ huān 更喜欢 *v* prefer

gèng yuǎn 更远 *adv* farther

gèng zāo（de） 更糟（的）*adj* worse

gōng chǎng 工厂 *n* factory

gōng chéng shī 工程师 *n* engineer

gōng jiàng 工匠 *n* artisan, craftsman

gōng jù 工具 *n* tool

gōng tóu 工头 *n* foreman

gōng yè 工业 *n* industry

gōng yì 工艺 *n* craft

gōng zī dān 工资单 *n* pay slip

gōng zuò 工作 *n* job, work

gōng zuò 工作 *v* work

gōng zuò rén yuán 工作人员 *n* staff

gōng zuò zhě 工作者 *n* worker

gōng 弓 *n* bow

gōng bù 公布 *v* announce

gōng bù 公布 *n* proclamation

gōng gào 公告 *n* announcement, notice

gōng gòng de 公共的 *adj* public

gōng gòng qì chē 公共汽车 *n* bus

gōng huì huì zhǎng 公会会长 *n* deacon

gōng jī 公鸡 *n* rooster

gōng jīn 公斤 *n* kilogram

gōng jué 公爵 *n* duke

gōng jué fū rén 公爵夫人 *n* duchess

gōng kāi biǎo shì 公开表示 *v* air

gōng kāi de 公开的 *adj* open

gōng kāi de 公开地 *adv* publicly

gōng kāi wǔ rǔ 公开侮辱 *v* affront

gōng kāi wǔ rǔ 公开侮辱 *n* affront

gōng kāi xìng 公开性 *n* openness

gōng kāi xuān bù de 公开宣布的 *adj* avowed

gōng kāi xuān chēng 公开宣称 *v* profess

gōng lǐ 公里 *n* kilometer

gōng lǐ 公理 *n* axiom

gōng mín 公民 *n* citizen

gōng mín de 公民的 *adj* civic, civil

gōng mín shēn fen 公民身份 *n* citizenship

gōng mín tóu piào 公民投票 *n* referendum

gōng mù 公墓 *n* cemetery

gōng niú 公牛 *n* bull

gōng píng 公平 *adj* fair

gōng píng 公平 *n* fairness
gōng píng de 公平的 *adj* impartial
gōng rèn 公认 *n* recognition
gōng shēng 公升 *n* liter
gōng shì 公式 *n* formula
gōng shì bāo 公事包 *n* briefcase
gōng sī 公司 *n* company, corporation, firm, house
gōng wù shàng de 公务上的 *adj* official
gōng yáng 公羊 *n* ram
gōng yù 公寓 *n* apartment, flat
gōng yuán 公园 *n* park
gōng yuē 公约 *n* convention
gōng zhèng 公正 *n* candor
gōng zhèng de 公正的 *adj* disinterested, impartial, unbiased
gōng zhèng de 公正地 *adv* justly
gōng zhèng 公证 *n* notary
gōng zhì de 公制的 *adj* metric
gōng zhòng de 公众的 *adj* public
gōng zhū 公猪 *n* boar
gōng zhǔ 公主 *n* princess
gōng jì 功绩 *n* exploit
gōng kè 功课 *n* homework
gōng néng 功能 *n* function
gōng jī 攻击 *n* assault, attack
gōng jī 攻击 *v* assault, attack
gōng jī zhě 攻击者 *n* assailant, attacker
gōng nuǎn 供暖 *n* heating
gōng yìng 供应 *v* supply
gōng diàn 宫殿 *n* palace
gōng shùn de 恭顺地 *adv* humbly

gǒng gù 巩固 *v* consolidate
gǒng 汞 *n* mercury
gǒng 拱 *n* arch
gòng chǎn zhǔ yì 共产主义 *n* communism
gòng chǎn zhǔ yì de 共产主义的 *adj* communist
gòng fàn 共犯 *n* accomplice
gòng hé dǎng 共和党 *n* republic
gòng hé guó 共和国 *n* republic
gòng móu zhě 共谋者 *n* conspirator
gòng shí 共识 *n* consensus
gòng tóng de 共同的 *adj* common
gòng tóng kàn fǎ 共同看法 *n* consensus
gòng xiǎng 共享 *n* communion
gòng yòng 共用 *v* pool
gòng guò yú qiú 供过于求 *n* glut
gòng rén huà xiàng huò pāi zhào qī jiān 供人画像或拍照期间 *n* sitting
gòng yìng shāng 供应商 *n* supplier
gòng xiàn 贡献 *v* contribute
gòng xiàn 贡献 *n* contribution
gòng xiàn zhě 贡献者 *n* contributor
gōu 沟 *n* ditch
gōu tōng 沟通 *v* communicate
gōu tōng 沟通 *n* communication
gōu zi 钩子 *n* hook
gōu huǒ 篝火 *n* bonfire, campfire
gǒu 狗 *n* dog
gǒu wō 狗窝 *n* kennel

G

gòu chéng 构成 *v* comprise, consist, constitute

gòu chéng ...de jī chǔ （huò qǐ yīn） 构成...的基础（或起因）*v* underlie

gòu sī 构思 *v* conceive

gòu zào 构造 *n* constitution

gòu mǎi 购买 *iv* buy, purchase

gòu mǎi 购买 *n* purchase

gòu wù 购物 *n* shopping

gòu wù chē 购物车 *n* cart

gū jì 估计 *v* estimate, size up

gū jì 估计 *n* estimation

gū 姑 *n* aunt

yí yí 姨 *n* aunt

jiù mā 舅妈 *n* aunt

shěn 婶 *n* aunt

gū xī 姑息 *v* appeasement

gū dú 孤独 *n* solitude

gū dú de 孤独的 *adj* solitary

gū ér 孤儿 *n* orphan

gū ér yuàn 孤儿院 *n* orphanage

gū jiā guǎ rén 孤家寡人 *adv* lonely

gū lì 孤立 *v* isolate

gū zhù yī zhì de 孤注一掷的 *adj* desperate

gū fù 辜负 *v* let down

gǔ dài 古代 *n* antiquity

gǔ guài de 古怪的 *adj* eccentric, nutty, weird

gǔ lǎo 古老 *n* antiquity

gǔ lǎo de 古老的 *adj* ancient, archaic

gǔ lóng xiāng shuǐ 古龙香水 *n* cologne

gǔ tóng sè de 古铜色的 *adj* tanned

gǔ cāng 谷仓 *n* barn

gǔ wù 谷物 *n* cereal

gǔ dōng 股东 *n* shareholder

gǔ fèn 股份 *n* stake

gǔ piào 股票 *n* stock

gǔ xī 股息 *n* dividend

gǔ 骨 *n* bone

gǔ gàn 骨干 *n* backbone

gǔ jià 骨架 *n* skeleton

gǔ ròu 骨肉 *n* flesh

gǔ suǐ 骨髓 *n* bone marrow, marrow

gǔ huò 蛊惑 *v* bewitch

gǔ 鼓 *n* drum

gǔ dòng zhě 鼓动者 *n* agitator

gǔ lì 鼓励 *v* encourage

gǔ mó 鼓膜 *n* eardrum

gǔ qǐ 鼓起 *v* muster

gǔ wǔ 鼓舞 *v* hearten, inspire

gǔ wǔ de 鼓舞的 *adj* rousing

gǔ wǔ rén xīn de rén （huò shì wù） 鼓舞人心的人（或事物）*n* inspiration

gǔ zhǎng huān yíng 鼓掌欢迎 *v* applaud

hè cǎi děng 喝彩等 *v* applaud

gù de 固的 *adj* solid

gù dìng 固定 *v* affix, immobilize

gù dìng de 固定的 *adj* immobile, stationary

gù yǒu de 固有的 *adj* innate

gù zhí 固执 *n* tenacity

gù zhí jǐ jiàn 固执己见 *adj* opinionated

gù zhí jǐ jiàn de 固执己见的 *adj* pushy

gù shi 故事 *n* story, tale

gù xiāng 故乡 *n* hometown

gù yì de 故意的 *adj* deliberate

gù yì de 故意的 *adv* willfully

gù yì de 故意地 *adv* purposely

gù yì pò huài 故意破坏 *n* vandalism

gù zhàng 故障 *v* break down

gù zhàng 故障 *n* breakdown, fault, malfunction

gù jì 顾忌 *n* scruples

gù kè 顾客 *n* customer

gù wèn 顾问 *n* adviser, counselor

gù yōng 雇佣 *v* hire

gù yòng 雇用 *v* employ

gù yuán 雇员 *n* employee

gù zhǔ 雇主 *n* employer

guā 刮 *v* scrape

guǎ fù 寡妇 *n* widow

guà chē 挂车 *n* trailer

guà duàn diàn huà 挂断电话 *v* hang up

guà suǒ 挂锁 *n* padlock

guà tǎn 挂毯 *n* tapestry

guǎi zhàng 拐杖 *n* crutch

guài dàn 怪诞 *adj* grotesque

guài dàn de 怪诞的 *adj* bizarre, eerie

guài pǐ de 怪癖的 *adj* eccentric

guài wù 怪物 *n* monster

guān 冠 *n* crest

guān bì 关闭 *v* close, shut off

guān bì 关闭 *n* closure

guān bì de 关闭的 *adj* closed

guān diào 关掉 *v* switch off, turn off

guān huái 关怀 *v* care for

guān jiàn 关键 *n* key

guān jiàn de 关键的 *adj* critical, crucial

guān jié yán 关节炎 *n* arthritis

guān lián 关联 *n* conjunction

guān shuì 关税 *n* tariff

guān xì 关系 *n* connection, relationship

guān xì dào 关系到 *v* concern

guān xīn 关心 *v* care, care about

guān xīn 关心 *n* concern

guān yú 关于 *pre* about, concerning, regarding

guān zhù 关注 *n* concern

guān chá 观察 *n* observation

guān chá 观察 *v* observe

guān diǎn 观点 *n* perspective, viewpoint

guān guāng 观光 *v* sightseeing

guān niàn 观念 *n* perception

guān zhòng 观众 *n* audience, spectator

guān fāng de 官方的 *adj* official

guān liáo 官僚 *n* bureaucrat

guān liáo zhǔ yì 官僚主义 *n* bureaucracy

guān si 官司 *n* lawsuit

guān cai 棺材 *n* casket, coffin

guān fū 鳏夫 *n* widower

guǎn zhǎng 馆长 *n* curator

guǎn yuán 馆员 *n* librarian

G

guǎn 管 *n* duct
guǎn dào 管道 *n* pipeline
guǎn jiā 管家 *n* housekeeper
guǎn yuè qì 管乐器 *n* pipe
guǎn lǐ 管理 *v* administer, govern, manage, management
guǎn lǐ bù dàng 管理不当 *v* mismanage
guǎn lǐ rén 管理人 *n* caretaker
guǎn zi 管子 *n* pipe
guàn de 冠的 *adj* coronary
guàn jūn 冠军 *n* champ, champion
guàn zhuàng de 冠状的 *adj* coronary
guàn lì 惯例 *n* routine, rule
guàn xìng 惯性 *adj* habitual
guàn gài 灌溉 *n* irrigation
guàn mù 灌木 *n* bush, shrub
guàn shū 灌输 *v* indoctrinate, instill
guàn shuǐ 灌水 *v* irrigate
guàn 鹳 *n* stork
guàn 罐 *n* canister, pot
guàn tou 罐头 *n* can, tin
guàn zhuāng de 罐装的 *adj* canned
guāng 光 *n* light, ray
guāng gù 光顾 *n* patronage
guāng gù 光顾 *v* patronize
guāng huá 光滑 *n* smoothness
guāng liàng de 光亮的 *adj* luminous
guāng róng 光荣 *adj* glorious
guāng tū de 光秃的 *adj* bare

guāng xiàn 光线 *n* beam
guāng xué de 光学的 *adj* optical
guāng zé 光泽 *n* gloss
guāng zǐ 光子 *n* corpuscle
guǎng bō 广播 *v* broadcast
guǎng bō 广播 *n* broadcast
guǎng bō diàn tái 广播电台 *n* broadcaster
guǎng bō qì 广播器 *n* broadcaster
guǎng bō yuán 广播员 *n* broadcaster
guǎng chǎng 广场 *n* square
guǎng fàn de 广泛的 *adj* wide
guǎng fàn de 广泛地 *adv* widely
guǎng gào 广告 *v* advertise
guǎng gào 广告 *n* advertising
guàng jiē 逛街 *v* shop
guī huán 归还 *n* restitution
guī jié dào 归结到 *v* boil down to
guī 龟 *n* turtle
guī dìng 规定 *v* ordain, prescribe, stipulate
guī fàn 规范 *v* standardize
guī lǜ xìng 规律性 *n* regularity
guī mó 规模 *n* scale
guī zé 规则 *n* precept, regulation, rule
guī zhāng 规章 *n* regulation
guī yī zhě 皈依者 *n* convert
guī yú 鲑鱼 *n* salmon
guǐ dào 轨道 *n* orbit
guǐ jì 轨迹 *n* trajectory
guǐ jì 诡计 *n* ruse
guǐ 鬼 *n* apparition, ghost
guǐ liǎn 鬼脸 *n* grimace

guì tái 柜台 *n* counter
guì zú 贵族 *n* aristocrat, nobility
guì zú 贵族 *adj* nobleman
guì zú de 贵族的 *adj* noble
guì zú jiē jí 贵族阶级 *n* aristocracy
guì zú quán lì 贵族权力 *n* lordship
guì bài 跪拜 *v* genuflect
gǔn 滚 *v* roll
guō lú 锅炉 *n* boiler
guó fáng 国防 *n* defense
guó huì 国会 *n* congress
guó jí 国籍 *n* nationality
guó jì xiàng qí 国际象棋 *n* chess
guó jiā 国家 *n* country, nation, state
guó nèi 国内 *adj* domestic
guó nèi de 国内的 *adj* civil
guó wáng 国王 *n* king
guó yǒu huà 国有化 *v* nationalize
guó 摑 *n* slap
guǒ duàn de 果断的 *adj* deciding, decisive
guǒ jiàng 果酱 *n* jam, marmalade
guǒ pí 果皮 *n* peel
guǒ wèi de 果味的 *adj* fruity
guǒ yuán 果园 *n* orchard
guǒ zhī 果汁 *n* juice
guǒ zhù 裹住 *v* muffle
guò chéng 过程 *n* course, process
guò dào 过道 *n* aisle
guò dù 过度 *n* excess
guò dù de 过度地 *adj* undue
guò dù yōng jǐ de 过度拥挤的 *adj* overcrowded
guò dù 过渡 *n* transition

guò duō de 过多的 *adj* excessive
guò fèn de 过分的 *adj* excessive, exorbitant
guò fèn yāo qiú de 过分要求的 *adj* demanding
guò fèn zuò 过分做 *v* overdo
guò fèn gāo gū 过份高估 *v* overrate
guò gāo suǒ jià 过高索价 *v* overcharge
guò huǒ 过火 *adv* overboard
guò jī fèn zǐ 过激分子 *adj* extremist
guò lái 过来 *v* come over
guò liàng 过量 *n* excess, glut, overdose
guò lǜ 过滤 *v* filter, sift
guò mǐn 过敏 *n* allergy
guò mǐn de 过敏的 *adj* allergic
guò qī 过期 *n* expiration
guò qù 过去 *v* elapse
guò qù cháng cháng 过去常常 *adj* used to
guò qù de 过去的 *adj* last, past
guò shèng de 过剩的 *adj* redundant, superfluous
guò shī shā rén（zuì） 过失杀人（罪）*n* manslaughter
guò shí de 过时的 *adj* antiquated, old-fashioned
guò shì 过世 *v* pass away

G

H

hā mì guā 哈密瓜 *n* cantaloupe

hā qian 哈欠 *n* yawn

hái zi 孩子 *n* brat; kid

hái zi qì de 孩子气的 *adj* childish

hǎi 海 *n* sea

hǎi àn 海岸 *n* coast

hǎi àn de 海岸的 *adj* coastal

hǎi àn xiàn 海岸线 *n* coastline

hǎi bá 海拔 *n* altitude

hǎi bào 海报 *n* postcard, poster

hǎi biān de 海边的 *adj* seaside

hǎi bīn 海滨 *n* seashore

hǎi dào 海盗 *n* pirate

hǎi gǎng 海港 *n* harbor

hǎi guān 海关 *n* custom

hǎi jiǎo 海角 *n* cape

hǎi jūn 海军 *n* navy

hǎi jūn shàng jiàng 海军上将 *n* admiral

hǎi lí 海狸 *n* beaver

hǎi luò yīn 海洛因 *n* heroin

hǎi mián 海绵 *n* sponge

hǎi ōu 海鸥 *n* gull, seagull

hǎi tān 海滩 *n* beach

hǎi tún 海豚 *n* dolphin

hǎi wài 海外 *adv* overseas

hǎi wān 海湾 *n* gulf

hǎi xiá 海峡 *n* strait

hǎi xiān 海鲜 *n* seafood

hǎi xiàng 海象 *n* walrus

hǎi yàn 海燕 *v* swallow

hǎi yáng 海洋 *n* ocean

hǎi yáng de 海洋的 *adj* marine

hài rén de 骇人的 *adj* appalling

hài pà 害怕 *adj* afraid

hài xiū 害羞 *n* shyness

hài xiū de 害羞的 *adj* bashful, shy

hán hu bù qīng de shuō 含糊不清地说 *v* babble

hán lèi de 含泪的 *adj* tearful

hán qiān 含铅 *adj* leaded

hán shuǐ de 含水的 *adj* watery

hán xù de 含蓄的 *adj* implicit

hán yì 含义 *n* meaning

hán yǒu 含有 *v* contain

hán lěng 寒冷 *adj* frigid

hán lěng de 寒冷的 *adj* chilly

hǎn 喊 *v* cry, shout

hǎn 喊 *n* shout

hǎn jiào 喊叫 *n* outcry

hàn bǎo bāo 汉堡包 *n* burger, hamburger

hàn shuǐ 汗水 *n* perspiration, sweat

hàn zāi 旱灾 *n* drought

hàn gōng 焊工 *n* welder

hàn jiē 焊接 *v* weld

hàn liào 焊料 *v* solder

háng huì 行会 *n* guild

háng bān 航班 *n* flight

háng hǎi zhě 航海者 *n* voyager

háng kōng 航空 *n* aviation

háng xiàn 航线 *n* airline

háo bù hán hu de 毫不含糊的 *adj* unequivocal

háo huá de 毫华的 *adj* posh

háo kè 毫克 *n* milligram

háo mǐ 毫米 *n* millimeter

háo wú yí wèn de 毫无疑问的 *adj* undisputed

háo 嗥 *v* howl

háo shēng 嗥声 *n* howl

háo huá de 豪华的 *adj* deluxe, luxurious, regal

háo zhái 豪宅 *n* mansion

háo zhū 豪猪 *n* porcupine

háo táo 嚎啕 *v* wail

háo táo shēng 嚎啕声 *n* wail

hǎo 好 *adj* fine, good

hǎo 好 *adv* nicely

hǎo ba 好吧 *adv* alright

hǎo chī de 好吃的 *adj* tasteful

hǎo chù 好处 *n* benefit

hǎo de 好的 *adj* nice

hǎo gǎn 好感 *n* favor

hǎo jí de 好极的 *adj* great

hǎo kàn de 好看的 *adj* good-looking

hǎo píng 好评 *n* praise

hǎo shì 好事 *n* favor

hǎo shǒu 好手 *n* ace

hǎo wán de 好玩的 *adj* playful

hǎo xiào de 好笑的 *adj* comical

hǎo xīn 好心 *n* kindness

hǎo xīn de 好心的 *adj* kind

hǎo xīn de 好心地 *adv* kindly

hǎo yǒu 好友 *n* buddy

hào biàn de 好辩的 *adj* contentious

hào guǎn xián shì de 好管闲事的 *adj* nosy

hào jiāo jì de 好交际的 *adj* sociable

hào kè 好客 *n* hospitality

hào qí de 好奇的 *adj* curious

hào qí xīn 好奇心 *n* curiosity

hào zhàn de 好战的 *adj* belligerent, militant

hào zhēng lùn de 好争论的 *adj* quarrelsome

hào mǎ 号码 *n* number

hào zhào 号召 *v* call on

hào dà 浩大 *n* gall bladder

hào dà de 浩大的 *adj* vast

hào jìn 耗尽 *v* deplete, sap

hē 喝 *iv* drink

hè cǎi 喝彩 *v* acclaim

hé bìng 合并 *n* annexation, fusion, merger

hé bìng 合并 *v* merge

hé chàng 合唱 *n* chorus

hé chàng tuán 合唱团 *n* choir

hé chéng 合成 *n* synthesis

hé fǎ de 合法的 *adj* lawful, legitimate

hé fǎ huà 合法化 *v* legalize

hé fǎ xìng 合法性 *n* legality

hé jīn 合金 *n* alloy

hé lǐ de 合理的 *adj* rational, reasonable

hé lǐ huà 合理化 *v* rationalize

hé shí yí de 合时宜的 *adj* opportune

hé tong 合同 *n* contract

hé yì de 合意的 *adj* pleasing

hé zuò 合作 *v* cooperate

hé zuò 合作 *n* cooperation

hé zuò de 合作的 *adj* cooperative

hé zuò huǒ bàn 合作伙伴 *n* partner

hé zuò zhě 合作者 *n* collaborator

hé 和 *c* and

hé 和 *pre* with

hé ǎi de 和蔼的 *adj* bland

hé ǎi kě qīn 和蔼可亲 *adj* amiable

hé ǎi kě qīn de 和蔼可亲的 *adj* affable

hé jiě 和解 *v* reconcile

hé mù de 和睦的 *adj* amicable

hé píng 和平 *n* peace

hé píng de 和平的 *adj* peaceful

hé shang 和尚 *n* monk

hé xié 和谐 *n* harmony

hé 河 *n* river

hé néng de 核能的 *adj* nuclear

hé shí 核实 *v* verify

hé tao 核桃 *n* walnut

hé xīn 核心 *n* core

hé zǐ de 核子的 *adj* nuclear

hé lán 荷兰 *n* Holland, Netherlands

hé lán de 荷兰的 *adj* Dutch

hé zi 盒子 *n* box

hēi àn 黑暗 *n* darkness

hēi àn de 黑暗的 *adj* dark

hēi bǎn 黑板 *n* blackboard, chalkboard

hēi dù 黑度 *n* blackness

hēi kè rù qīn 黑客入侵 *v* hack

hēi mài 黑麦 *n* rye

hēi méi 黑莓 *n* blackberry

hēi sè de 黑色的 *adj* black

hēi xīng xing 黑猩猩 *n* chimpanzee

hén jì 痕迹 *n* vestige

hěn 很 *adv* grossly

hěn báo de 很薄的 *adj* meager

hěn chà 很差 *adv* poorly

hěn duō 很多 *adv* lot, much

hěn duō 很多 *adj* lots

hěn shǎo de 很少地 *adv* rarely, seldom

hěn dú de 狠毒的 *adj* diabolical, vicious

hèn 恨 *v* hate

hēng qǔ zi 哼曲子 *v* hum

héng jiǔ 恒久 *n* constancy

héng wēn qì 恒温器 *n* thermostat

héng fú 横幅 *n* banner

hōng zhà 轰炸 *v* bomb

hōng zhà 轰炸 *n* bombing

hǒng piàn 哄骗 *v* coax

hōng 烘 *v* bake, parch

hōng gān 烘干 *v* dry

hōng gān de 烘干的 *adj* dried

hōng gān jī 烘干机 *n* dryer

hōng kǎo 烘烤 *v* roast

hōng xiāng 烘箱 *n* oven

hóng bǎo shí 红宝石 *n* ruby

hóng lì 红利 *n* dividend

hóng sè de 红色的 *adj* red

hóng wěi 宏伟 *adj* grand

hóng wěi de 宏伟的 *adj* magnificent, noble

hóng liú 洪流 *n* torrent

hóng shuǐ 洪水 *n* deluge

hóng 虹 *n* bow

hóu 喉 *n* larynx

hóu lóng 喉咙 *n* throat

hóu 猴 *n* monkey
hǒu shēng 吼声 *n* roar
hòu dài 后代 *n* offspring
hòu fāng 后方 *n* rear
hòu fāng de 后方的 *adj* rear
hòu guǒ 后果 *n* consequence
hòu huǐ 后悔 *v* regret
hòu huǐ 后悔 *n* remorse
hòu huǐ de 后悔的 *adj* remorseful
hòu lái 后来 *adv* afterwards, later
hòu lái de 后来的 *adj* later
hòu mén 后门 *n* backdoor
hòu miàn 后面 *n* back
hòu tuì 后退 *v* back up, rear,
   recede
hòu tuì 后退 *n* recession
hòu wèi 后卫 *n* guard
hòu yì 后裔 *n* descendant
hòu yuàn 后院 *n* backyard, yard
hòu zhě 后者 *adj* latter
hòu de 厚的 *adj* thick
hòu dù 厚度 *n* thickness
hǒu yán wú chǐ de 厚颜无耻的
   adj cheeky
hòu xuǎn rén 候选人 *n* candidate
hòu xuǎn zī gé 候选资格 *n*
   candidacy
hū 呼 *n* call
hū hǎn 呼喊 *n* call
hū hǎn 呼喊 *v* call
hū jiào 呼叫 *v* call
hū jiào 呼叫 *n* call, calling, appeal
hū xī 呼吸 *n* breath, breathing
hū xī 呼吸 *v* breathe
hū xī zuò yòng 呼吸作用 *n*
   respiration

hū yìng 呼应 *v* evoke
hū yù 呼吁 *n* appeal
hū yù 呼吁 *v* appeal
hū shì 忽视 *v* ignore, neglect,
   overlook
hū shì 忽视 *n* neglect
hú 弧 *n* arc
hú li 狐狸 *n* fox
hú luó bo 胡萝卜 *n* carrot
hú shuō bā dào 胡说八道 *n*
   nonsense
hú sī luàn xiǎng de 胡思乱想的
   adj cranky
hú táo ké 胡桃壳 *adv* nut-shell
hú tòng 胡同 *n* alley
hú xū 胡须 *n* beard
hú yán 胡言 *n* crap
hú 湖 *n* lake
hú 糊 *v* paste
hú tú 糊涂 *n* muddle
hú tú de 糊涂的 *adj* silly
hú dié 蝴蝶 *n* butterfly
hù huàn 互换 *v* interchange
hù huàn 互换 *n* interchange
hù xiāng yǒu guān xì 互相有关系
   v correlate
hù zhù 互助 *adj* fraternal
hù wài 户外 *adv* outdoors
hù wài de 户外的 *adv* outdoor
hù háng jiàn 护航舰 *n* frigate
hù lǐ 护理 *v* nurse
hù mù jìng 护目镜 *n* goggles
hù shi 护士 *n* nurse
hù sòng 护送 *n* convoy, escort
hù wèi 护卫 *n* convoy

hù zhào 护照 *n* passport
huā 花 *n* flower
huā （shí jiān děng） 花（时间等） *iv* spend
huā bàn 花瓣 *n* petal
huā biān 花边 *n* lace
huā fèi 花费 *iv* cost
huā fěn 花粉 *n* pollen
huā gǎng yán 花岗岩 *n* granite
huā guān de 花冠的 *adj* coronary
huā huán 花环 *n* garland
huā lěi 花蕾 *n* bud
huā pén 花盆 *n* flowerpot
huā píng 花瓶 *n* vase
huā quān 花圈 *n* wreath
huā shēng 花生 *n* peanut
huā yuán 花园 *n* garden
huá ěr zī 华尔兹 *n* waltz
huá lì 华丽 *adj* flashy, gorgeous
huá bīng 滑冰 *v* ice skate
huá dào yī biān 滑到一边 *iv* slide
huá de 滑的 *adj* slippery
huá dòng 滑动 *v* slip
huá dòng 滑动 *n* slip
huá ji de 滑稽的 *adj* comical
huá lún 滑轮 *n* pulley
huá xiáng 滑翔 *v* glide
huá xuě 滑雪 *v* ski
huà hé wù 化合物 *n* compound
huà shí 化石 *n* fossil
huà xué 化学 *n* chemistry
huà xué de 化学的 *adj* chemical
huà xué jiā 化学家 *n* chemist
huà yóu qì 化油器 *n* carburetor
huà zhuāng pǐn 化妆品 *n*

cosmetic, makeup
huá jiǎng 划桨 *v* paddle
huá pò 划破 *v* skin
huá qù 划去 *v* cross out
huà 画 *n* painting
huà bǐ 画笔 *n* paintbrush
huà bù 画布 *n* canvas
huà jiā 画家 *n* painter
huà juàn 画卷 *n* scroll
huà láng 画廊 *n* gallery
huà xiàng 画像 *n* portrait
huà tí 话题 *n* topic
huái hèn de 怀恨的 *adj* spiteful
huái jiù 怀旧 *n* nostalgia
huái róu 怀柔 *v* conciliate
huái róu de 怀柔的 *adj* conciliatory
huái yí 怀疑 *n* disbelief, doubt
huái yí 怀疑 *v* discredit
huái yí 怀疑 *v* doubt, suspect
huái yí de 怀疑的 *adj* skeptic
huái yí lùn zhě 怀疑论者 *adj* skeptic
huái yí zhě 怀疑者 *adj* skeptic
huái yǒu xī wàng de 怀有希望的 *adj* hopeful
huái yùn 怀孕 *n* pregnancy
huái yùn de 怀孕的 *adj* pregnant
huái 踝 *n* ankle
huài de 坏的 *adj* bad
huài diào de 坏掉的 *adj* broken
huài jū 坏疽 *n* gangrene
huān hū 欢呼 *v* acclaim, cheer
huān kuài 欢快 *adj* jubilant
huān lè de 欢乐的 *adj* joyful

huān lè zhī gē 欢乐之歌 *n* carol

huān yíng 欢迎 *v* herald, welcome

huān yíng 欢迎 *n* welcome

hái 还 *adv* also

hái hǎo 还好 *adv* okay

hái wèi 还未 *c* yet

huán jī 还击 *v* hit back

huán jìng 环境 *n* circumstance, environment, setting

huán rào 环绕 *v* circle, surround

huǎn chōng 缓冲 *v* cushion

huǎn hé 缓和 *v* appeasement, deaden, defuse

huǎn jiě 缓解 *v* ease

huǎn jiě (chú) 缓解（除）*n* relief

huǎn xíng 缓刑 *n* reprieve, respite

huàn jué 幻觉 *v* hallucinate

huàn miè 幻灭 *n* disillusion

huàn xiǎng 幻想 *n* fantasy

huàn xiàng 幻象 *n* illusion

huàn yǐng 幻影 *n* apparition, mirage

huàn qǐ 唤起 *v* call out

huàn xǐng 唤醒 *n* awakening

huàn xǐng 唤醒 *v* rouse

huàn xǐng de 唤醒的 *adj* rousing

huàn dòng 换动 *v* switch

huàn dòng 换动 *n* switch

huàn xióng 浣熊 *n* raccoon

huàn ái de 患癌的 *adj* cancerous

huàn biàn mì zhèng de 患便秘症的 *adj* constipated

huàn bìng 患病 *adj* ailing

huàn táng niào bìng de 患糖尿病的 *adj* diabetic

huàn fā 焕发 *v* glow

huāng liáng 荒凉 *adj* desolate

huāng liáng 荒凉 *n* desolation

huāng liáng de 荒凉的 *adj* bleak, deserted, stark, wild, derelict, dilapidated

huāng miù de 荒谬的 *adj* absurd

huáng dì 皇帝 *n* emperor

huáng guān 皇冠 *n* crown

huáng jiā de 皇家的 *adj* imperial, royal

huáng zú 皇族 *n* royalty

huáng fēng 黄蜂 *n* wasp

huáng guā 黄瓜 *n* cucumber

huáng hūn 黄昏 *n* dusk

huáng jīn 黄金 *n* gold

huáng niú 黄牛 *n* oxen

huáng sè 黄色 *adj* yellow

huáng sè zhà yào 黄色炸药 *n* dynamite

huáng yóu 黄油 *n* butter

huáng chóng 蝗虫 *n* locust

huáng zāi de 蝗灾的 *adj* infested

huǎng yán 谎言 *n* lie

huǎng zi 幌子 *n* pretense

huī 灰 *n* ash

huī àn 灰暗 *adj* gloomy

huī àn de 灰暗的 *adj* murky

huī bái de 灰白的 *adj* grayish

huī chén 灰尘 *n* dust

huī sè de 灰色的 *adj* gray, grayish, deft, skillful

huī xié de 诙谐的 *adj* humorous

huī fù 恢复 *n* comeback, recovery, restoration

huī fù 恢复 v recover, recuperate, regain, restore, revert

huī fù jīng shén 恢复精神 v revive

huī fù yuán zhuàng 恢复原状 v rehabilitate

huī dòng 挥动 v wield

huī fā xìng 挥发性 adj volatile

huī huò 挥霍 v squander

huī huáng de 辉煌的 adj splendid

huī zhāng 徽章 n badge

huí 回 adv back

huí bào 回报 v repay

huí bì 回避 v dodge, evade, sidestep

huí dá 回答 v answer

huí dá de 回答的 adj responsive

huí fù 回复 v reply

huí fù 回复 n reply

huí gù 回顾 v review

huí gù 回顾 n review

huí guī 回归 v return

huí guī 回归 n return

huí jī 回击 v pay back

huí kòu 回扣 n kickback

huí kuì 回馈 v pay back

huí lái 回来 v come back

huí láng 回廊 n cloister

huí lǐ 回礼 n recompense

huí qiān 回迁 v move back

huí qù 回去 v go back

huí shēng 回声 n echo

huí shōu lì yòng （fèi wù děng） 回收利用（废物等） v recycle

huí tóu 回头 v turn back

huí xiǎng de 回响的 adj resounding

huí xíng zhēn 回形针 n paperclip

huí yì 回忆 v recall, recollect

huí yì 回忆 n recollection

huí yì lù 回忆录 n memoirs

huǐ hèn 悔恨 n contrition

huǐ wù 悔悟 v repent

huǐ wù 悔悟 n repentance

huì jí 汇集 v pool

huì jì 汇寄 v remit

huì jì 汇寄 n remittance

huì piào 汇票 n money order

huì chuán bō de 会传播的 adj contagious

huì huī 会徽 n emblem

huì jí 会集 n congregation

huì kū wěi de 会枯萎的 adj perishable

huì pò de 会破的 adj breakable

huì yì 会议 n conference, meeting, session

huì yuán 会员 n member

huì zhòng 会众 n congregation

huì huà 绘画 iv draw

huì huà 绘画 n drawing

huì tú yuán 绘图员 n draftsman

huì zhì （dòng huà piān） 绘制（动画片）v animate

huì lù 贿赂 n bribe

huì lù 贿赂 v buy off

huì lù xíng wéi 贿赂行为 n bribery

huì xīng 彗星 n comet

huǐ huài 毁坏 v ravage, ruin, wreck

huǐ huài de 毁坏的 adj dilapidated

huǐ miè 毁灭 *n* destruction, devastation

huǐ miè xìng de 毁灭性的 *adj* devastating

hūn àn de 昏暗的 *adj* dim

hūn guò qù 昏过去 *v* pass out

hūn hūn yù shuì 昏昏欲睡 *adj* drowsy

hūn mí 昏迷 *n* coma, trance

hūn lǐ 婚礼 *n* wedding

hūn lǐ de 婚礼的 *adj* bridal

hūn yīn 婚姻 *n* marriage, matrimony

hūn yīn de 婚姻的 *adj* marital

hún dàn 混蛋 *n* jerk

hùn hé 混合 *n* blend, mixture, mix-up

hùn hé 混合 *v* blend, mingle, mix

hùn hé jì 混合剂 *n* mixture

hùn hé wù 混合物 *n* compost, compound

hùn luàn 混乱 *n* chaos, confusion, disorder, muddle

hùn luàn de 混乱的 *adj* chaotic

hùn níng tǔ 混凝土 *n* concrete

hùn xiáo 混淆 *v* confound

hùn zá 混杂 *n* cross

hùn zá de 混杂的 *adj* assorted, mixed-up

huò miǎn 豁免 *adj* exempt

huò miǎn 豁免 *n* exemption

huó 活 *v* live

huó de cháng 活得长 *v* outlive

huó de 活的 *adj* alive

huó dòng 活动 *n* activity, campaign, exertion

huó pō de 活泼的 *adj* brisk, lively, vivacious

huó yuè 活跃 *adj* active

huó yuè de 活跃的 *adj* bustling, dashing

huǒ 火 *n* fire

huǒ chái 火柴 *n* match

huǒ chē 火车 *n* train

huǒ chē chū guǐ 火车出轨 *n* derailment

huǒ chē huò qì chē zhàn 火车或汽车站 *n* depot

huǒ guāng 火光 *n* flare

huǒ guō 火锅 *n* pot

huǒ huā sāi 火花塞 *n* spark plug

huǒ jiàn 火箭 *n* rocket

huǒ jù 火炬 *n* torch

huǒ lì wǎng 火力网 *n* barrage

huǒ rè 火热 *adj* fiery

huǒ shān 火山 *n* volcano

huǒ shān kǒu 火山口 *n* crater

huǒ tuǐ 火腿 *n* ham

huǒ xīng 火星 *n* Mars

huǒ yàn 火焰 *n* flame

huǒ yào 火药 *n* gunpowder

huǒ zàng 火葬 *v* cremate

huǒ zàng chǎng 火葬场 *n* crematorium

huǒ bàn 伙伴 *n* mate, pal

huǒ bàn guān xì 伙伴关系 *n* partnership

huò 或 *c* or

huò xǔ 或许 *adv* perhaps

huò bì 货币 *n* currency

huò tān 货摊 *n* booth

H

huò wù 货物 *n* cargo

huò yùn 货运 *n* freight

huò dé 获得 *v* acquire, gain, get, obtain, secure

huò dé 获得 *n* acquisition, attainment, gain

huò dé kuài lè 获得快乐 *v* relish

huò qǔ 获取 *v* derive

huò luàn 霍乱 *n* cholera

J

jī 击 *iv* hit

jī huǒ huā 击火花 *v* spark off

jī jiàn 击剑 *n* fencing

jī kuì 击溃 *v* zap

jī luò 击落 *v* shoot down

jī tuì 击退 *v* repulse

jī tuì 击退 *n* repulse

jī xiǎng 击响 *n* smack

jī xiǎng 击响 *v* smack

jī zhòng 击中 *n* hit

jī zhòng 击中 *iv* hit

jī è 饥饿 *n* hunger, starvation

jī è de 饥饿的 *adj* hungry

jī huāng 饥荒 *n* famine

jī chǎng 机场 *n* airfield, airport

jī dòng 机动 *n* maneuver

jī gōng 机工 *n* mechanic

jī gòu 机构 *n* institution

jī guān pào 机关炮 *n* cannon

jī huì 机会 *n* chance, opportunity

jī jǐng de 机警的 *adj* wary

jī jǐng de 机警地 *adv* knowingly

jī lǐ 机理 *n* mechanism

jī mì de 机密的 *adj* confidential

jī piào fèi 机票费 *n* airfare

jī qì 机器 *n* machine

jī qiāng 机枪 *n* machine gun

jī qiǎo 机巧 *n* ingenuity

jī xiè huà 机械化 *v* mechanize

jī xiè zhuāng zhì 机械装置 *n* mechanism

jī zhì 机制 *n* mechanism

jī zhì 机智 *n* tact, wit

jī zhì de 机智的 *adj* tactful, witty

jī ròu 肌肉 *n* muscle

jī 鸡 *n* chicken

jī dàn 鸡蛋 *n* egg

jī wěi jiǔ 鸡尾酒 *n* cocktail

jì xiàng 迹象 *n* indication

jī lěi 积累 *n* buildup

jī qiàn （**zhàng kuǎn**、**zhài wù děng**）积欠（账款、债务等）*v* run up

jī yā dài bàn shì xiàng 积压待办事项 *n* backlog

jī běn de 基本的 *adj* basic, fundamental, rudimentary

jī céng 基层 *adj* grassroots

jī chǔ 基础 *n* foundation

jī chǔ zhī shi 基础知识 *n* basics

jī dì 基地 *n* base

jī dū de 基督的 *adj* Christian

jī dū jiào 基督教 *n* Christianity

jī dū jiào de 基督教的 *adj* Christian

jī jīn 基金 *n* fund

jī jīn huì 基金会 *n* foundation

jī shí 基石 *n* cornerstone

jī yīn 基因 *n* gene

jì xiào 绩效 *n* performance

jī xíng 畸形 *n* deformity

jī dòng 激动 *n* concussion

jī dòng rén xīn de 激动人心的 *adj* breathtaking

jī guāng 激光 *n* laser

jī huó 激活 *v* activate

jī huó 激活 *n* activation

jī lì 激励 *v* galvanize, goad, motivate, spur

jī lì 激励 *n* spur

jī liè 激烈 *adj* fierce

jī nù 激怒 *v* enrage, exasperate

jī qǐ 激起 *v* arouse, inspire, set off

jī qíng 激情 *n* passion

jī qíng de 激情的 *adj* passionate

jī sù 激素 *n* hormone

jí shí de 及时的 *adj* timely

jí pǔ sài rén 吉普赛人 *n* gypsy

jí tā 吉他 *n* guitar

jí xiáng de 吉祥的 *adj* auspicious

jí jí kě wēi de 岌岌可危的 *adj* precarious

jí 级 *n* level

jí 即 *adv* namely

jí jiāng dào lái de 即将到来的 *adj* forthcoming

jí jiāng fā shēng de 即将发生的 *adj* imminent

jí jiāng lái lín de 即将来临的 *adj* upcoming

jí kè 即刻 *adv* instantly

jí shǐ 即使 *c* even if

jí xìng 即兴 *adv* impromptu

jí xìng chuàng zuò 即兴创作 *v* improvise

jí dà de 极大的 *n* incalculable

jí dì de 极地的 *adj* polar

jí diǎn 极点 *n* pole

jí duān 极端 *adj* extreme

jí duān zhǔ yì zhě 极端主义者 *adj* extremist

jí hǎo de 极好的 *adj* fabulous, splendid, superb, terrific, wonderful

jí hēi de 极黑的 *adj* pitch-black

jí jiǎn dān 极简单 *adj* foolproof

jí lè 极乐 *n* bliss

jí lè de 极乐的 *adj* blissful

jí qí 极其 *adv* exceedingly

jí qí chǒu lòu de 极其丑陋的 *adj* hideous

jí quán zhǔ yì de 极权主义的 *adj* totalitarian

jí tòng kǔ de 极痛苦的 *adj* excruciating

jí wéi jù dà de 极为巨大的 *adj* fabulous

jí wéi zhòng yào de 极为重要的 *adj* paramount

jí wú lǐ de 极无礼的 *adj* outrageous

jí xiàn 极限 *n* limit, limitation

jí xíng lǚ rén 急行旅人 *n* poster

jí xìng de 急性的 *adj* acute

jí zào de 急躁的 *adj* impatient

J

jí zhuǎn zhí xià 急转直下 *adv* nosedive

jí chí 疾驰 *v* gallop

jí fēng 疾风 *n* blast

jí shǒu de 棘手的 *adj* thorny, tricky

jí 集 *n* episode

jí chéng 集成 *v* integrate

jí hé 集合 *v* congregate, muster

jí hé 集合 *n* congregation

jí hé gōng yù 集合公寓 *n* condo

jí huì 集会 *n* assembly, rally

jí shì 集市 *n* bazaar, fair

jí zhōng 集中 *v* centralize, concentrate

jí zhōng 集中 *n* concentration

jí zhōng yú 集中于 *v* focus on

jí zhuāng xiāng 集装箱 *n* container

jí dù 嫉妒 *n* envy, jealousy

jí dù 嫉妒 *v* envy

jí dù de 嫉妒的 *adj* envious, jealous

jǐ gè 几个 *adj* several

jǐ hé 几何 *n* geometry

jī hū 几乎 *adv* almost, nearly

jī hū bù 几乎不 *adv* barely, hardly

jī hū méi yǒu 几乎没有 *adv* scarcely

jǐ yǔ 给予 *v* bestow, give, hold out

jǐ yǔ bāng zhù 给予帮助 *v* minister

jǐ jìn 挤进 *v* squeeze in

jǐ yā 挤压 *v* mash, mob, squeeze, squeeze up

jǐ yǎn 挤眼 *n* wink

jǐ yǎn 挤眼 *v* wink

jǐ 脊 *n* ridge

jǐ gǔ 脊骨 *n* backbone

jǐ zhù 脊柱 *n* spine

jì cè 计策 *n* ruse

jì huà 计划 *v* plan, project

jì huà 计划 *n* plan, resolution, scheme

jì shù 计数 *v* count

jì shù 计数 *n* count

jì shù qì 计数器 *n* counter

jì suàn 计算 *v* calculate, compute

jì suàn 计算 *n* calculation

jì suàn jī 计算机 *n* computer

jì suàn qì 计算器 *n* calculator

jì lù 记录 *v* record, write down

jì lù qì 记录器 *n* recorder

jì lù yuán 记录员 *n* recorder

jì rì qī 记日期 *v* date

jì shí 记时 *v* time

jì xià 记下 *v* write down

jì yì 记忆 *n* memory, recollection, remembrance

jì yì lì 记忆力 *n* recollection

jì yì quē shī 记忆缺失 *n* amnesia

jì zhàng yuán 记帐员 *n* bookkeeper

jì zhě 记者 *n* journalist, reporter

jì zhù 记住 *v* remember

jì liǎng 伎俩 *n* ploy, trick

jì zhù 系住 *v* affix

jì zhù 系住 *n* hitch

jì lù 纪录 *n* record

jì lù piān 纪录片 *n* documentary

jì lǜ 纪律 *n* discipline

jì niàn 纪念 *v* commemorate

jì niàn bēi 纪念碑 *n* monument

jì niàn bēi de 纪念碑的 *adj* monumental

jì niàn pǐn 纪念品 *n* memento, souvenir

jì nǚ 妓女 *n* tart

jì yuàn 妓院 *n* brothel

jì qiǎo 技巧 *n* skill

jì qiǎo 技巧 *n* technique

jì shù de 技术的 *adj* technical

jì shù mì jué 技术秘诀 *n* know-how

jì shù xìng 技术性 *n* technicality

jì shù yuán 技术员 *n* technician

jì liàng 剂量 *n* dosage

jì dù 季度 *n* quarter

jì jié 季节 *n* season

jì jié xìng de 季节性的 *adj* seasonal

jì bù 既不 *adj* neither

jì chéng 继承 *v* inherit

jì chéng 继承 *n* inheritance

jì chéng rén 继承人 *n* heir

jì fù 继父 *n* stepfather

jì jiě mèi 继姐妹 *n* stepsister

jì mǔ 继母 *n* stepmother

jì nǚ 继女 *n* stepdaughter

jì rèn zhě 继任者 *n* successor

jì xiōng dì 继兄弟 *n* stepbrother

jì xù 继续 *v* continue, go ahead, go on, keep on

jì zǐ 继子 *n* stepson

jì jìng 寂静 *n* hush

jì mò 寂寞 *v* loiter

jì mò 寂寞 *n* loneliness

jì mò de 寂寞的 *adj* loner

jì shēng chóng 寄生虫 *n* parasite

jì shòu 寄售 *n* consignment

jì tuō 寄托 *n* sustenance

jì sī 祭司 *n* priestess

jì tán 祭坛 *n* altar

jì yí 祭仪 *n* cult

jiā bān 加班 *adv* overtime

jiā bèi 加倍 *v* redouble

jiā dà 加大 *v* intensify

jiā diàn rù 加垫褥 *v* cushion

jiā kǔ wèi 加苦味 *v* embitter

jiā kuài 加快 *v* accelerate, hurry, hurry up, quicken, step up

jiā kuān 加宽 *v* broaden, widen

jiā lún 加仑 *n* gallon

jiā mǎn 加满 *v* refill

jiā miǎn 加冕 *n* coronation, crowning

jiā miǎn 加冕 *v* crown

jiā nóng pào 加农炮 *n* cannon

jiā qiáng 加强 *v* beef up, enhance, reinforce, strengthen

jiā rán liào（**yóu**）加燃料（油）*v* fuel

jiā rè 加热 *v* heat

jiā rè 加热 *n* heating

jiā rè qì 加热器 *n* heater

jiā rù 加入 *n* affiliation

jiā rù 加入 *v* join

jiā rù xǔ kě 加入许可 *n* admission

jiā shàng 加上 *v* add

jiā shàng 加上 *n* addition

J

jiā shàng jì hào 加上记号 v earmark

jiā sù 加速 v step up

jiā sù qì 加速器 n accelerator

jiā yóu 加油 v refuel

jiā zhī 加之 pre besides

jiā zhòng 加重 v aggravate

jiā zhòng 加重 n aggravation

jiá 夹 v clip, pinch

jiā bǎn 夹板 n splint

jiá kè 夹克 n jacket

jiā qián 夹钳 n clamp, cramp

jiā zi 夹子 n clamp, pinch

jiā 家 n home

jiā zhǎng 家长 n parents

jiā cháng de 家常的 adj homely

jiā huo 家伙 n fellow, guy

jiā jiào 家教 n tutor

jiā jū 家居 n household

jiā jù 家具 n furniture

jiā qín 家禽 n poultry

jiā shì 家世 n ancestry

jiā tíng 家庭 n family

jiā tíng nèi bù de 家庭内部的 adj domestic

jiā tíng zhǔ fù 家庭主妇 n housewife

jiā wù 家务 n housework

jiā wù zá shì 家务杂事 n chore

jiā chù 家畜 n livestock

jiā yuán 家园 n homeland

jiā shā 袈裟 n cassock

jiá xū 颊须 n whiskers

jiǎ bǎn 甲板 n deck

jiǎ chóng 甲虫 n beetle

jiǎ ké lèi dòng wù 甲壳类动物 n shellfish

jiǎ zhuàng xiàn 甲状腺 n thyroid

jiǎ de 假的 adj dummy, phony

jiǎ dìng 假定 v presume, presuppose, suppose

jiǎ dìng de 假定的 adj conditional

jiǎ fà 假发 n hairpiece, wig

jiǎ mào 假冒 v fake

jiǎ mào de 假冒的 adj counterfeit, fake

jiǎ méi mao 假眉毛 n hairpiece

jiǎ rén 假人 n dummy

jiǎ shè 假设 v assume

jiǎ shè 假设 n assumption, supposition

jiǎ shè 假设 c supposing

jiǎ shuō 假说 n hypothesis

jiǎ xiàng 假象 n semblance

jiǎ yá 假牙 n dentures

jiǎ zhuāng 假装 v counterfeit, feign, pretend

jiǎ zhuāng 假装 n guise

jiǎ zhuāng de 假装的 adj counterfeit

jià gé 价格 n price

（jià gé děng）guò gāo de（价格等）过高的 adj exorbitant

jià zhí 价值 n value

jià zhí guān 价值观 n value

jià shǐ cāng 驾驶舱 n cockpit

jià shǐ shì 驾驶室 n cab

jià zi 架子 n shelf, shelves

jià qī 假期 n vacation

jià rì 假日 n holiday

jià jiē 嫁接 *v* graft

jià jiē 嫁接 *n* graft

jià zhuang 嫁妆 *n* dowry

jiān zhà 奸诈 *n* treachery

jiān zhà de 奸诈的 *adj* treacherous

jiān jiào 尖叫 *v* scream, shriek

jiān jiào 尖叫 *n* scream

jiān jiào shēng 尖叫声 *n* shriek

jiān kū 尖哭 *v* screech

jiān ruì de 尖锐的 *adj* poignant

jiān chí 坚持 *v* adhere, assert, insist, persist; hang on, hold on to, stick to

jiān chí 坚持 *n* insistence, assertion

jiān chí bù xiè de 坚持不懈的 *adj* persistent

jiān chí de 坚持的 *adj* constant

jiān dìng 坚定 *adj* firm

jiān dìng 坚定 *v* fortify

jiān dìng bù yí de 坚定不移的 *adj* adamant

jiān dìng de 坚定的 *adj* committed, decisive

jiān dìng xìng 坚定性 *n* firmness

jiān gù de 坚固的 *adj* sturdy, substantial

jiān guǒ 坚果 *n* nut

jiān guǒ ké 坚果壳 *n* nutrition

jiān jué de 坚决的 *adj* adamant

jiān qiáng de 坚强的 *adj* adamant, strong, tough

jiān rěn bù bá 坚忍不拔 *n* fortitude

jiān rěn kè jǐ de 坚忍克己的 *adj* stoic

jiān miè 歼灭 *v* annihilate

jiān miè 歼灭 *n* annihilation

jiān jù 间距 *n* interval

jiān 肩 *n* shoulder

jiān dài 肩带 *n* strap

jiān jù de 艰巨的 *adj* arduous

jiān kǔ de 艰苦的 *adj* strenuous

jiān nán de 艰难的 *adj* rough

jiān róng de 兼容的 *adj* compatible

jiān róng xìng 兼容性 *n* compatibility

jiān chá 监察 *n* surveillance

jiān chá yuán 监察员 *n* inspector, warden

jiān dū 监督 *v* monitor, oversee, supervise

jiān dū 监督 *n* supervision

jiān hù 监护 *n* custody

jiān hù rén 监护人 *n* custodian, guardian

jiān jìn 监禁 *n* custody

jiān jìn 监禁 *v* imprison

jiān shì 监视 *v* monitor, spy

jiān shì 监视 *n* watch

jiān tīng 监听 *v* monitor

jiān yù 监狱 *n* prison

jiān yù zhǎng 监狱长 *n* warden

jiān mò de 缄默的 *adj* mute

jiān dàn 煎蛋 *n* omelet

jiān guō 煎锅 *n* frying pan

jiǎn pǔ 俭朴 *adj* frugal

jiǎn 减 *v* subtract

jiǎn chú 减除 n deduction
jiǎn chú é 减除额 n deduction
jiǎn fǎ 减法 n subtraction
jiǎn qīng 减轻 v alleviate, mitigate
jiǎn qīng 减轻 n relax
jiǎn qù 减去 v extract
jiǎn qù de 减去的 adj minus
jiǎn ruò 减弱 v waver, weaken
jiǎn shǎo 减少 v bring down, decline, decrease, ebb, reduce, wane
jiǎn shǎo 减少 n decline, decrease
jiǎn xiǎo 减小 v downsize
jiǎn xiǎo de 减小的 adj attenuating
jiǎn 剪 iv cut, shear
jiǎn dāo 剪刀 n scissors
jiǎn yǐng 剪影 n silhouette
jiǎn chá 检查 v check, inspect
jiǎn chá 检查 n inspection
jiǎn chá yuán 检查员 n inspector
jiǎn chá guān 检察官 n prosecutor
jiǎn kòng 检控 v prosecute
jiǎn xiū 检修 v overhaul
jiǎn yàn 检验 n check up
jiǎn yàn 检验 v screen
jiǎn bào 简报 n briefing
jiǎn dān 简单 n simplicity
jiǎn dān de 简单的 adj plain, simple
jiǎn dān de 简单地 adv plainly, simply
jiǎn duǎn de 简短的 adj brief
jiǎn duǎn de 简短地 adv briefly

jiǎn huà 简化 v simplify
jiǎn jié 简洁 n brevity
jiǎn jié de 简洁的 adj concise, terse
jiǎn jiè 简介 n profile
jiǎn lòu de 简陋的 adj austere
jiǎn pǔ de 简朴的 adj austere
jiǎn xùn 简讯 n bulletin
jiàn 见 iv see
jiàn miàn 见面 iv meet
jiàn zhèng rén 见证人 n eyewitness
jiàn 件 n piece
jiàn lì 建立 v establish
jiàn shè 建设 iv build
jiàn shè 建设 n construction
jiàn shè xìng de 建设性的 adj constructive
jiàn shè zhě 建设者 n builder
jiàn yì 建议 n advice, proposal, suggestion
jiàn yì 建议 v advise, suggest
jiàn zào 建造 iv build
jiàn zào 建造 v construct
jiàn zhù 建筑 n architecture, building
jiàn zhù gōng rén 建筑工人 n builder
jiàn zhù shī 建筑师 n architect
jiàn zhù zhě 建筑者 n builder
jiàn dié 间谍 n spy
jiàn dié huó dòng 间谍活动 n espionage
jiàn gé 间隔 n break, interval
jiàn jiē de 间接的 adj indirect

jiàn 剑 *n* sword
jiàn bǐng 剑柄 *n* hilt
jiàn kāng 健康 *n* health
jiàn kāng 健康 *adj* healthy
jiàn shēn 健身 *n* fitness
jiàn shēn 健身 *v* work out
jiàn shēn fáng 健身房 *n* gymnasium
jiàn tán 健谈 *adj* talkative
jiàn wàng zhèng 健忘症 *n* amnesia
jiàn zhuàng de 健壮的 *adj* robust
jiàn duì 舰队 *n* fleet
jiàn jìn shì de 渐进式的 *adj* progressive
jiàn 溅 *v* splash
jiàn tà 践踏 *v* trample
jiàn dìng 鉴定 *v* identify
jiàn pán 键盘 *n* keyboard
jiàn 箭 *n* arrow
jiàn yú 箭鱼 *n* swordfish
jiāng fā shēng de 将发生的 *adj* impending
jiāng lái de 将来的 *adj* coming
jiàng hu 浆糊 *n* paste
jiāng jú 僵局 *adj* deadlock
jiāng jú 僵局 *n* stalemate
jiāng yìng de 僵硬的 *v* iron
jiǎng dào 讲道 *n* homily
jiǎng huà 讲话 *n* speech
jiǎng jià 讲价 *n* bargaining
jiǎng tái 讲台 *n* lectern
jiǎng tán 讲坛 *n* pulpit
jiǎng 奖 *n* award, prize
jiǎng bēi 奖杯 *n* trophy
jiǎng jīn 奖金 *n* bonus
jiǎng lì 奖励 *v* award, reward
jiǎng lì 奖励 *n* incentive
jiǎng pǐn 奖品 *n* award, garland, reward
jiǎng xué jīn 奖学金 *n* fellowship, scholarship
jiǎng zhāng 奖章 *n* medallion
jiǎng 桨 *n* oar
jiàng 匠 *n* smith
jiàng dī 降低 *v* debase, diminish
jiàng dī shēn fèn 降低身份 *v* degrade
jiàng dī shēn fèn de 降低身份的 *adj* demeaning
jiàng gé 降格 *n* degradation
jiàng jí 降级 *v* demote
jiàng lín 降临 *v* descend
jiàng luò sǎn 降落伞 *n* parachute
jiàng wēn 降温 *v* cool down
jiàng xuě 降雪 *n* snowfall
jiàng yǔ liàng 降雨量 *n* rainfall
jiàng zhí 降职 *v* demote
jiāo 交 *v* turn in
jiāo chā 交叉 *n* crossing
jiāo chā diǎn 交叉点 *n* crossing
jiāo cuò 交错 *v* cross
jiāo cuò de 交错的 *adj* cross
jiāo gěi 交给 *v* hand in
jiāo huàn 交换 *v* exchange, swap
jiāo huàn 交换 *n* swap, bargain, deal
jiāo huǒ 交火 *n* crossfire
jiāo liú 交流 *v* communicate
jiāo liú 交流 *n* communication, communion

jiāo péng yǒu 交朋友 *v* befriend
jiāo shè 交涉 *v* intercede
jiāo tán 交谈 *n* conversation
jiāo tán 交谈 *v* converse, talk
jiāo tì 交替 *v* alternate
jiāo tì de 交替的 *adj* alternate
jiāo tōng （liàng） 交通（量） *n* traffic
jiāo tuō 交托 *n* commitment
jiāo wǎng huò guān xì 交往或关系 *n* dealings
jiāo xiǎng qǔ 交响曲 *n* symphony
jiāo yì 交易 *iv* deal
jiāo yì 交易 *n* transaction
jiāo zhī 交织 *v* intertwine
jiāo 教 *iv* teach
jiāo qū 郊区 *n* outskirts, suburb
jiāo yóu 郊游 *n* outing
jiāo ruò 娇弱 *n* delicacy
jiāo shuǐ 浇水 *v* water
jiāo ào 骄傲 *n* pride
jiāo ào de 骄傲的 *adj* proud
jiāo ào zì dà de 骄傲自大的 *adj* overbearing
jiāo guǎn 胶管 *n* hose
jiāo náng 胶囊 *n* capsule
jiāo shuǐ 胶水 *n* glue
jiāo zhān 胶粘 *v* glue
jiāo diǎn 焦点 *n* focus
jiāo lǜ 焦虑 *n* anxiety
jiāo yóu 焦油 *n* tar
jiāo shí 礁石 *n* reef
jiāo dù 角度 *n* angle
jiāo luò 角落 *n* corner
jiāo huá 狡猾 *adj* foxy

jiǎo huá de 狡猾的 *adj* cunning
jiǎo huá de 狡猾的 *adj* devious, sly
jiǎo xiá de 狡黠地 *adv* knowingly
jiǎo 绞 *iv* wring
jiǎo jià 绞架 *n* gallows
jiǎo tòng 绞痛 *n* colic
jiǎo zhèng 矫正 *v* rectify
jiǎo 脚 *n* feet, foot
jiǎo bù 脚步 *n* footstep
jiǎo jiān 脚尖 *n* tiptoe
jiǎo shǒu jià 脚手架 *n* scaffolding
jiǎo tà shí dì 脚踏实地 *adj* down-to-earth
jiǎo zhǐ 脚趾 *n* toe
jiǎo zhù 脚注 *n* footnote
jiǎo liàn 铰链 *v* hinge
jiǎo liàn 铰链 *n* hinge
jiǎo bàn 搅拌 *v* scramble, stir
jiǎo bàn jī 搅拌机 *n* blender, mixer
jiǎo huò wù 缴获物 *n* booty
jiǎo xiè 缴械 *n* disarmament
jiào 叫 *v* cry
jiào hǎn 叫喊 *v* yell
jiào shēng 叫声 *n* cry, crying
jiào chē 轿车 *n* saloon
jiào gāo de 较高的 *adj* superior
jiào shǎo de 较少的 *adj* lesser
jiào duì 校对 *n* check up
jiào zhǔn 校准 *v* calibrate
jiào kē shū 教科书 *n* textbook
jiào liàn 教练 *n* coach, trainer
jiào qū 教区 *n* parish
jiào qū jū mín 教区居民 *n* parishioner

jiào shī 教师 *n* teacher
jiào shì 教室 *n* classroom
jiào shòu 教授 *n* professor
jiào táng 教堂 *n* church
jiào tiáo huà 教条化 *adj* dogmatic
jiào xùn 教训 *n* lesson
jiào yì 教义 *n* creed, doctrine
jiào yì wèn dá shū 教义问答书 *n* catechism
jiào yù 教育 *v* educate
jiào yù de 教育的 *adj* educational
jiào yù xué 教育学 *n* pedagogy
jiào zhí gōng 教职工 *n* faculty
jiào zōng 教宗 *n* pontiff, Pope
jiào mǔ 酵母 *n* yeast
jiē duàn 阶段 *n* phase, stage
jiē jí 阶级 *n* class
jiē tī 阶梯 *n* ladder, stepladder
jiē 接 *v* pick
jiē chù 接触 *v* touch on
jiē guǎn 接管 *v* take over
jiē jìn 接近 *n* access, approach, proximity
jiē jìn 接近 *v* approach
jiē jìn 接近 *pre* close to
jiē lì bàng 接力棒 *n* baton
jiē nà 接纳 *v* admit
jiē rǎng 接壤 *v* border on
jiē shēng pó 接生婆 *n* midwife
jiē shòu 接受 *v* accept, take in, undergo
jiē shòu 接受 *n* acceptance
jiē shòu néng lì qiáng de 接受能力强的 *adj* receptive
jiē shòu péi xùn rén yuán 接受培训人员 *n* trainee

jiē xià de 接下的 *adj* next
jiē xià lái 接下来 *c* whereupon
jiē zhòng 接种 *v* vaccinate
jiē chuān 揭穿 *v* debunk
jiē lù 揭露 *v* expose, uncover
jiē mù 揭幕 *v* unveil
jiē 街 *n* street
jiē chē 街车 *n* streetcar
jiē qū 街区 *n* block
jié jiǎn 节俭 *n* austerity, frugality
jié jiǎn de 节俭的 *adj* thrifty
jié jiǎn de 节俭地 *adv* sparingly
jié lù 节录 *v* brief
jié lù 节录 *n* excerpt
jié mù 节目 *n* program
jié rì 节日 *adj* festive
jié rì 节日 *n* festivity
jié yuē 节约 *v* economize
jié zhì 节制 *v* abstain, mortify
jié zhì 节制 *n* abstinence, mortification
jié zòu 节奏 *n* pace, rhythm
jié chí （yóu zhǐ jié jī） 劫持（尤指劫机） *v* hijack
jié chí （yóu zhǐ jié jī） 劫持（尤指劫机） *n* hijack
jié jī fàn 劫机犯 *n* hijacker
jié chū de 杰出的 *adj* illustrious
jié zuò 杰作 *n* masterpiece
jié jìng 洁净 *n* cleanliness
jié 结 *n* knot
jié cháng 结肠 *n* colon
jié gòu 结构 *n* structure, texture
jié guǒ 结果 *n* effect, outcome, result

J

jié guǒ 结果 *v* end up
jié guǒ shì 结果是 *v* turn out
jié hé 结合 *v* combine, conjugate
jié hūn 结婚 *v* marry, wed
jié hūn de 结婚的 *adj* conjugal
jié kuài 结块 *v* agglomerate
jié lùn 结论 *n* conclusion
jié lùn xìng de 结论性的 *adj* demonstrative
jiē shi de 结实的 *adj* burly, compact
jié shù 结束 *v* conclude, wind up
jié shù 结束 *n* conclusion
jié wěi 结尾 *n* conclusion, ending
jié bào 捷豹 *n* jaguar
jié jìng 捷径 *n* shortcut
jié máo 睫毛 *n* eyelash
jié zhī 截肢 *v* amputate
jié zhī 截肢 *n* amputation
jié zhǐ qī xiàn 截止期限 *n* deadline
tā 她 *adj* her
tā 她 *pro* she
tā de 她的 *pro* hers
tā zì jǐ 她自己 *pro* herself
jiě fu 姐夫 *n* brother-in-law
jiě chú 解除 *v* relieve
jiě chú wǔ zhuāng 解除武装 *v* disarm
jiě dòng 解冻 *v* thaw
jiě dòng 解冻 *n* thaw
jiě dú jì 解毒剂 *n* antidote
jiě fàng 解放 *v* emancipate, liberate
jiě fàng 解放 *n* liberation
jiě gù 解雇 *n* dismissal

jiě gù 解雇 *v* sack
jiě jiù 解救 *v* extricate
jiě jué 解决 *v* resolve, solve, tackle, workout
jiě jué 解决 *n* settlement
jiě jué fāng àn 解决方案 *n* solution
jiě kāi 解开 *v* disentangle, undo, unfasten, unleash, unravel, untie, unwind
jiě kě 解渴 *v* quench
jiě kòu 解扣 *v* unbutton
[jiě]luǎn cháo [解]卵巢 *n* ovary
jiě pōu 解剖 *n* anatomy
jiě pōu xué 解剖学 *n* anatomy
jiě sàn 解散 *v* disband, dismiss, dissolve
jiě sàn 解散 *n* dissolution
jiě shì 解释 *v* account for, explain, fathom out, interpret
jiě tǐ 解体 *n* disintegration
jiè cí 介词 *n* preposition
jiè rù 介入 *v* intervene
jiè shào 介绍 *v* introduce
jiè shào 介绍 *n* introduction
jiè yì 介意 *v* mind
jiè 戒 *iv* quit
jiè jiǔ 戒酒 *n* abstinence
jiè jué 戒绝 *v* abstain
jiè lù 戒律 *n* commandment
jiè yán 戒严 *n* curfew
jiè zhi 戒指 *n* ring
jiè mo 芥末 *n* mustard
jiè 借 *v* borrow
jiè 借 *n* debit

jiè chū 借出 _iv_ lend
jiè fāng 借方 _n_ debit
jiè kǒu 借口 _n_ excuse
jīn tiān 今天 _adv_ today
jīn wǎn 今晚 _adv_ tonight
jīn （huáng）sè de 金（黄）色
  的 _adj_ golden
jīn de 金的 _adj_ golden
jīn é 金额 _n_ amount
jīn fà de 金发的 _adj_ blond
jīn qiāng yú 金枪鱼 _n_ tuna
jīn róng 金融 _adj_ financial
jīn sī què 金丝雀 _n_ canary
jīn yín cái bǎo 金银财宝 _n_
  treasure
jīn zhì de 金制的 _adj_ golden
jīn shǔ 金属 _n_ metal
jīn shǔ de 金属的 _adj_ metallic
jīn zì tǎ 金字塔 _n_ pyramid
jīn tiē 津贴 _n_ allowance
jǐn jǐn 仅仅 _adv_ barely
jǐn còu de 紧凑的 _adj_ compact
jǐn de 紧的 _adj_ tight
jǐn gù 紧固 _v_ fasten
jǐn jí 紧急 _n_ emergency, urgency
jǐn jí de 紧急的 _n_ instant
jǐn jí de 紧急的 _adj_ urgent
jǐn mì de 紧密的 _adj_ compact
jǐn tiē 紧贴 _iv_ cling
jǐn zhān 紧粘 _v_ adhere
jǐn zhāng 紧张 _adj_ strained
jǐn zhāng 紧张 _n_ tension
jǐn zhāng de 紧张的 _adj_ intense,
  tense, uptight
jǐn zhuā 紧抓 _v_ clinch

jǐn shèn 谨慎 _n_ caution,
  discretion, prudence
jǐn shèn de 谨慎的 _adj_ cautious,
  discreet, prudent
jǐn biāo sài 锦标赛 _n_ tournament
jǐn guǎn 尽管 _c_ despite
jǐn guǎn 尽管 _n_ spite
jǐn guǎn rú cǐ 尽管如此 _c_
  nonetheless
jìn lì 尽力 _v_ endeavor
jìn lì 尽力 _n_ endeavor
jìn liàng jiǎn shǎo 尽量减少 _v_
  minimize
jìn tóu 尽头 _n_ dead end
jìn 近 _pre_ near
jìn chù 近处 _n_ vicinity
jìn lái 近来 _adv_ lately
jìn shi de 近视的 _adj_ myopic,
  nearsighted
jìn sì de 近似的 _adj_ approximate
jìn 进 _v_ get in
jìn gōng 进攻 _n_ aggression,
  offense
jìn gōng de 进攻的 _adj_ offensive
jìn kǒu 进口 _v_ import
jìn kǒu 进口 _n_ importation
jìn kǒu shuì 进口税 _n_ customs
jìn lái 进来 _v_ come in
jìn rù 进入 _n_ admittance, entree,
  entry
jìn rù 进入 _v_ enter
jìn rù de quán lì 进入的权利 _n_
  access
jìn shuǐ zhá 进水闸 _n_ intake
jìn tuì liǎng nán de 进退两难的
  adj stranded

J

jìn xíng 进行 *v* carry on, conduct, proceed, process

jìn yī bù 进一步 *adv* further

jìn zhǎn 进展 *n* headway, progress

jìn zhǎn 进展 *v* progress

jìn shēng 晋升 *v* elevate

jìn shēng 晋升 *n* elevation

jìn pào 浸泡 *v* soak

jìn tòu 浸透 *v* soak up

jìn bì 禁闭 *v* confine, incarcerate

jìn bì 禁闭 *n* confinement

jìn lìng 禁令 *n* ban

jìn shí 禁食 *n* abstinence

jìn yù 禁欲 *n* celibacy

jìn yù de 禁欲的 *adj* stoic

jìn zhǐ 禁止 *v* ban, forbid, outlast, prohibit, refrain, restrict

jìn zhǐ 禁止 *n* prohibition

jīng diǎn de 经典的 *adj* classic

jīng dù 经度 *n* longing

jīng jì 经济 *n* economy

jīng jì shí huì 经济实惠 *adj* economical

jīng jì shuāi tuì 经济衰退 *n* recession

jīng jiǔ 经久 *v* outlaw

jīng jiǔ bú shuāi de 经久不衰的 *adj* unfailing

jīng lǐ 经理 *n* manager

jīng lì 经历 *v* go through

jīng xiāo 经销 *n* agency

jīng xiāo shāng 经销商 *n* agent, dealer

jīng yàn 经验 *n* experience

jīng yàn bú zú de 经验不足的 *adj* inexperienced

jīng yíng 经营 *v* operate

jīng è 惊愕 *n* dismay

jīng hài de 惊骇的 *adj* aghast

jīng kǒng 惊恐 *n* horror

jīng qí 惊奇 *n* amazement, surprise

jīng rén de 惊人的 *adj* alarming, astonishing, breathtaking, stunning, wonderful

jīng sǒng de 惊悚的 *adj* spooky

jīng tàn 惊叹 *v* exclaim

jīng xǐ 惊喜 *v* surprise

jīng xià 惊吓 *v* startle

jīng xiǎn de 惊险的 *adj* breathtaking

jīng zhuàng tǐ 晶状体 *n* lens

jīng cǎi de 精彩的 *adj* marvelous

jīng dù 精度 *n* accuracy

jīng lì 精力 *n* energy

jīng lì chōng pèi 精力充沛 *adj* energetic

jīng liàn chǎng 精炼厂 *n* refinery

jīng měi 精美 *n* delicacy

jīng měi de 精美的 *adj* delicate

jīng mì 精密 *n* precision

jīng míng 精明 *adj* astute, shrewd

jīng pí lì jìn 精疲力尽 *adj* exhausting

jīng pí lì jìn 精疲力尽 *n* exhaustion

jīng què de 精确的 *adj* precise

jīng què dù 精确度 *n* definition

jīng shén 精神 *n* mentality, spirit

jīng shén biàn tài zhě 精神变态者 *n* psychopath

jīng shén bìng xué 精神病学 *n* psychiatry

jīng shén cuò luàn 精神错乱 *n* lunacy

jīng shén de 精神的 *adj* mental, spiritual

jīng shén kē yī shī 精神科医师 *n* psychiatrist

jīng shén shàng 精神上 *adv* mentally

jīng tōng 精通 *n* mastery, proficiency

jīng tōng de 精通的 *adj* proficient

jīng zhì de 精致的 *adj* exquisite

jīng zǐ 精子 *n* sperm

jīng yú 鲸鱼 *n* whale

jǐng 井 *n* well

jǐng bù 颈部 *n* neck

jǐng diǎn 景点 *n* attraction

jǐng guān 景观 *n* landscape

jǐng qì 景气 *n* boom

jǐng sè de 景色的 *adj* scenic

（jǐng wù děng de） qián jǐng （景物等的）前景 *n* foreground

jǐng bào 警报 *n* alarm, alert

jǐng bào qì 警报器 *n* siren

jǐng chá 警察 *n* cop, police, policeman

jǐng gào 警告 *v* warn

jǐng gào 警告 *n* warning

jǐng gùn 警棍 *n* baton

jǐng jiè xiàn 警戒线 *n* cordon

jìng 净 *n* net

jìng huà 净化 *n* purification

jìng huà 净化 *v* purify

jìng xiàng 径向 *v* drive at

jìng luán 痉挛 *n* convulsion, spasm

jìng jì chǎng 竞技场 *n* arena

jìng sài 竞赛 *n* contest

jìng zhēng 竞争 *v* compete, contend

jìng zhēng 竞争 *n* competition, rivalry

jìng zhēng de 竞争的 *adj* competitive

jìng zhēng duì shǒu 竞争对手 *n* competitor

jìng zhēng zhě 竞争者 *n* contender

jìng wèi 敬畏 *n* awe

jìng yì 敬意 *n* homage

jìng jì xià lái 静寂下来 *v* hush up

jìng mài 静脉 *n* vein

jìng mài nèi de 静脉内的 *adj* intravenous

jìng zhǐ bù dòng de 静止不动的 *adj* stationary

jìng zhǐ de 静止的 *adj* still

jìng zi 镜子 *n* looking glass, mirror

jiū chán 纠缠 *iv* dwell, entangle

jiū fēn 纠纷 *n* tangle

jiū zhèng 纠正 *v* correct

jiū 鸠 *n* dove

jiǔ 九 *adj* nine

jiǔ shí 九十 *adj* ninety

jiǔ yuè 九月 *n* September

jiǔ 酒 *n* booze, liquor, wine

jiǔ ba 酒吧 *n* bar

jiǔ ba nǚ 酒吧女 *n* barmaid

jiǔ ba shì zhě 酒吧侍者 *n* bartender

jiǔ bǎo 酒保 *n* barman

jiǔ diàn 酒店 *n* hotel

jiǔ guǎn 酒馆 *n* tavern

jiǔ jīng de 酒精的 *adj* alcoholic

jiǔ jīng zhòng dú 酒精中毒 alcoholism

jiù bù 旧布 *n* rag

jiù 救 *v* put out

jiù hù chē 救护车 *n* ambulance

jiù jì 救济 *n* alms

jiù shēng yuán 救生员 *n* lifeguard

jiù shì zhǔ 救世主 *n* Messiah, savior

jiù shú 救赎 *n* salvation

jiù yuán 救援 *v* rescue

jiù cān shí duàn 就餐时段 *n* sitting

jiù yào lái de 就要来的 *adj* coming

jiù yè 就业 *n* employment

jiù zhí 就职 *n* inauguration

jiù 鹫 *n* buzzard

jū liú dì 居留地 *n* settlement

jū mín 居民 *n* inhabitant

jū zhōng 居中 *v* center

jū zhù 居住 *iv* dwell, inhabit, reside

jū zhù 居住 *n* residence

jū zhù zhě 居住者 *n* occupant

jū liú 拘留 *n* custody, detention

jū shù 拘束 *n* uneasiness

jū jī shǒu 狙击手 *n* sniper

jū gōng 鞠躬 *v* bow

jū gōng 鞠躬 *n* bow

jú 局 *n* bureau

jú cù de 局促的 *adj* cramped

jú wài rén 局外人 *n* outsider

jú zi 桔子 *n* tangerine

jǔ jué 咀嚼 *v* munch

jǔ sàng 沮丧 *n* depression, dismay, frustration

jǔ sàng de 沮丧的 *adj* dejected, despondent

jǔ bàn 举办 *v* stage

jǔ bào rén 举报人 *n* informer

jǔ dòng 举动 *n* conduct

jǔ lì 举例 *n* example

jǔ lì zhèng míng 举例证明 *v* exemplify

jǔ qǐ 举起 *v* elevate, hoist

jǔ zhǐ 举止 *n* demeanor

jù 句 *n* sentence

jù biàn 巨变 *n* cataclysm

jù dà 巨大 *adj* enormous, huge

jù dà 巨大 *n* immensity

jù dà de 巨大的 *adj* colossal, immense, monstrous, prodigious, stupendous, tremendous

jù kū 巨窟 *n* cavern

jù mǎng 巨蟒 *n* python

jù rén 巨人 *n* giant

jù xíng 巨型 *adj* gigantic

jù jué 拒绝 *n* denial, rebuff, refusal, refuse, rejection

jù jué 拒绝 *v* rebuff, refuse, reject, turn down

jù tǐ de 具体的 *adj* concrete, specific

jù lè bù 俱乐部 *n* club
jù běn 剧本 *n* scenario, script
jù liè de 剧烈的 *adj* acute
jù qíng shuō míng shū 剧情说明书 *n* scenario
jù tòng 剧痛 *n* pang
jù bào dào 据报道 *adv* reportedly
jù chēng 据称 *adv* allegedly
jù shuō 据说 *adv* reputedly
jù lí 距离 *n* distance
jù fēng 飓风 *n* hurricane
jù 锯 *iv* saw
jù liàn 锯链 *n* chainsaw
jù zi 锯子 *n* saw
jù guāng dēng 聚光灯 *n* spotlight
jù hé 聚合 *v* converge
jù huì 聚会 *v* gather
jù huì 聚会 *n* gathering
jù jī 聚积 *n* buildup
jù jí 聚集 *v* congregate
juān zèng 捐赠 *v* donate
juān zèng 捐赠 *n* donation
juān zèng rén 捐赠人 *n* donor
juān zèng zhě 捐赠者 *n* benefactor
juān liú 涓流 *v* trickle
juǎn 卷 *v* roll
juǎn qū 卷曲 *v* curl
juǎn qū 卷曲 *n* curl
juǎn qū de 卷曲的 *adj* curly
juàn zhóu 卷轴 *n* reel, scroll
jué dìng 决定 *v* decide
jué dìng 决定 *n* decision
jué dìng xìng de 决定性的 *adj* conclusive, deciding, decisive

jué dòu 决斗 *n* duel
jué xīn 决心 *n* determination
jué yì 决议 *n* resolution
jué qiào 诀窍 *n* know-how
jué bù huì cuò de 绝不会错的 *adj* infallible
jué duì 绝对 *adj* absolute
jué duì bù kě kào de 绝对不可靠的 *adj* infallible
jué jì de 绝迹的 *adj* extinct
jué wàng 绝望 *n* despair
jué wàng de 绝望的 *adj* desperate, hopeless
jué yuán 绝缘 *v* insulate
jué yuán tǐ 绝缘体 *n* insulation
jué chá（lì） 觉察（力）*n* perception
jué xǐng 觉醒 *n* disillusion
jué jiàng de 倔强的 *adj* adamant
jiáo 嚼 *v* chew
jué dòu shì 角斗士 *n* gladiator
jūn bèi 军备 *n* armaments
jūn duì 军队 *n* army
jūn huǒ 军火 *n* ammunition
jūn jiàn 军舰 *n* warship
jūn shì 军士 *n* sergeant
jūn tuán 军团 *n* legion, regiment
jūn xiè kù 军械库 *n* arsenal
jūn yíng 军营 *n* barracks
jūn zhǔ 君主 *n* monarch
jūn zhǔ lì xiàn zhì 君主立宪制 *n* monarchy
jūn yī 均一 *n* uniformity
jūn yún de 均匀的 *adj* even

J

K

kā fēi 咖啡 *n* coffee

kā fēi yīn 咖啡因 *n* caffeine

kǎ 卡 *n* card

kǎ chē 卡车 *n* truck

kǎ chē sī jī 卡车司机 *n* trucker

kǎ lù lǐ 卡路里 *n* calorie

kǎ tōng 卡通 *n* cartoon

kāi 开 *n* carat

kāi chē 开车 *iv* drive

kāi chú 开除 *n* expulsion

kāi chǔ fāng 开处方 *v* prescribe

kāi fā 开发 *v* develop

kāi fā lì yòng 开发利用 *n* exploitation

kāi fàng 开放 *v* open up

kāi guān 开关 *v* switch

kāi guān 开关 *n* switch

kāi guàn qì 开罐器 *n* can opener

kāi huā 开花 *v* blossom

kāi huǒ 开火 *v* fire

kāi kěn 开垦 *v* reclaim

kāi míng de 开明的 *adj* open-minded

kāi mù 开幕 *n* opening

kāi qiāng dǎ shāng 开枪打伤 *v* gun down

kāi qiú 开球 *n* kickoff

kāi shǐ 开始 *iv* begin, commerce, get down to, set about, set out, start

kāi shǐ 开始 *n* beginning, start

kāi shǐ de 开始的 *adj* initial

kāi shǐ gōng zuò 开始工作 *v* embark

kāi shì 开释 *v* acquit

kāi suǒ 开锁 *v* unlock

kāi wán xiào 开玩笑 *v* joke

kāi wèi jiǔ 开胃酒 *n* aperitif

kāi wèi shí pǐn 开胃食品 *n* appetizer

kāi xiāo 开销 *n* spending

kāi xiǎo chāi 开小差 *v* space out

kǎi xuán 凯旋 *n* triumph

kǎi tǐ zì 楷体字 *adj* italics

kàn 看 *n* look

kàn 看 *v* look, look at, view, watch

kàn chū 看出 *v* discern

kàn chuān 看穿 *adj* see-through

kàn dào 看到 *iv* saw

kān de jiàn de 看得见的 *adj* visible

kàn fǎ 看法 *n* view

kān guǎn rén 看管人 *n* custodian

kàn jiàn 看见 *v* spot

kàn lái 看来 *v* appear, seem

kān shǒu 看守 *n* watch

kān shǒu rén 看守人 *n* caretaker

kàn tái 看台 *n* grandstand

kāng fù zhōng de 康复中的 *adj* convalescent

kāng nǎi xīn 康乃馨 *n* carnation

kāng kǎi 慷慨 *n* bounty, generosity

kàng shēng sù 抗生素 *n* antibiotic

kàng yì 抗议 *v* protest

kàng yì 抗议 *n* protest

kǎo gǔ xué 考古学 *n* archaeology

kǎo lǜ 考虑 *v* consider
kǎo lǜ 考虑 *n* consideration
kǎo shì 考试 *n* examination
kǎo bèi 拷贝 *n* copy
kǎo bèi 拷贝 *v* copy
kǎo jià 烤架 *n* barbecue
kǎo lú 烤炉 *n* baker
kǎo miàn bāo 烤面包 *v* toast
kǎo miàn bāo 烤面包 *n* toast
kǎo miàn bāo de rén 烤面包的人 *n* toaster
kǎo miàn bāo jī 烤面包机 *n* toaster
kǎo qì 烤器 *n* broiler
kǎo ròu 烤肉 *n* barbecue
kǎo shú de ròu 烤熟的肉 *n* roast
kào 靠 *n* leaning
kào chuán wù 靠船坞 *v* dock
kào diàn 靠垫 *n* cushion
kào jìn de 靠近的 *adj* close
kào zài 靠在 *v* lean on
kē kè 苛刻 *adj* harsh
kē kè 苛刻 *n* harshness
kē qiú de 苛求的 *adj* demanding
kē zé 苛责 *n* culpability
kē jì 科技 *n* technology
kē xué 科学 *n* science
kē xué de 科学的 *adj* scientific
kē xué jiā 科学家 *n* scientist
kē shuì 瞌睡 *n* doze
ké 壳 *n* shell
ké sou 咳嗽 *n* cough
ké sou 咳嗽 *v* cough
kě ài de 可爱的 *adj* adorable, cunning, cute, lovable, lovely

kě bǐ de 可比的 *adj* comparable
kě cǎi nà de 可采纳的 *adj* admissible
kě chāi xiè de 可拆卸的 *adj* detachable
kě chéng shòu de 可承受的 *adj* bearable
kě chǐ de 可耻的 *adj* disgraceful, shameful
kě chǔ lǐ de 可处理的 *adj* manageable
kě chù zhī de 可触知的 *adj* palpable
kě tiáo de 可调的 *adj* adjustable
kě fá de 可罚的 *adj* punishable
kě fèn kāi de 可分开的 *adj* divisible
kě gēng zhòng de 可耕种的 *adj* arable
kě guān de 可观的 *adj* considerable
kě guǎn lǐ de 可管理的 *adj* manageable
kě hèn 可恨 *adj* hateful
kě jì chéng de 可继承的 *adj* hereditary
kě jiàn xìng 可见性 *n* visibility
kě jiē jìn de 可接近的 *adj* accessible, approachable
kě jiē shòu de 可接受的 *adj* acceptable
kě jiě shì de 可解释的 *adj* accountable
kě jìn rù de 可进入的 *adj* accessible

K

kě jìng zhòng de 可敬重的 *adj*
adorable

kě jū zhù 可居住 *adj* habitable

kě jū zhù de 可居住的 *adj*
inhabitable

kě kǎ yīn 可卡因 *n* cocaine

kě kào de 可靠的 *adj* dependable,
reliable

kě kě fěn 可可粉 *n* cocoa

kě kòu chú de 可扣除的 *adj*
deductible

kě lián de 可怜的 *adj* pathetic,
pitiful, wretched

kě néng de 可能的 *adv* likely

kě néng de 可能的 *adj* possible,
probable

kě néng fā shēng de shì 可能发
生的事 *n* eventuality

kě néng xìng 可能性 *n*
eventuality, likelihood, odds,
possibility

kě nì zhuǎn de 可逆转的 *adj*
reversible

kě pà 可怕 *adj* dreadful, fearful,
frightening, ghastly

kě pà de 可怕的 *adj* appalling,
awful, dire, dreaded, eerie,
horrendous, horrible, scary,
shocking, terrible, terrific,
terrifying

kě qǔ de 可取的 *adj* advisable,
desirable

kě rán wù 可燃物 *n* combustible

kě rèn yì chǔ lǐ de 可任意处理的
adj disposable

kě róng rěn de 可容忍的 *adj*
tolerable

kě róng de 可溶的 *adj* soluble

kě shí de 可食的 *adj* edible

kě shǐ yòng de 可使用的 *adj*
accessible

kě tīng jiàn de 可听见的 *adj*
audible

kě xī 可惜 *n* pity

kě xī 可惜 *v* shame

kě xǐ de 可洗的 *adj* washable

kě xǐ de 可喜的 *adj* gratifying

kě xiào de 可笑的 *adj* laughable,
ludicrous, ridiculous

kě xìn de 可信的 *adj* believable,
credible

kě xìn dù 可信度 *n* credibility

kě xìn lài de 可信赖的 *adj*
dependable

kě xíng 可行 *adj* feasible

kě xíng de 可行的 *adj* workable

kě yí de 可疑的 *adl* doubtful, fishy,
questionable, suspicious

kě yǐ 可以 *iv* can

kě yǐ 可以 *adv* okay

kě yǐ bì miǎn de 可以避免的 *adj*
avoidable

kě yǐ lǐ jiě de 可以理解的 *adj*
understandable

kě yǐ rèn xuǎn de 可以任选的 *adj*
optional

kě yǐ shí xiàn de 可以实现的 *adj*
attainable

kě yǐ yuán liàng 可以原谅 *adj*
forgivable

kě yǐ zuò 可以做 *iv* may

kě yǐn yòng de 可饮用的 *adj* drinkable

kě yòng de 可用的 *adj* available

kě yòng xìng 可用性 *n* availability

kě zēng de 可憎的 *adj* detestable, heinous

kě zhēng lùn de 可争论的 *adj* debatable

kě zhī pèi de 可支配的 *adj* disposable

kě zhì yù de 可治愈的 *adj* curable

kě qiú 渴求 *n* craving

kě wàng 渴望 *v* aspire, covet, crave, desire

kě wàng 渴望 *n* desire, eagerness, lust, aspiration

kě wàng 渴望 *adj* long

kě wàng 渴望 *v* thirst, yearn

kě wàng de 渴望的 *adj* eager

kè 克 *n* gram

kè fú 克服 *v* overcome

kè lā 克拉 *n* carat

kè lóng 克隆 *v* clone

kè lóng 克隆 *n* cloning

kè zhì 克制 *n* restraint

kè bó 刻薄 *n* meanness

kè bó de 刻薄的 *adj* mean

kè hén yú 刻痕于 *v* score

kè miàn 刻面 *n* facet

kè cāng 客舱 *n* cabin

kè chē xiāng 客车厢 *n* carriage

kè guān de 客观的 *adj* impersonal

kè guān de 客观的 *n* objective

kè hù 客户 *n* client, clientele

kè rén 客人 *n* guest

kè tīng 客厅 *n* living room

kè zhàn 客栈 *n* inn

kè 课 *n* class

kè chéng 课程 *n* course, lesson

kěn dìng 肯定 *adj* sure

kěn dìng 肯定 *adv* surely

kěn dìng de 肯定的 *adj* affirmative

kěn qǐng 恳请 *v* implore

kěn qiú 恳求 *iv* beseech, plead

kěn 啃 *v* gnaw

kēng 坑 *n* pit

kēng dòng 坑洞 *n* pothole

kōng de 空的 *adj* empty, hollow, vacant

kōng jiān 空间 *n* space

kōng qì 空气 *n* air

kōng shǒu dào 空手道 *n* karate

kōng xū 空虚 *n* emptiness

kōng yóu 空邮 *n* airmail

kōng zhōng xiǎo jiě 空中小姐 *n* stewardess

kǒng què 孔雀 *n* peacock

kǒng xì 孔隙 *n* pore

kǒng bù 恐怖 *adj* grisly

kǒng bù 恐怖 *n* terror

kǒng bù zhèng 恐怖症 *n* phobia

kǒng bù zhǔ yì 恐怖主义 *n* terrorism

kǒng bù zhǔ yì zhě 恐怖主义者 *n* terrorist

kǒng huāng 恐慌 *n* panic

kǒng jù 恐惧 *v* dread, horrify

kǒng jù 恐惧 *n* fear, fright

kǒng lóng 恐龙 *n* dinosaur

K

kǒng hè 恐吓 *v* intimidate, terrify, terrorize

kòng bái de 空白的 *adj* blank

kòng chū 空出 *v* vacate

kòng wèi 空位 *n* vacancy

kòng xián de 空闲的 *adj* idle, unoccupied

kòng gào 控告 *v* sue

kòng zhì 控制 *v* command, control, dominate, restrain

kòng zhì 控制 *n* control, domination, dominion, helm

kǒu 口 *n* mouth

kǒu cái 口才 *n* eloquence

kǒu chī 口吃 *v* stammer, stutter

kǒu dài 口袋 *n* pocket

kǒu hào 口号 *n* catchword, slogan

kǒu jìng 口径 *n* caliber

kǒu kě 口渴 *v* thirst

kǒu shào 口哨 *n* whistle

kǒu shòu 口授 *v* dictate

kǒu tóu de 口头地 *adv* orally

kǒu tóu shàng de 口头上地 *adv* verbally

kǒu wù 口误 *n* indiscretion

kǒu xiāng táng 口香糖 *n* gum

kǒu yīn 口音 *n* accent

kòu chú 扣除 *v* deduct, dock

kòu chú 扣除 *n* deduction

kòu fèn 扣分 *v* mark down

kòu liú 扣留 *v* detain

kòu yā 扣压 *iv* withhold

kòu yā 扣押 *v* impound

kòu yā 扣押 *n* seizure

kòu yǎn 扣眼 *n* buttonhole

kū wěi 枯萎 *v* wither

kū zào wú wèi 枯燥无味 *adj* dull

kū 哭 *v* cry

kū shēng 哭声 *n* cry

kū shēng 哭声 *adj* crying

kǔ de 苦的 *adj* bitter

kǔ nàn 苦难 *n* misery

kǔ nǎo 苦恼 *n* affliction

kǔ sè de 苦涩地 *adv* bitterly

kǔ wèi 苦味 *n* bitterness

kǔ xíng 苦行 *n* austerity

kǔ xíng de 苦行的 *adj* ascetic, austere

kù cún 库存 *n* inventory

kù 裤 *n* pants

kù 酷 *adj* cool

kuā dà 夸大 *v* exaggerate, overstate

kuā yào 夸耀 *v* boast

kuà dù 跨度 *n* span

kuà guò 跨过 *v* span

kuài 块 *n* bar

kuài 快 *adj* fast

kuài dì 快递 *n* express

kuài huo de 快活的 *adj* jolly, jovial

kuài lè 快乐 *adj* happy

kuài lè de 快乐的 *adj* cheerful

kuài lè de 快乐地 *adv* joyfully

kuài sù de 快速的 *adj* quick

kuài sù de 快速地 *adv* quickly

kuài jì shī 会计师 *n* accountant

kuài zhào 快照 *n* snapshot

kuān chǎng de 宽敞的 *adj* roomy, spacious

kuān dà 宽大 *n* bounty

kuān dà de 宽大的 *adj* lenient
kuān de 宽的 *adj* broad, wide
kuān dù 宽度 *n* breadth, width
kuān guǎng de 宽广地 *adv* broadly
kuān hòu 宽厚 *n* clemency
kuān róng 宽容 *n* decency, tolerance
kuān shù 宽恕 *v* condone
kuān shù 宽恕 *n* forgiveness, remission
kuān wèi 宽慰 *n* relief
kuān xiàn qī 宽限期 *n* grace
kuān guān jié 髋关节 *n* hip
kuǎn dài 款待 *n* treat
kuáng ào de 狂傲的 *adj* cocky
kuáng bào de 狂暴的 *adj* berserk, frenzied
kuáng bào xíng wéi 狂暴行为 *v* rampage
kuáng huān zuò lè 狂欢作乐 *v* revel
kuáng nù 狂怒 *n* furor
kuáng nù de 狂怒的 *adj* berserk
kuáng quǎn bìng 狂犬病 *n* rabies
kuáng rè 狂热 *adj* fanatic, frenetic
kuáng rè de 狂热的 *adj* wild
kuáng xǐ 狂喜 *n* ecstasy
kuáng xǐ 狂喜 *v* exult
kuàng chǎn 矿产 *n* mineral
kuàng gōng 矿工 *n* miner
kuàng jǐng 矿井 *n* mine
kuàng shí 矿石 *n* ore
kuàng 框 *v* frame
kuàng jià 框架 *n* frame, framework

kuī jiǎ 盔甲 *n* armor
kuí wú de 魁梧的 *adj* burly
kuǐ lěi 傀儡 *n* dummy
kuì làn 溃烂 *v* fester
kuì yáng 溃疡 *n* ulcer
kūn chóng 昆虫 *n* insect
kǔn 捆 *n* bundle
kǔn 捆 *v* bundle
kǔn bǎng 捆绑 *iv* bind, tie
kùn huò 困惑 *n* confusion, quandary
kùn jìng 困境 *n* dead end, dilemma, predicament
kùn juàn 困倦 *n* tiredness
kùn nan 困难 *n* difficulty, discomfort, hardship, hassle
kùn nan de 困难的 *adj* difficult, hard, tough
kùn rǎo 困扰 *iv* beset
kuò dà 扩大 *n* enlargement, expansion
kuò dà 扩大 *v* expand
kuò sàn 扩散 *v* diffuse
kuò zhǎn 扩展 *v* widen
kuò zhǎn fàn wéi 扩展范围 *v* branch out
kuò zhāng 扩张 *v* sprawl
kuò de 阔的 *adj* broad

K

L

lā jī 垃圾 n garbage, junk, rubbish, trash

lā jī chǎng 垃圾场 n dump

lā jī tǒng 垃圾桶 n trash can

lā 拉 v pull

lā cháng 拉长 v lengthen

lā liàn 拉链 n zipper

lā shǐ 拉屎 n crap

lā xià 拉下 v pull down

lǎ ba 喇叭 n horn, trumpet

là 蜡 n wax

là bǐ 蜡笔 n crayon

là zhú 蜡烛 n candle

là de 辣的 adj spicy

là jiāo 辣椒 n pepper

lái 来 iv come

lái fǎng 来访 v drop in

lái lín 来临 n coming

lán jié 拦截 v intercept

lán 栏 n column

lán jià 栏架 n hurdle

lán wěi yán 阑尾炎 n appendicitis

lán sè de 蓝色的 adj blue

lán tú 蓝图 n blueprint

lán lǚ de 褴褛的 adj ragged

lán qiú 篮球 n basketball

lán zi 篮子 n basket

lǎn 懒 n laziness

lǎn duò de 懒惰的 adj lazy

lǎn hàn 懒汉 n bum

lǎn hàn 懒汉 adj slob

lǎn sǎn de 懒散的 adj idle, lax

làn jiāo 滥交 n screw

làn jiāo de 滥交的 adj promiscuous

làn yòng 滥用 v abuse

làn yòng 滥用 n abuse, misuse

làn yòng de 滥用的 adj abusive

láng 狼 n wolf

láng zhū 狼蛛 n tarantula

lǎng mǔ jiǔ 朗姆酒 n rum

làng cháo 浪潮 n tidal wave, tide

làng fèi 浪费 v waste

làng fèi de 浪费的 adj wasteful

làng yǒng 浪涌 n surge

láo dòng 劳动 n labor

láo dòng zhě 劳动者 n laborer

láo lèi de 劳累的 adj tiresome

láo gù de 牢固的 adj strong

láo kào de 牢靠的 adj secure

láo sāo 牢骚 n gripe

lǎo 老 adj old

lǎo bǎn 老板 n boss

lǎo chǔ nǔ 老处女 n spinster

lǎo hǔ 老虎 n tiger

lǎo liàn de 老练的 adj diplomatic, tactful

lǎo nián de 老年的 adj senior

lǎo rén 老人 adj elderly

lǎo shī 老师 n master

lǎo shì de 老式的 adj old-fashioned, outmoded

liáo cǎo de 潦草的 adj sloppy

lè guān 乐观 n optimism

lè guān de 乐观的 adj optimistic, positive

lè qù 乐趣 n pleasure

lè mǎ 勒马 _v_ rein

lè suǒ 勒索 _n_ blackmail, extortion

lēi zhù 勒住 _v_ curb

lēi zhù 勒住 _n_ curb

léi dá 雷达 _n_ radar

léi diàn 雷电 _n_ thunderbolt

léi guǎn 雷管 _n_ detonator

léi zhèn yǔ 雷阵雨 _n_ thunderstorm

lèi gǔ 肋骨 _n_ rib

lèi 泪 _n_ tear

lèi bié 类别 _n_ category

lèi sì 类似 _n_ analogy

lèi sì 类似 _v_ resemble

lèi sì 类似 _adj_ similar

lèi sì yú 类似于 _adj_ akin

lèi tuī 类推 _n_ analogy

lèi xíng 类型 _n_ type

lèi de 累的 _adj_ tired

lěi jī 累积 _v_ accumulate, amass

lèi rén de 累人的 _adj_ shattering

léi zhui de 累赘的 _adj_ burdensome, cumbersome

léng jìng 棱镜 _n_ prism

lěng 冷 _n_ chill, coldness

lěng 冷 _adj_ cool

lěng cáng 冷藏 _v_ refrigerate

lěng cháo rè fěng 冷嘲热讽 _n_ cynicism

lěng dàn 冷淡 _n_ coolness

lěng dàn de 冷淡的 _adj_ aloof, brittle, cooling, frosty

lěng de 冷的 _adj_ cold

lěng dòng 冷冻 _v_ chill

lěng dòng jī 冷冻机 _n_ freezer

lěng jìng 冷静 _v_ chill out, cool down

lěng jìng xià lái 冷静下来 _v_ calm down

lěng kù wú qíng de 冷酷无情的 _adj_ callous

lěng luò 冷落 _v_ snub

lěng luò 冷落 _n_ snub

lěng mò 冷漠 _n_ apathy, indifference

lěng mò de 冷漠的 _adj_ indifferent

lěng què 冷却 _v_ cool

lí mǐ 厘米 _n_ centimeter

lí 梨 _n_ pear

lí hé qì 离合器 _n_ clutch

lí hūn 离婚 _n_ divorce

lí hūn 离婚 _v_ divorce

lí hūn de nǚ rén 离婚的女人 _n_ divorcee

lí kāi 离开 _v_ depart, leave

lí qì 离弃 _v_ desert

lí qún de 离群的 _adj_ withdrawn

lí 犁 _v_ plow

lí gōu 犁沟 _n_ furrow

lí pá 犁耙 _n_ rake

lí míng 黎明 _n_ dawn

lǐ bài 礼拜 _n_ cult

lǐ bài shì 礼拜式 _n_ cult

lǐ bài yí shì 礼拜仪式 _n_ liturgy

lǐ mào 礼貌 _n_ decency, politeness

lǐ pǐn 礼品 _n_ gift

lǐ táng 礼堂 _n_ auditorium

lǐ yí 礼仪 _n_ courtesy, etiquette, manners

lǐ chéng 里程 _n_ mileage

L

lǐ chéng bēi 里程碑 *n* milestone

lǐ chéng biǎo 里程表 *n* odometer

<俚>yì shàng dàng de rén <俚>易上当的人 *n* sap

lǐ fà 理发 *n* haircut

lǐ fà shī 理发师 *n* barber

lǐ jiě 理解 *v* apprehend, comprehend, fathom out, figure out, understand

lǐ lùn 理论 *n* theory

lǐ shì huì 理事会 *n* council

lǐ xiǎng de 理想的 *adj* ideal

lǐ zhì 理智 *n* sanity

lì liang 力量 *n* force, power, strength

lì quàn 力劝 *v* exhort

lì zhēng 力争 *iv* strive

lì shǐ 历史 *n* history

lì shǐ xué jiā 历史学家 *n* historian

lì shū 历书 *n* almanac

lì chǎng 立场 *n* position, stand, standpoint

lì fǎ zhě 立法者 *n* lawmaker

lì fǎ 立法 *v* legislate

lì fǎ 立法 *n* legislation

lì fǎ jī guān 立法机关 *n* legislature

lì fāng tǐ 立方体 *n* cube

lì fāng tǐ de 立方体的 *adj* cubic

lì jí 立即 *adv* immediately

lì jí de 立即的 *n* instant

lì hài guān xì 利害关系 *n* stake

lì jǐ de 利己的 *n* egoist

lì jǐ zhǔ yì 利己主义 *n* egoism

lì qì 利器 *n* cutlery

lì rùn 利润 *n* margin, profit

lì rùn fēng hòu de 利润丰厚的 *adj* lucrative

lì xī 利息 *n* interest

lì yòng 利用 *v* avail, capitalize, exploit, utilize

lì qīng 沥青 *n* asphalt

lì wài 例外 *n* exception

lì zhèng 例证 *n* illustration

lì zi 例子 *n* instance

lì shí 砾石 *n* gravel

lì zǐ 粒子 *n* particle

lián gēn bá qǐ 连根拔起 *v* uproot

lián guàn de 连贯的 *adj* coherent

lián jiē 连接 *v* connect, converge

lián jiē 连接 *n* connection

lián jiē cí 连接词 *n* conjunction

lián kù wà 连裤袜 *n* pantyhose

lián suǒ diàn 连锁店 *n* chain

lián tóng yī qǐ 连同一起 *adv* together

lián xù 连续 *n* sequence

lián xù bù duàn de 连续不断的 *adj* incessant

lián xù de 连续的 *adj* consecutive, continuous

lián xù měng jī 连续猛击 *v* batter

lián xù xìng 连续性 *n* continuity

lián zì hào 连字号 *n* hyphen

lián mǐn 怜悯 *n* compassion

lián bāng 联邦 *adj* federal

lián hé 联合 *n* alignment, conjunction, fusion, joint, union

lián hé 联合 *v* club

lián hé 联合 *adv* jointly

lián luò 联络 *n* liaison

lián méng 联盟 *n* alliance, coalition

lián méng 联盟 *v* ally

lián méng de 联盟的 *adj* allied

lián xì 联系 *v* contact

lián xì 联系 *n* contact

lián xiǎng 联想 *v* associate

lián xiǎng 联想 *n* association

lián jià de 廉价的 *adj* cheap, inexpensive

lián dāo 镰刀 *n* sickle

liǎn 脸 *n* face

liǎn hóng 脸红 *v* blush

liǎn hóng 脸红 *n* blush

liǎn sè 脸色 *n* complexion

liàn xí 练习 *n* exercise

liàn xí 练习 *v* exercise, practice

liàn jīn shù de 炼金术的 *adj* hermetic

liàn yù 炼狱 *n* purgatory

liàn 链 *n* chain

liàn jiē 链接 *v* link

liàn jiē 链接 *n* link

liáng xīn 良心 *n* conscience

liáng xìng de 良性的 *adj* benign

liáng kuài 凉快 *n* coolness

liáng kuài de 凉快的 *adj* cooling

liáng xié 凉鞋 *n* sandal

liáng 梁 *n* beam

liáng shi 粮食 *n* grain

liǎng cì 两次 *adv* twice

liǎng gè 两个 *adj* both

liǎng gè 两个 *n* couple

liǎng qī de 两栖的 *adj* amphibious

liàng dù 亮度 *n* brightness

liàng zé 亮泽 *adj* glossy

liáo fǎ 疗法 *n* therapy

liáo yǎng yuàn 疗养院 *n* infirmary

liáo tiān 聊天 *v* chat

liào wàng tái 了望台 *n* observatory

liào xiǎng 料想 *v* suppose

liè 列 *v* list

liè 列 *n* row

liè jǔ 列举 *v* enumerate

liè fēng 烈风 *n* gale

liè jiǔ 烈酒 *n* liqueur

liè shì 烈士 *n* martyr

liè quǎn 猎犬 *n* hound

liè rén 猎人 *n* hunter

liè wù 猎物 *n* prey, quarry

liè fèng 裂缝 *n* cleft, crack, crevice, fracture

liè fèng 裂缝 *iv* slit

liè hén 裂痕 *n* fracture

liè kāi 裂开 *v* come apart, rip

liè kǒu 裂口 *n* chasm, rift

liè gǒu 鬣狗 *n* hyena

lín jìn de 邻近的 *adj* adjacent

lín jū 邻居 *n* neighbor

lín lǐ 邻里 *n* neighborhood

lín yīn dà dào 林荫大道 *n* boulevard

lín bié 临别 *n* parting

lín jìn de 临近的 *adj* imminent

lín shí de 临时的 *adj* provisional, temporary

lín sǐ suǒ wò zhī chuáng 临死所卧之床 *n* deathbed

lín zhōng de 临终的 *adj* dying

L

lín zhōng zhī shí 临终之时 *n* deathbed

lín yù 淋浴 *n* shower

lín 磷 *n* phosphorus

lìn sè de 吝啬的 *adj* stingy

lìn xī de 吝惜地 *adv* grudgingly

líng yá lì chǐ 伶牙俐齿 *adj* garrulous

líng chē 灵车 *n* hearse

líng gǎn 灵感 *n* inspiration

líng hún 灵魂 *n* soul

líng huó 灵活 *adj* flexible

líng jià 凌驾 *v* override

líng luàn 凌乱 *n* disorder

líng luàn de 凌乱的 *adj* messy

líng 铃 *n* bell

líng yáng 羚羊 *n* antelope

líng 零 *n* zero

líng bù jiàn 零部件 *n* spare part

líng gōng 零工 *n* chore

líng suì de 零碎的 *adv* piecemeal

líng xīng de 零星的 *adj* sporadic

líng yòng de 零用的 *adj* petty

lǐng dài 领带 *n* necktie, tie

lǐng dǎo 领导 *n* chief, leader; leadership

lǐng dǎo 领导 *iv* lead

lǐng dǎo rén 领导人 *n* leader

lǐng dǎo zhě 领导者 *n* rudder

lǐng huì 领会 *v* comprehend, fathom out

lǐng kōng 领空 *n* airspace

lǐng shì 领事 *n* consul

lǐng shì guǎn 领事馆 *n* consulate

lǐng tǔ 领土 *n* realm, territory

lǐng xiān de 领先的 *adj* leading

lǐng xiù 领袖 *n* chief

lǐng xiù mèi lì de 领袖魅力的 *adj* charismatic

lǐng yù 领域 *n* area

lìng pái 令牌 *n* token

lìng rén bù ān 令人不安 *adj* disturbing

lìng rén bù kuài de 令人不快的 *adj* unpleasant

lìng rén bù yuè de 令人不悦的 *adj* displeasing, undesirable

lìng rén fán nǎo 令人烦恼 *adj* worrisome

lìng rén fèi jiě de 令人费解的 *adj* puzzling

lìng rén jīng jù de 令人惊惧的 *adj* horrendous

lìng rén jīng qí de 令人惊奇的 *adj* amazing

lìng rén jīng qí de shì wù 令人惊奇的事物 *n* surprise

lìng rén jīng tàn 令人惊叹 *adj* astounding

lìng rén jìng wèi 令人敬畏 *adj* awesome

lìng rén jǔ sàng de 令人沮丧的 *adj* depressing

lìng rén kùn huò de 令人困惑的 *adj* confusing

lìng rén mǎn zú de 令人满足的 *adj* gratifying

lìng rén máo gǔ sǒng rán 令人毛骨悚然 *adj* gruesome

lìng rén qīn pèi de 令人钦佩的 *adj* admirable

lìng rén shēng wèi de 令人生畏的 *adj* daunting

lìng rén shī wàng de 令人失望的 *adj* disappointing

lìng rén tǎo yàn de 令人讨厌的 *adj* bothersome

lìng rén xiè qì de 令人泄气的 *adj* discouraging

lìng rén xìn fú de 令人信服的 *adj* stringent

lìng rén yàn wù de 令人厌恶的 *adj* detestable, disgusting, distasteful, ungrateful

lìng rén yàn fán de 令人厌烦的 *adj* irritating

lìng rén zhèn fèn 令人振奋 *adj* exciting, exhilarating

lìng rén zhèn jīng de 令人震惊的 *adj* devastating, shocking

lìng rén zhì xī de 令人窒息的 *adj* stifling

lìng rén zháo mí 令人着迷 *v* fascinate

lìng rén zuò ǒu 令人作呕 *adj* sickening

lìng jiā 另加 *adv* plus

lìng wài 另外 *adj* another

liū bīng 溜冰 *v* skate

liū bīng 溜冰 *n* skate

liū jìn 溜进 *v* sneak

liú lǎn 浏览 *v* browse, look through, navigate

liú lǎn qì 浏览器 *n* browser

liú 流 *v* flow

liú 流 *n* flow, stream

liú chǎn 流产 *v* abort, miscarry

liú chǎn 流产 *n* abortion, miscarriage

liú chū 流出 *v* exude

liú fàng 流放 *v* banish

liú fàng 流放 *n* banishment

liú gǎn 流感 *n* flu, influenza

liú hàn 流汗 *n* perspiration

liú làng hàn 流浪汉 *n* bum, wanderer, drifter, vagrant

liú lèi 流泪 *iv* tear

liú lì 流利 *adv* fluently

liú lián 流连 *v* hang around

liú lù 流露 *n* outpouring

liú máng 流氓 *n* hoodlum, hooligan, mobster, rascal

liú shā 流沙 *n* quicksand

liú shī 流失 *v* drain

liú shì 流逝 *n* lapse

liú shì 流逝 *v* lapse

liú tǐ 流体 *n* fluid

liú tōng 流通 *v* circulate

liú tōng 流通 *n* circulation

liú wáng 流亡 *v* exile

liú wáng 流亡 *n* exile

liú xīng 流星 *n* meteor

liú xíng 流行 *n* vogue

liú xíng bìng 流行病 *n* epidemic

liú xíng de 流行的 *adj* fashionable, popular, prevalent

liú xíng yǔ 流行语 *n* catchword

liú xuè 流血 *iv* bleed

liú yán 流言 *n* buzz

liú xīn de 留心的 *adj* mindful

liú yì de 留意的 *adj* attentive

L

liú （**huáng**） 硫（磺）*n* sulfur

liù 六 *adj* six

liù shí 六十 *adj* sixty

liù yuè 六月 *n* June

gē zhī shēng 咯吱声 *n* creak

lóng 龙 *n* dragon

lóng xiā 龙虾 *n* lobster

lóng zi 笼子 *n* cage

lóng 聋 *n* deafness

lóng de 聋的 *adj* deaf

lóng lóng shēng 隆隆声 *n* rumble

lǒng 垄 *n* ridge

lǒng duàn 垄断 *v* monopolize

lǒng duàn 垄断 *n* monopoly

lǒng duàn wù （**shāng pǐn**） 垄断物（商品）*n* monopoly

lóu céng 楼层 *n* story

lóu tī 楼梯 *n* stair, staircase, stairs

lóu xià 楼下 *adv* downstairs

lòu dòng 漏洞 *n* loophole

lù shuǐ 露水 *n* dew

lù tái 露台 *n* patio

lù tiān de 露天的 *adv* outdoor

lú sǔn 芦笋 *n* asparagus

lú wěi 芦苇 *n* reed

lú zào 炉灶 *n* stove

lǔ mǎng 鲁莽 *n* audacity

lǔ mǎng de 鲁莽的 *adj* audacious, reckless

lù dì de 陆地的 *adj* terrestrial

lù yīn 录音 *n* recording

lù yīn jī 录音机 *n* tape recorder

lù 鹿 *n* deer

lù ròu 鹿肉 *n* venison

lǜ bō qì 滤波器 *n* filter

lǜ guāng jì 滤光剂 *n* sun block

lǜ wǎng 滤网 *n* mesh, strainer

lù chéng 路程 *n* route

lù dēng 路灯 *n* streetlight

lù guǐ 路轨 *n* rail

lù guò 路过 *v* stop by

lù jìng 路径 *n* path

lù kǒu 路口 *n* junction

lù miàn 路面 *n* pavement

lù rén 路人 *n* passer-by

lù xiàn 路线 *n* route

lù zhàng 路障 *n* barricade

lǘ 驴 *n* donkey

lǚ 旅 *n* brigade

lǚ xíng 旅行 *v* travel

lǚ xíng duì 旅行队 *n* caravan

lǚ xíng zhě 旅行者 *n* traveler

lǚ yóu yè 旅游业 *n* tourism

lǚ yóu zhě 旅游者 *n* tourist

lǚ 铝 *n* aluminum

lǚ xíng 履行 *n* fulfillment

lǜ shī 律师 *n* attorney, counsel, counselor, lawyer

lǜ 率 *n* rate

shuài zhí de 率直的 *adj* candid

lǜ bǎo shí 绿宝石 *n* emerald

lǜ dòu 绿豆 *n* green bean

lǜ sè 绿色 *adj* green

lǜ zhōu 绿洲 *n* oasis

luǎn huáng zhì 卵黄质 *n* yolk

luǎn shí 卵石 *n* boulder, pebble

luàn hōng hōng de 乱哄哄的 *adj* tumultuous

luàn mà 乱骂 *v* cuss

lüè duó 掠夺 *v* pillage, plunder, ravage

lüè duó 掠夺 *n* raven
lüè qù 略去 *v* omit
lún 轮 *n* turn
lún bān 轮班 *n* shift
lún kuò 轮廓 *n* contour
lún kuò fēn míng de 轮廓分明的 *adj* clear-cut
lún liú 轮流 *v* alternate
lún liú de 轮流的 *adj* alternate
lún yǐ 轮椅 *n* wheelchair
lún zi 轮子 *n* wheel
lùn jù 论据 *n* argument
lùn wén 论文 *n* thesis
lùn zhèng 论证 *v* demonstrate
lùn zhèng de 论证的 *adj* demonstrative
luó mǎ jiào huáng de zhí wèi （quán lì、rèn qī） 罗马教皇的职位（权力、任期） *n* papacy
luó pán 罗盘 *n* compass
luō suō 啰嗦 *v* nag
luō suō de 啰嗦的 *adj* nagging
luó bo 萝卜 *n* radish
luó jí 逻辑 *v* log
luó zi 骡子 *n* mule
luó dīng 螺钉 *n* screw
luó mǔ 螺母 *n* nut
luó shuān 螺栓 *n* bolt
luó sī dāo 螺丝刀 *n* screwdriver
luó wén 螺纹 *n* thread
luǒ tǐ 裸体 *n* nudity
luǒ tǐ de 裸体的 *adj* nude
luǒ tǐ zhǔ yì 裸体主义 *n* nudism
luǒ tǐ zhǔ yì zhě 裸体主义者 *n* nudist

luò tuó 骆驼 *n* camel
luò cháo 落潮 *v* ebb
luò hòu 落后 *v* fall behind
luò jiǎo chù 落脚处 *n* whereabouts
luò kōng 落空 *v* fall through
luò shí 落实 *v* implement

M

L
M

mā ma 妈妈 *n* mom
mā 抹 *v* wipe
má dài jiě gù 麻袋[the～]解雇 *n* sack
má fan 麻烦 *n* trouble
má fan de 麻烦的 *adj* cumbersome, troublesome
má fēng bìng 麻风病 *n* leprosy
má fēng bìng huàn zhě 麻疯病患者 *n* leper
má mù 麻木 *n* numbness
má mù de 麻木的 *adj* callous, insensitive, numb
má què 麻雀 *n* sparrow
má zhěn 麻疹 *n* measles
má zuì 麻醉 *n* anesthesia, narcotic
mǎ 马 *n* horse
mǎ ān 马鞍 *n* saddle
mǎ bù tíng tí 马不停蹄 *adv* nonstop
mǎ chē 马车 *n* carriage

mǎ jiù 马厩 *n* stable

mǎ kè sī zhǔ yì zhě 马克思主义者 *adj* Marxist

mǎ lè 马勒 *n* bridle, rein

mǎ líng shǔ 马铃薯 *n* potato

mǎ sài kè 马赛克 *n* mosaic

mǎ xì tuán 马戏团 *n* circus

mǎ 码 *n* yard

mǎ tóu 码头 *n* pier, wharf

mǎ yǐ 蚂蚁 *n* ant

mà 骂 *v* scold

mà 骂 *n* scolding

mǎ fēi 吗啡 *n* morphine

mái zàng 埋葬 *n* burial

mái zàng 埋葬 *v* bury

mǎi de qǐ 买得起 *v* afford

mǎi de qǐ de 买得起的 *adj* affordable

mǎi fāng 买方 *n* buyer

mǎi jiā 买家 *n* buyer

mài kè fēng 麦克风 *n* microphone

mài zi 麦子 *n* wheat

mài guó zéi 卖国贼 *n* traitor

mài jiā 卖家 *n* seller

mài nòng xué wèn de 卖弄学问的 *adj* pedantic

mài chōng 脉冲 *n* pulse

mǎn mǎn de 满满的 *adj* full

mǎn yì 满意 *n* satisfaction

mǎn yì de 满意的 *adj* content, satisfactory

mǎn zài de 满载的 *adj* loaded

mǎn zú 满足 *v* appeasement, gratify, meet

mǎn zuò de 满座的 *adj* sold-out

màn de 慢的 *adj* slow

màn dòng zuò 慢动作 *n* slow motion

màn màn de 慢慢地 *adv* slowly

màn xìng de 慢性的 *adj* chronic

màn bù 漫步 *v* stroll, wander

màn huà 漫画 *n* caricature, cartoon

màn yóu 漫游 *v* roam

màn yán 蔓延 *iv* spread

máng lù 忙碌 *adj* hectic

máng lù 忙碌 *n* hustle

máng lù de 忙碌的 *adj* busy, engaged

máng lù de 忙碌地 *adv* busily

máng luàn de 忙乱的 *adj* bustling

máng mù de 盲目的 *adj* aimless, blind

máng mù de 盲目地 *adv* blindly

máng rán de 茫然的 *adj* dazed

mǎng zhuàng de 莽撞的 *adj* pushy

māo 猫 *n* cat

māo tóu yīng 猫头鹰 *n* owl

máo gǔ sǒng rán de 毛骨悚然的 *adj* creepy

máo jīn 毛巾 *n* towel

máo mao chóng 毛毛虫 *n* caterpillar

máo mao yǔ 毛毛雨 *n* drizzle

máo róng de 毛绒的 *adj* plush

máo róng róng 毛茸茸 *adj* furry

máo shuā 毛刷 *n* hairbrush

máo tǎn 毛毯 *n* blanket

máo xiàn 毛线 *n* yarn

máo yī 毛衣 *n* sweater

M

máo 矛 *n* spear

máo dùn 矛盾 *n* contradiction, paradox

máo dùn de 矛盾的 *adj* ambivalent

máo wèi 锚位 *n* berth

mào mì de 茂密的 *adj* lush

mào fàn 冒犯 *v* affront

mào fàn 冒犯 *n* affront

mào hào 冒号 *n* colon

mào xiǎn 冒险 *n* adventure

mào xiǎn 冒险 *v* risk, venture

mào xiǎn （shì yè） 冒险（事业） *n* venture

mào xiǎn lǚ xíng 冒险旅行 *n* odyssey

mào yì 贸易 *n* trade

mào yì 贸易 *v* trade

mào yì shāng 贸易商 *n* trader

mào zi 帽子 *n* hat

méi bì yào de 没必要的 *adj* unnecessary

méi rén zhù de 没人住的 *adj* unoccupied

méi yǒu 没有 *pre* without

méi yǒu rén 没有人 *pro* no one, nobody

méi yǒu shòu hài de 没有受害的 *adj* unhurt

méi yǒu xī wàng de 没有希望的 *adj* hopeless

méi gui huā 玫瑰花 *n* rose

méi gui jīng jīng wén shū 玫瑰经经文书 *n* rosary

méi gui sè 玫瑰色 *adj* rosy

méi mao 眉毛 *n* brow, eyebrow

méi 莓 *n* raspberry

méi dú 梅毒 *n* syphilis

méi zi 梅子 *n* plum

méi 煤 *n* coal

méi cāng 煤仓 *n* bunker

méi zhā 煤渣 *n* cinder

méi 霉 *n* mildew

méi biàn de 霉变的 *adj* moldy

měi 每 *adj* each, every

měi 每 *pre* per

měi dāng 每当 *adv* whenever

měi gè 每个 *adv* apiece

měi jì de 每季的 *adj* quarterly

měi nián de 每年的 *adv* yearly

měi rén 每人 *adv* apiece

měi rì 每日 *adv* daily

měi xiǎo shí 每小时 *adv* hourly

měi yuè de 每月的 *adv* monthly

měi yuè yī cì de 每月一次的 *adv* monthly

měi zhōu 每周 *adv* weekly

měi dé 美德 *n* virtue

měi fà shī 美发师 *n* hairdresser

měi guó de 美国的 *adj* American **（měi guó 、jiā ná dà de）1fēn zhù bì** （美国、加拿大的）1分铸币 *n* dime

měi huà 美化 *v* beautify, embellish

měi lì 美丽 *n* beauty

měi lì x 美丽x *adj* beautiful

měi miào 美妙 *adv* fine

měi rén yú 美人鱼 *n* mermaid

<měi >tān wū <美>贪污 *v* graft

M

měi wèi de 美味的 *adj* delicious, tasty

měi xué de 美学的 *adj* aesthetic

měi yuán 美元 *n* dollar, buck

měi zhōng bù zú 美中不足 *n* imperfection

měi zhōu de 美洲的 *adj* American

mèi mei 妹妹 *n* sister

mèi lì 魅力 *n* charm

mén 门 *n* door, gate

mén bà 门把 *n* handle

mén dì 门第 *n* ancestry

mén kǎn 门槛 *n* threshold

mén jiē 门阶 *n* doorstep

mén kǒu 门口 *n* doorway, threshold

mén láng 门廊 *n* porch

mén líng 门铃 *n* buzzer, doorbell

mén shuān 门闩 *n* latch

mén tú 门徒 *n* disciple

mén wài hàn 门外汉 *n* layman

mén zhěn bìng rén 门诊病人 *n* outpatient

méng fā 萌发 *v* sprout

méng yǒu 盟友 *n* ally

méng yuē 盟约 *n* covenant

méng lóng 朦胧 *adj* hazy

méng lóng 朦胧 *n* obscurity

méng lóng de 朦胧的 *adj* dim

měng chōng 猛冲 *v* dash

měng liè de 猛烈的 *adj* boisterous, drastic

méng bì 蒙蔽 *v* blindfold

méng yǎn wù 蒙眼物 *n* blindfold

mèng 梦 *n* dream

mèng jiàn 梦见 *iv* dream

mèng yǎn 梦魇 *n* nightmare

mí bǔ 弥补 *v* atone, make up for

mí bǔ 弥补 *n* atonement

mí 迷 *n* fan

mí gōng 迷宫 *n* labyrinth, maze

mí huò 迷惑 *v* bewilder, captivate, enchant

mí liàn 迷恋 *v* obsess

mí lù 迷路 *v* stray

mí lù de 迷路的 *adj* stray

mí nǐ de 迷你的 *adj* petite

mí nǐ qún 迷你裙 *n* miniskirt

mí rén de 迷人的 *adj* catching, charming, enchanting

mí tú 迷途 *adv* astray

mí xìn 迷信 *n* superstition

mí zhù 迷住 *v* captivate, mesmerize

mí 谜 *n* mystery

mí yǔ 谜语 *n* riddle

mǐ 米 *n* meter

mǐ fàn 米饭 *n* rice

mì jué 秘诀 *n* tip

mì mì 秘密 *n* secrecy, secret

mì mì de 秘密的 *adj* clandestine, confidential, hidden, stealthy

mì mì de 秘密地 *adv* secretly

mì mì huó dòng de chǎng suǒ 秘密活动的场所 *n* den

mì shū 秘书 *n* secretary

mì bù kě fēn de 密不可分的 *adj* inseparable

mì dù 密度 *n* density

mì fēng de 密封的 *adj* hermetic

mì jí de 密集的 *adj* dense, intensive

mì lín 密林 *n* jungle

mì mǎ 密码 *n* password

mì mǎ xíng shì de 密码形式的 *adj* scrambled

mì móu 密谋 *v* conspire

mì qiè de 密切地 *adv* closely

mì yǒu 密友 *n* confidant, crony

mì fēng 蜜蜂 *n* bee

mì yuè 蜜月 *n* honeymoon

mián bèi 棉被 *n* quilt

mián huā 棉花 *n* cotton

miǎn chú 免除 *v* exonerate

miǎn fèi 免费 *adj* free

miǎn fèi dā （**chē lǚ xíng**） 免费搭（车旅行） *n* hitch

miǎn fèi zèng sòng de 免费赠送的 *adj* complimentary

miǎn yì de 免疫的 *adj* immune

miǎn yì jiē zhòng 免疫接种 *v* immunize

miǎn yì lì 免疫力 *n* immunity

miǎn lì 勉励 *v* exhort

miǎn qiǎng de 勉强的 *adj* narrow, reluctant

miǎn qiǎng de 勉强地 *adv* narrowly, reluctantly

miàn bāo 面包 *n* bread, loaf

miàn bāo diàn 面包店 *n* bakery

miàn bāo pí 面包皮 *n* crust

miàn bāo shī 面包师 *n* baker

miàn bāo xiè 面包屑 *n* crumb

miàn bù biǎo qíng 面部表情 *n* countenance

miàn duì 面对 *v* face up to

miàn duì 面对 *pre* facing

miàn fěn 面粉 *n* flour

miàn jī 面积 *n* area

miàn jiá 面颊 *n* cheek

miàn jù 面具 *n* mask

miàn róng 面容 *n* countenance

miàn shā 面纱 *n* veil

miàn shuāng 面霜 *n* cream

miàn tuán 面团 *n* dough

miàn xiàng 面向 *adj* oriented

miáo pǔ 苗圃 *n* nursery

miáo tiao de 苗条的 *adj* slender, slim

miáo huì 描绘 *v* depict, portray, represent

miáo shù 描述 *v* depict, describe

miáo shù 描述 *n* description

miáo shù de 描述的 *adj* descriptive

miáo zhǔn 瞄准 *v* aim

miǎo shì 藐视 *v* defy

miǎo shì de 藐视的 *adj* defiant

miào 庙 *n* temple

miè jué 灭绝 *v* exterminate, extinguish

miè wáng 灭亡 *v* die out

miè shì 蔑视 *n* contempt, defiance

mín jiān de 民间的 *adj* civil

mín yì cè yàn dà xuǎn 民意测验[pl.]大选 *n* poll

mín zhǔ 民主 *n* democracy

mín zhǔ de 民主的 *adj* democratic

mǐn gǎn de 敏感的 *adj* sensitive

M

mǐn jié de 敏捷的 *adj* agile

mǐn ruì de 敏锐的 *adj* acute, brisk

míng cí 名词 *n* noun

míng dān 名单 *n* list

míng lì 名利 *n* fame

míng rén 名人 *n* celebrity

míng yù 名誉 *n* reputation

míng bai 明白 *v* figure out

míng liàng 明亮 *n* clearness

míng liàng de 明亮的 *adj* bright

míng què 明确 *adj* explicit

míng què de 明确的 *adj* clear, definite, demonstrative, distinct

míng què de 明确地 *adv* expressly

míng tiān 明天 *adv* tomorrow

míng xī 明晰 *n* clarity, clearness

míng xiǎn de 明显的 *adj* apparent

míng xìn piàn 明信片 *n* postage

míng xīng 明星 *n* star

míng zhì de 明智的 *adj* advisable, judicious, wise

mìng lìng 命令 *v* command, dictate

mìng lìng 命令 *n* mandate, order

mìng tí 命题 *n* proposition

mìng yùn 命运 *n* destiny, fate

miù jiàn 谬见 *n* delusion

miù lùn 谬论 *n* fallacy

mó fàn 模范 *adj* exemplary

mó fǎng 模仿 *v* imitate, mime

mó hu 模糊 *v* blur

mó hu 模糊 *adj* fuzzy

mó hu de 模糊的 *adj* blurred, vague

mó kuài 模块 *n* module

mó nǐ 模拟 *v* simulate

mó shì 模式 *n* mode; mold

mó tè 模特 *n* model

mó xíng 模型 *n* model; mold

mú zi 模子 *n* mold

mó 膜 *n* membrane

mó cā 摩擦 *n* friction

mó tiān lóu 摩天楼 *n* skyscraper

mó tuō chē 摩托车 *n* motorcycle

mó cā 磨擦 *v* rub

mò fáng 磨房 *n* mill

mó lì 磨砺 *v* harden

mó nàn 磨难 *n* ordeal, tribulation

mó shā 磨砂 *v* scrub

mó suì 磨碎 *iv* grind

mó xuē qì 磨削器 *n* sharpener

mó gu 蘑菇 *n* mushroom

mó fǎ shī 魔法师 *n* sorcerer

mó guǐ 魔鬼 *n* devil

mó shù 魔术 *n* magic

mó shù shī 魔术师 *n* magician

mǒ diào 抹掉 *v* erase

mǒ shā 抹杀 *v* obliterate

mò shōu 没收 *v* confiscate

mò shōu 没收 *n* confiscation

mò lì huā 茉莉花 *n* jasmine

mò shēng rén 陌生人 *n* stranger

mò shì 漠视 *v* disregard

mò jìng 墨镜 *n* sunglasses

mò xī gē de 墨西哥的 *adj* Mexican

móu shā 谋杀 *n* homicide, murder

mǒu 某 *adj* certain

mǒu rén 某人 *pro* somebody, someone

mǒu yī tiān 某一天 *adv* someday

mǒu zhǒng fāng fǎ 某种方法 *adv* someway

mǔ jī 母鸡 *n* hen

mǔ mǎ 母马 *n* mare

mǔ qīn 母亲 *n* mother

mǔ shī zi 母狮子 *n* lioness

mǔ xìng 母性 *n* motherhood

mǔ lì 牡蛎 *n* oyster

mǔ zhǐ 拇指 *n* thumb

mù cái 木材 *n* lumber, timber

mù de 木的 *adj* wooden

mù fá 木筏 *n* raft

mù gōng 木工 *n* carpentry

mù jiang 木匠 *n* carpenter

mù jiang yè 木匠业 *n* carpentry

mù nǎi yī 木乃伊 *n* mummy

mù ǒu 木偶 *n* puppet

mù qì 木器 *n* carpentry

mù tàn 木炭 *n* charcoal

mù tou 木头 *n* wood

mù biāo 目标 *n* goal, target

mù dì 目的 *n* purpose

mù dì dì 目的地 *n* destination

mù jī zhě 目击者 *n* eyewitness

mù jī zhèng rén 目击证人 *n* witness

mù lù 目录 *n* catalog, contents, directory

mù qián 目前 *adv* currently

mù qián de 目前的 *adj* present

mù xuàn de 目眩的 *adj* dazed

mù yù 沐浴 *n* bath

mù cǎo 牧草 *n* pasture

mù shī 牧师 *n* chaplain, clergyman, pastor, priest

mù yáng rén 牧羊人 *n* shepherd

mù 墓 *n* tomb

mù bēi 墓碑 *n* gravestone, tombstone

mù yuán 墓园 *n* graveyard

mù zhì míng 墓志铭 *n* epitaph

mù sī lín de 穆斯林的 *adj* Muslim

N

ná 拿 *iv* hold, take

ná qǐ 拿起 *v* pick up

ná zǒu 拿走 *v* take away

nǎ gè 哪个 *adj* which

nèi 内 *adj* inside

nèi bù de 内部的 *adj* interior, inward

nèi dì 内弟 *n* brother-in-law

nèi gé 内阁 *n* cabinet

nèi jiù de 内疚的 *adj* guilty

nèi lù 内陆 *adv* inland

nèi lù de 内陆的 *adj* inland, landlocked

nèi luàn 内乱 *n* strife

nèi xiàng de 内向的 *adj* introvert

nèi xiōng 内兄 *n* brother-in-law

nèi yī 内衣 *n* underwear, lingerie

nèi zài de 内在的 *adj* inner, intrinsic

nèi zhì de 内置的 *adj* built-in

nà 那 *adj* that

M
N

nà lǐ 那里 *adv* there

nà xiē 那些 *adj* those

nà rù 纳入 *v* incorporate

nǎi lào 奶酪 *n* cheese

nǎi nai 奶奶 *n* grandmother, granny

nǎi niú 奶牛 *n* cow

nǎi niú chǎng 奶牛场 *n* dairy farm

nǎi yóu 奶油 *n* cream

nǎi yóu de 奶油的 *adj* creamy

nài jiǔ 耐久 *n* longitude

nài xīn 耐心 *n* patience

nài yòng de 耐用的 *adj* durable

nán 男 *n* men

nán àn mó shī 男按摩师 *n* masseur

nán dà xué shēng lián yì huì 男大学生联谊会 *n* fraternity

nán gāo yīn 男高音 *n* tenor

nán guǎn jiā 男管家 *n* butler

nán hái 男孩 *n* boy

nán péng yǒu 男朋友 *n* boyfriend

nán xìng 男性 *n* male

nán xìng de 男性的 *adj* masculine, virile

nán xìng shēng zhí qì guān 男性生殖器官 *adj* wily

nán xiū dào shì 男修道士 *n* friar

nán xiū dào yuàn yuàn zhǎng 男修道院院长 *n* abbot

nán zǐ 男子 *n* man

nán zǐ de 男子的 *adj* masculine

nán zǐ hàn de 男子汉的 *adj* manly

nán zǐ qì de 男子气的 *adj* masculine

nán 南 *n* south

nán bù de 南部的 *adj* southern

nán fāng rén 南方人 *n* southerner

nán guā 南瓜 *n* pumpkin

nán miàn 南面 *adv* southbound

nán dǒng de 难懂的 *adj* elusive

nán jiē jìn de 难接近的 *adj* inaccessible

nán jiě de 难解的 *adj* obscure

nán kàn de 难看的 *adj* hideous

nán lǐ jiě de 难理解的 *adj* inexplicable

nán miǎn de 难免的 *adj* unavoidable

nàn mín 难民 *n* refugee

nán píng xī de 难平息的 *adj* implacable

nán shòu de 难受的 *adj* wretched

nán wàng de 难忘的 *adj* memorable, unforgettable

nán yǐ biàn rèn 难以辨认 *adj* illegible

nán yǐ fù dān de 难以负担的 *adj* burdensome

nán yǐ shuō chū kǒu de 难以说出口的 *adj* unspeakable

nán yǐ xiāng xìn de 难以相信的 *adj* unbelievable

nán yǐ xiǎng xiàng de 难以想象的 *adj* unthinkable

nán yǐ zhì xìn de 难以置信的 *adj* incredible

nán yǐ zhuō mō de 难以捉摸的 *adj* evasive

nán zhuō mō de 难捉摸的 *adj* elusive

náng zhǒng 囊肿 *n* cyst

nǎo de 脑的 *adj* cerebral

nǎo mó yán 脑膜炎 *n* meningitis

nào jù 闹剧 *n* farce

nào zhōng 闹钟 *n* alarm clock

néng 能 *adj* able

néng 能 *iv* can

néng gàn de 能干的 *adj* capable, competent

néng gòu 能够 *iv* can

néng lì 能力 *n* ability, capability, capacity, competence, faculty

néng xī shōu de 能吸收的 *adj* absorbent

néng xùn sù jiē shòu de 能迅速接受的 *adj* receptive

néng yuán 能源 *n* energy

ní gū 尼姑 *n* nun

ní gǔ dīng 尼古丁 *n* nicotine

ní 泥 *n* mud

ní gōng 泥工 *n* mason

ní nìng de 泥泞的 *adj* muddy

ní tán 泥潭 *n* quagmire

nǐ 你 *pro* you

nǐ de 你的 *adj* your

nǐ de 你的 *pro* yours

nǐ hǎo 你好 *e* hello

nǐ zì jǐ 你自己 *pro* yourself

nǐ rén huà 拟人化 *v* personify

nì chēng 昵称 *n* nickname

nì huǒ 逆火 *v* backfire

nì jìng 逆境 *n* adversity, reverse

nì zhuǎn 逆转 *n* reversal

nì míng 匿名 *n* anonymity

nì míng de 匿名的 *adj* anonymous

nì ài 溺爱 *v* spoil

nì sǐ 溺死 *v* drown

niān zhe 拈着 *v* stick

nián 年 *n* year

nián biǎo 年表 *n* chronology

nián dài xué 年代学 *n* chronology

nián dù de 年度的 *adj* annual

nián jiàn 年鉴 *n* almanac

nián lǎo de 年老的 *adj* senile

nián líng 年龄 *n* age

nián qīng de 年轻的 *adj* young

nián qīng rén 年轻人 *n* cub, youngster

nián tǔ 粘土 *n* clay

nián xìng de 粘性的 *adj* sticky

nián yè 粘液 *n* mucus

niǎn xiàn jī 捻线机 *n* twister

niǎn guò 碾过 *v* run over

niàng jiǔ chǎng 酿酒厂 *n* winery

niàng zào 酿造 *v* brew

niǎo 鸟 *n* bird

niǎo huì 鸟喙 *n* beak

niǎo qiāng 鸟枪 *n* shotgun

niào 尿 *n* urine

niào bù 尿布 *n* diaper

niē zào 捏造 *v* concoct

niē zào 捏造 *n* concoction

niē zào de 捏造的 *adj* trumped-up

niè chǐ lèi dòng wù（**rú shǔ děng**）啮齿类动物（如鼠等）*n* rodent

niè zi 镊子 *n* tweezers

niè 镍 *n* nickel

níng jìng 宁静 *n* serenity

níng jìng de 宁静的 *adj* pastoral, restful, serene

N

N

nìng kě 宁可 *adv* rather
nǐng jǐn 拧紧 *v* screw
níng méng 柠檬 *n* lemon
níng méng shuǐ 柠檬水 *n* lemonade
níng gù 凝固 *v* curdle
níng jié 凝结 *v* coagulate, condense, curdle
níng jié wù 凝结物 *n* coagulation
níng jù 凝聚 *v* agglomerate
níng jù lì 凝聚力 *n* cohesion
níng kuài 凝块 *n* clot
níng shì 凝视 *v* gaze
níng suō 凝缩 *n* condensation
niú 牛 *n* cattle, ox
niú cáo 牛槽 *n* manger
niú fèn 牛粪 *n* dung
niú nǎi 牛奶 *n* milk
niú nǎn 牛腩 *n* sirloin
niú pái 牛排 *n* steak
niú ròu 牛肉 *n* beef
niú zǎi 牛仔 *n* cowboy, jeans
niǔ ní de 忸怩的 *adj* self-conscious
niǔ dǎ 扭打 *n* scuffle
niǔ dòng 扭动 *v* wiggle, writhe
niǔ qū 扭曲 *v* distort
niǔ qū 扭曲 *n* distortion
niǔ qū de 扭曲的 *adj* twisted
niǔ shāng 扭伤 *v* sprain
niǔ zhù duì shǒu 扭住对手 *v* clinch
nóng chǎng 农场 *n* farm, ranch
nóng cūn 农村 *n* countryside
nóng cūn de 农村的 *adj* rural
nóng jiā chǎng yuàn 农家场院 *n* farmyard

nóng mín 农民 *n* farmer, peasant
nóng yào 农药 *n* pesticide
nóng yè 农业 *n* agriculture
nóng yè de 农业的 *adj* agricultural
nóng de 浓的 *adj* thick
nóng dù 浓度 *n* concentration
nóng suō 浓缩 *v* condense
nóng yè 浓液 *n* dope
nóng 脓 *n* pus
nòng āo 弄凹 *v* dent
nòng fān 弄翻 *v* capsize
nòng qīng 弄清 *v* ascertain
nòng qīng chǔ 弄清楚 *v* sort out
nòng xū 弄虚 *v* falsify
nòng zāng 弄脏 *v* blot, defile
nòng zāo 弄糟 *v* mess up
nú lì 奴隶 *n* slave
nú yì 奴役 *n* bondage, slavery
nǔ lì 努力 *n* effort, endeavor, exertion
nǔ lì 努力 *v* endeavor
nǔ lì de 努力的 *adj* diligent
nǚ àn mó shī 女按摩师 *n* masseuse
nǚ bó jué 女伯爵 *n* countess
nǚ chèn shān 女衬衫 *n* blouse
nǚ ér 女儿 *n* daughter
nǚ fáng dōng 女房东 *n* landlady
nǚ fú wù yuán 女服务员 *n* waitress
nǚ gōng jué 女公爵 *n* duchess
nǚ hái 女孩 *n* girl
nǚ huáng 女皇 *n* empress
nǚ jì chéng rén 女继承人 *n* heiress

nǚ pú 女仆 *n* maid
nǚ rén 女人 *n* woman, women
nǚ shén 女神 *n* goddess
nǚ shì 女士 *n* madam
nǚ shuì páo 女睡袍 *n* nightgown
nǚ wáng 女王 *n* queen
nǚ xìng de 女性的 *adj* feminine
nǚ xiū dào yuàn 女修道院 *n* convent
nǚ xu 女婿 *n* son-in-law
nǚ yǎn yuán 女演员 *n* actress
nǚ yǒu 女友 *n* girlfriend
nǚ zhǔ chí rén 女主持人 *n* hostess
nǚ zǐ 女子 *n* female
nüè ji 疟疾 *n* malaria
nüè dài 虐待 *v* abuse, mistreat
nüè dài 虐待 *n* abuse, mistreatment
nüè dài kuáng zhě 虐待狂者 *n* sadist
nuǎn qì piàn 暖气片 *n* radiator
nuó wēi 挪威 *n* Norway
nuó wēi de 挪威的 *adj* Norwegian
nuó yòng 挪用 *v* embezzle
nuò yán 诺言 *n* promise
nuò fū 懦夫 *n* coward
nuò ruò 懦弱 *n* cowardice
nuò ruò de 懦弱的 *adv* cowardly

ōu zhōu 欧洲 *n* Europe
ōu zhōu de 欧洲的 *adj* European
ōu dǎ 殴打 *v* maul
ǒu tù 呕吐 *v* throw up, vomit
ǒu tù wù 呕吐物 *n* vomit
ǒu ěr 偶尔 *adv* occasionally
ǒu fā shì jiàn 偶发事件 *n* contingency
ǒu rán 偶然 *n* contingency
ǒu rán de 偶然的 *adj* circumstantial, contingent
ǒu rán pèng dào 偶然碰到 *v* come across
ǒu xiàng 偶像 *n* idol
ǒu xiàng chóng bài 偶像崇拜 *n* idolatry

N O P

pā xià 趴下 *v* get down
pā zhe zǒu de 趴着走的 *adj* creepy
pá 爬 *v* climb, crawl
pá xíng 爬行 *v* scramble
pá xíng dòng wù 爬行动物 *n* reptile
pà 怕 *v* creep
pāi jī 拍击 *v* slap

pāi jī shēng 拍击声 *n* flop, slap
pāi mài 拍卖 *n* auction
pāi mài 拍卖 *v* auction
pāi mài rén 拍卖人 *n* auctioneer
pāi shè 拍摄 *n* shot
pāi shǒu 拍手 *v* clap
pāi zhào 拍照 *v* photograph
pāi zi 拍子 *n* beat
pái huái 徘徊 *v* linger
pái huái 徘徊 *n* prowler
pái 排 *n* platoon
pái chì 排斥 *v* repel
pái chū 排出 *v* discharge
pái chū 排出 *n* discharge
pái chú 排除 *v* exclude
pái duì 排队 *v* line up
（**pái fēng**）**zhào** （排风）罩 *n* hood
pái liàn 排练 *n* rehearsal
pái liàn 排练 *v* rehearse
pái liè 排列 *v* align, row
pái míng 排名 *v* rank
pái qì 排气 *v* exhaust
pái qiú 排球 *n* volleyball
pái shuǐ 排水 *n* drainage
pái shuǐ gōu 排水沟 *n* gutter
pái shuǐ xì tǒng 排水系统 *n* drainage
pái xiè guǎn 排泄管 *n* duct
pái xù 排序 *n* sort
pái 牌 *n* tablet
pài duì 派队 *n* party
pài qiǎn 派遣 *v* detach, dispatch
pān dēng 攀登 *n* climbing
pán xuán 盘旋 *v* circle

pán shān 蹒跚 *v* stumble
pàn duàn 判断 *n* judgment
pàn duàn 判断 *v* size up
pàn jué 判决 *v* sentence
pàn jué 判决 *n* sentence
pàn xíng 判刑 *v* condemn
pàn guó 叛国 *n* treason
pàn luàn 叛乱 *n* insurgency, rebellion
pàn tú 叛徒 *n* traitor
páng dà de 庞大的 *adj* bulky
páng guān zhě 旁观者 *n* bystander, onlooker, spectator
páng lù 旁路 *n* bypass
pàng 胖 *adj* fat
pāo 抛 *iv* cast, toss
pāo qì 抛弃 *v* discard, forsake
pāo qì de 抛弃的 *adj* outcast
páo xiāo 咆哮 *v* growl, roar
páo zi 袍子 *n* gown
pǎo 跑 *iv* run
pǎo bù zhě 跑步者 *n* runner
pǎo dào 跑道 *n* runway
pào mò 泡沫 *n* bubble, foam, lather
pào pao táng 泡泡糖 *n* bubble gum
pào zài 泡在 *v* soak in
pào bīng bù duì 炮兵部队 *n* artillery
pào tái 炮台 *n* fort
pēi tāi 胚胎 *n* embryo
pēi yá 胚芽 *n* germ
péi bàn 陪伴 *n* companionship, company

péi shěn tuán 陪审团 *n* jury

péi xùn 培训 *n* training

péi yǎng 培养 *v* bring up, cultivate, foster, raise

péi yù 培育 *v* nurture

péi cháng 赔偿 *n* compensation, indemnity, recompense, reparation, restitution

péi cháng 赔偿 *v* indemnify, redress

pèi dài 佩戴 *v* adorn

pèi fú 佩服 *v* admire

pèi 配 *v* match

pèi（yào） 配（药）*v* dispense

pèi cài 配菜 *n* trimmings

pèi duì wù 配对物 *n* counterpart

pèi guǎn 配管 *n* plumbing

pèi hé 配合 *v* conjugate

pèi jìng shī 配镜师 *n* optician

pèi ǒu 配偶 *n* mate, spouse

pèi ǒu de 配偶的 *adj* conjugal

pēn 喷 *v* spray

pēn chū 喷出 *v* belch, emit

pēn chū wù 喷出物 *n* belch

pēn fā 喷发 *v* erupt

pēn fā 喷发 *n* eruption

pēn quán 喷泉 *n* fountain, geyser

pēn quán 喷泉 *iv* spring

pēn quán 喷泉 *n* spring

pēn tì 喷嚏 *n* sneeze

pēn zuǐ 喷嘴 *n* nozzle

pén dì 盆地 *n* basin

pēng jī 抨击 *v* lash out

pēng tiáo fǎ 烹调法 *n* cuisine

pēng tiáo fēng gé 烹调风格 *n* cuisine

pēng rèn 烹饪 *v* cook

pēng rèn 烹饪 *n* cooking, cuisine

péng yǒu 朋友 *n* friend

péng zi 棚子 *n* shack

péng bó fā zhǎn 蓬勃发展 *v* flourish, prosper

péng chē 篷车 *n* caravan

péng zhàng 膨胀 *v* bloat, inflate

péng zhàng 膨胀 *n* bulge

péng zhàng de 膨胀的 *adj* bloated, puffy

pèng dào 碰到 *v* run into

pèng shāng 碰伤 *n* bruise

pèng zhuàng 碰撞 *v* collide

pèng zhuàng 碰撞 *n* collision

pī fā 批发 *n* wholesale

pī píng 批评 *n* criticism, critique

pī píng 批评 *v* criticize

pī zhǔn 批准 *n* approval, ratification

pī zhǔn 批准 *v* approve, ratify

pī jiān 披肩 *n* cape

pī lù 披露 *v* disclose

pī dāo 劈刀 *n* chopper

pī lì 霹雳 *n* thunderbolt

pí bāo gǔ tou de 皮包骨头的 *adj* skinny

pí cǎo 皮草 *n* fur

pí dài 皮带 *n* leash

pí de 皮的 *adj* skinny

pí fū 皮肤 *n* skin

pí gé 皮革 *n* leather

pí lián 毗连 *v* adjoin

pí lián de 毗连的 *adj* adjoining

pí juàn de 疲倦的 *adj* weary

P

pí láo 疲劳 *n* fatigue
pí jiǔ 啤酒 *n* beer
pí jiǔ chǎng 啤酒厂 *n* brewery
pí qi 脾气 *n* temper
pí qi bào zào de 脾气暴躁的 *adj* crusty
pí qi huài 脾气坏 *adj* grumpy
pì gu 屁股 *n* butt
pì jìng de 僻静的 *adj* secluded
piàn duàn 片段 *n* fragment
piān chā 偏差 *n* aberration, deviation
piān hào 偏好 *n* predilection, preference
piān jiàn 偏见 *n* bias, prejudice
piān lí zhǔ tí 偏离主题 *v* digress
piān tóu tòng 偏头痛 *n* migraine
piān zhí 偏执 *n* bigotry
piān zhí de 偏执的 *adj* paranoid
piān zhí de rén 偏执的人 *n* bigot
piàn jú 骗局 *n* hoax, scam, swindle
piàn jú 骗局 *v* swindle
piàn rén de 骗人的 *adj* deceitful
piàn zi 骗子 *n* cheater, con man, crook, swindler
piǎo bái 漂白 *v* bleach, whiten
piǎo bái jì 漂白剂 *n* bleach
piāo fú 漂浮 *adv* adrift
piāo fú zhe 漂浮着 *adv* afloat
piào liang de 漂亮的 *adj* pretty
piāo liú wù 漂流物 *n* drifter
piāo yí 漂移 *v* drift
piào fáng 票房 *n* box office
piào gēn 票根 *n* stub

piào jià 票价 *n* fare
piě hào 撇号 *n* apostrophe
pīn tú 拼图 *n* jigsaw
pīn xiě 拼写 *iv* spell
pīn xiě 拼写 *n* spelling
pín jí de 贫瘠的 *adj* barren
pín kùn 贫困 *adj* needy
pín kùn 贫困 *n* poverty
pín kùn de 贫困的 *adj* destitute, indigent
pín mín kū 贫民窟 *n* slum
pín qióng de 贫穷的 *adj* impoverished, indigent
pín xuè 贫血 *n* anemia
pín xuè de 贫血的 *adj* anemic
pín dào 频道 *n* channel
pín fán 频繁 *adj* frequent
pín fán de 频繁的 *v* frequent
pín lǜ 频率 *n* frequency
pǐn cháng 品尝 *v* savor, taste
pǐn pái 品牌 *n* brand
pǐn tuō 品脱 *n* pint
pǐn wèi 品味 *n* taste
pǐn zhì dī liè de 品质低劣的 *adj* crappy
pǐn zhǒng 品种 *n* breed, variety
píng 平 *adj* flat
píng bǎn 平板 *n* slab
píng cháng de 平常的 *adj* normal, usual
píng dàn de 平淡的 *adj* bland, insipid
píng děng 平等 *adj* equal
píng děng 平等 *n* equality
píng dǐ guō 平底锅 *n* pan, saucepan

píng fán 平凡 *n* banality

píng fán de 平凡的 *adj* homely, uneventful

píng hé de 平和的 *adj* placid

píng héng 平衡 *v* balance

píng héng 平衡 *n* balance, equilibrium

píng héng de 平衡的 *v* level

píng jià 平价 *n* parity

píng jìng 平静 *n* calm

píng jìng de 平静的 *adj* calm

píng jūn 平均 *n* average

píng tái 平台 *n* platform

píng tǎn de 平坦地 *adv* plainly

píng xī 平息 *v* appeasement, quell

píng yì jìn rén de 平易近人的 *adj* approachable

píng yōng 平庸 *n* mediocrity

píng yōng de 平庸的 *adj* mediocre

píng yuán 平原 *n* plain

píng fēn 评分 *n* score

píng gū 评估 *v* assess

píng gū 评估 *n* assessment

píng jià 评价 *n* appraisal

píng jià 评价 *v* appraise, evaluate

píng lùn 评论 *v* comment, remark

píng lùn 评论 *n* comment, observation, remark

píng dān 凭单 *n* voucher

píng guǒ 苹果 *n* apple

píng guǒ zhī 苹果汁 *n* cider

píng mù 屏幕 *n* screen

píng 瓶 *n* bottle

píng jǐng 瓶颈 *n* bottleneck

pō 泼 *v* splash

pó po 婆婆 *n* mother-in-law

pò hài 迫害 *v* persecute

pò jìn de 迫近的 *adj* pending

pò qiè de 迫切的 *adj* pressing

pò shǐ 迫使 *v* compel, oblige

pò chǎn 破产 *v* bankrupt

pò chǎn 破产 *n* bankruptcy

pò chǎn de 破产的 *adj* bankrupt, broke

pò huài 破坏 *n* demolition, destruction

pò huài 破坏 *v* devastate, ravage, undermine, vandalize

pò huài xìng 破坏性 *adj* destructive

pò huài xìng de 破坏性的 *adj* damaging

pò huài zhě 破坏者 *n* destroyer

pò jiù 破旧 *adj* shabby

pò jiù de 破旧的 *adj* dilapidated, worn-out

pò liè 破裂 *n* break, rupture

pò liè 破裂 *v* break up, rupture

pò suì 破碎 *n* break

pò suì 破碎 *v* crumble

pò suì de 破碎的 *adj* crushing

pò yì 破译 *v* decipher

pò lì 魄力 *n* charisma

pú rén 仆人 *n* servant

pú táo 葡萄 *n* grape, grapevine

pú táo gàn 葡萄干 *n* raisin

pú táo táng 葡萄糖 *n* glucose

pú táo yá 葡萄牙 *n* Portugal

pú táo yá de 葡萄牙的 *adj* Portuguese

P

pú táo yuán 葡萄园 *n* vineyard

pǔ sù 朴素 *n* austerity

pǔ biàn de 普遍的 *adj* prevalent, universal, widespread

pǔ chá 普查 *n* census

pǔ jí 普及 *v* popularize

pǔ tōng de 普通的 *adj* ordinary

pù bù 瀑布 *n* chute, waterfall

Q

qī 七 *adj* seven

qī shí 七十 *adj* seventy

qī yuè 七月 *n* July

qī zǐ 妻子 *n* wife, wives

qī cǎn de 凄惨的 *adj* miserable

qī dài 期待 *v* look forward

qī kān 期刊 *n* journal

qī wàng 期望 *v* expect

qī wàng 期望 *n* expectation

qī xiàn 期限 *n* duration

qī piàn 欺骗 *n* deception

qī piàn 欺骗 *v* cheat, deceive, delude, dupe, victimize

qī piàn 欺骗 *n* deceit, guile

qī piàn de 欺骗的 *adj* deceptive

qī yā 欺压 *v* oppress

qī zhà 欺诈 *v* defraud

qī zhà 欺诈 *n* fiddle

qī zhà 欺诈 *adj* fraudulent

qī hēi de 漆黑的 *adj* pitch-black

qí tā 其他 *adj* other

qí yú de rén 其余的人 *n* remainder

qí zhōng yī gè 其中一个 *adj* either

qí jì 奇迹 *n* marvel, miracle, prodigy, wonder

qí jì bān de 奇迹般的 *adj* miraculous

qí miào 奇妙 *n* oddity

jī shù 奇数 *adj* odd

qí yì de 奇异的 *adj* eerie, singular, strange, odd, peculiar, queer, strange

qí shì 歧视 *v* discriminate

qí shì 歧视 *n* discrimination

qí dǎo 祈祷 *n* litany, prayer

qí dǎo 祈祷 *v* pray

qí qū bù píng de 崎岖不平的 *adj* bumpy

qí (mǎ) 骑（马） *iv* ride

qí bīng 骑兵 *n* cavalry

qí bīng bù duì 骑兵部队 *n* cavalry

qí shì 骑士 *n* knight

qí zì xíng chē de rén 骑自行车的人 *n* cyclist

qí 旗 *n* flag

qí gān 旗杆 *n* flagpole

qí zhì 旗帜 *n* banner

qǐ gài 乞丐 *n* beggar

qǐ qiú 乞求 *v* beg

qǐ é 企鹅 *n* penguin

qǐ tú 企图 *v* attempt

qǐ tú 企图 *n* attempt

qǐ tú yǎn gài 企图掩盖 *n* cover-up

qǐ yè 企业 *n* enterprise

qǐ yè jiā 企业家 *n* entrepreneur
qǐ chéng 启程 *v* set off
qǐ dí 启迪 *v* enlighten
qǐ dòng 启动 *v* activate, initiate
qǐ dòng 启动 *n* activation
qǐ fā de 启发的 *adj* suggestive
qǐ háng 启航 *v* sail
qǐ háng 启航 *n* sail
qǐ shì 启示 *n* apocalypse, revelation
qǐ shì lù 启示录 *n* apocalypse
qǐ cǎo 起草 *v* draft
qǐ chéng 起程 *v* depart, set out
qǐ chū 起初 *adv* initially
qǐ chuáng 起床 *v* get up
qǐ fǎn yìng 起反应 *v* react
qǐ huò gōu 起货钩 *n* crowbar
qǐ lì 起立 *v* stand up
qǐ shǐ 起始 *n* onset
qǐ shǐ diǎn 起始点 *n* threshold
qǐ sù 起诉 *v* indict
qǐ yì 起义 *n* uprising
qǐ yīn 起因 *n* cause
qǐ yuán 起源 *v* derive
qǐ yuán yú 起源于（from） *v* stem
qǐ zhě hén 起褶痕 *v* crease
qǐ zhòng jī 起重机 *n* crane, hoist
qì fēn 气氛 *n* atmosphere
qì guǎn 气管 *n* windpipe
qì hòu 气候 *n* climate
qì hòu de 气候的 *adj* climatic
qì něi 气馁 *v* discouragement, dishearten
qì qiú 气球 *n* balloon

qì wèi 气味 *n* odor
qì xī 气息 *n* wind
qì xiàng tái 气象台 *n* observatory
qì quán 弃权 *v* forfeit
qì chē 汽车 *n* auto, automobile, car
qì chē lǚ guǎn 汽车旅馆 *n* motel
qì huà 汽化 *v* vaporize
qì yóu 汽油 *n* gasoline
qì yuē 契约 *n* bond, deed
qì guān 器官 *n* organ
qì jù 器具 *n* appliance
qì wù 器物 *n* utensil
qiān nián 千年 *n* millennium
qiān wǎ 千瓦 *n* kilowatt
qiān chū 迁出 *v* move out
qiān yí 迁移 *v* migrate
qiān lián 牵连 *v* implicate, incriminate
qiān yǐn 牵引 *n* traction
qiān 铅 *n* lead
qiān bǐ 铅笔 *n* pencil
qiān bēi 谦卑 *n* humility
qiān bēi de 谦卑地 *adv* humbly
qiān xū 谦虚 *adj* modest
qiān xū 谦虚 *n* modesty
qiān xùn 谦逊 *v* condescend
qiān xùn de 谦逊的 *adj* humble
qiān míng 签名 *v* sign
qiān míng yú ...bèi miàn 签名于...背面 *v* endorse
qiān zì 签字 *n* signature
qián 前 *adv* before
qián 前 *adj* former
qián é 前额 *n* forehead

Q

qián jìn 前进 *v* advance

qián jìn 前进 *n* advance

qián jìn 前进 *adv* forward

qián liè 前列 *n* forefront

qián liè xiàn 前列腺 *n* prostate

qián mian 前面 *n* front

qián mian de 前面的 *adj* front

qián qíng 前情 *n* antecedent

qián qū 前驱 *n* precursor

qián rèn 前任 *n* predecessor

qián sū lián de 前苏联的 *adj* soviet

qián suǒ wèi wén de 前所未闻的 *adj* unheard-of

qián tí 前提 *n* premise

qián tí shì 前提是 *c* providing that

qián wǎng 前往 *adj* bound for

qián xī 前夕 *n* eve

qián yán 前言 *n* foreword, preface

qián zhào 前兆 *n* omen

qián zhuì 前缀 *n* prefix

qián zòu 前奏 *n* prelude

qián chéng 虔诚 *n* piety

qián chéng de 虔诚的 *adj* devout, pious

qián 钱 *n* money

qián bāo 钱包 *n* purse, wallet

qián de sú chēng 钱的俗称 *n* dough

qián zi 钳子 *n* pincers, pliers, tongs

qián kǒu wù 箝口物 *n* gag

qián shuǐ 潜水 *v* dive

qián shuǐ 潜水 *n* diving

qián shuǐ yuán 潜水员 *n* diver

qiǎn 浅 *adj* shallow

qiǎn hēi sè de 浅黑色的 *adj* brunette

qiǎn fǎn huí guó 遣返回国 *v* repatriate

qiǎn zé 谴责 *v* condemn, denounce, deplore, rebuke

qiǎn zé 谴责 *n* condemnation, rebuke

qiàn 欠 *v* owe

qiàn quē de 欠缺的 *adj* defective

qiāng 枪 *n* gun

qiāng dàn 枪弹 *n* gunshot

qiāng kǒu 枪口 *n* muzzle

qiāng shā 枪杀 *v* gun down

qiāng shēng 枪声 *n* gunfire

qiāng shǒu 枪手 *n* gunman

qiāng táng 枪膛 *n* chamber

qiāng xiè 枪械 *n* firearm

qiáng dà 强大 *adj* formidable

qiáng dà de 强大的 *adj* mighty, powerful

qiáng dào 强盗 *n* bandit, robber

qiáng diào 强调 *v* emphasize, underline

qiáng dù 强度 *n* intensity, strength

qiáng hàn de 强悍的 *adj* intrepid

qiáng jiā 强加 *n* imposition

qiáng jiān 强奸 *v* rape

qiáng jiān 强奸 *n* rape

qiáng jiān fàn 强奸犯 *n* rapist

qiáng jìn 强劲 *adj* gusty

qiáng liè de 强烈的 *adj* fervent, intense

qiáng liè fǎn duì 强烈反对 *v* deplore

qiáng pò 强迫 *v* bludgeon, constrain, force

qiáng pò 强迫 *n* coercion

qiáng pò de 强迫的 *adj* compulsive

qiáng qiú de 强求的 *adj* pushy

qiáng xíng 强行 *adv* forcibly

qiáng xíng 强行 *v* ram

qiáng zhàn 强占 *v* usurp

qiáng zhì 强制 *v* coerce, obligate

qiáng zhì 强制 *n* coercion, compulsion

qiáng zhì de 强制的 *adj* compelling, compulsive, obligatory

qiáng zhì zhí xíng 强制执行 *v* enforce

qiáng zhuàng 强壮 *adj* hardy

qiáng zhuàng de 强壮的 *adj* strong

qiáng bì 墙壁 *n* wall

qiǎng duó 抢夺 *v* rob

qiǎng jié 抢劫 *n* robbery

qiǎng jiù 抢救 *n* rescue

qiǎng zhàn 抢占 *v* preempt

qiāo 敲 *n* knock

qiāo 敲 *v* knock

qiāo dǎ 敲打 *n* beat

qiāo zhà 敲诈 *v* extort

qiāo zhà 敲诈 *n* extortion, racketeering

qiáo zhuāng 乔装 *v* disguise

qiáo zhuāng 乔装 *n* disguise

qiáo 桥 *n* bridge

qiáo liáng 桥梁 *n* viaduct

qiáo bù qǐ 瞧不起 *v* look down

qiǎo hé 巧合 *n* coincidence

qiǎo hé de 巧合的 *adj* coincidental

qiǎo kè lì 巧克力 *n* chocolate

qiǎo miào de 巧妙的 *adj* cunning

qiào pí 俏皮 *n* impertinence

qiē 切 *v* slice

qiē duàn 切断 *v* cut off

qiē duàn 切断 *n* severance

qiē gē zhě 切割者 *n* cutter, cyanide

qiē kǒu 切口 *n* incision

qiè pàn 切盼 *v* yearn

qiē piàn 切片 *n* slice

qiè qǔ 窃取 *v* pilfer, steal

qiè zéi 窃贼 *n* burglar

qiè yì de 惬意的 *adj* agreeable

qīn ài de 亲爱的 *adj* darling, dear

qīn bǐ qiān míng 亲笔签名 *n* autograph

qīn hé lì 亲和力 *n* affinity

qīn mì de 亲密的 *adj* close, intimate

qīn mì dù 亲密度 *n* intimacy

qīn qi 亲戚 *n* relative

qīn qiè 亲切 *adj* folksy

qīn qiè de 亲切的 *adj* approachable, cordial

qīn qíng 亲情 *n* kinship

qīn shàn 亲善 *n* goodwill

qīn xìn 亲信 *n* henchman

qīn fàn 侵犯 *v* encroach

qīn lüè 侵略 *n* aggression

Q

qīn lüè xìng de 侵略性的 *adj* aggressive

qīn lüè zhě 侵略者 *n* aggressor, invader

qīn shí 侵蚀 *v* eat away

qīn pèi 钦佩 *n* admiration

qín cài 芹菜 *n* celery

qín fèn 勤奋 *n* diligence

qín fèn de 勤奋的 *adj* diligent

qín láo de 勤劳的 *adj* industrious

qǐn jù 寝具 *n* bedding

qǐn shì 寝室 *n* dormitory

qīng chūn de 青春的 *adj* youthful

qīng chūn qī 青春期 *n* adolescence, heyday, puberty

qīng méi sù 青霉素 *n* penicillin

qīng nián shí qī 青年时期 *n* youth

qīng shǎo nián 青少年 *n* adolescent

qīng tái 青苔 *n* moss

qīng tóng 青铜 *n* bronze

qīng wā 青蛙 *n* frog

qīng yù 青玉 *n* sapphire

qīng qì 氢气 *n* hydrogen

qīng de 轻的 *adj* light

qīng liàng jí 轻量级 *n* lightweight

qīng shuài de 轻率的 *adj* indiscreet

qīng miáo dàn xiě 轻描淡写 *v* trivialize

qīng miè 轻蔑 *v* scorn

qīng miè de 轻蔑的 *n* scornful

qīng pāi 轻拍 *n* pat, tap

qīng shēng de xiào 轻声地笑 *v* chuckle

qīng shì 轻视 *v* belittle

qīng sōng 轻松 *n* relief

qīng tiāo 轻佻 *adj* frivolous

qīng wēi 轻微 *adv* lightly

qīng wēi de 轻微的 *adj* minor

qīng xìn 轻信 *adj* gullible

qīng yì dé lái de qián 轻易得来的钱 *n* gravy

qīng zuì 轻罪 *n* misdemeanor

qīng dǎo 倾倒 *v* dump, pour

qīng fù 倾覆 *v* capsize

qīng jiǎo 倾角 *n* inclination

qīng mò 倾没 *v* plunge

qīng mò 倾没 *n* plunge

qīng pén dà yǔ 倾盆大雨 *n* downpour

qīng tīng 倾听 *v* heed

qīng xiàng 倾向 *n* propensity

qīng xiàng de 倾向的 *adj* prone

qīng xiāo 倾销 *v* dump

qīng xié 倾斜 *n* declension

qīng xié 倾斜 *v* incline, lean, tilt

qīng xié de 倾斜的 *adj* oblique, slanted

qīng xiè 倾卸 *v* dump

qīng bái de 清白的 *adj* blameless

qīng chú 清除 *n* clearance, purge

qīng chú 清除 *v* purge

qīng chǔ de 清楚的 *adj* crisp, distinct, lucid

qīng chǔ de fā yīn 清楚的发音 *n* articulation

qīng chǔ de 清楚地 *adv* clearly

qīng chǔ de jiǎng huà 清楚地讲话 *v* articulate

qīng jié 清洁 *v* clean
qīng jié de 清洁的 *adj* clean
qīng jié gōng 清洁工 *n* cleaner
qīng jié jì 清洁剂 *n* cleanser
qīng suàn 清算 *v* liquidate
qīng suàn 清算 *n* liquidation
qīng xī de 清晰的 *adj* plain
qīng xī dù 清晰度 *n* definition
qīng xǐ 清洗 *v* cleanse
qīng xīn de 清新的 *adj* refreshing
qīng xǐng 清醒 *adj* sober
qīng xǐng de 清醒的 *adj* sane
qīng zhēn sì 清真寺 *n* mosque
qíng fù 情妇 *n* mistress
qíng gǎn 情感 *n* emotion
qíng kuàng 情况 *n* case, situation
qíng rén 情人 *n* lover, sweetheart
qíng xù 情绪 *n* sentiment
qíng xù huà de 情绪化的 *adj* moody
qíng yǒu kě yuán de 情有可原的 *adj* extenuating
qíng tiān de 晴天的 *adj* sunny
qíng yǔ biǎo 晴雨表 *n* barometer
qǐng qiú 请求 *v* call on, request
qǐng qiú 请求 *n* request
qǐng yuàn shū 请愿书 *n* petition
qìng zhù 庆祝 *v* celebrate
qìng zhù 庆祝 *n* celebration
qióng rén 穷人 *n* poor
qióng dǐng 穹顶 *n* dome
qiū zhěn 丘疹 *n* pimple
qiū jì 秋季 *n* autumn
qiū tiān 秋天 *n* fall
qiú fàn 囚犯 *n* prisoner

qiú jìn 囚禁 *n* captivity
qiú ài 求爱 *v* court
qiú ài 求爱 *n* courtship
qiú hūn 求婚 *v* propose
qiú zhù （huò píng jiè）（duì xiàng） 求助（或凭借）（对象） *v* resort
qiú 球 *n* ball, sphere
qiú jīng 球茎 *n* bulb
qiú pāi 球拍 *n* bat, racket
qū 区 *n* borough, district
qū fēn 区分 *n* distinction
qū fēn 区分 *v* distinguish
qū huà 区划 *n* compartment
qū yù 区域 *n* region, zone
qū yù de 区域的 *adj* regional
qū bǐng 曲柄 *n* crank
qū qí bǐng 曲奇饼 *n* cookie
qū xiàn 曲线 *n* curve
qū dòng 驱动 *n* drive
qū dòng 驱动 *iv* drive
qū gǎn 驱赶 *v* chase away
qū mó rén 驱魔人 *n* exorcist
qū sàn 驱散 *v* dispel, disperse
qū zhú 驱逐 *v* evict, expel, oust
qū zhú chū jìng 驱逐出境 *v* deport
qū zhú chū jìng 驱逐出境 *n* deportation
qū zhú jiàn 驱逐舰 *n* destroyer
qū cóng de 屈从的 *adj* subdued
qū fú 屈服 *v* capitulate, succumb, yield
qū xī 屈膝 *v* genuflect
qū zūn 屈尊 *v* condescend, deign

Q

qū gàn 躯干 *n* torso

qū shì 趋势 *n* tendency, trend

qú dào 渠道 *n* channel

qǔ chū 取出 *v* dislodge

qǔ dài 取代 *v* displace, supersede

qǔ huí 取回 *v* get back

qǔ huí 取回 *n* retrieval, withdrawal

qǔ xiāo 取消 *v* call off, cancel, revoke, disqualify

qǔ xiāo 取消 *n* cancellation

qǔ xiāo zhǒng zú gé lí 取消种族隔离 *v* desegregate

qǔ yuè 取悦 *v* please

qù 去 *iv* go

qù chú 去除 *v* remove

qù pí 去皮 *v* peel

quān 圈 *n* circle

quān tào 圈套 *v* snare

quān tào 圈套 *n* snare

quán bù yù shòu wán de 全部预售完的 *adj* sold-out

quán guó de 全国的 *adj* national

quán jǐng 全景 *n* panorama

quán miàn de 全面的 *adj* comprehensive

quán shén guàn zhù 全神贯注 *n* preoccupation

quán shén guàn zhù de 全神贯注的 *adj* engrossed

quán shèng shí qī 全盛时期 *n* heyday

quán shì jiè de 全世界的 *adj* worldwide

quán shū 全书 *n* testament

quán tǐ chéng wù yuán 全体乘务员 *n* crew

quán tǐ chuán yuán 全体船员 *n* crew

quán tǐ tóng háng 全体同行 *n* fraternity

quán tǐ yī zhì 全体一致 *n* unanimity

quán wú de 全无的 *adj* devoid

quán xīn 全新 *adj* brand-new

quán guì 权贵 *n* dignitary

quán lì 权力 *n* authority

quán lì zhǔ yì zhě de 权力主义者的 *adj* authoritarian

quán lì 权利 *n* right

quán shì 权势 *n* ascendancy

quán wēi 权威 *n* authority

quán yí de 权宜的 *adj* expedient

quán yí zhī jì 权宜之计 *n* expediency

quán dǎ 拳打 *v* punch

quán dǎ 拳打 *n* punch

quán jī shǒu 拳击手 *n* boxer; boxing

quán tóu 拳头 *n* fist

quán suō 蜷缩 *v* huddle

quán gǔ 颧骨 *n* cheekbone

quǎn chǐ 犬齿 *n* fang

quǎn rú zhǔ yì 犬儒主义 *n* cynicism

quàn gào 劝告 *v* counsel

quàn gào 劝告 *n* counsel

quàn zǔ 劝阻 *v* discourage, dissuade

quē diǎn 缺点 *n* drawback, fault, shortcoming, vice

quē fá 缺乏 *n* deficiency, lack
quē fá 缺乏 *v* lack
quē fá de 缺乏的 *adj* deficient, devoid
quē kǒu 缺口 *n* dent
quē xí 缺席 *n* absence
quē xí 缺席 *adj* absent
quē xiàn 缺陷 *n* defect
qué zi 瘸子 *adj* cripple
què bān 雀斑 *n* freckle
què bǎo 确保 *v* ensure
què dìng 确定 *v* ascertain, determine
què dìng de 确定的 *adj* certain
què dìng xìng 确定性 *n* certainty
què qiè de 确切的 *adj* definitive, exact
què rèn 确认 *v* confirm, validate
què rèn 确认 *n* confirmation
què shí de 确实的 *adj* conclusive
què zhèng 确证 *v* corroborate
qún zi 裙子 *n* skirt
qún 群 *n* cluster, flock, swarm
qún jū 群居 *adj* gregarious

R

rán ér 然而 *c* however
rán ér 然而 *adv* nevertheless
rán hòu 然后 *adv* afterwards, then
rán liào 燃料 *n* fuel

rán liào kù 燃料库 *n* bunker
rán qǐ 燃起 *v* flare-up
rán qì 燃气 *n* gas
rán shāo 燃烧 *v* blaze
rán shāo 燃烧 *n* combustion
rán shāo de 燃烧的 *adj* ablaze
rǎn liào 染料 *n* dye
ràng 让 *iv* let, let in, let out
ràng bù 让步 *v* back down, concede, give in
ràng bù 让步 *n* concession
ràng chū 让出 *v* give out
ràng rén gǎn jué wú liáo de 让人感觉无聊的 *adj* boring
ràng rén jí dù tòng kǔ de 让人极度痛苦的 *adj* agonizing
ràng rén nán yǐ zhì xìn 让人难以置信 *adj* mind-boggling
ràng rén shàng yǐn de 让人上瘾的 *adj* addictive
ràng xíng 让行 *n* yield
ráo shù 饶恕 *v* spare
rào 绕 *iv* wind
rào 绕 *adj* winding
rào guò 绕过 *v* bypass
rào xíng de lù 绕行的路 *n* detour
rě má fán 惹麻烦 *v* trouble
rě nù 惹怒 *v* infuriate
rě rén zhù mù de 惹人注目的 *n* striking
rè 热 *adj* hot
rè chén 热忱 *n* ardor, zeal
rè chéng 热诚 *adj* hearty
rè dài de 热带的 *adj* tropical
rè làng 热浪 *n* heat wave

Q
R

rè liè de huān yíng 热烈的欢迎 *n* ovation

rè qì 热气 *n* heat

rè qíng 热情 *n* enthusiasm

rè qíng de 热情的 *adj* ardent, fervent

rè qíng yáng yì 热情洋溢 *adj* effusive

rè shēn 热身 *v* warm up

rè shuǐ qì 热水器 *n* water heater

rè xīn 热心 *n* zest

rè xīn de 热心的 *adj* ardent, zealous

rè zhōng de 热衷的 *adj* avid, zealous

rén 人 *n* creature, people, person

rén cái 人才 *n* talent

rén gōng de 人工的 *adj* artificial

rén gōng tuī dòng 人工推动 *v* manhandle

rén kǒu 人口 *n* population

rén lèi 人类 *n* human being, humankind, mankind

rén lèi de 人类的 *adj* human

rén lì 人力 *n* manpower

rén qún 人群 *n* crowd, throng

rén rén 人人 *pro* everybody, everyone

rén shì bù mén 人事部门 *n* personnel

rén shì dàng àn 人事档案 *n* dossier

rén wén 人文 *n* humanities

rén xíng dào 人行道 *n* sidewalk

rén xíng héng dào 人行横道 *n* crosswalk

rén zhì 人质 *n* hostage

rén ài 仁爱 *n* benevolence

rén cí 仁慈 *n* clemency

rén cí de 仁慈的 *adj* benevolent, lenient

rěn nài 忍耐 *v* put up with

rěn shòu 忍受 *iv* bear, endure, put up

rèn chū 认出 *v* identify, recognize

rèn kě 认可 *v* acknowledge

rèn kě 认可 *n* approbation, concession

rèn zhēn 认真 *n* seriousness

rèn zhēn de 认真的 *adv* earnestly

rèn zhēn de 认真的 *adj* intense, serious

rèn zhèng 认证 *v* certify

rèn zuì 认罪 *n* plea

rèn hé 任何 *adj* any

rèn hé rén 任何人 *pro* anybody, anyone

rèn hé shì /wù 任何事/物 *pro* anything

rèn mìng 任命 *v* appoint

rèn mìng 任命 *n* appointment

rèn qī 任期 *n* term

rèn wù 任务 *n* task

rèn xìng de 任性的 *adj* arbitrary

rèn xìng de 任性的 *adv* willfully

rèn yì de 任意的 *adj* arbitrary

rèn yì de 任意地 *adv* randomly

rèn shēn 妊娠 *n* gestation

rèn shēn de 妊娠的 *adj* pregnant

rèn dài 韧带 *n* ligament

rèn xìng de 韧性的 *adj* resilient

R

rēng diào 扔掉 *v* throw away
rì 日 *n* day
rì bào 日报 *n* journal
rì běn 日本 *n* Japan
rì chū 日出 *n* sunrise
rì jì 日记 *n* diary
rì lì 日历 *n* calendar
rì luò 日落 *n* sundown
rì qī 日期 *n* date
rì yǔ 日语 *adj* Japanese
rì zhì 日志 *n* log
róng yào 荣耀 *n* glory
róng yù 荣誉 *n* honor
róng liàng 容量 *n* capacity, volume
róng nà 容纳 *v* accommodate
róng rěn 容忍 *v* tolerate
róng xǔ de 容许的 *adj* admissible
róng yì de 容易的 *adj* easy
róng yì de 容易地 *adv* easily
róng jì de 溶剂的 *adj* solvent
róng jiě 溶解 *n* dissolution
róng 熔 *v* melt
róng lú 熔炉 *n* furnace
róng qià de guān xì 融洽的关系 *n* rapport
róu rèn de 柔韧的 *adj* pliable
róu ruǎn 柔软 *n* tenderness
róu ruǎn de 柔软的 *adj* supple, tender
ròu guì 肉桂 *n* cinnamon
ròu lèi 肉类 *n* meat
ròu tāng 肉汤 *n* broth
ròu tǐ de 肉体的 *adj* bodily, carnal, corporal

ròu wán 肉丸 *n* meatball
ròu yù de 肉欲的 *adj* carnal
ròu zhī 肉汁 *n* gravy
rú guǒ 如果 *c* if
rú hé 如何 *adv* how
rú shí de 如实的 *adj* truthful
rú chóng 蠕虫 *n* worm
rú dòng 蠕动 *v* creep
rǔ fáng 乳房 *n* breast
rǔ gē 乳鸽 *n* pigeon
rǔ lào 乳酪 *n* cream
rǔ tóu 乳头 *n* nipple
rǔ zhuàng de 乳状的 *adj* milky
rǔ mà de 辱骂的 *adj* abusive
rù chǎng quàn 入场券 *n* admission
rù chǎng xǔ kě 入场许可 *n* admittance, entree
rù diàn xíng qiè 入店行窃 *n* shoplifting
rù kǒu 入口 *n* entrance, way in
rù kǒu chù 入口处 *n* entry
rù qí tú 入歧途 *adv* astray
rù qīn 入侵 *v* intrude, invade
rù qīn 入侵 *n* intrusion, invasion, intruder
rù qīn zhě 入侵者 *n* intruder, raider
rù yè 入夜 *n* nightfall
ruǎn 软 *n* softness
ruǎn de 软的 *adj* soft
ruǎn gāo 软膏 *n* ointment
ruǎn huà 软化 *v* soften
ruǎn mù sāi 软木塞 *n* cork
ruǎn ruò 软弱 *adj* feeble

R

ruǎn ruò de 软弱的 *adj* weak
ruǎn ruò wú lì 软弱无力 *adj* wimp
ruì diǎn 瑞典 *n* Sweden
ruì diǎn de 瑞典的 *adj* Swedish
ruì shì 瑞士 *n* Switzerland
ruì shì de 瑞士的 *adj* Swiss
（**ruì shì de**）木屋 （瑞士
的）木屋 *n* chalet
rùn nián 闰年 *n* leap year
rùn huá 润滑 *v* grease, lubricate
rùn huá 润滑 *n* lubrication
rùn huá zhī 润滑脂 *n* grease
ruò rén xǐ huān de 若人喜欢的
adj likable
ruò de 弱的 *adj* lean
ruò diǎn 弱点 *n* vice, weakness
ruò huà 弱化 *v* attenuate

S

sǎ 撒 *v* sprinkle
sǎ 洒 *v* sprinkle
sāi dōng xi 塞东西 *v* stuff
sāi mǎn 塞满 *v* cram
sāi zhù kǒu bù 塞住口部 *v* gag
sāi xiàn yán 腮腺炎 *n* mumps
sài pǎo 赛跑 *v* race
sān 三 *adj* three
sān bèi de 三倍的 *adj* triple
sān jiǎo 三角 *n* triangle
sān jiǎo jià 三脚架 *n* tripod
sān lián de 三联的 *adj* triple
sān míng zhì 三明治 *n* sandwich
sān shí 三十 *adj* thirty
sān yuè 三月 *n* March
sǎn 伞 *n* umbrella
sǎn bīng 伞兵 *n* paratrooper
sàn 散 *adv* asunder
sàn bù 散步 *n* walk
sàn luò 散落 *n* fallout
sàn rè qì 散热器 *n* radiator
sǎn wén 散文 *n* prose
sàng qīn 丧亲 *n* bereavement
sàng shī 丧失 *v* incapacitate
sàng shī de 丧失的 *adj* bereaved
sàng yǒu 丧友 *n* bereavement
sāo dòng 骚动 *n* commotion
sāo luàn 骚乱 *n* disorder, uproar
sāo rǎo 骚扰 *v* harass, molest
sāo rǎo 骚扰 *n* harassment
sǎo miáo 扫描 *v* scan
sào zhou 扫帚 *n* broom
sǎo zi 嫂子 *n* sister-in-law
sè cǎi 色彩 *n* color
sè qíng de 色情的 *adj* obscene
sēn lín 森林 *n* forest
shā 杀 *v* kill
shā hài 杀害 *n* killing
shā jūn 杀菌 *v* pasteurize
shā rén fàn 杀人犯 *n* murderer
shā shǒu 杀手 *n* assassin, killer
shā 沙 *n* sand
shā bù 沙布 *n* gauze
shā dīng yú 沙丁鱼 *n* sardine
shā fā 沙发 *n* sofa
shā huáng 沙皇 *n* czar

R
S

shā kēng 沙坑 *n* bunker
shā lā 沙拉 *n* salad
shā mò 沙漠 *n* desert
shā chē 刹车 *n* brake
shā chē 刹车 *v* brake
shā guō 砂锅 *n* casserole
shā jiāng 砂浆 *n* mortar
shā zhǐ 砂纸 *n* sandpaper
shā yú 鲨鱼 *n* shark
shǎ de 傻的 *adj* silly
shǎ guā 傻瓜 *adj* sucker
shǎ zi 傻子 *adj* fool
shāi 筛 *v* sift
shài shāng 晒伤 *n* sunburn
shān 山 *n* hill, mountain
shān gōu 山沟 *n* ravine
shān gǔ 山谷 *n* valley
shān jǐ 山脊 *n* ridge
shān pō 山坡 *n* hillside
shān yáng 山羊 *n* goat
shān chú 删除 *v* delete
shān jié 删节 *v* abridge
shān qù 删去 *v* cut out
shān dòng 煽动 *v* incite, instigate
shān dòng 煽动 *n* incitement
shǎn diàn 闪电 *n* lightning
shǎn guāng 闪光 *n* flash
shǎn liàng 闪亮 *v* glimpse
shǎn liàng de 闪亮的 *adj* shiny
shǎn shǎn fā guāng 闪闪发光 *v* sparkle
shǎn shuò 闪烁 *v* blink, flicker, glimpse, glitter
shàn qì 疝气 *n* hernia
shàn 善 *n* goodness

shàn jiě rén yì de 善解人意的 *adj* understanding
shàn chuǎng 擅闯 *v* trespass
shàn lí zhí shǒu 擅离职守 *v* desert
shāng 伤 *n* injury
shāng gǎn de 伤感的 *adj* sorrowful
shāng hài 伤害 *v* harm, hurt
shāng hài 伤害 *n* harm
shāng hài 伤害 *adj* hurt
shāng hén 伤痕 *n* scar
shāng kǒu 伤口 *n* gash, wound
shāng nǎo jīn 伤脑筋 *adj* grueling
shāng wáng zhě 伤亡者 *n* casualty
shāng xīn 伤心 *v* grieve
shāng xīn 伤心 *adj* sad
shāng biāo 商标 *n* trademark
shāng chéng 商城 *n* mall
shāng diàn 商店 *n* shop, store
shāng jiā 商家 *n* merchant
shāng pǐn 商品 *n* goods, merchandise
shāng rén 商人 *n* businessman
shāng shù 商数 *n* quotient
shāng wù 商务 *n* business
shāng wù de 商务的 *adj* commercial
shāng yè 商业 *n* commerce
shāng yè de 商业的 *adj* commercial
shāng yì 商议 *n* counsel
shàng àn 上岸 *adv* ashore
shàng bù de 上部的 *adj* upper

S

shàng céng shè huì 上层社会 *n* aristocracy

shàng chē 上车 *v* board

shàng chuán 上船 *v* board

shàng chuán （huò fēi jī děng） 上船（或飞机等） *v* embark

shàng děng de 上等的 *adj* classy

shàng dì 上帝 *n* God, providence

shàng è 上颚 *n* palate

shàng jí de 上级的 *adj* superior

shàng liàn 上链 *v* chain

shàng liú shè huì de 上流社会的 *adj* genteel

shàng sè 上色 *v* color

shàng shēng 上升 *v* ascend, come up, go up, raise, rise

shàng shēng 上升 *n* raise

shàng shēng 上升 *adv* uphill

shàng shǒu kào 上手拷 *v* handcuff

shàng sù 上诉 *n* appeal

shàng sù 上诉 *v* appeal

shàng wǔ 上午 *n* morning

shàng xià wén 上下文 *n* context

shàng xiào 上校 *n* colonel

shàng yǎn 上演 *v* stage

shàng yǐn de 上瘾的 *adj* addicted

shāo 烧 *iv* burn

shāo jiāo 烧焦 *v* scorch

shāo kǎo 烧烤 *n* barbecue, grill

shāo kǎo 烧烤 *v* broil, grill

shāo shāng 烧伤 *n* burn

shāo wēi 稍微 *adv* slightly

shāo wēi yī dòng 稍微一动 *v* budge

sháo zi 勺子 *n* spoon

shǎo de 少的 *adj* less

shǎo liàng 少量 *n* morsel

shǎo liàng de 少量的 *adj* marginal

shǎo liàng de fā fàng 少量地发放 *v* dole out

shào nián 少年 *n* juvenile, teenager

shào nián de 少年的 *adj* juvenile

（shào nián）fàn zuì （少年）犯罪 *n* delinquency

shào nián qī 少年期 *n* boyhood

shào nǚ 少女 *n* maiden

shǎo shù 少数 *adj* few

shǎo shù mín zú 少数民族 *n* minority

shǎo yǒu de 少有的 *adj* infrequent

shào bīng 哨兵 *n* sentry

shē chǐ 奢侈 *n* extravagance

shē chǐ de 奢侈的 *adj* extravagant

shē chǐ pǐn 奢侈品 *n* luxury

shē huá 奢华 *adj* lavish

shē huá 奢华 *v* lavish

shē lì 猞猁 *n* lynx

shé 舌 *n* tongue

shé duàn 折断 *iv* cut

shé duàn 折断 *n* fracture

shé 蛇 *n* serpent, snake

shé xiē 蛇蝎 *n* viper

shè bèi 设备 *n* equipment, furnishings

shè dìng 设定 *iv* set

shè dìng 设定 *n* setup

shè jì 设计 *n* design

shè jì 设计 *v* devise

shè jì 设计 v project
shè xiǎng 设想 v envisage
shè xiǎng 设想 adj fancy
shè zhì 设置 iv set
shè huì 社会 n society
shè huì zhǔ yì 社会主义 n socialism
shè huì zhǔ yì de 社会主义的 adj socialist
shè jiāo 社交 v socialize
shè qū 社区 n community
shè jī 射击 iv shoot
shè shā 射杀 v zap
shè shǒu 射手 n marksman
shè jí 涉及 v concern, involve
shè miǎn 赦免 n absolution
shè miǎn 赦免 v absolve, condone
shè yǐng 摄影 n photography
shè yǐng shī 摄影师 n photographer
shēn bào 申报 v declare
shēn míng 申明 v affirm
shēn qǐng 申请 n application
shēn qǐng 申请 v apply, apply for
shēn qǐng rén 申请人 n applicant
shēn shù 申述 n allegation, electricity, power
shēn shù 申述 v allege
shēn shǒu 伸手 v reach
shēn shǒu kě jí de jù lí 伸手可及的距离 n reach
shēn suō 伸缩 v flex
shēn cái 身材 n figure, shape
shēn fèn 身份 n identity
shēn gāo 身高 n height

shēn tǐ 身体 n body
shēn tǐ bù shì de 身体不适的 adj indisposed
shēn tǐ de 身体的 adj bodily
（shēn tǐ huò zhì lì de）quē xiàn （身体或智力的）缺陷 n handicap
shēn tǐ shàng de 身体上地 adj physically
shēn wú fēn wén de 身无分文的 adj penniless
shēn yín 呻吟 v groan, moan
shēn yín 呻吟 n groan, moan
shēn shì 绅士 n gentleman
shēn 砷 n arsenic
shēn bú kě cè 深不可测 adj abysmal
shēn de 深的 adj deep
shēn dù 深度 n depth
shēn huà 深化 v deepen
shēn kǎn 深砍 n slash
shēn kǎn 深砍 v slash
shēn kè de 深刻的 adj profound
shēn kēng 深坑 n chasm
shēn lán sè（de）深蓝色（的）adj navy blue
shēn rù 深入 adv in depth
shēn rù liǎo jiě 深入了解 v tap into
shēn shēn de 深深地 adv dearly
shēn sī shú lù 深思熟虑 v deliberate
shēn sī shú lù de 深思熟虑的 adj deliberate
shēn yuān 深渊 n abyss

S

shén 神 *n* deity, divinity

shén cì néng lì de 神赐能力的 *adj* charismatic

shén de 神的 *adj* divine

shén fù 神父 *n* rector

shén huà 神化 *v* mystify

shén huà 神话 *n* myth

shén jīng 神经 *n* nerve

shén jīng jǐn zhāng de 神经紧张的 *adj* nervous

shén jīng xì tǒng de 神经系统的 *adj* nervous

shén jīng zhì de 神经质的 *adj* neurotic

shén mì de 神秘的 *adj* mysterious, mystic, occult

shén qí 神奇 *adj* fantastic

shén qí de 神奇的 *adj* magical

shén shèng 神圣 *n* holiness, sanctify

shén shèng de 神圣的 *adj* holy, sacred

shén shòu de néng lì 神授的能力 *n* charisma

shén xìng 神性 *n* divinity

shén xué 神学 *n* theology

shén xué jiā 神学家 *n* theologian

shén yù 神谕 *n* oracle

shén zhí rén yuán 神职人员 *n* clergy, priesthood

shén zhì zhèng cháng de 神志正常的 *adj* sane

shěn chá 审查 *n* censorship

shěn hé 审核 *v* examine

shěn jì 审计 *v* audit

shěn měi de 审美的 *adj* aesthetic

shěn pàn 审判 *n* trial

shěn shì 审视 *v* scan

shěn wèn 审问 *v* interrogate

shěn xùn 审讯 *n* inquest

shěn yì 审议 *n* scrutiny

shèn zàng 肾脏 *n* kidney

shèn chū 渗出 *v* exude

shèn rù 渗入 *v* permeate

shèn tòu 渗透 *v* infiltrate, penetrate

shèn tòu 渗透 *n* infiltration

shēng 升 *v* lift

shēng 升 *n* liter

shēng gāo 升高 *v* hoist

shēng gāo 升高 *n* hoist

shēng jí 升级 *v* escalate, upgrade

shēng qǐ 升起 *iv* arise

shēng zhí 升职 *v* move up

shēng zhí 升职 *n* promotion

shēng bìng 生病 *adj* ill

shēng cài 生菜 *n* lettuce

shēng chǎn 生产 *v* produce

shēng chǎn 生产 *n* produce, production

shēng cún 生存 *v* subsist, survive

shēng cún 生存 *n* survival

shēng de 生的 *adj* raw

shēng dòng de 生动的 *adj* dynamic, vivid

shēng huán zhě 生还者 *n* survivor

shēng huó 生活 *n* life

shēng huó fāng shì 生活方式 *n* lifestyle

shēng jì 生计 *n* livelihood

S

shēng jiāng 生姜 *n* ginger
shēng mìng 生命 *n* being, life
shēng mìng lì 生命力 *n* vitality
shēng rì 生日 *n* birthday
shēng tài xué 生态学 *n* ecology
shēng wù 生物 *n* being
shēng wù xué 生物学 *n* biology
shēng wù xué de 生物学的 *adj* biological
shēng xiù 生锈 *v* rust
shēng xiù de 生锈的 *adj* rusty
shēng yá 生涯 *n* career
shēng yù 生育 *n* fertility
shēng yù 生育 *v* procreate
shēng zhěn 生疹 *v* rash
shēng chēng 声称 *v* assert, claim
shēng chēng 声称 *n* assertion, claim
shēng diào 声调 *n* tone
shēng míng láng jí de 声名狼藉的 *adj* notorious
shēng míng 声明 *n* declaration, statement
shēng míng 声明 *v* state
shēng míng duàn jué guān xì 声明断绝关系 *v* disown
shēng shì hào dà 声势浩大 *n* mammoth
shēng xué de 声学的 *adj* acoustic
shēng yīn 声音 *n* sound, voice
shēng yuán 声援 *n* solidarity
shèng guò 胜过 *v* outdo, outshine, outweigh
shèng lì 胜利 *n* victory
shèng lì de 胜利的 *adj* triumphant, victorious

shèng rèn 胜任 *n* competence
shèng zhě 胜者 *n* victor
shéng 绳 *n* tie
shéng suǒ 绳索 *n* rope
shéng zi 绳子 *n* cord
shěng 省 *n* province
shěng （luó mǎ dì guó de xíng zhèng qū huà）省（罗马帝国的行政区划）*n* diocese
shěng qù 省去 *v* leave out
shèng cān bēi 圣餐杯 *n* chalice
shèng cān bù 圣餐布 *n* corporal
shèng dàn 圣诞 *n* Christmas
shèng dàn jié 圣诞节 *n* X-mas
shèng dì 圣地 *n* shrine
shèng gē 圣歌 *n* anthem, chant, hymn
shèng gōng huì de 圣公会的 *adj* Anglican
shèng huà 圣化 *v* sanctify
shèng jié 圣洁 *n* sanctity
shèng jīng 圣经 *n* bible
shèng jīng de 圣经的 *adj* biblical
shèng lǐ 圣礼 *n* sacrament
shèng rén 圣人 *n* saint
shèng suǒ 圣所 *n* sanctuary
shèng tán 圣坛 *n* shrine
shèng xià 盛夏 *n* midsummer
shèng yàn 盛宴 *n* feast
shèng cài 剩菜 *n* leftovers
shèng yú 剩余 *n* surplus
shèng yú de 剩余的 *n* remains
shèng yú wù 剩余物 *n* remainder
shī jiǎn 尸检 *n* autopsy
shī tǐ 尸体 *n* carcass, corpse

S

shī bài 失败 *v* break down, fail, go under

shī bài 失败 *n* defeat, failure

shī cháng de 失常的 *adj* deranged

shī dàng xíng wéi 失当行为 *n* misconduct

shī héng 失衡 *n* imbalance

shī mián 失眠 *n* insomnia

shī míng 失明 *n* blindness

shī qù 失去 *iv* lose

shī qù lián luò 失去联络 *v* drift apart

shī qù zhī jué de 失去知觉的 *adj* unconscious

shī shì（chuán děng） 失事（船等）*n* wreckage

shī wàng 失望 *n* disappointment

shī xiū 失修 *n* disrepair

shī yè 失业 *n* unemployment

shī yè de 失业的 *adj* jobless, unemployed

shī zhí 失职 *n* delinquency

shī zhí de 失职的 *adj* delinquent

shī zōng de 失踪的 *adj* missing

shī zi 虱子 *n* lice, louse

shī 诗 *n* poem

shī gē 诗歌 *n* poetry, verse

shī rén 诗人 *n* poet

shī cuī mián shù 施催眠术 *v* hypnotize

shī féi 施肥 *v* fertilize, soil

shī guò féi de 施过肥的 *adj* soiled

shī jiā 施加 *v* exert, impose

shī shě 施舍 *n* alms, handout

shī xǐ 施洗 *v* baptize

shī yā 施压 *v* pressure

shī yǐ cuī mián shù 施以催眠术 *v* mesmerize

shī yǐ tú yóu lǐ 施以涂油礼 *v* anoint

shī yǔ 施与 *n* dispensation

shī zi 狮子 *n* lion

shī de 湿的 *adj* wet

shī dù 湿度 *n* humidity

shí 十 *adj* ten

shí bā 十八 *adj* eighteen

shí è bù shè de 十恶不赦的 *adj* heinous

shí èr 十二 *adj* twelve

shí èr gè 十二个 *n* dozen

shí èr yuè 十二月 *n* December

shí jìn wèi de 十进位的 *adj* decimal

shí jiǔ 十九 *adj* nineteen

shí liù 十六 *adj* sixteen

shí měi fēn 十美分 *n* nickel

shí nián 十年 *n* decade

shí qī 十七 *adj* seventeen

shí sān 十三 *adj* thirteen

shí sì 十四 *adj* fourteen

shí wǔ 十五 *adj* fifteen

shí yī 十一 *adj* eleven

shí yī yuè 十一月 *n* November

shí yì 十亿 *n* billion

shí yuè 十月 *n* October

shí zì jià 十字架 *n* crucifix

shí zì jiāo chā 十字交叉 *v* crisscross

shí zì jūn zhàn shì 十字军战士 *n* crusader

shí zì lù kǒu 十字路口 *n* crossroads

shí jǐn wù 什锦物 *n* assortment

shén me 什么 *adj* what

shí huà de 石化的 *adj* petrified

shí huī 石灰 *n* lime

shí huī shí 石灰石 *n* limestone

shí liu 石榴 *n* pomegranate

shí tou 石头 *n* rock, stone

shí yóu 石油 *n* oil, petroleum

shí cháng 时常 *adv* regularly

shí cháng fā shēng de 时常发生的 *v* frequent

shí dài 时代 *n* era

shí jiān 时间 *n* time

shí jiān biǎo 时间表 *n* timetable

shí jiān jì huà 时间计划 *n* schedule

（**shí jiān**）**xiāo shì** （时间）消逝 *v* elapse

shí kè 时刻 *n* moment

shí máo 时髦 *n* vogue

shí shàng 时尚 *n* fad, fashion

shí shì fěng cì jù 时事讽刺剧 *n* revue

shí zhōng 时钟 *n* clock

shí zhuāng wǔ tái 时装舞台 *n* runway

shí bié 识别 *v* discern

shí jì de 实际的 *adj* actual

shí jì shàng 实际上 *adv* actually, virtually

shí jiàn de 实践的 *adj* practicing

shí jiàn zhī shi 实践知识 *n* know-how

shí lì 实力 *n* strength

shí xí shēng 实习生 *v* intern

shí xiàn 实现 *v* achieve, live up

shí xiàn 实现 *n* fulfillment

shí yàn 实验 *n* experiment

shí yàn shì 实验室 *n* lab

shí yòng de 实用的 *adj* practical

shí yòng zhǔ yì zhě 实用主义者 *adj* pragmatist

shí zhì de 实质的 *adj* substantial

shí dào 食道 *n* esophagus

shí pǐn 食品 *n* food, foodstuff

shí pǔ 食谱 *n* recipe

shí rén zhě 食人者 *n* cannibal

shí táng 食堂 *n* canteen

shí yú 鲥鱼 *n* anchovy

shǐ qián de 史前的 *adj* prehistoric

shǐ 使 *v* enable

（**shǐ**）**ān jìng xià lái** （使）安静下来 *n* hush

shǐ（**gè rén、shè tuán、jī gòu děng**）**lì shǔ yú yī jiào dà zǔ zhī** 使（个人、社团、机构等）隶属於一较大组织 *v* affiliate

shǐ（**zuì xíng**）**jiǎn qīng de** 使（罪行）减轻的 *adj* extenuating

shǐ ……shòu yì 使……受益 *v* benefit

（**shǐ**）**àn dàn** （使）暗淡 *v* dim

shǐ ān quán 使安全 *v* secure

shǐ biàn tián 使变甜 *v* sweeten

shǐ bù gāo xìng 使不高兴 *v* displease

shǐ cháo shī 使潮湿 *v* dampen

shǐ chén zhuó 使沉着 *v* sedate

S

shǐ chéng wéi bì yào 使成为必要
v entail

shǐ chéng yī háng 使成一行 *v*
align

shǐ chéng dān 使承担 *v* entail

shǐ chī jīng 使吃惊 *v* astonish,
astound

shǐ chí dùn 使迟钝 *v* constipate

shǐ chǒu lòu 使丑陋 *v* disfigure

shǐ diū liǎn 使丢脸 *n* shame

shǐ duì kàng 使对抗 *v* antagonize

shǐ duò luò 使堕落 *adj* deprave

shǐ è huà 使恶化 *v* aggravate

shǐ è huà 使恶化 *adj* deprave

shǐ ěr lóng 使耳聋 *v* deafen

shǐ fán nǎo 使烦恼 *v* pester

shǐ féi wò 使肥沃 *v* fertilize

shǐ fēn lí 使分离 *v* detach

shǐ fèn nù 使愤怒 *v* anger

shǐ fēng fù 使丰富 *v* fertilize

shǐ fú cóng 使服从 *v* subject

shǐ fú shuǐ tǔ 使服水土 *v*
acclimatize

shǐ fǔ bài 使腐败 *adj* deprave

shǐ fǔ làn 使腐烂 *v* decompose

shǐ gān gà 使尴尬 *v* embarrass

shǐ gāo xìng 使高兴 *v* rejoice

shǐ hán xīn 使寒心 *v* chill

shǐ hú tu 使糊涂 *v* confuse

shǐ hù xiāng guān lián 使互相关
联 *v* correlate

shǐ huà hé 使化合 *v* compound

shǐ jí dù tòng kǔ 使极度痛苦 *v*
agonize

shǐ jí zhōng 使集中 *v* center

shǐ jiān gù 使坚固 *v* corroborate

shǐ jiē nà wéi chéng yuán 使接纳
为成员 *v* affiliate

shǐ jié méng 使结盟 *v* align

(shǐ) jìn huà (使)进化 *v*
evolve

shǐ jīng hài huò jǔ sàng 使惊骇或
沮丧 *v* appall

shǐ jīng qí 使惊奇 *v* amaze

shǐ jìng luán 使痉挛 *v* convulse

shǐ jiù rèn yào zhí 使就任要职 *v*
chair

shǐ jǔ sàng 使沮丧 *v* dismay

shǐ jù jí 使聚集 *v* aggregate

shǐ kōng de 使空的 *v* empty

shǐ kū jié 使枯竭 *v* deplete

shǐ kū zào 使枯燥 *v* bore

shǐ kǔ nǎo 使苦恼 *v* haunt

shǐ kùn huò 使困惑 *v* baffle

shǐ lì shǔ 使隶属 *v* subject

shǐ mǎn yì 使满意 *v* content,
satisfy

shǐ máng mù 使盲目 *v* blind

shǐ máng rán 使茫然 *v* daze

shǐ miàn duì 使面对 *v* confront

shǐ míng liàng 使明亮 *v* brighten

shǐ mìng 使命 *n* mission

(shǐ) mó hu (使)模糊 *v* dim

shǐ mù xuàn 使目眩 *v* dazzle

shǐ rè xīn 使热心 *v* enthuse

shǐ rén nǎo hǎi zhōng fú xiàn chū
使人脑海中浮现出 *v* conjure up

shǐ rén xìn fú de 使人信服的 *adj*
convincing

S

shǐ rén yú kuài de 使人愉快的 *adj* agreeable, pleasing

shǐ rù zuò 使入座 *v* chair

shǐ shāng xīn 使伤心 *v* sadden

shǐ shī miàn zi 使失面子 *v* deface

shǐ shī qù dòu zhì 使失去斗志 *v* demoralize

shǐ shī wàng 使失望 *v* disappoint

shǐ shì qì dī luò 使士气低落 *v* demoralize

shǐ shì yìng xīn huán jìng 使适应新环境 *v* acclimatize

shǐ shú xī 使熟悉 *v* acquaint

shǐ shùn cóng 使顺从 *v* subdue

shǐ shùn lì 使顺利 *v* smooth

shǐ suō xiǎo 使缩小 *v* deflate

shǐ tān huàn 使瘫痪 *v* cripple

shǐ tòng kǔ （**yōu lǜ**） 使痛苦 （忧虑） *v* distress

shǐ tú 使徒 *n* apostle

shǐ tú de 使徒的 *adj* apostolic

shǐ wú xiào 使无效 *v* nullify

shǐ xí guàn yú 使习惯于 *v* accustom

shǐ xǐ yuè 使喜悦 *v* delight

shǐ xiǎn xiàn 使显现 *v* manifest

shǐ xiāng xìn 使相信 *v* convince

shǐ xiè qì 使泄气 *v* discourage

shǐ xīng fèn 使兴奋 *v* excite

shǐ xiū kuì 使羞愧 *n* shame

shǐ yǎn huā 使眼花 *v* dazzle

shǐ yōng jǐ 使拥挤 *v* crowd

shǐ yòng 使用 *n* access, use

shǐ yòng 使用 *v* avail, employ, use, utilize

shǐ yòng zhě 使用者 *n* user

shǐ yòng zhōng de 使用中的 *adj* engaged

shǐ yǒu lián xì 使有联系 *v* associate

shǐ yǒu shēng qì 使有生气 *v* animate

shǐ yǒu zūn yán 使有尊严 *v* dignify

shǐ yù nàn 使遇难 *v* wreck

shǐ yūn xuàn 使晕眩 *v* daze

shǐ zài jié hé 使再结合 *v* rejoin

shǐ zhě 使者 *n* herald

shǐ zhèn zuò 使振作 *v* cheer up

shǐ zhèn dòng 使震动 *v* convulse

shǐ zhèn jīng 使震惊 *v* shock

shǐ chóng shēng 使重生 *v* revive

shǐ zháo mí 使着迷 *v* bewitch

shí zì jià 使字架 *n* cross

shì bīng 士兵 *n* soldier

shì zú 氏族 *n* clan

shì gù 世故 *n* poise

shì jì 世纪 *n* century, epoch

shì jiān de 世间的 *adj* worldly

shì jiè 世界 *n* world

shì xí 世袭 *n* patrimony

shì zhǎng 市长 *n* mayor

shì chǎng 市场 *n* market

shì de 市的 *adj* civic

shì mín de 市民的 *adj* civic

shì zhèng tīng 市政厅 *n* city hall, town hall

shì zhōng xīn 市中心 *n* downtown

shì ài de 示爱的 *adj* affectionate

shì wēi yóu xíng 示威游行 *v* demonstrate

shì yì 示意 *v* beckon

shì 事 *n* matter

shì gù 事故 *n* accident

shì hòu fēn xī 事后分析 *n* hindsight

shì jiàn 事件 *n* circumstance, event, incident

shì shí 事实 *n* fact

shì shí 事实 *adj* factual

shì shí shàng 事实上 *adv* virtually

shì wù 事务 *n* affair

shì xiān 事先 *adv* beforehand

shì xiān de 事先的 *adj* prior

shì jiǎo 视角 *n* perspective

shì jué 视觉 *n* vision

shì jué de 视觉的 *adj* visual

shì lì 视力 *n* eyesight

shì xiàn 视线 *n* sight

shì yě 视野 *n* view

shì zuò 视作 *v* deem

shì diǎn 试点 *n* pilot

shì tàn 试探 *n* probing

shì tàn 试探 *v* sound out

shì tú 试图 *v* attempt

shì tú 试图 *n* attempt

shì máo 饰毛 *n* crest

shì pǐn 饰品 *n* ornament

shì 室 *n* chamber

shì nèi 室内 *adv* indoor

shì nèi zhuāng shì pǐn 室内装饰品 *n* upholstery

shì qiáng líng ruò zhě 恃强凌弱者 *adj* bully

shì 是 *iv* be

shì 是 *adv* yes

shì ...de biāo zhì 是...的标志 *v* denote

shì fǒu 是否 *c* whether

shì zi jiāo 柿子椒 *n* bell pepper

shì dàng de 适当的 *adj* appropriate, expedient, proper

shì dé qí fǎn 适得其反 *v* backfire

shì hé 适合 *v* fit

shì hé de 适合的 *adj* fitting, suitable

shì pèi qì 适配器 *n* adapter

shì yì 适意 *n* amenities

shì yìng 适应 *v* adapt

shì yìng 适应 *n* adaptation

shì yìng xìng qiáng 适应性强 *adj* adaptable

shì yòng 适用 *v* apply

shì yòng de 适用的 *adj* applicable

shì fàng 释放 *v* discharge, free, release

shì fàng 释放 *n* discharge

shì yì 释义 *n* interpretation

shì hào 嗜好 *n* hobby

shì xuè de 嗜血的 *adj* bloodthirsty

shōu cáng 收藏 *n* collection

shōu cáng jiā 收藏家 *n* collector

shōu dào 收到 *v* receive

shōu duì 收兑 *n* redemption

shōu fèi 收费 *n* toll

shōu fèi 收费 *v* toll

shōu gē 收割 *v* reap

shōu gòu 收购 *v* acquire

shōu gòu 收购 *n* acquisition

shōu huí 收回 *v* recoup, regain, retrieve, take back, withdraw

S

shōu jí 收集 *v* collect
shōu jiàn rén 收件人 *n* addressee
shōu jǐn 收紧 *v* tighten
shōu jù 收据 *n* receipt, voucher
shōu kuǎn rén 收款人 *n* payee
shōu mǎi 收买 *v* buy off
shōu rù 收入 *n* income, revenue
shōu suō 收缩 *n* contraction
shōu suō 收缩 *iv* shrink
shōu yǎng 收养 *v* adopt, foster
shōu yǎng 收养 *n* adoption
shōu yǎng guān xì de 收养关系的 *adj* adoptive
shōu yì 收益 *n* gain, proceeds
shōu yīn jī 收音机 *n* radio
shōu yín yuán 收银员 *n* cashier
shǒu 手 *n* hand
shǒu bì 手臂 *n* arm
shǒu biǎo 手表 *n* watch
shǒu cè 手册 *n* handbook, manual
shǒu dài 手袋 *n* handbag
shǒu diàn tǒng 手电筒 *n* flashlight
shǒu dòng de 手动的 *adj* manual
shǒu duàn 手段 *n* means
shǒu fēng qín 手风琴 *n* accordion
shǒu gǎo 手稿 *n* manuscript
shǒu gōng zhì zuò 手工制作 *adj* handmade
shǒu jī 手机 *n* cell phone
shǒu kào 手铐 *n* cuff, handcuffs
shǒu liú dàn 手榴弹 *n* grenade
shǒu pà 手帕 *n* handkerchief
shǒu qiāng 手枪 *n* handgun, pistol
shǒu qiǎo de 手巧的 *adj* handy

shǒu shì cāi zì 手势猜字 *n* charade
shǒu tào 手套 *n* glove
shǒu tí xiāng 手提箱 *n* suitcase
shǒu wàn 手腕 *n* wrist
shǒu wú cùn tiě de 手无寸铁的 *adj* unarmed
shǒu xià 手下 *adj* underlying
shǒu yì 手艺 *n* craft
shǒu zhǎng 手掌 *n* palm
shǒu zhàng 手杖 *n* cane
shǒu zhǐ 手指 *n* finger
shǒu zhuó 手镯 *n* bracelet
shǒu cái nú 守财奴 *n* miser
shǒu fǎ de 守法的 *adj* law-abiding
shǒu héng 守恒 *n* conservation
shǒu mén yuán 守门员 *n* goalkeeper
shǒu yè 守夜 *v* vigil
shǒu cì lòu miàn 首次露面 *n* debut
shǒu dū 首都 *n* capital
shǒu shì hé 首饰盒 *n* casket
shǒu xiàng 首相 *n* chancellor
shǒu yào 首要 *adj* foremost
shǒu yào 首要 *n* primacy
shǒu yào de 首要的 *adj* premier, prime
shǒu yào de 首要地 *adv* chiefly
shòu yī 寿衣 *n* shroud
shòu yī 寿衣 *adj* shrouded
shòu hài zhě 受害者 *n* victim
shòu huì 受贿 *n* bribery
shòu jīng xià de 受惊吓的 *adj* startled

S

shòu kǔ 受苦 *v* suffer

shòu nüè kuáng 受虐狂 *n* masochism

shòu shāng 受伤 *v* injure, wound

shòu xī yǐn 受吸引 *v* gravitate

shòu yì 受益 *v* benefit

shòu yì rén 受益人 *n* beneficiary

shòu liè 狩猎 *v* hunt

shòu liè 狩猎 *n* hunting

shòu xìng 兽性 *n* bestiality

shòu xué 兽穴 *n* den

shòu yī 兽医 *n* veterinarian

shòu huò dān 售货单 *n* sale slip

shòu piào chù 售票处 *n* box office

shòu (**quán**) **gěi** 授（权）给 *v* delegate

shòu quán 授权 *n* authorization

shòu quán 授权 *v* authorize

shòu yǔ 授予 *v* bestow, confer, grant

shòu yǔ xǔ kě 授予许可 *v* license

shòu ruò 瘦弱 *adj* emaciated

shū 书 *n* book

shū diàn 书店 *n* bookstore

shū guì 书柜 *n* bookcase

shū jià 书架 *n* bookcase

shū miàn de 书面的 *adj* written

shū mù 书目 *n* bibliography

shū shāng 书商 *n* bookseller

shū xiě 书写 *n* handwriting

shū xìn 书信 *n* epistle

shū shu 叔叔 *n* uncle

shū niǔ 枢纽 *n* hub

shū 梳 *v* comb

shū zi 梳子 *n* comb

shū nǚ bān de 淑女般的 *adj* ladylike

shū hu 疏忽 *n* negligence, oversight

shū hu de 疏忽的 *adj* negligent

shū sàn 疏散 *n* dispersal

shū sàn 疏散 *v* evacuate

shū shuǐ dào 疏水道 *n* aqueduct

shū yuǎn de 疏远的 *adj* aloof, estranged

shū shì 舒适 *n* amenities, comfort, ease

shū shì de 舒适的 *adj* comfortable, cozy

shū zhǎn 舒展 *n* stretch

shū zhǎn 舒展 *v* stretch

shū 输 *iv* lose

shū chū 输出 *n* output

shū jiā 输家 *n* loser

shū rù 输入 *n* input

shū sòng guǎn 输送管 *n* duct

shū xuè 输血 *n* transfusion

shū cài 蔬菜 *v* vegetable

shú huí 赎回 *v* redeem

shú jīn 赎金 *v* ransom

shú zuì 赎罪 *v* atone, expiate

shú zuì 赎罪 *n* atonement, expiation

shú liàn de 熟练的 *adj* versed

shú rén 熟人 *n* acquaintance

shú xī 熟悉 *n* acquaintance

shú xī 熟悉 *adj* familiar

shǔ 鼠 *n* mouse, rat

shǔ biāo 鼠标 *n* mouse

shǔ yì 鼠疫 *n* plague

S

shǔ lèi 薯类 *n* yam

shǔ piàn 薯片 *n* chip

shǔ tiáo 薯条 *n* fries

shǔ guāng 曙光 *n* twilight

shù yǔ 术语 *n* terminology

shù yǔ xué 术语学 *n* terminology

shù 束 *n* bunch, bundle

shù fù/fú 束缚 *n* bondage, tie; curb

shù fù /fú 束缚 *v* curb

shù 树 *n* tree

shù gàn 树干 *n* trunk

shù pí 树皮 *n* bark

shù yè 树液 *n* sap

shù zhī 树枝 *n* branch

shù lì 竖立 *v* erect

shù qín 竖琴 *n* harp

shù jù 数据 *n* data

shù jù kù 数据库 *n* database

shù liàng 数量 *n* amount, quantity

shù xué 数学 *n* math

shù zì 数字 *n* digit, figure, number

shù kǒu 漱口 *v* gargle

shuā 刷 *v* brush

shuā qù 刷去 *v* brush aside

shuā xīn 刷新 *v* brush up

shuā xīn 刷新 *v* refresh

shuā zi 刷子 *n* brush

shuāi bài 衰败 *v* decay

shuāi bài 衰败 *n* decay

shuāi lǎo de 衰老的 *adj* decrepit

shuāi luò 衰落 *v* decline

shuāi luò 衰落 *n* decline

shuāi ruò 衰弱 *v* languish

shuāi tuì 衰退 *v* decline, degenerate

shuāi tuì 衰退 *n* decline

shuāi tuì de 衰退的 *adj* degenerate

shuāi 摔 *v* tumble

shuāi jiāo 摔跤 *n* wrestling

shuāi jiāo shǒu 摔跤手 *n* wrestler

shuān zhù 闩住 *v* bar

shuān hǎo 拴好 *v* bolt

shuān zhù 拴住 *v* hitch up

shuāng 双 *adj* double

shuāng bāo tāi 双胞胎 *n* twin

shuāng bìn 双鬓 *n* sideburns

shuāng céng chuáng 双层床 *n* bunk bed

shuāng de 双的 *adj* dual

shuāng tǒng wàng yuǎn jìng 双筒望远镜 *n* binoculars

shuāng yǔ de 双语的 *adj* bilingual

shuāng yuán yīn 双元音 *n* diphthong

shuāng yuè yī cì de 双月一次的 *adj* bimonthly

shuāng dòng 霜冻 *n* frost

shuí /shéi 谁 *pro* who, whom

shuǐ 水 *n* water

shuǐ bīng 水兵 *n* sailor

shuǐ dòu 水痘 *n* chicken pox

shuǐ fèn 水分 *n* moisture

shuǐ guǎn gōng 水管工 *n* plumber

shuǐ guàn 水罐 *n* jug

shuǐ guǒ 水果 *n* fruit

shuǐ hú 水壶 *n* kettle

shuǐ jīng 水晶 *n* crystal

shuǐ kù 水库 *n* reservoir

shuǐ lì de 水力的 *adj* hydraulic

S

shuǐ lóng tóu 水龙头 *n* faucet

shuǐ mì de 水密的 *adj* waterproof, watertight

shuǐ ní 水泥 *n* cement, concrete

shuǐ niú 水牛 *n* buffalo

shuǐ pào 水泡 *n* blister

shuǐ píng de 水平的 *adj* horizontal

shuǐ shēng de 水生的 *adj* aquatic

shuǐ tǎ 水塔 *n* cistern

shuǐ tǎ 水獭 *n* otter

shuǐ zhì 水蛭 *n* leech

shuǐ zhū 水珠 *n* globule

shuǐ zú guǎn 水族馆 *n* aquarium

shuì 税 *n* duty, tax

shuì 睡 *iv* sleep

shuì mián 睡眠 *n* sleep

shuì yī 睡衣 *n* pajamas

shuì zháo 睡着 *adj* asleep

shǔn 吮 *v* suck

shùn biàn 顺便 *adv* incidentally

shùn cóng de 顺从的 *adj* amenable

shùn lì de 顺利的 *adj* smooth

shùn lì de 顺利地 *adv* smoothly

shùn biàn de 瞬变的 *adj* transient

shùn jiān 瞬间 *adv* momentarily

shuō 说 *iv* say, speak, utter

shuō fǎ 说法 *n* saying

shuō fú 说服 *v* convince, persuade

shuō fú lì 说服力 *n* persuasion

shuō fú lì de 说服力的 *adj* persuasive

shuō huǎng 说谎 *v* lie

shuō huǎng zhě 说谎者 *adj* liar

shuō jiào 说教 *v* preach

shuō jiào 说教 *n* preaching

shuō míng 说明 *v* demonstrate, illustrate

shuō míng 说明 *n* illustration

shuō xián huà 说闲话 *v* gossip

shuō xiào 说笑 *adv* jokingly

shuò shì 硕士 *n* master

sī chóu 丝绸 *n* silk

sī dài 丝带 *n* ribbon

sī jīn 丝巾 *n* scarf

sī mián 丝棉 *n* floss

sī xiàn 丝线 *n* floss

sī 司 *n* division

sī fǎ 司法 *n* justice

sī jī 司机 *n* chauffeur, driver

sī rén de 私人的 *adj* private

sī shēng de 私生的 *adj* illegitimate

sī shēng zǐ /nǚ 私生子/女 *n* bastard

sī shì 私室 *n* den

sī xià chéng rèn de 私下承认的 *adj* off-the-record

sī xíng chǔ sǐ 私刑处死 *v* lynch

sī yǔ 私语 *n* murmur

sī xiǎng 思想 *n* mind

sī yǎ 嘶哑 *adj* hoarse

sī 撕 *iv* tear

sī chéng suì piàn 撕成碎片 *v* shred

sī xià miàn jù 撕下面具 *v* unmask

sǐ 死 *v* die

sǐ de 死的 *adj* dead, lifeless

sǐ qù de 死去的 *adj* deceased

sǐ wáng 死亡 *n* death, demise

sǐ wáng lǜ 死亡率 *n* mortality

sǐ wáng rén shù 死亡人数 *n* death toll

sǐ wáng xiàn jǐng 死亡陷阱 *n* death trap

sì 四 *adj* four

sì chù mì shí 四处觅食 *v* prowl

sì fēn zhī yī 四分之一 *n* quarter

sì shí 四十 *adj* forty

sì yuè 四月 *n* April

sì zhī 四肢 *n* extremities

sì yuàn de 寺院的 *adj* monastic

sì nüè 肆虐 *n* havoc

sōng chí de 松弛的 *adj* lax

sōng chí de 松驰的 *adj* slack

sōng chuí de 松垂的 *adj* baggy

sōng kāi 松开 *v* unwind

sōng sǎn de 松散的 *adj* lame, loose

sōng shǔ 松鼠 *n* squirrel

sōng shù 松树 *n* pine

sǒng jiān 耸肩 *v* shrug

sǒng lì de 耸立的 *adj* towering

sòng gē 颂歌 *n* carol

sōu suǒ 搜索 *v* search

sōu suǒ 搜索 *n* search

sōu xún 搜寻 *n* quest

sū xǐng 苏醒 *iv* awake

sù sòng 诉讼 *n* litigation, proceedings

sù miáo 素描 *v* sketch

sù miáo 素描 *n* sketch

sù shí zhǔ yì zhě 素食主义者 *v* vegetarian

sù dù 速度 *n* velocity

sù jì 速记 *n* shorthand

sù yuàn 宿怨 *n* feud

sù liào 塑料 *n* plastic

sù zào 塑造 *v* shape

suān 酸 *n* acid

suān dù 酸度 *n* acidity

suān liū liū de 酸溜溜的 *adj* sour

suàn cuò 算错 *v* miscalculate

suàn shù 算术 *n* arithmetic

suī rán 虽然 *c* although, though

suí hòu de 随后的 *adj* subsequent

suí jī de 随机地 *adv* randomly

suì 碎 *adv* asunder

suì piàn 碎片 *n* debris, shred

suì ròu 碎肉 *n* mincemeat

suì dào 隧道 *n* tunnel

sūn zi 孙子 *n* grandson

sǔn hài 损害 *n* detriment, disadvantage, harm

sǔn hài 损害 *v* harm, impair

sǔn huài 损坏 *n* damage

sǔn huài 损坏 *v* damage

sǔn huǐ （wài mào） 损毁（外貌） *v* disfigure

sǔn shāng wài guān 损伤外观 *v* deface

sǔn shī 损失 *n* loss

sǔn wū 损污 *v* defile

suō duǎn 缩短 *v* abbreviate, condense, contract, shorten

suō huí 缩回 *v* retract

suō xiǎo 缩小 *v* dwindle

suō xiě 缩写 *v* abbreviate

shuǐ lóng tóu 缩写 *n* abbreviation, initials

S

suō xiě cí 缩写词 *n* abbreviation
suō yǐng 缩影 *n* miniature
suǒ wèi de 所谓的 *adj* so-called
suǒ yǒu 所有 *adj* all
suǒ yǒu quán 所有权 *n* ownership
suǒ jià 索价 *v* charge
suǒ yǐn 索引 *n* bibliography
suǒ suì de 琐碎的 *adj* paltry, trivial
suǒ 锁 *v* lock
suǒ 锁 *n* lock
suǒ gǔ 锁骨 *n* collarbone
suǒ jiàng 锁匠 *n* locksmith
suǒ qǐ lái 锁起来 *v* lock up
suǒ shàng 锁上 *v* lock up

T

tā 他 *pro* he
tā de 他的 *adj* his
tā de 他的 *pro* his
tā men 他们 *pro* they
tā men zì jǐ 他们自己 *pro* themselves
tā huǐ 塌毁 *n* disrepair
tā xiàn 塌陷 *v* cave in
tǎ 塔 *n* tower
tǎ lóu 塔楼 *n* turret
tà bǎn 踏板 *n* pedal
tà bǎn chē 踏板车 *n* scooter
tāi ér 胎儿 *n* fetus

tái 台 *n* stand
tái qiú 台球 *n* billiards
tài 太 *adv* too
tài guò fèn de 太过份的 *adj* overdone
tài píng jiān 太平间 *n* mortuary
tài xián 太咸 *adj* salty
tài yáng 太阳 *n* sun
tài yáng néng de 太阳能的 *adj* solar
tài du 态度 *n* attitude
tān cái 贪财 *n* avarice
tān lán 贪婪 *n* avarice, greed
tān lán de 贪婪的 *adj* avaricious
tān tú 贪图 *v* covet
tān wū 贪污 *n* graft
tān xīn 贪心 *adj* greedy
tān xīn de 贪心的 *adj* insatiable
tān zāng wǎng fǎ 贪赃枉法 *v* pervert
tān 摊 *n* stand
tān huán 摊还 *v* amortize
tān pái 摊牌 *n* showdown
tān xiāo 摊销 *v* amortize
tān huàn 瘫痪 *n* paralysis
tān huàn 瘫痪 *v* paralyze
tán huà 谈话 *v* converse
tán pàn 谈判 *v* negotiate
tán pàn 谈判 *n* negotiation
tǎn bái 坦白 *n* admission, confession
tǎn bái 坦白 *v* confess
tǎn bái de 坦白的 *adj* candid
tǎn bái de 坦白地 *adv* frankly
tǎn kè 坦克 *n* tank

tǎn shuài 坦率 *adj* frank
tǎn shuài 坦率 *n* frankness
tǎn shuài de 坦率的 *adj* plain,
　straight
tàn xī 叹息 *n* sigh
tàn xī 叹息 *v* sigh
tàn jìn 炭烬 *n* embers
tàn cè qì 探测器 *n* detector
tàn chá 探查 *v* probe
tàn suǒ 探索 *v* explore
tàn xiǎn jiā 探险家 *n* explorer
tāng 汤 *n* soup
tāng chí 汤匙 *n* tablespoon
táng tū de 唐突的 *adj* brusque
táng xiōng dì zǐ mèi 堂兄弟姊妹
　 n cousin
táng 糖 *n* sugar
táng guǒ 糖果 *n* candy
táng jiāng 糖浆 *n* syrup
táng niào bìng 糖尿病 *n* diabetes
táng niào bìng huàn zhě 糖尿病
　患者 *adj* diabetic
tǎng 躺 *iv* lay, lie
tàng shāng 烫伤 *v* scald
táo bì 逃避 *v* dodge, duck, elude,
　escape, evade, evasion
táo bì de 逃避的 *adj* evasive
táo fàn (**bīng**) 逃犯（兵） *n*
　deserter
táo pǎo 逃跑 *v* defect, escape,
　run away
táo tuō 逃脱 *v* outrun
táo wáng 逃亡 *iv* flee
táo wáng zhě 逃亡者 *n* deserter,
　fugitive

táo 桃 *n* peach
táo huā xīn mù 桃花心木 *n*
　mahogany
táo cí 陶瓷 *n* ceramic
táo qì 陶器 *n* crockery
táo zuì 陶醉 *v* revel
táo zuì de 陶醉的 *adj* intoxicated
táo qì guǐ 淘气鬼 *n* rascal
tǎo hǎo 讨好 *v* ingratiate
tǎo jià huán jià 讨价还价 *v*
　bargain, haggle
tǎo lùn 讨论 *v* debate, discuss
tǎo lùn 讨论 *n* debate, discussion
tǎo rén xǐ huān de 讨人喜欢的
　adj delightful
tǎo yàn 讨厌 *v* dislike, loathe
tǎo yàn 讨厌 *n* dislike, nuisance
tǎo yàn de 讨厌的 *adj*
　cumbersome, nasty, repugnant,
　undesirable
tào 套 *v* wrap
tè bié de 特别的 *adj* special
tè cǐ 特此 *adv* hereby
tè diǎn 特点 *n* dimension, feature
tè jì yǎn yuán 特技演员 *n* acrobat
tè quán 特权 *n* franchise,
　prerogative, privilege
tè shè 特赦 *n* amnesty
tè shǐ 特使 *n* envoy
tè shū 特殊 *adj* exceptional
tè xǔ 特许 *n* concession
tè xǔ jīng xiāo quán 特许经销权
　n franchise
tè xǔ shè lì 特许设立 *v* charter
tè yǒu de 特有的 *adj*
　characteristic, peculiar

T

tè zhēng 特征 *n* trait

téng tòng 疼痛 *n* ache, pain, disease, illness, sickness

téng 藤 *n* vine

téng tiáo 藤条 *n* cane

tī chú 剔除 *v* strike out

tī 踢 *v* kick

tí 啼 *v* crow

tí chàng 提倡 *v* advocate

tí chū 提出 *v* address, bring up, come forward

tí chū ... zuò wéi fǎn duì de lǐ yóu 提出 ... 作为反对的理由 *v* object

tí dào 提到 *v* mention

tí dào 提到 *n* mention

tí gāo 提高 *v* enhance, heighten

tí gōng 提供 *v* offer, provide

tí gōng 提供 *n* offer, offering, provision

tí jiàn yì 提建议 *v* propose

tí jiāo 提交 *v* submit

tí jiāo dàng àn 提交档案 *v* file

tí kuǎn 提款 *n* withdrawal

tí liàn 提炼 *v* refine

tí míng 提名 *v* nominate

tí qián 提前 *v* pull ahead

tí shēng 提升 *v* elevate

tí shì 提示 *n* reminder

tí wèn 提问 *v* question

tí wèn dá 提问答 *v* quiz

tí xǐng 提醒 *v* remind

tí yì 提议 *v* counsel

tí yì 提议 *n* proposition

tí gū 鹈鹕 *n* pelican

tí cí 题词 *n* inscription

tí xiàn 题献 *v* dedicate

tí 蹄 *n* hoof

tǐ huì dào 体会到 *v* realize

tǐ jī 体积 *n* bulk

tǐ jī dà de 体积大的 *adj* bulky

tǐ tiē de 体贴的 *adj* considerate

tǐ xì de 体系的 *adj* systematic

tǐ xiàn 体现 *v* embody

tǐ yàn 体验 *n* experience

tǐ yù 体育 *n* sport

tì 剃 *v* shave

tì dāo 剃刀 *n* razor

tì dài 替代 *v* substitute

tì dài 替代 *n* substitute

tì dài huò gòng xuǎn zé de rén huò wù 替代或供选择的人或物 *n* alternative

tì huàn 替换 *v* refill, replace

tì huàn 替换 *n* replacement

tì zuì yáng 替罪羊 *n* scapegoat

tiān 天 *n* day

tiān cái 天才 *n* genius

tiān chuāng 天窗 *n* skylight

tiān de 天的 *adj* celestial

tiān é 天鹅 *n* swan

tiān é róng 天鹅绒 *n* velvet

tiān fù de 天赋的 *adj* innate

tiān guó de 天国的 *adj* celestial

tiān huā 天花 *n* smallpox

tiān huā bǎn 天花板 *n* ceiling

tiān kōng 天空 *n* sky

tiān kōng de 天空的 *adj* celestial

tiān qì 天气 *n* weather

tiān rán de 天然的 *adj* crude

tiān shēng de 天生的 *adj* innate
tiān shǐ 天使 *n* angel
tiān shǐ bān de 天使般的 *adj* angelic
tiān táng 天堂 *n* heaven, paradise
tiān táng de 天堂的 *adj* heavenly
tiān tiān 天天 *adj* everyday
tiān wén de 天文的 *adj* astronomic
tiān wén tái 天文台 *n* observatory
tiān wén xué 天文学 *n* astronomy
tiān wén xué jiā 天文学家 *n* astronomer
tiān xiàn 天线 *n* antenna
tiān xiàn de 天线的 *adj* terrestrial
tiān zhēn de 天真的 *adj* naive
tiān zhǔ jiào 天主教 *n* Catholicism
tiān zhǔ jiào de 天主教的 *adj* catholic
（**tiān zhǔ jiào de**）**méi gui jīng** （天主教的）玫瑰经 *n* rosary
tiān jiā 添加 *v* add
tiān jiā 添加 *n* addition
tián dì 田地 *n* field
tián jìng 田径 *n* track
tián yuán shēng huó de 田园生活的 *adj* pastoral
tián 甜 *n* sweetness
tián cài 甜菜 *n* beet
tián de 甜的 *adj* sweet
tián guā 甜瓜 *n* melon
tián pǐn 甜品 *n* dessert
tián shí 甜食 *n* sweets
tián xīn 甜心 *n* honey
tián bǔ 填补 *v* fill

tián chōng 填充 *v* populate
tián liào 填料 *n* padding
tián mái chǎng 填埋场 *n* landfill
tǎn 舔 *v* lick
tiǎo dòng 挑动 *n* dare
tiǎo qǐ 挑起 *v* stir up
tiāo ti 挑剔 *adj* fussy
tiāo ti de 挑剔的 *adj* choosy, nitpicking
tiǎo xìn 挑衅 *n* defiance, provocation
tiǎo xìn 挑衅 *v* defy, provoke
tiǎo zhàn 挑战 *v* challenge
tiǎo zhàn 挑战 *n* challenge, dare
tiǎo zhàn xìng de 挑战性的 *adj* challenging
tiáo 条 *n* strip
tiáo jiàn 条件 *n* condition
tiáo kuǎn 条款 *n* clause, terms
tiáo wén 条纹 *n* stripe
tiáo wén de 条纹的 *adj* striped
tiáo yuē 条约 *n* treaty
tiáo dà 调大 *v* turn up
tiáo hǎo 调好 *v* tune
tiáo hé 调和 *n* accord
tiáo jié qì 调节器 *n* conditioner
tiáo jiě 调解 *v* mediate
tiáo jiě yuán 调解员 *n* mediator
tiáo kòng 调控 *v* regulate
tiáo lǐ yuán 调理员 *n* conditioner
diào qiān 调迁 *v* relocate
tiáo qíng 调情 *v* flirt
tiáo wèi pǐn 调味品 *n* condiment, seasoning
tiáo wèi zhī 调味汁 *n* sauce

T

tiáo yǎng de 调养的 *adj* convalescent

tiáo zhěng 调整 *v* adjust

tiáo zhěng 调整 *n* adjustment

tiáo zhì 调制 *v* concoct

tiáo zhì 调制 *n* concoction

tiào 跳 *v* jump

tiào 跳 *n* jump

tiào bǎn 跳板 *n* springboard

tiào dòng 跳动 *n* throb

tiào dòng 跳动 *v* throb

tiào dòng de 跳动的 *adj* jumpy

tiào guò 跳过 *v* skip

tiào guò 跳过 *n* skip

tiào lán 跳栏 *n* hurdle

tiào sǎn 跳伞 *v* bail out

tiào shuǐ 跳水 *v* dive

tiào wǔ 跳舞 *n* dancing

tiào yuè 跳跃 *v* hop

tiào zǎo 跳蚤 *n* flea

tiē 贴 *v* paste

tiē shàng 贴上 *v* affix

tiē zhǐ 贴纸 *n* sticker

tiě 铁 *n* iron

tiě gùn 铁棍 *n* crowbar

tiě jiàng 铁匠 *n* blacksmith

tiě liàn 铁链 *n* shackle

tiě lù 铁路 *n* railroad

tiě qiāo 铁锹 *n* spade

tiě qiāo 铁橇 *n* crowbar

tiě xiù 铁锈 *n* rust

tiě zhēn 铁砧 *n* anvil

tīng 听 *v* listen

tīng bù qīng 听不清 *n* deafness

tīng dào 听到 *iv* hear

tīng qǐ lái 听起来 *v* sound

tīng zhèng huì 听证会 *n* hearing

tīng zhòng 听众 *n* audience, listener

tíng 亭 *n* pavilion

tíng yuàn 庭院 *n* courtyard

tíng bó 停泊 *v* moor, park

tíng bó chù 停泊处 *n* berth

tíng chē 停车 *n* parking

tíng chē chǎng 停车场 *n* parking

tíng dùn 停顿 *adj* standstill

tíng huǒ 停火 *n* cease-fire

tíng liú 停留 *v* stop over

tíng xià 停下 *n* holdup

tíng zhàn 停战 *n* armistice

tíng zhǐ 停止 *v* cease, desist, discontinue, halt, stop

tíng zhǐ 停止 *n* recess, stop

tíng zhì 停滞 *v* stagnate

tíng zhì 停滞 *n* stagnation

tíng zhì de 停滞的 *adj* stagnant

tǐng zhí de 挺直的 *adj* upright

tōng cháng 通常 *adv* normally, ordinarily

tōng dào 通道 *n* admittance, passage

tōng fēng 通风 *v* air, ventilate

tōng fēng 通风 *n* ventilation

tōng guò 通过 *v* get by, pass

tōng guò 通过 *n* pass

tōng guò 通过 *pre* through

tōng huò péng zhàng 通货膨胀 *n* inflation

tōng jiān 通奸 *n* adultery

tōng qín 通勤 *v* commute

tōng xìn 通信 *v* correspond

tōng xìn zhě 通信者 *n* correspondent

tōng xíng zhèng 通行证 *n* pass

tōng xùn 通讯 *v* communicate

tōng xùn 通讯 *n* communication

tōng xùn jì zhě 通讯记者 *n* correspondent

tōng yòng 通用 *adj* generic

tōng zhī 通知 *v* inform, notify

tōng zhī 通知 *n* notification

tóng bān tóng xué 同班同学 *n* classmate

tóng bàn 同伴 *n* companion

tóng bāo 同胞 *n* brethren, compatriot, countryman

tóng bù 同步 *v* synchronize

tóng děng 同等 *adj* tantamount to

tóng děng de 同等的 *adj* equivalent

tóng huì 同会 *n* brethren

tóng jū 同居 *v* cohabit

tóng méng 同盟 *n* league

tóng móu 同谋 *n* complicity

tóng qíng 同情 *n* compassion, sympathy

tóng qíng 同情 *v* sympathize, agree, consent

tóng rén 同人 *n* fraternity

tóng shēng chuán yì 同声传译 *adj* simultaneous

tóng shí 同时 *adj* simultaneous

tóng shí fā shēng 同时发生 *v* coincide

tóng shì 同事 *n* colleague

tóng táng 同堂 *n* brethren

tóng háng 同行 *n* peer

tóng xìng zhì de 同性质的 *adj* congenial

tóng yàng 同样 *adv* likewise

tóng yàng de 同样的 *adj* alike

tóng yè gōng huì 同业公会 *n* guild

tóng yì 同意 *n* consent

tóng zhì 同志 *n* comrade

tóng zhōng xīn de 同中心的 *adj* concentric

tóng 铜 *n* copper

tóng huà 童话 *n* fairy

tóng jūn 童军 *n* scout

tóng nián 童年 *n* childhood

tóng kǒng 瞳孔 *n* pupil

tǒng jì 统计 *n* statistic

tǒng yī 统一 *n* unification

tǒng yī 统一 *v* unify

tǒng zhì 统治 *n* domination, dominion, rule

tǒng zhì 统治 *v* govern, rule

tǒng 桶 *n* barrel, bucket, pail

tǒng 筒 *n* canister

tòng 痛 *n* sore

tòng de 痛的 *adj* sore

tòng fēng 痛风 *n* gout

tòng hèn 痛恨 *v* abhor

tòng kū 痛哭 *v* cry out

tòng kǔ 痛苦 *n* agony, anguish, distress, suffering

tòng kǔ 痛苦 *adj* hurt

tòng kǔ de 痛苦的 *adj* harrowing, painful

T

tòng xīn 痛心 *adj* distressing

tòng yǐn 痛饮 *v* guzzle

tōu kàn 偷看 *v* peep

tōu qiè 偷窃 *n* heist, larceny

tōu qiè 偷窃 *v* rip off

tōu tīng 偷听 *v* eavesdrop

tōu tōu mō mō de 偷偷摸摸的 *adj* covert

tóu bù 头部 *n* head

tóu fà 头发 *n* hair

（**tóu fa de**）一缕（头发的）*n* lock

tóu gǔ 头骨 *n* skull

tóu kuī 头盔 *n* helmet

tóu mù 头目 *n* ringleader

tóu pí 头皮 *n* scalp

tóu pí xiè 头皮屑 *n* dandruff

tóu tòng 头痛 *n* headache

tóu yūn 头晕 *n* dizziness

tóu yūn de 头晕的 *adj* dizzy

tóu 投 *iv* cast

tóu bǎo 投保 *v* insure

tóu chǎn 投产 *v* inaugurate

tóu dì 投递 *n* delivery

tóu dì jiāo 投递交 *v* deliver

tóu jī 投机 *n* speculation

tóu xiáng 投降 *v* surrender

tóu xiáng 投降 *n* surrender

tóu piào 投票 *n* vote, voting

tóu piào yòng zhǐ 投票用纸 *n* ballot

tóu shí tou 投石头 *v* stone

tóu sù 投诉 *n* complaint

tóu sù 投诉 *v* lodge

tóu zhì 投掷 *v* hurl, throw

tóu zī 投资 *v* invest

tóu zī 投资 *n* investment

tóu zī zhě 投资者 *n* investor

tóu zǐ 骰子 *n* dice

tòu lù nèi qíng de 透露内情的 *adj* revealing

tòu míng de 透明的 *adj* transparent

tū 凸 *v* protrude

tū tóu de 秃头的 *adj* bald

tū yīng 秃鹰 *n* vulture

tū biàn 突变 *n* revulsion

tū chū 突出 *v* stand out, stick out

tū chū de 突出的 *adj* prominent

tū fā 突发 *v* break out, burst

tū jìn 突进 *v* dash

tū pò 突破 *n* breakthrough

tū rán 突然 *adv* abruptly

tū rán de 突然的 *adj* sudden

tū rán de 突然地 *adv* suddenly

tū rán kāi shǐ 突然开始 *v* burst into

tū rán lí kāi 突然离开 *v* break away

tū wéi 突围 *v* break out

tú 图 *n* diagram

tú biāo 图标 *n* icon

tú biǎo 图表 *n* chart

（**tú huà**）（图画）*n* foreground

tú jiě 图解 *adj* graphic

tú jiě 图解 *n* illustration

tú piàn 图片 *n* picture

tú shū guǎn 图书馆 *n* library

tú bù lǚ xíng 徒步旅行 *v* hike

tú bù lǚ xíng 徒步旅行 *n* hike

tú láo 徒劳 *adj* futile

tú láo 徒劳 *n* futility

tú gāo yào 涂膏药 *v* plaster

tú huà 涂画 *v* paint

tú liào 涂料 *n* dope; paint

tú piàn 涂片 *v* smear

tú xiāng yóu 涂香油 *v* embalm

tú yǐ yóu huò ruǎn gāo 涂以油或软膏 *v* anoint

tú chǎng 屠场 *n* butchery

tú fū 屠夫 *n* butcher

tú shā 屠杀 *n* butchery, massacre

tú zǎi 屠宰 *v* slaughter

tú zǎi 屠宰 *n* slaughter

tǔ 土 *n* dirt

tǔ dì 土地 *n* land

tǔ ěr qí 土耳其 *n* Turkey

tǔ ěr qí de 土耳其的 *adj* Turk

tǔ rǎng 土壤 *n* soil

tǔ lù 吐露 *v* confide

tǔ tán 吐痰 *iv* spit

tù zi 兔子 *n* rabbit

tuān liú 湍流 *n* turbulence

tuán duì 团队 *n* team

tuán jié 团结 *v* unite

tuán jié 团结 *n* unity

tuán jù 团聚 *n* reunion

tuī 推 *v* push, shove

tuī 推 *n* shove

tuī cè 推测 *v* suspect

tuī chí 推迟 *v* defer, postpone, put off

tuī chí 推迟 *n* postponement

tuī dìng 推定 *n* presumption

tuī duàn 推断 *n* corollary

tuī duàn 推断 *v* infer

tuī fān 推翻 *v* bring down, overthrow, overturn, topple

tuī fān 推翻 *n* overthrow

tuī guǎng 推广 *v* promote

tuī guǎng 推广 *n* promotion

tuī jiàn 推荐 *v* commend, recommend

tuī jiàn 推荐 *n* commendation

tuī jiàn rén 推荐人 *n* referee

tuī jìn 推进 *v* boost, propel

tuī jìn 推进 *n* boost

tuī jìn de 推进的 *adj* impulsive

tuī lǐ 推理 *n* reasoning

tuī lùn 推论 *v* deduce, reason

tuī xiāo yuán 推销员 *n* salesman

tuī xiè 推卸 *v* shirk

tuí fèi 颓废 *n* decadence

tuǐ 腿 *n* leg

tuì cháo 退潮 *v* ebb

tuì chū 退出 *v* bow out, pull out

tuì huà 退化 *n* degeneration, degradation

tuì huí 退回 *v* fall back

tuì kuǎn 退款 *v* refund

tuì kuǎn 退款 *n* refund

tuì kuǎn 退款 *n* reimbursement

tuì suō 退缩 *v* chicken out

tuì wèi 退位 *v* abdicate

tuì wèi 退位 *n* abdication

tuì wǔ jūn rén 退伍军人 *n* veteran

tuì xiū 退休 *v* retire

tuì xiū 退休 *n* retirement

T

tuì xiū jīn 退休金 *n* pension

tuì sè 褪色 *adj* faded

tūn bìng 吞并 *v* gobble

tūn mò 吞没 *v* engulf

tūn shí 吞食 *v* devour

tūn xià 吞下 *v* ingest

tuō ér suǒ 托儿所 *n* nursery

tuō fù 托付 *n* commitment

tuō jià 托架 *n* bracket

tuō pán 托盘 *n* tray

tuō 拖 *v* drug

tuō chē 拖车 *n* caravan, tow truck

tuō lā 拖拉 *v* haul

tuō lā jī 拖拉机 *n* tractor

tuō xié 拖鞋 *n* slipper

tuō yán de 拖延的 *adj* lingering

tuō yè 拖曳 *v* drag, shuffle, tow

tuō 脱 *iv* shed

tuō dǎng 脱党 *n* defection

tuō guāng yī fu 脱光衣服 *v* strip

tuō guǐ 脱轨 *v* derail

tuō lí 脱离 *v* break away, defect, secede

tuō pí 脱皮 *v* skim

tuō shēn 脱身 *v* get away

tuō shuǐ 脱水 *v* dehydrate

tuō yī 脱衣 *v* undress

tuó bèi 驼背 *n* hunchback

tuó bèi de 驼背的 *adj* hunched

tuó fēng 驼峰 *n* hump

tuó niǎo 鸵鸟 *n* ostrich

tuǒ dang de 妥当地 *adv* duly

tuǒ shàn de 妥善地 *adv* properly

tuǒ xié 妥协 *n* compromise

tuǒ xié 妥协 *v* compromise

tuǒ yuán xíng de 椭圆形的 *adj* oval

tuò zhí 拓殖 *v* colonize

tuò yè 唾液 *n* saliva

wā 挖 *iv* dig

wā jué 挖掘 *v* excavate

wā kuàng 挖矿 *v* mine

wǎ guàn 瓦罐 *n* jar

wǎ jiě 瓦解 *v* disintegrate

wǎ jiě de 瓦解的 *adj* prostrate

wǎ lì 瓦砾 *n* rubble

wǎ tè 瓦特 *n* watt

wà dài 袜带 *n* garter

wà zi 袜子 *n* sock

wài biǎo de 外表的 *adj* exterior

wài bù de 外部的 *adj* exterior, external

wài gōng 外公 *n* granddad, grandfather

wài guān 外观 *n* appearance

wài guó de 外国的 *adj* foreign

wài guó rén 外国人 *n* alien, foreigner

wài jiāo 外交 *n* diplomacy

wài jiāo de 外交的 *adj* diplomatic

wài jiāo guān 外交官 *n* diplomat

wài kē de 外科的 *adv* surgical

wài kē yī shēng 外科医生 *n* surgeon

wài ké 外壳 *n* crust
wài miàn 外面 *adv* out, outside
wài miàn （biǎo） de 外面（表）的 *adj* outer
wài miàn de 外面的 *adj* exterior
wài shāng xìng 外伤性 *adj* traumatic
wài sūn 外孙 *n* grandson
wài xiàng de 外向的 *adj* extroverted, outgoing
wài xīng rén 外星人 *n* alien
wài yuán 外缘 *n* rim
wān qū 弯曲 *v* curve, flex, warp
wān qū chù 弯曲处 *n* crook
wān qū de 弯曲的 *adj* crooked, warped
wān xià lái 弯下来 *v* bend down
wān 湾 *n* bay
wān dòu 豌豆 *n* pea
wán 丸 *n* pill
wán 完 *n* end
wán chéng 完成 *v* accomplish, achieve, complete, finish, fulfill, wrap up
wán chéng 完成 *n* accomplishment, achievement, completion, fulfillment
wán hǎo wú sǔn de 完好无损的 *adj* intact
wán jié 完结 *v* end
wán měi 完美 *n* perfection, polish
wán měi de 完美的 *adj* perfect
wán quán 完全 *adv* solely
wán quán de 完全的 *adj* perfect
wán quán de 完全地 *adv* completely, entirely

wán zhěng de 完整的 *adj* complete, unbroken
wán 玩 *v* play
wán jiā 玩家 *n* player
wán nòng 玩弄 *v* mess around
wán shì bù gōng 玩世不恭 *n* cynicism
wán gù de 顽固的 *adj* crusty, obstinate, stubborn
wán pí de 顽皮的 *adj* naughty
wán tóng 顽童 *n* brat
wǎn huí 挽回 *v* retrieve
wǎn 晚 *adv* late
wǎn fàn 晚饭 *n* supper
wǎn nián 晚年 *n* old age
wǎn shàng 晚上 *n* evening
wǎn yàn 晚宴 *n* dinner
wǎn zhōng 晚钟 *n* curfew
wǎn 碗 *n* bowl
wǎn guì 碗柜 *n* dresser
wàn 万 *n* million
wàn néng de 万能的 *adj* almighty
wáng cháo 王朝 *n* dynasty, reign
wáng guó 王国 *n* kingdom
wáng shì de 王室的 *adj* royal
wáng zǐ 王子 *n* prince
wáng zuò 王座 *n* throne
wǎng 网 *n* web
wǎng qiú 网球 *n* tennis
wǎng zhàn 网站 *n* site, web site, network, web
wǎng hòu kào 往后靠 *v* lean back
wǎng qián 往前 *adv* onwards
wàng xiǎng 妄想 *n* delusion

wàng ēn fù yì 忘恩负义 n
ingratitude

wàng jì 忘记 v forget

wàng què 忘却 v raze

wàng què de 忘却的 adj oblivious

wàng yuǎn jìng 望远镜 n
telescope

wēi hài 危害 v endanger,
jeopardize

wēi jī 危机 n crisis

wēi wáng 危亡 n peril

wēi xiǎn 危险 n danger, hazard

wēi xiǎn de 危险的 adj dangerous,
hazardous, perilous

wēi hè 威吓 v daunt

wēi lì dà de 威力大的 adj potent

wēi shè 威慑 v deter

wēi shè （**lì liang**、**yīn sù**、**wù**）
威慑（力量、因素、物）n
deterrence

wēi wàng 威望 n prestige

wēi xié 威胁 n menace, threat

wēi xié 威胁 v threaten

wēi àn de 微暗的 adj obscure

wēi bō lú 微波炉 n microwave

wēi bù zú dào de 微不足道的 adj
insignificant

wēi fēng 微风 n breeze

wēi guāng 微光 n gleam, glimmer

wēi lì 微粒 n corpuscle

wēi miào de 微妙的 adj delicate,
subtle

wēi shēng wù 微生物 n microbe

wēi xiǎo 微小 n pettiness

wēi xiǎo de 微小的 adj petty

wēi xiào 微笑 v smile

wēi xiào 微笑 n smile

wéi 为 v deem

wèi 为 pre for

wèi dān bǎo 为担保 v vouch for

wèi shén me 为什么 adv why

wéi chǎng 围场 n compound,
enclosure

wéi gōng 围攻 iv besiege

wéi kùn 围困 n siege

wéi kùn 围困 v siege

wéi lán 围栏 n fence

wéi qún 围裙 n apron

wéi（**fǎn**）**kàng** 违（反）抗 n
disobedience

wéi bèi 违背 n infraction

wéi fǎ de 违法的 adj illegitimate

wéi fǎn de 违反的 adj repugnant

wéi fàn 违犯 v violate

wéi jìn pǐn 违禁品 n contraband

wéi kàng 违抗 n defiance

wéi kàng 违抗 v disobey

wéi kàng de 违抗的 adj defiant

wéi yuē 违约 n breach

wéi gān 桅杆 n mast

wéi wù zhǔ yì 唯物主义 n
materialism

wéi yī 唯一 n sole

wéi yī 唯一 adj sole

wéi chí 维持 v sustain

wéi chí shēng huó 维持生活 v
subsist

wéi hù 维护 n safeguard

wéi hù 维护 v uphold

wéi shēng sù 维生素 n vitamin

W

wéi xiū 维修 *n* maintenance
wěi dà 伟大 *n* greatness
wěi dà de 伟大的 *adj* great
wěi jūn zǐ 伪君子 *adj* hypocrite
wěi liè 伪劣 *adj* shoddy
wěi shàn 伪善 *n* hypocrisy, insincerity
wěi zào 伪造 *v* counterfeit, forge
wěi zào 伪造 *n* forgery
wěi zào de 伪造的 *adj* phony
wěi zhèng zuì 伪证罪 *n* perjury
wěi zhuāng 伪装 *v* camouflage, masquerade
wěi zhuāng 伪装 *n* camouflage
wěi ba 尾巴 *n* tail
wěi dù 纬度 *n* latitude
wěi pài dài biǎo 委派代表 *v* delegate
wěi qū 委屈 *n* grievance
wěi tuō 委托 *v* commit, entrust
wěi yuán huì 委员会 *n* commission, committee
wěi suō 萎缩 *v* atrophy
wěi xiè 猥亵 *n* indecency
wèi shēng jiān 卫生间 *n* lavatory
wèi shēng xué 卫生学 *n* hygiene
wèi xīng 卫星 *n* satellite
wèi bèi chá jué de 未被察觉的 *adj* unnoticed
wèi chá jué de 未察觉的 *adj* unaware
wèi chéng nián rén de 未成年人的 *adj* minor
wèi chéng shú de 未成熟的 *adj* crude

wèi hūn de 未婚的 *adj* unmarried
wèi hūn fū 未婚夫 *n* fiancé
wèi hūn nǚ rén 未婚女人 *n* spinster
wèi jiā gōng de 未加工的 *adj* raw
wèi jué dìng de 未决定的 *adj* debatable
wèi lái 未来 *n* future
wèi què dìng de 未确定的 *adj* undecided
wèi shòu shāng de 未受伤的 *adj* unharmed
wèi wán chéng de 未完成的 *adj* unfurnished
wèi yù jiàn dào de 未预见到的 *adj* unforeseen
wèi zhī de 未知的 *adj* unknown
wèi yú 位于 *v* locate
wèi yú 位于 *adj* located
wèi zhi 位置 *n* lay
（**wèi dao huò qì wèi**）**xiàng yú de** （味道或气味）象鱼的 *adj* fishy
wèi 胃 *n* stomach
wèi（**xīn**）**zhuó rè** 胃（心）灼热 *n* heartburn
wèi de 胃的 *adj* gastric
wèi kǒu 胃口 *n* appetite
wèi（**yǎng**）喂（养）*iv* feed
wèi jiè 慰藉 *n* consolation
wèi wèn zhě 慰问者 *n* comforter
wēn dù 温度 *n* temperature
wēn dù jì 温度计 *n* thermometer
wēn hé 温和 *n* clemency
wēn hé de 温和的 *adj* balmy, bland, mild

wēn nuǎn 温暖 *adj* genial

wēn nuǎn 温暖 *n* warmth

wēn nuǎn de 温暖的 *adj* warm

wēn quán 温泉 *n* spa

wēn rè 温热 *adj* lukewarm

wēn rè de 温热的 *adj* tepid

wēn róu 温柔 *adj* gentle

wēn róu 温柔 *n* gentleness, tenderness

wēn róu de 温柔的 *adj* mild, softly, tender

wēn shì 温室 *n* greenhouse

wēn shùn 温顺 *n* docility, meekness

wēn shùn de 温顺的 *adj* docile, meek

wēn shùn de 温顺的 *v* tame

wén běn 文本 *n* text

wén huà 文化 *n* culture

wén huà de 文化的 *adj* cultural

wén jiàn 文件 *n* document, documentation, paper, paperwork

wén jiàn jiá 文件夹 *n* folder

wén jù 文具 *n* stationery

wén máng 文盲 *adj* illiterate

wén míng 文明 *n* civilization

wén míng huà 文明化 *v* civilize

wén píng 文凭 *n* diploma

wén shū 文书 *n* clerk

wén shū huò bàn shì yuán de 文书或办事员的 *adj* clerical

wén xiàn 文献 *n* bibliography

wén xiōng 文胸 *n* bra

wén xué 文学 *n* literature

wén zhāng 文章 *n* article

wén zì 文字 *n* character

wén 闻 *iv* smell

wén zi 蚊子 *n* mosquito

wěn 吻 *v* kiss

wěn 吻 *n* kiss

wěn luàn de 紊乱的 *adj* disorganized

wěn dìng 稳定 *n* stability

wěn dìng de 稳定的 *adj* stable

wěn zhòng de 稳重的 *adj* steady

wèn 问 *v* ask

wèn dá jí 问答集 *n* catechism

wèn hòu 问候 *n* greetings, regards

wèn hòu de 问候的 *adj* complimentary

wèn juàn 问卷 *n* questionnaire

wèn tí 问题 *n* issue, problem, question

wēng wēng shēng 嗡嗡声 *n* buzz

wō lún 涡轮 *n* turbine

wō niú 蜗牛 *n* snail

wǒ 我 *pro* I

wǒ de 我的 *pro* mine

wǒ de 我的 *adj* my

wǒ men 我们 *pre* us

wǒ men 我们 *pro* we

wǒ men de 我们的 *adj* our

wǒ men de 我们的 *pro* ours

wǒ men zì jǐ 我们自己 *pro* ourselves

wǒ zì jǐ 我自己 *pro* myself

wò dǎo de 卧倒的 *adj* prostrate

wò shì 卧室 *n* bedroom

W

wò jǐn 握紧 v clench

wò shǒu 握手 n handshake

wū yā 乌鸦 n crow

wū diǎn 污点 n blemish, blot, stain

wū diǎn 污点 v stain

wū diǎn de 污点的 adj tainted

wū gòu 污垢 n dirt

wū huì 污秽 adj filthy

wū huì wù 污秽物 n grime

wū jì 污迹 n smear

wū miè 污蔑 v denigrate

wū rǎn 污染 v contaminate, pollute

wū rǎn 污染 n contamination, pollution

wū shuǐ 污水 n sewage

wū sǔn 污损 v blot

wū wù 污物 n filth

wū yè 呜咽 v sob, whine

wū yè 呜咽 n sob

wū pó 巫婆 n witch

wū shī 巫师 n wizard

wū shù 巫术 n sorcery, witchcraft

wū dǐng 屋顶 n roof

wú 无 pre none

wú bǎo hù de 无保护的 adj unprotected

wú biān mào 无边帽 n cap

wú chǐ de 无耻的 adj shameless

wú chù 无处 adv nowhere

wú dǐ de 无底的 adj bottomless

wú dìng xíng de 无定形的 adj amorphous

wú fǎ jiě shì de 无法解释的 adj inexplicable

wú fǎ rěn shòu de 无法忍受的 adj intolerable, unbearable

wú fáng yù de 无防御的 adj defenseless

wú fèng de 无缝的 adj seamless

wú gài huò chē 无盖货车 n wagon

wú gēn jù 无根据 adj groundless

wú gēn jù de 无根据的 adj baseless

wú gū 无辜 n innocence

wú gū de 无辜的 adj innocent

wú guān 无关 n nothing

wú guān de 无关的 adj unrelated

wú hài 无害 adj harmless

wú huā guǒ 无花果 n fig

wú jǐ zhù de 无脊柱的 adj spineless

wú jiā kě guī 无家可归 adj homeless

wú jià de 无价的 adj invaluable

wú jié zhì 无节制 n incontinence

wú jié zhì de 无节制的 adj dissolute

wú kā fēi yīn de 无咖啡因的 adj decaf

wú kě bì miǎn de 无可避免的 adj inevitable

wú kě biàn bó de 无可辩驳的 adj irrefutable

wú kě zé nàn de 无可责难的 adj blameless

wú kě zhēng biàn de 无可争辩 adj indisputable

wú lǐ 无礼 n discourtesy

W

wú lǐ de 无礼的 *adj* impertinent

wú lì rùn de 无利润的 *adj* unprofitable

wú liáo 无聊 *n* boredom

wú liáo de 无聊的 *adj* bored

wú lùn shén me 无论什么 *adj* whatever

wú lùn shuí/shéi 无论谁 *pro* whoever

wú lùn zài nǎ 无论在哪 *c* wherever

wú míng 无名 *pro* nobody

wú néng 无能 *n* inability, incompetence

wú néng de 无能的 *adj* impotent, incapable, incompetent, inept

wú néng wéi lì de 无能为力的 *adj* powerless, unable

wú pàn duàn lì de 无判断力的 *adj* disoriented

wú qiān de 无铅的 *adj* unleaded

wú qíng 无情 *adj* heartless, ruthless

wú qíng de 无情的 *adj* merciless

wú róng zhì yí de 无容置疑地 *adv* undoubtedly

wú shén lùn 无神论 *n* atheism

wú shén lùn 无神论 *adj* godless

wú shén lùn zhě 无神论者 *n* atheist

wú shéng de 无绳的 *adj* cordless

wú shì shí gēn jù de 无事实根据的 *adj* unfounded

wú sī de 无私的 *adj* unselfish

wú tòng de 无痛的 *adj* painless

wú wèi de 无味的 *adj* tasteless

wú xiá cī 无瑕疵 *adj* flawless

wú xiá cī de 无瑕疵的 *adj* impeccable

wú xiá de 无瑕的 *adj* immaculate

wú xiàn de 无线的 *adj* wireless

wú xiàn de 无限的 *adj* boundless, infinite, unlimited

wú xiàn qī de 无限期的 *adj* indefinite

wú xiào de 无效的 *adj* ineffective, null, void, countless, innumerable, numerous

wú xiào de 无效的 *n* invalid

wú xíng de 无形的 *adj* invisible

wú xiù de 无袖的 *adj* sleeveless

wú yán yǐ duì de 无言以对的 *adj* speechless

wú yào kě jiù de 无药可救的 *adj* incurable

wú yī kào de 无依靠的 *adj* helpless

wú yí de 无疑的 *adj* deciding

wú yì de 无意的 *adj* unconscious

wú yì shí de 无意识的 *adj* mindless

wú yì yì 无意义 *adj* senseless

wú yì yì de 无意义的 *adj* meaningless, pointless

wú yòng de 无用的 *adj* idle, useless

wú yōu wú lǜ de 无忧无虑的 *adj* carefree

wú yún de 无云的 *adj* cloudless

wú zhèng fǔ zhǔ yì zhě 无政府主义者 *n* anarchist

wú zhèng fǔ zhuàng tài 无政府状态 *n* anarchy

wú zhī 无知 *n* ignorance

wú zhī de 无知的 *adj* ignorant, uneducated

wú zhǐ jìng de 无止境的 *adj* unending

wú zhòng dà shì jiàn de 无重大事件的 *adj* uneventful

wú zhù de 无助的 *adj* helpless

wú zǐ 无籽 *adj* seedless

wú zǐ nǚ de 无子女的 *adj* childless

wú zǔ zhī de 无组织的 *adj* disorganized

wú zuì shì fàng 无罪释放 *n* acquittal

wǔ 五 *adj* five

wǔ jiǎo dà lóu 五角大楼 *n* pentagon

wǔ shí 五十 *adj* fifty

wǔ yuè 五月 *n* May

wǔ cān 午餐 *n* lunch

wǔ shuì 午睡 *n* nap

wǔ yè 午夜 *n* midnight

wǔ lì 武力 *n* force

wǔ qì 武器 *n* armaments, weapon

wǔ zhuāng 武装 *v* arm

wǔ zhuāng de 武装的 *adj* armed

wǔ rǔ 侮辱 *v* insult, slap

wǔ rǔ 侮辱 *n* insult, slap

wǔ dǎo 舞蹈 *n* dance

wǔ dǎo 舞蹈 *v* dance

wǔ tái 舞台 *n* arena, stage

wǔ tīng 舞厅 *n* ballroom

wù yīng 兀鹰 *n* vulture

wù 物 *n* object, thing

wù lǐ xué 物理学 *n* physics

wù pǐn 物品 *n* article

wù wù jiāo huàn 物物交换 *v* barter

wù zhì 物质 *n* substance

wù zhǒng 物种 *n* species

wù dǎo 误导 *v* mislead

wù dǎo de 误导的 *adj* misleading

wù huì 误会 *v* misunderstand

wù jiě 误解 *v* misconstrue, misinterpret

wù rù qí tú de 误入歧途的 *adj* misguided

wù 雾 *n* fog

xī yáng 夕阳 *n* sunset

xī bān yá 西班牙 *n* Spain

xī bān yá de 西班牙的 *adj* Spanish

xī bān yá rén 西班牙人 *n* Spaniard

xī bān yá yì 西班牙裔 *adj* Hispanic

xī bù de 西部的 *adj* western

xī fāng 西方 *n* west

xī fāng de 西方的 *adj* western

xī fāng rén 西方人 *adj* westerner

xī guā 西瓜 *n* watermelon

xī nán 西南 *n* southwest

xī zhuāng 西装 *n* suit

xī 吸 *v* inhale

xī guǎn 吸管 *adj* sucker

xī pán 吸盘 *adj* sucker

xī shōu 吸收 *v* absorb, assimilate, take in

xī shōu 吸收 *n* assimilation

xī xuè guǐ 吸血鬼 *n* vampire

xī yān 吸烟 *v* smoke

xī yān zhě 吸烟者 *n* smoker

xī yǐn 吸引 *v* attract, charm, enthrall

xī yǐn （zhù yì lì） 吸引（注意力） *v* rivet

xī yǐn de 吸引的 *adj* enthralling

xī yǐn lì 吸引力 *n* attraction, magnetism

xī yǐn rén de 吸引人的 *adj* intriguing, tempting

xī là 希腊 *n* Greece

xī là de 希腊的 *adj* Greek

xī wàng 希望 *n* hope

xī shēng 牺牲 *n* sacrifice

xī niú 犀牛 *n* rhinoceros

xī bó de 稀薄的 *adj* tenuous

xī quē 稀缺 *n* scarcity

xī quē de 稀缺的 *adj* scarce

xī shǎo de 稀少的 *adj* sparse

xī shì 稀释 *v* dilute

xī yǒu de 稀有的 *adj* rare

xī gǔ 溪谷 *n* valley

xī 锡 *n* tin

xī yì 蜥蜴 *n* lizard

xī xiào 嘻笑 *v* giggle

xī bù 膝部 *n* lap

xī guān jié 膝关节 *n* knee

xí guàn 习惯 *n* custom, habit

xí guàn de 习惯的 *adj* customary

xí jī 袭击 *v* assail, raid

xí jī 袭击 *n* raid

xǐ de diào de 洗得掉的 *adj* washable

xǐ dí 洗涤 *v* wash

xǐ dí jì 洗涤剂 *n* detergent

xǐ jì 洗剂 *n* lotion

xǐ jié 洗劫 *v* sack

xǐ jié 洗劫 *n* sack

xǐ lǐ 洗礼 *n* baptism, christening

xǐ lǐ 洗礼 *v* christen

xǐ nǎo 洗脑 *v* brainwash

xǐ shǒu jiān 洗手间 *n* rest room

xǐ wǎn jī 洗碗机 *n* dishwasher

xǐ yī 洗衣 *n* laundry

xǐ zǎo 洗澡 *v* bathe

xǐ ài 喜爱 *n* affection

xǐ huān 喜欢 *adj* fond

xǐ huān 喜欢 *n* fondness, liking

xǐ huān 喜欢 *v* like

xǐ huān zhēng chǎo de 喜欢争吵的 *adj* quarrelsome

xǐ jù 喜剧 *n* comedy

xǐ jù yǎn yuán 喜剧演员 *n* comedian

xǐ yuè 喜悦 *n* delight, joy

xì jù 戏剧 *n* play

xì jù huà 戏剧化 *v* dramatize

xì jù xìng de 戏剧性的 *adj* dramatic

xì 系 *n* department

xì chū de pài shēng de shì wù 系出的n. 派生的事物 *adj* derivative

xì liè 系列 *n* series
xì shù 系数 *n* coefficient
xì tǒng 系统 *n* system
xì tǒng de 系统的 *adj* systematic
xì de 细的 *adj* attenuating
xì jūn 细菌 *n* bacteria
xì kàn 细看 *v* scan
xì wēi chā bié 细微差别 *n* nuance
xì wēi de jì xiàng 细微的迹象 *n* inkling
xì zhì de 细致的 *adj* meticulous
xiā 虾 *n* shrimp
xiā de 瞎的 *adj* blind
xiá gǔ 峡谷 *n* canyon, gorge
xiá wān 峡湾 *n* fjord
xiá ài de 狭隘的 *adj* parochial
xiá zhǎi （ài） de 狭窄（隘）的 *adj* narrow
xiá cī 瑕疵 *n* flaw
xià 下 *adv* off
xià ba 下巴 *n* chin
xià bǎi 下摆 *n* hem
xià bīng báo 下冰雹 *v* hail
xià chē 下车 *v* get off
xià chén 下沉 *v* gravitate, sink, sink in
xià chuán 下船 *v* disembark
xià dá fǎ lìng 下达法令 *v* decree
xià děng de 下等的 *adj* inferior
xià dìng jué xīn de 下定决心的 *adj* single-minded
xià dú 下毒 *v* poison
xià guì 下跪 *iv* kneel
xià hé de 下颌的 *n* jaw
xià jiàn de 下贱的 *adj* crappy

xià jiàng 下降 *v* decline, descend
xià jiàng 下降 *n* decline, decent
xià lái 下来 *v* come down, get down, go down
xià liú de 下流的 *adj* dirty
xià liú de 下流地 *adv* grossly
xià luò 下落 *n* whereabouts
xià máo mao yǔ 下毛毛雨 *v* drizzle
xià mian 下面 *adv* below
xià pō 下坡 *adv* downhill
xià qián 下潜 *v* submerge
xià qīng 下倾 *n* descent
xià shì 下士 *n* corporal
xià shuǐ dào 下水道 *n* drainage, sewer
xià tái 下台 *n* downfall
xià tái 下台 *v* step down
xià wǔ 下午 *n* afternoon
xià xuě 下雪 *v* snow
xià yǔ 下雨 *v* rain
xià shǔ 下属 *adj* underlying
xià dāi de 吓呆的 *adj* aghast
xià hu 吓唬 *v* frighten, scare
xià hu 吓唬 *n* scare
xià zǒu 吓走 *v* scare away
xià tiān 夏天 *n* summer
xiān fēng 先锋 *n* pioneer, vanguard
xiān jué tiáo jiàn 先决条件 *n* prerequisite
xiān lì 先例 *n* precedent
xiān sheng 先生 *n* mister, sir
xiān xíng cí 先行词 *n* antecedent
xiān yú de 先于的 *adj* previous

X

xiān zhī 先知 *n* prophet

xiān wéi 纤维 *n* fiber

xián huà 闲话 *n* gossip

xián hùn 闲混 *v* goof

xián shú de 娴熟的 *adj* skillful

xián tī 舷梯 *n* ramp

xiǎn ér yì jiàn de 显而易见的 *adj* noticeable, obvious

xiǎn lù 显露 *v* reveal

xiǎn lù 显露 *n* revelation

xiǎn rán 显然 *adv* apparently, obviously

xiǎn shì 显示 *v* display, indicate

xiǎn shì（chū） 显示（出）*v* exhibit

xiǎn shì qì 显示器 *n* display

xiǎn wēi jìng 显微镜 *n* microscope

xiǎn yǎn de 显眼的 *adj* conspicuous

xiǎn zhù de 显著的 *adj* conspicuous, gross, patent

xiǎn zhù de 显著的 *n* striking

xiǎn zhe 显着 *adv* notably

xiǎn è 险恶 *n* sinister

xiàn 县 *n* county

xiàn 现 *v* represent

xiàn chǎng 现场 *n* scene

xiàn chǎng de 现场的 *adj* live

xiàn dài de 现代的 *adj* modern

xiàn dài huà 现代化 *v* modernize

xiàn jīn 现金 *n* cash

xiàn shí 现实 *n* reality

xiàn shí zhǔ yì 现实主义 *n* realism

xiàn xiàng 现象 *n* phenomenon

xiàn zài 现在 *adv* now

xiàn 线 *n* line, string

xiàn rén 线人 *n* informant

xiàn suǒ 线索 *n* clue

xiàn dù 限度 *n* extent

xiàn zhì 限制 *v* confine, constipate, limit

xiàn zhì 限制 *n* confinement, restraint

xiàn fǎ 宪法 *n* constitution

xiàn zhāng 宪章 *n* charter

xiàn hài 陷害 *v* frame

xiàn jǐng 陷阱 *n* noose, pitfall, trap

xiàn rù kùn jìng 陷入困境 *v* bog down

xiàn rù zhǎo zé de 陷入沼泽的 *adj* swamped

xiàn 馅 *n* stuffing

xiàn bǐng 馅饼 *n* pie

xiàn mù 羡慕 *n* envy

xiàn mù 羡慕 *v* envy

xiàn 献 *v* dedicate

xiàn cí 献辞 *n* dedication

xiàn shēn 献身 *v* devote

xiàn yīn qín 献殷勤 *v* court

xiàn 腺 *n* gland

xiāng cūn 乡村 *n* country

xiāng cūn de 乡村的 *adj* rustic

xiāng qīn 乡亲 *n* folks

xiāng xià rén 乡下人 *n* countryman

xiāng chà 相差 *n* discrepancy

xiāng chǔ 相处 *v* get along

xiāng dāng dà de 相当大的 *adj* sizable

xiāng dāng de 相当的 *adj* comparative

xiāng dāng shù liàng de 相当数量的 *adj* significant

xiāng duì de 相对的 *adj* relative

xiāng fǎn 相反 *adv* opposite

xiāng fǎn 相反 *n* opposite

xiāng fǎn de 相反的 *adj* contrary, opposite

xiāng fǎn de 相反地 *adv* conversely

xiāng guān 相关 *adj* related

xiāng guān de 相关的 *adj* pertinent, relevant

xiāng hù 相互 *adv* mutually

xiāng hù de 相互的 *adj* reciprocal

xiāng jiāo 相交 *v* intersect

xiāng jù 相聚 *v* get together

xiāng máo dùn de 相矛盾的 *adj* conflicting

xiàng mào píng yōng de 相貌平庸的 *adj* homely

xiāng sì 相似 *n* analogy, resemblance, similarity

xiāng tóng 相同 *adj* identical

xiāng xiàng 相像 *n* likeness

xiāng xìn 相信 *v* believe

xiāng yīng de 相应的 *adj* corresponding

xiāng zhuàng 相撞 *n* crash

xiāng zhuàng 相撞 *v* crash

xiāng cài 香菜 *n* parsley

xiāng cháng 香肠 *n* sausage

xiāng guā 香瓜 *n* cantaloupe

xiāng huǒ 香火 *n* incense

xiāng jiāo 香蕉 *n* banana

xiāng liào 香料 *n* spice

xiāng shuǐ 香水 *n* fragrance, perfume

xiāng yān 香烟 *n* cigarette

xiāng yóu 香油 *n* balm

xiāng zi 箱子 *n* bin, box

xiāng qiàn de 镶嵌的 *adj* inlaid

xiāng zhù 镶住 *v* mount

xiáng shěn 详审 *v* sift

xiáng shù 详述 *v* detail

xiáng xì 详细 *n* detail

xiáng xì shuō míng 详细说明 *v* define, detail

xiǎng shòu 享受 *v* enjoy

xiǎng shòu 享受 *n* enjoyment

xiǎng liàng de 响亮地 *adv* loudly

xiǎng yìng de 响应的 *adj* responsive

xiǎng 想 *v* ponder, think

xiǎng chéng wéi 想成为 *adj* would-be

xiǎng chū 想出 *v* figure out

xiǎng fǎ 想法 *n* thought

xiǎng jiā 想家 *adj* homesick

xiǎng niàn 想念 *v* miss

xiǎng xiàng 想象 *v* imagine

xiǎng xiàng de 想象的 *adj* ideal

xiǎng xiàng lì 想象力 *adj* fancy

xiǎng xiàng lì 想象力 *n* imagination

xiǎng xiàng 想像 *v* picture

xiàng 向 *pre* towards

xiàng ...tí gòng 向...提供 *iv* feed

xiàng àn 向岸 *adv* ashore

xiàng chuán wài 向船外 *adv* overboard

xiàng dōng 向东 *adv* eastward

xiàng hòu 向后 *adv* backwards

xiàng hòu de 向后的 *adj* backward

xiàng qián 向前 *pre* ahead

xiàng qián 向前 *v* move forward

xiàng shàng 向上 *v* move up

xiàng shàng 向上 *n* upturn

xiàng wài 向外 *adj* outward

xiàng wài shēn zhǎn 向外伸展 *adj* outstretched

xiàng wǎng 向往 *v* desire, long for

xiàng xī 向西 *adv* westbound

xiàng xià （de） 向下（的） *adv* down

xiàng liàn 项链 *n* necklace

xiàng mù 项目 *n* item, program, project

xiàng jī 相机 *n* camera

（xiàng） cháng yá （象）长牙 *n* tusk

xiàng fù qīn bān 象父亲般 *adj* fatherly

xiàng yá 象牙 *n* ivory

xiàng zhēng 象征 *n* token

xiàng zhēng de 象征的 *adj* symbolic

xiàng 像 *pre* like

xiàng jiāo 橡胶 *n* rubber

xiàng pí cā 橡皮擦 *n* eraser

xiàng shù 橡树 *n* oak

xiàng zǐ 橡子 *n* acorn

xuē （mù tou） 削（木头） *v* whittle

xuē jiān 削尖 *v* sharpen

xuē jiǎn 削减 *v* curtail, cut, cut back, cut down, whittle

xuē jiǎn 削减 *n* cut

xiāo jìn 宵禁 *n* curfew

xiāo chú 消除 *v* deaden, eliminate

xiāo chú wēi xiǎn 消除危险 *v* defuse

xiāo dú 消毒 *v* disinfect, sterilize

xiāo dú jì 消毒剂 *v* disinfectant

xiāo fáng duì yuán 消防队员 *n* firefighter

xiāo fáng yuán 消防员 *n* fireman

xiāo fèi 消费 *v* consume

xiāo fèi 消费 *n* consumption, spending

xiāo fèi zhě 消费者 *n* consumer

xiāo hào 消耗 *v* exhaust

xiāo huà 消化 *v* digest

xiāo huà 消化 *n* digestion

xiāo huà bù liáng 消化不良 *n* indigestion

xiāo huà de 消化的 *adj* digestive

xiāo jí de 消极的 *adj* negative, passive

xiāo miè 消灭 *v* perish

xiāo qiǎn 消遣 *n* diversion, pastime

xiāo sàn 消散 *v* dissipate, scatter

xiāo shēng qì 消声器 *n* muffler

xiāo shī 消失 *v* disappear, vanish

xiāo shī 消失 *n* disappearance

xiāo sè de 萧瑟的 *adj* bleak

xiǎo bèi de 小辈的 *adj* junior

xiǎo biàn 小便 *v* urinate

X

xiǎo cè zi 小册子 *n* booklet, pamphlet

xiǎo chē 小车 *n* trolley

xiǎo chōng tū 小冲突 *n* skirmish

xiǎo chǒu 小丑 *n* clown

xiǎo dǎo 小岛 *n* isle

xiǎo de 小的 *adj* little, small

xiǎo duàn děng 小段等 *n* bit

xiǎo fāng kuài 小方块 *n* lump

xiǎo fèi 小费 *n* tip

xiǎo gōng jù 小工具 *n* gadget

xiǎo gǒu 小狗 *n* puppy

xiǎo hái 小孩 *n* toddler

xiǎo hǎi wān 小海湾 *n* cove

xiǎo huǒ zi 小伙子 *n* lad

xiǎo jī 小鸡 *n* chick

xiǎo jiě 小姐 *n* miss

xiǎo kǒu de hē 小口地喝 *v* sip

xiǎo kuài 小块 *n* scrap

xiǎo kūn chóng 小昆虫 *n* bug

xiǎo lǐ bài táng 小礼拜堂 *n* chapel

xiǎo mǎ 小马 *n* colt

xiǎo māo 小猫 *n* kitten

xiǎo niú 小牛 *n* calf

xiǎo niú ròu 小牛肉 *n* veal

xiǎo piàn 小片 *n* bit

xiǎo píng miàn 小平面 *n* facet

xiǎo pù bù 小瀑布 *n* cascade

xiǎo qì 小憩 *n* break

xiǎo qiǎo de 小巧的 *adj* compact

xiǎo qiú 小球 *n* globule

xiǎo shān dǐng 小山顶 *n* hilltop

xiǎo shēng bào yuàn 小声抱怨 *v* murmur

xiǎo shēng shuō（huà） 小声说（话）*v* murmur

xiǎo shí 小时 *n* hour

xiǎo shū zi 小叔子 *n* brother-in-law

xiǎo shǔ 小鼠 *n* mice

xiǎo shù de 小数的 *adj* decimal

xiǎo shuō 小说 *n* fiction, novel

xiǎo shuō jiā 小说家 *n* novelist

xiǎo tí qín 小提琴 *n* fiddle, violin

xiǎo tí qín shǒu 小提琴手 *n* violinist

xiǎo tí dà zuò 小题大做 *n* fuss

xiǎo tǐ 小体 *n* corpuscle

xiǎo tíng 小亭 *n* kiosk

xiǎo tǒng 小桶 *n* keg

xiǎo tōu 小偷 *n* thief

xiǎo wò shì 小卧室 *n* cubicle

xiǎo wū 小屋 *n* cottage, hut

xiǎo xī 小溪 *n* creek

xiǎo xiàng 小巷 *n* alley

xiǎo xiǎo de 小小的 *adj* tiny

xiǎo xīn 小心 *v* beware

xiǎo xīn de 小心的 *adj* careful

xiǎo xīn jǐn shèn de 小心谨慎地 *adv* gingerly

xiǎo xíng xīng 小行星 *n* asteroid

xiǎo xíng dù jiǎ wū 小型度假屋 *n* chalet

xiǎo xíng mó tuō chē 小型摩托车 *n* scooter

xiǎo yè qǔ 小夜曲 *n* serenade

xiǎo yuán miàn bāo 小圆面包 *n* bun

xiǎo zhū 小珠 *n* globule

xiǎo zì 小字 *n* fine print, small print

xiǎo zǔ 小组 *n* group

xiào xiàng 肖像 *n* effigy

xiào chuǎn 哮喘 *n* asthma

xiào chuǎn de 哮喘的 *adj* asthmatic

xiào lì 效力 *n* effectiveness

xiào lǜ 效率 *n* efficiency

xiào zhōng 效忠 *n* allegiance

xiào gōng 校工 *n* janitor

xiào 笑 *v* laugh

xiào 笑 *n* laugh

xiào bǐng 笑柄 *n* laughing stock

xiào hua 笑话 *n* gag, joke

xiào shēng 笑声 *n* laughter

xiē zi 楔子 *n* wedge

xiē sī dǐ lǐ 歇斯底里 *adj* hysterical

xiē xi 歇息 *v* repose

xiē xi 歇息 *n* repose

xiē zi 蝎子 *n* scorpion

xié tiáo 协调 *v* coordinate, correspond, harmonize

xié tiáo 协调 *n* coordination

xié tiáo yuán 协调员 *n* coordinator

xié huì 协会 *n* association

xié yì 协议 *n* accord, agreement, pact, protocol, settlement

xié zhù 协助 *v* assist

xié zuò 协作 *v* club, collaborate

xié zuò 协作 *n* collaboration

xié zuò de 协作的 *adj* concurrent

xié è 邪恶 *n* evil, wickedness

xié è de 邪恶的 *adj* evil, satanic, wicked

xié dào 斜道 *n* chute

xié de 斜的 *adj* diagonal

xié pō 斜坡 *n* descent, slope

xié xiàng yī biān 斜向一边 *adv* sideways

xié yǐ 斜倚 *v* recline

xié dài 携带 *v* carry

xié 鞋 *n* shoe

xié dài 鞋带 *n* shoelace

xié diàn 鞋店 *n* shoe store

xié lèi 鞋类 *n* footwear

xiě 写 *iv* write

xiě dì zhǐ 写地址 *v* address

xiě gāng yào 写纲要 *v* outline

xiě xià 写下 *v* get down

xiě zài ……xià mian 写在……下面 *v* underwrite

xiè lòu 泄漏 *v* leak

xiè lòu 泄漏 *n* leak, leakage

xiè lòu 泄露 *v* divulge

xiè de 泻的 *adj* laxative

xiè xià 卸下 *v* dismount

xiè zǎi 卸载 *v* unload

xiè dú 亵渎 *v* blaspheme, desecrate

xiè dú 亵渎 *n* blasphemy

xiè dú（shén wù、shén líng）zuì 亵渎（神物、神灵）罪 *n* sacrilege

xiè dú de 亵渎的 *adj* profane

xiè xie 谢谢 *n* thanks

xiè 蟹 *n* crab

xīn ài de 心爱的 *adj* beloved

xīn fán 心烦 *n* hanger

xīn fù 心腹 *n* henchman

xīn jiǎo tòng 心绞痛 *n* angina

xīn lǐ de 心理的 *adj* psychic

xīn lǐ xué 心理学 *n* psychology

xīn qíng 心情 *n* mood

xīn shén bú ān de 心神不安的 *adj* uneasy

xīn tiào 心跳 *n* heartbeat

xīn tòng 心痛 *n* heartburn

xīn xiōng kāi kuò de 心胸开阔的 *adj* broadminded

xīn yuàn 心愿 *n* aspiration

xīn zàng 心脏 *n* heart

xīn zàng bìng xué 心脏病学 *n* cardiology

xīn zàng de 心脏的 *adj* cardiac

xīn zàng tíng tiào 心脏停跳 *n* cardiac arrest

xīn piàn 芯片 *n* chip

xīn kǔ cóng shì 辛苦从事 *v* toil

xīn shǎng 欣赏 *v* appreciate, savor

xīn shǎng 欣赏 *n* appreciation

xīn xǐ ruò kuáng 欣喜若狂 *adj* ecstatic

xīn 锌 *n* zinc

xīn bīng 新兵 *n* recruit

xīn cháo de 新潮的 *adj* trendy

xīn chéng yuán 新成员 *n* recruit

xīn de 新的 *adj* new

xīn hūn 新婚 *adj* newlywed

xīn jìn de 新近地 *adv* newly

xīn láng 新郎 *n* bridegroom, groom

xīn niáng 新娘 *n* bride

xīn niáng de 新娘的 *adj* bridal

xīn qí (**gǎn**) 新奇（感）*n* novelty

xīn qí shì wù 新奇事物 *n* novelty

xīn rén 新人 *n* newcomer

xīn rèn de 新任的 *adj* incoming

xīn shēng ér 新生儿 *n* newborn

xīn shǒu 新手 *n* novice

xīn wén 新闻 *n* news, newscast, press

xīn wén bào dǎo 新闻报导 *n* coverage

xīn wén jiǎn bào 新闻简报 *n* newsletter

xīn xiān 新鲜 *adj* fresh

xīn xiān 新鲜 *n* freshness

xīn zé xī 新泽西 *n* jersey

xīn chóu 薪酬 *n* pay

xīn jīn 薪金 *n* salary

xīn shuǐ 薪水 *n* wage

xīn zī 薪资 *n* paycheck

xìn 信 *n* letter

（**xìn de**）**fù jiàn** （信的）附件 *n* enclosure

xìn fēng 信封 *n* envelope

xìn hào 信号 *n* signal

xìn lài 信赖 *n* dependence, reliance

xìn niàn 信念 *n* conviction

xìn rèn 信任 *v* trust

xìn rèn 信任 *n* trust

xìn rèn de 信任的 *adj* unsuspecting

xìn shǐ 信使 *n* courier, messenger

xìn tiáo 信条 *n* creed

xìn tú 信徒 *n* believer

xìn tuō 信托 *v* confide

xìn tuō 信托 *n* trust

X

xìn xī 信息 *n* message
xìn xiāng 信箱 *n* mailbox
xìn xīn 信心 *n* confidence
xìn yǎng 信仰 *n* belief, faith
xìn yòng 信用 *n* credit
xìn yù 信誉 *n* goodwill
xīng fèn 兴奋 *n* excitement, thrill
xīng fèn 兴奋 *v* thrill
xīng fèn jì 兴奋剂 *n* stimulant
xīng wàng 兴旺 *v* thrive
xīng hào 星号 *n* asterisk
xīng huǒ 星火 *n* spark
xīng qī 星期 *n* week
xīng qī èr 星期二 *n* Tuesday
xīng qī liù 星期六 *n* Saturday
xīng qī sān 星期三 *n* Wednesday
xīng qī sì 星期四 *n* Thursday
xīng qī wǔ 星期五 *n* Friday
xīng qī yī 星期一 *n* Monday
xīng qiú 星球 *n* planet
xīng xing 星星 *n* star
xīng zuò 星座 *n* constellation
xīng xing 猩猩 *n* orangutan
xíng shì bèi gào 刑事被告 *n* culprit
xíng chéng 行程 *n* itinerary, trip
xíng chéng 行程 *v* trip
xíng dòng 行动 *v* act
xíng dòng 行动 *n* action, proceedings
xíng huì 行贿 *v* bribe
xíng huì 行贿 *n* bribery
xíng li 行李 *n* baggage, luggage
xíng rén 行人 *n* pedestrian
xíng shǐ 行使 *n* exertion

xíng wéi 行为 *v* behave
xíng wéi 行为 *n* behavior, conduct, deed, demeanor
xíng wéi bù duān 行为不端 *v* misbehave
xíng wéi wú lǐ mào 行为无礼貌 *v* misbehave
xíng zhèng bù mén 行政部门 *n* executive
xíng zhèng guān 行政官 *n* executive, magistrate
xíng chéng 形成 *n* formation
xíng chéng āo xiàn 形成凹陷 *v* dent
xíng róng cí 形容词 *n* adjective
xíng shì 形式 *n* form, shape
xíng xiàng 形象 *n* image
xíng xiàng huà 形象化 *v* visualize
xíng zhuàng 形状 *n* shape
xǐng lái 醒来 *iv* wake up
xǐng zhe de 醒着的 *adj* awake
xìng 杏 *n* apricot
xìng rén 杏仁 *n* almond
xìng gāo cǎi liè 兴高采烈 *adj* elated
xìng qù 兴趣 *n* interest
xìng zhì bó bó 兴致勃勃 *n* gusto
xìng 姓 *n* surname
xìng míng 姓名 *n* name
xìng shì 姓氏 *n* last name
xìng fú 幸福 *n* happiness
xìng fú gǎn 幸福感 *n* euphoria
xìng yùn 幸运 *adj* fortunate
xìng yùn de 幸运的 *adj* lucky
xìng bié 性别 *n* gender

xìng bié 性别 *n* sex
xìng gé 性格 *n* character
xìng néng lì 性能力 *n* virility
xìng nüè dài kuáng zhě 性虐待狂者 *n* sadist
xìng yù 性欲 *n* sexuality
xìng yù de 性欲的 *adj* lustful
xìng zhì 性质 *n* nature
xiōng cán 凶残 *n* ferocity
xiōng měng 凶猛 *adj* ferocious
xiōng dì 兄弟 *n* brother
xiōng dì bān de 兄弟般的 *adj* brotherly
xiōng dì de 兄弟的 *adj* brotherly
xiōng dì guān xì 兄弟关系 *n* brotherhood
xiōng bù 胸部 *n* bosom, bust
xiōng huái 胸怀 *n* bosom
xiōng kǒu 胸口 *n* chest
xióng háo de 雄豪的 *adj* valiant
xióng lù 雄鹿 *n* buck
xióng wěi de 雄伟的 *adj* majestic
xióng xīn 雄心 *n* ambition
xióng yīng 雄鹰 *n* eagle
xióng 熊 *n* bear
xióng zhǎng 熊掌 *n* paw
xiū huì 休会 *v* adjourn
xiū xi 休息 *v* rest
xiū xi 休息 *n* rest
xiū xi shì 休息室 *n* lounge
xiū xián 休闲 *n* leisure, recreation
xiū xián de 休闲的 *adj* casual
xiū xián kù 休闲裤 *n* slacks
xiū zhàn 休战 *n* truce
xiū dào yuàn 修道院 *n* abbey, cloister, monastery, seminary

xiū dìng 修订 *n* amendment, revision
xiū fù 修复 *v* mend
xiū gǎi 修改 *v* amend, modify, revise
xiū jiǎn 修剪 *v* prune, trim
xiū jiǎn 修剪 *n* prune
xiū lǐ 修理 *v* fix, repair
xiū yǎng 修养 *n* culture
xiū yǎng de 修养的 *adj* cultural
xiū chǐ 羞耻 *v* shame
xiū rǔ 羞辱 *v* humiliate
xiù kǒu 袖口 *n* cuff
xiù zi 袖子 *n* sleeve
xū gòu 虚构 *adj* fictitious
xū gòu de 虚构的 *adj* dummy
xū huàn de 虚幻的 *adj* unreal
xū jiǎ 虚假 *n* falsehood
xū nǐ de 虚拟的 *adj* dummy
xū róng 虚荣 *n* vanity
xū ruò 虚弱 *adj* frail
xū ruò de 虚弱的 *adj* impoverished
xū wěi de 虚伪的 *adj* insincere
xū zhāng shēng shì 虚张声势 *v* bluff
xū yào 需要 *v* demand, necessitate, need
xū yào 需要 *n* demand, need
xū yào de 需要的 *adj* needy
xǔ duō 许多 *adj* many
xǔ duō 许多 *n* multitude
xǔ kě 许可 *n* license, permission
xù mù 序幕 *n* prologue
xù yán 序言 *n* preamble

xù shuō 叙说 v narrate

xù jí 续集 n sequel

xù jiǔ 酗酒 n alcoholism

xiù 嗅 v sniff

xiù jué 嗅觉 n scent

xù shuǐ chí 蓄水池 n cistern

xù yì pò huài 蓄意破坏 v sabotage

xù yì pò huài 蓄意破坏 n sabotage

xuān chēng 宣称 v declare

xuān chuán 宣传 n propaganda, publicity

xuān chuán 宣传 v propagate

xuān chuán cè 宣传册 n brochure

xuān gào 宣告 v proclaim

xuān gào wú zuì 宣告无罪 v acquit

xuān pàn 宣判 v pronounce

xuān shì 宣誓 n oath

xuān shì 宣誓 iv swear

xuān yán 宣言 n proclamation

xuān huá 喧哗 adv noisily

xuān huá de 喧哗的 adj tumultuous

xuān nào 喧闹 v clamor

xuān nào de 喧闹的 adj boisterous, noisy

xuán chuí 悬垂 n drape

xuán diào zhe huò bǎi dòng bù dìng 悬吊着或摆动不定 v dangle

xuán fú yè 悬浮液 n suspension

xuán guà 悬挂 iv hang

xuán yá 悬崖 n cliff, precipice

xuán yí 悬疑 n suspense

xuàn fēng 旋风 n cyclone

xuán lǜ 旋律 n chant, melody

xuán lǜ de 旋律的 adj melodic

xuán lǜ yōu měi de 旋律优美的 adj melodic

xuán niǔ 旋钮 n knob

xuán rào de 旋绕的 adj convoluted

xuán wō 旋涡 n whirlpool

xuán zhuǎn 旋转 v revolve, whirl

xuǎn chū 选出 v elect

xuǎn jǔ 选举 n election

xuǎn jǔ quán 选举权 n franchise

xuǎn piào 选票 n ballot

xuǎn xiàng 选项 n option

xuǎn zé 选择 n choice

xuǎn zé 选择 iv choose

xuǎn zé 选择 v opt for, select

xuǎn zé 选择 n selection

xuàn yào 炫耀 v show off

xuàn guāng 眩光 n glare

xuàn yūn de 眩晕的 adj dizzy

xuē 靴 n boot

xué fèi 学费 n tuition

xué huì 学会 v institute

xué kē 学科 n discipline

xué pài 学派 n sect

xué qī 学期 n semester

xué qī 学期 n term

xué shēng 学生 n pupil, student

xué shì 学士 n bachelor

xué shù de 学术的 adj academic

xué shuō 学说 n doctrine

xué tú 学徒 n apprentice

xué wèi 学位 *n* degree
xué xí 学习 *iv* learn, study
xué xí 学习 *n* learning
xué xí zhě 学习者 *n* learner
xué xiào 学校 *n* school
xué yuán 学员 *n* trainee
xué yuàn 学院 *n* academy, college, faculty, institution
xué zhě 学者 *n* scholar
xuě 雪 *n* snow
xuě bēng 雪崩 *n* avalanche
xuě huā 雪花 *n* snowflake
xuě lì jiǔ 雪利酒 *n* sherry
xuě qiāo 雪橇 *n* sleigh
xuě jiā 雪茄 *n* cigar
xuě yú 鳕鱼 *n* cod
xuè 血 *n* blood
xiě līn līn 血淋淋 *adj* gory
xuè qīng 血清 *n* serum
xuè qiú 血球 *n* corpuscle
xuè shuān zhèng 血栓症 *n* thrombosis
xuè tǒng 血统 *n* ancestry
xuè xīng 血腥 *adj* bloody
xūn zhāng 勋章 *n* medal
xūn 熏 *v* fumigate
xūn de 熏的 *adj* smoked
xūn zhū ròu 熏猪肉 *n* bacon
xún huí 寻回 *v* locate
xún qiú 寻求 *iv* seek
xún zhǎo 寻找 *v* look for
xún zhǎo 寻找 *n* search
xún háng 巡航 *v* cruise
xún luó 巡逻 *n* patrol
xún yóu 巡游 *n* parade

xùn fú 驯服 *v* conciliate
xùn huà 驯化 *v* domesticate
xùn lù 驯鹿 *n* reindeer
xún wèn 询问 *v* demand
xún wèn 询问 *n* inquiry
xún wèn zhí xíng rèn wu de qíng kuàng 询问执行任务的情况 *v* debrief
xún xù jiàn jìn 循序渐进 *adj* gradual
xùn jiè 训诫 *n* precept
xùn liàn 训练 *n* coaching
xùn liàn 训练 *v* train
xùn sù 迅速 *adv* speedily
xùn sù de 迅速的 *adj* prompt, rapid, speedy, swift
xùn dào 殉道 *n* martyrdom

yā 压 *v* squash
yā dǎo 压倒 *v* overpower, overwhelm
yā jǐn 压紧 *v* compact
yā lì 压力 *n* pressure, stress
yā píng 压平 *v* flatten
yā pò 压迫 *n* oppression
yā suì 压碎 *v* crush
yā suō 压缩 *v* compress
yā suō 压缩 *n* compression, condensation

yā yì 压抑 *v* depress
yā zhì 压制 *v* suppress
yā wǎng 押往 *v* commit
yā yùn 押韵 *n* rhyme
yā piàn 鸦片 *n* opium, poppy
yā zi 鸭子 *n* duck
yá chǐ 牙齿 *n* teeth, tooth
yá chǐ de 牙齿的 *adj* dental
yá kē de 牙科的 *adj* dental
yá qiān 牙签 *n* toothpick
yá tòng 牙痛 *n* toothache
yá yī 牙医 *n* dentist
yá 芽 *n* bud
yǎ de 哑的 *adj* mute
yà má bù 亚麻布 *n* linen
yàn xià 咽下 *v* ingest
yān cǎo 烟草 *n* tobacco
yān cōng 烟囱 *n* chimney
yān dǒu 烟斗 *n* pipe
yān huā 烟花 *n* fireworks
yān huī gāng 烟灰缸 *n* ashtray
yān wù dàn 烟雾弹 *n* smoking gun
yān mò 淹没 *n* flooding
yān mò 淹没 *v* inundate
yān mò 湮没 *n* oblivion
yán chǎng 延长 *v* extend, prolong, protect
yán chǎng 延长 *n* extension
yán chǎng de 延长的 *adj* protracted
yán chí 延迟 *v* procrastinate
yán huǎn 延缓 *n* stay
yán huǎn 延缓 *v* stay
yán wù 延误 *v* delay

yán wù 延误 *n* delay
yán xù 延续 *n* continuation
yán chéng 严惩 *v* chastise
yán chéng 严惩 *n* chastisement
yán gé de 严格的 *adj* strict
yán jùn 严峻 *adj* grim
yán kù de 严酷的 *adj* stark
yán lì 严厉 *adv* harshly
yán lì 严厉 *n* rigor
yán lì de 严厉的 *adj* severe, stern, stringent
yán lì de 严厉地 *adv* sternly
yán mì de 严密地 *adv* narrowly
yán zhòng 严重 *adj* grave
yán zhòng 严重 *adv* gravely
yán zhòng de 严重的 *adj* acute, heavy, serious, severe
yán zhòng de 严重地 *adv* badly
yán zhòng xìng 严重性 *n* seriousness, severity
yán qíng 言情 *n* romance
yán 沿 *pre* along
yán hǎi de 沿海的 *adj* coastal
yán rè de 炎热的 *adj* fervent, torrid
yán zhèng 炎症 *n* inflammation
yán jiū 研究 *v* research
yán jiū 研究 *n* research
yán jiū suǒ 研究所 *v* institute
yán tǎo huì 研讨会 *n* workshop
yán 盐 *n* salt
yán shuǐ hú 盐水湖 *n* lagoon
yǎn gài 掩盖 *v* cover up, cushion, overshadow
yǎn shì 掩饰 *v* camouflage

yǎn shì 掩饰 *n* camouflage

yǎn huā liáo luàn de 眼花缭乱的 *adj* dazzling

yǎn jiǎn 眼睑 *n* eyelid

yǎn jīng 眼睛 *n* eye

yǎn jìng 眼镜 *n* eyeglasses, glasses, speculate

yǎn 演 *v* act

yǎn biàn 演变 *n* evolution

yǎn biàn 演变 *v* evolve

yǎn chū 演出 *v* perform

yǎn chū 演出 *n* performance

yǎn jiǎng 演讲 *n* lecture

yǎn liàn 演练 *v* drill

yǎn liàn 演练 *n* drill

yǎn yì chū 演绎出 *v* deduce

yǎn yuán 演员 *n* actor

yàn wù 厌恶 *n* aversion, disgust, distaste, loathing

yàn wù 厌恶 *v* sicken

yàn wù de 厌恶的 *adj* averse, disagreeable, obnoxious, repulsive

yàn juàn 厌倦 *adj* fed up

yàn huì 宴会 *n* banquet

yàn xiǎng 宴飨 *n* treat

yàn shōu 验收 *n* acceptance

yàn zhèng 验证 *v* authenticate

yàn yǔ 谚语 *n* proverb

yàn 堰 *n* barrage

yàn mài piàn 燕麦片 *n* oatmeal

yáng shēng qì 扬声器 *n* loudspeaker

yáng 羊 *n* sheep

yáng máo 羊毛 *n* fleece, wool

yáng máo de 羊毛的 *adj* woolen

yáng máo wéi jīn 羊毛围巾 *n* comforter

yáng máo zhuàng wù 羊毛状物 *n* fleece

yáng pí zhǐ 羊皮纸 *n* parchment

yáng ròu 羊肉 *n* lamb

yáng tái 阳台 *n* balcony, terrace

yáng liǔ 杨柳 *n* willow

yáng cōng 洋葱 *n* onion

yáng wá wa 洋娃娃 *n* doll

yǎng liào 养料 *n* nourishment

yǎng yù 养育 *iv* breed

yǎng yù 养育 *n* upbringing

yǎng zhí 养殖 *n* cultivation

yǎng qì 氧气 *n* oxygen

yǎng yǎng 痒 *v* itch

yǎng yǎng 痒 *n* tickle

yǎng yǎng 痒 *adj* ticklish

yàng běn 样本 *n* sample

yàng shì 样式 *n* pattern

yāo diǎn 幺点 *n* ace

yāo zhé 夭折 *v* abort

yāo zhé 夭折 *n* abortion

yāo qiú 要求 *n* claim, demand, requirement

yāo qiú 要求 *v* claim, demand, require

yāo bù 腰部 *adj* logical

yāo bù 腰部 *n* waist

yāo qǐng 邀请 *n* invitation

yāo qǐng 邀请 *v* invite

yáo yán 谣言 *n* rumor

yáo 摇 *iv* shake

yáo bǎi 摇摆 *v* stagger, wag, waver

Y

yáo bǎi bù dìng de 摇摆不定的 *adj* ambivalent

yáo bǎi de 摇摆的 *adj* staggering

yáo huǎng bù wěn 摇晃不稳 *n* shambles

yáo lán 摇篮 *n* cradle

yáo líng 摇铃 *iv* ring

yáo yáo yù zhuì 摇摇欲坠 *adj* shaky

yáo yuǎn de 遥远的 *adj* distant, remote

yǎo 咬 *iv* bite, nip

yǎo 咬 *n* bite, nip

yào cǎo 药草 *n* herb

（**yào děng**）**xiào lì dà de** （药等）效力大的 *adj* potent

yào diàn 药店 *n* drugstore

yào jì 药剂 *n* pharmacy

yào jì diàn 药剂店 *n* pharmacy

yào jì shī 药剂师 *n* pharmacist

yào piàn 药片 *n* tablet

yào wán 药丸 *n* pellet

yào wù 药物 *n* drug

yào yòng de 药用的 *adj* medicinal

yào 要 *iv* must, want

yào me 要么 *adv* either

yào sù 要素 *n* element

yào yǎn de 耀眼的 *adj* dazzling, eye-catching

yē zi 椰子 *n* coconut

yē 噎 *v* choke

yé ye 爷爷 *n* granddad, grandfather

yě 也 *adv* also, too

yě bù 也不 *adv* neither

yě bù 也不 *c* nor

yě xǔ 也许 *adv* may-be

yě gōng zhū 野公猪 *n* wild boar

yě jī 野鸡 *n* pheasant

yě mán 野蛮 *n* barbarism, savagery

yě mán de 野蛮的 *adj* barbaric, savage

yě mán rén 野蛮人 *n* barbarian

yě niú 野牛 *n* bison

yě shēng de 野生的 *adj* wild

yě shēng wù 野生物 *n* wildlife

yě shòu 野兽 *n* beast

yě shòu bān de 野兽般的 *adj* bestial, brute

yě shòu de 野兽的 *adj* brute

yě tù 野兔 *n* hare

yě wài de 野外的 *adv* outdoor

yě xīn 野心 *n* ambition

yě yíng 野营 *n* camp

yè yú de 业余的 *adj* amateur

yè 叶 *n* leaf

yè 页 *n* page

yè 夜 *n* night

yè de 夜的 *adj* nocturnal

yè yīng 夜莺 *n* nightingale

yè huà 液化 *n* condensation

yè tǐ 液体 *n* liquid

yè xià 腋下 *n* armpit

yī 一 *adj* one

yī（**gè**、**zhī**、**jiàn děng**）一（个、只、件等）*a* a, an

yī bǎi 一百 *adj* hundred

yī bān 一般 *n* general

yī bàn 一半 *n* half

yī bàn 一半 *adj* half

yī chén bù rǎn de 一尘不染的 *adj* spotless

yī chéng bù biàn de 一成不变的 *adj* irrevocable

yī cì 一次 *adv* once

yī cì jiǎn dé de yáng máo 一次剪得的羊毛 *n* fleece

yī dà kǒu 一大口 *v* gulp

yī dà kǒu 一大口 *n* gulp

yī dà kǒu xià lái 一大口下来 *v* gulp down

yī dài rén （huò chǎn pǐn） 一代人（或产品）*n* generation

yī dàn 一旦 *adv* once

yī dàn 一旦 *c* once

yī dī 一滴 *n* drop

yī diǎn diǎn 一点点 *n* little bit

yī diǎn diǎn 一点点 *adv* little by little

yī diǎnr 一点儿 *n* fig

yī dìng de 一定的 *adj* certain

yī fēn zhōng 一分钟 *n* minute

yī fèn 一份 *n* copy

yī fū duō qī zhì 一夫多妻制 *n* polygamy

yī fū yī qī 一夫一妻 *n* monogamy

yī gài ér lùn 一概而论 *v* generalize

yī jī 一击 *n* hit

yī kǒu yǐn liào 一口饮料 *n* sip

yī lián chuàn 一连串 *n* sequence

yī lóu 一楼 *n* ground floor

yī nián yī dù de 一年一度的 *adv* yearly

yī pī 一批 *n* batch

yī piē 一瞥 *v* glance

yī piē 一瞥 *n* glance, glimpse

yī qiān 一千 *adj* thousand

yī qiè 一切 *pro* everything

yī sháo 一勺 *n* spoonful

yī shēng 一生 *adj* lifetime

yī shǒu 一手 *adj* singlehanded

yī shuāng 一双 *n* pair

yī sī bù gǒu 一丝不苟 *adj* scrupulous

yī tào 一套 *n* set

yī tǐ huà 一体化 *n* integration

yī tuán zāo 一团糟 *n* mess

yī xiǎo cuō 一小撮 *n* handful

yī xiē 一些 *adj* some

yī yàng 一样 *adv* as

yī yàng de 一样的 *adj* same

yī yì gū xíng 一意孤行 *n* obstinacy

yī yuè 一月 *n* January

yī zhèn 一阵 *n* fit

yī zhì 一致 *n* accord

yī zhì 一致 *v* concur

yī zhì de 一致的 *adj* concurrent, consistent

yī zhì xìng 一致性 *n* conformity, consistency

yī sī lán de 伊斯兰的 *adj* Islamic

yī chú 衣橱 *n* wardrobe

yī fu 衣服 *n* apparel, clothes

（yī fu de）zhǒu bù （衣服的）肘部 *n* elbow

yī lǐng 衣领 *n* collar

yī shēng 医生 *n* doctor

yī shī 医师 *n* physician

yī yào 医药 *n* medicine

yī yuàn 医院 *n* hospital

yī jù 依据 *n* basis

yī kào 依靠 *v* depend, rely on

yī kào găn 依靠感 *n* attachment

yī lài 依赖 *n* dependence, recourse

yī lài 依赖 *v* recourse

yī lài de 依赖的 *adj* dependent

yī rán 依然 *adv* still

yī yī bù shě de 依依不舍的 *adj* lingering

yí shì 仪式 *n* ceremony

yí rén de 宜人的 *adj* pleasant

yí xiàn 胰腺 *n* pancreas

yí dòng 移动 *v* move, shift

yí dòng 移动 *n* shift

yí dòng de 移动的 *adj* mobile

yí jiāo 移交 *v* hand over, turn over

yí mín 移民 *n* emigrant, immigrant, migrant; immigration

yí mín 移民 *v* emigrate, immigrate

yí qù 移去 *v* put away

yí zhí 移植 *n* graft

yí zhí 移植 *v* graft, transplant

yí chăn 遗产 *n* heritage, legacy

yí chuán 遗传 *adj* genetic

yí chuán xìng de 遗传性的 *adj* hereditary

yí hàn 遗憾 *n* regret

yí hàn de 遗憾的 *adj* regrettable

yí lòu 遗漏 *v* leave out

yí lòu 遗漏 *n* omission

yí qì 遗弃 *v* desert

yí qì de 遗弃的 *adj* derelict

yí wù 遗物 *n* relic

yí yán 遗言 *n* will

yí zèng 遗赠 *v* bequeath

yí zhǐ qì shǐ 颐指气使 *v* boss around

yí fàn 疑犯 *n* suspect

yí lǜ 疑虑 *n* qualm

yǐ guò shí 已过时 *adj* obsolete, outdated

yǐ hūn de 已婚的 *adj* married

yǐ jīng 已经 *adv* already

yǐ 以 *v* base

yǐ ...wéi jiāo diǎn 以…为焦点 *v* focus on

yǐ huò yì huò 以货易货 *v* barter

yǐ mǒu zhǒng fāng fǎ 以某种方法 *adv* somehow

yǐ qián de 以前的 *adj* previous

yǐ wéi 以为 *v* deem, suppose

yǐ wéi 以为 *n* sham

yǐ yān xūn 以烟熏 *v* smoke

yǐ zi 椅子 *n* chair

yì bù róng cí de 义不容辞的 *adj* obliged

yì wù 义务 *n* obligation

yì wù de 义务的 *adj* compulsory

yì wàn fù wēng 亿万富翁 *n* billionaire

yì shù 艺术 *n* art

yì shù de 艺术的 *adj* artistic

yì shù jiā 艺术家 *n* artist

yì shù pǐn 艺术品 *n* artwork

yì shù pǐn pò huài zhě 艺术品破坏者 *n* vandal

yì àn 议案 *n* motion

yì chéng 议程 *n* agenda
yì huì 议会 *n* parliament
yì yuàn （H-）议院 *n* house
yì cǎi 异彩 *n* splendor
yì cháng de 异常的 *adj* unusual
yì duān 异端 *n* heresy
yì duān de 异端的 *adj* heretic
yì guó qíng diào 异国情调 *adj* exotic
yì hū xún cháng de 异乎寻常的 *adj* eccentric
yì jiào de 异教的 *adj* heretic, pagan
yì jiào tú 异教徒 *n* heathen
yì jiào tú de 异教徒的 *adj* pagan
yì xiǎng tiān kāi 异想天开 *n* whim
yì yì 异议 *v* dissent
yì yù 抑郁 *n* depression
yì zhì 抑制 *v* constrain, curb, inhibit, repress, restrain
yì zhì 抑制 *n* curb, repression, restraint
yì zhě 译者 *n* translator
yì bào de 易爆的 *adj* explosive
yì biàn de 易变的 *adj* variable
yì chá jué 易察觉 *adj* sensible
yì chuán rǎn de 易传染的 *adj* catching
yì dú de 易读的 *adj* legible
yì fǔ làn de 易腐烂的 *adj* perishable
yì rán 易燃 *adj* flammable
yì shòu yǐng xiǎng de 易受影响的 *adj* susceptible
yì suì de 易碎的 *adj* breakable, crunchy, delicate

yì miáo 疫苗 *n* vaccine
yì shì 轶事 *n* anecdote
yì dà lì 意大利 *n* Italy
yì dà lì de 意大利的 *adj* Italian
yì jiàn 意见 *n* opinion
yì jiàn xiāng tóng 意见相同 *v* concur
yì jiàn yī zhì 意见一致 *n* consensus
yì qì xiāng tóu de 意气相投的 *adj* congenial
yì shí 意识 *n* awareness, consciousness
yì shí xíng tài 意识形态 *n* ideology
yì si shì 意思是 *v* denote
yì wài 意外 *n* accident
yì wài de 意外的 *adj* accidental
yì wài shì jiàn 意外事件 *n* bombshell
yì wài zhuàng dào 意外撞到 *v* bump into
yì wèi zhe 意味着 *v* connote
yì xiǎng bù dào de 意想不到的 *adj* unexpected
yì xiàng 意向 *n* intention
yì yì 意义 *n* sense, significance
yì yì zhòng dà de 意义重大的 *adj* significant
yì zhì 意志 *n* will
yì liú 溢流 *n* flooding
yì liú 溢流 *v* overflow
yì lòu 溢漏 *iv* spill
yì lòu 溢漏 *n* spill
yì xuè 溢血 *n* hemorrhage

yì lì 毅力 *n* persistence

yì zhèng 癔症 *n* hysteria

yīn cǐ 因此 *adv* hence, therefore, thus

yīn fèi yì chū 因沸溢出 *v* boil over

yīn sù 因素 *n* factor

yīn wèi 因为 *c* because, inasmuch as, since

yīn wèi 因为 *pre* because of

yīn xún shǒu jiù de 因循守旧的 *adj* conformist

yīn chén de 阴沉的 *adj* grayish

yīn liáng chù 阴凉处 *n* shade

yīn mái 阴霾 *n* haze

yīn móu 阴谋 *n* conspiracy, intrigue, plot, scheme

yīn móu 阴谋 *v* plot

yīn móu pò huài 阴谋破坏 *v* sabotage

yīn móu pò huài 阴谋破坏 *n* sabotage

yīn sēn 阴森 *adj* ghastly

yīn tiān de 阴天的 *adj* overcast

yīn qīn 姻亲 *n* in-laws

yīn 荫 *n* shade

yīn jié 音节 *n* syllable

yīn yuè 音乐 *n* music

yīn yuè huì 音乐会 *n* concert

yīn yuè jiā 音乐家 *n* musician

yīn liàng 音量 *n* volume

yīn xiǎng 音响 *n* speaker

yīn xiǎng de 音响的 *adj* acoustic

yīn qín 殷勤 *adj* gracious

yín sòng 吟诵 *n* recital

yín dàng de 淫荡的 *adj* prurient

yín de 淫的 *adj* lewd

yín huì 淫秽 *n* obscenity

yín hé 银河 *n* galaxy

yín qì 银器 *n* silverware

yín háng 银行 *n* bank

yǐn bào 引爆 *v* detonate

yǐn chū de 引出的 *adj* derivative

yǐn dù 引渡 *n* extradite, extradition

yǐn qǐ 引起 *v* cause, draw, underlie

yǐn qǐ hōng dòng de rén （huò wù） 引起轰动的人（或物） *n* dynamite

yǐn qǐ zhēng yì de 引起争议的 *adj* controversial

yǐn rén zhù mù de 引人注目的 *adj* eye-catching

yǐn yòng 引用 *v* invoke

yǐn yòu 引诱 *n* allure

yǐn yòu rén de 引诱人的 *adj* tempting

yǐn liào 饮料 *n* beverage, drink

yǐn shí 饮食 *n* diet

yǐn zhě 饮者 *n* drinker

yǐn bì 隐蔽 *v* conceal

yǐn bì de 隐蔽的 *adj* covert

yǐn cáng 隐藏 *v* conceal, hide, lurk

yǐn cáng de 隐藏的 *adj* hidden

yǐn huì de 隐晦的 *adj* vague

yǐn jū 隐居 *n* seclusion

yǐn jū dì 隐居地 *n* hideaway

yǐn jū zhě 隐居者 *n* recluse

yǐn mán 隐瞒 *v* conceal, hold back

yǐn shì 隐士 *n* hermit

yǐn sī 隐私 *n* privacy, secrecy

yǐn tuì de 隐退的 *adj* withdrawn

yǐn yù 隐喻 *n* metaphor

yǐn yǐn 瘾 *n* addiction

yìn běn 印本 *n* reprint

yìn shuā 印刷 *n* printing

yìn xiàng shēn de 印象深的 *adj* imposing, impressive

yìn zhāng 印章 *v* seal

yìn zhāng 印章 *n* seal

yīng dé wù 应得物 *n* dues

yīng fù de 应付的 *adj* payable

yīng fù zé de 应负责的 *adj* accountable

yīng gāi 应该 *iv* ought to

yīng shòu qiǎn zé de 应受谴责的 *adj* deplorable

yīng bàng 英镑 *n* pound

yīng cùn 英寸 *n* inch

yīng gé lán 英格兰 *n* England

yīng guó 英国 *n* Britain

yīng guó de 英国的 *adj* British, English

yīng jùn 英俊 *adj* handsome

yīng lǐ 英里 *n* mile

yīng mǔ 英亩 *n* acre

yīng xióng 英雄 *n* hero

yīng xióng de 英雄的 *adj* heroic

yīng xióng zhǔ yì 英雄主义 *n* heroism

yīng yǒng 英勇 *n* bravery

yīng yǒng de 英勇的 *adj* heroic

yīng yǒng xíng wéi 英勇行为 *n* exploit

yīng ér 婴儿 *n* infant

yīng ér bǎo mǔ 婴儿保姆 *n* babysitter

yīng ér chuáng 婴儿床 *n* crib

yīng ér qī 婴儿期 *n* infancy

yīng táo 樱桃 *n* cherry

yīng wǔ 鹦鹉 *n* parrot

yīng 鹰 *n* hawk

yíng hé 迎合 *v* cater to, pander

yíng jiē 迎接 *v* greet

yíng miàn 迎面 *adv* head-on

yíng tóu 迎头 *adv* head-on

yíng lì 盈利 *n* earnings

yíng lì 盈利 *v* profit

yíng 营 *n* battalion

yíng dì 营地 *n* camp

yíng jiù 营救 *v* rescue

yíng sī wǔ bì 营私舞弊 *v* malpractice

yíng yǎng bù liáng 营养不良 *n* malnutrition

yíng yǎng de 营养的 *adj* nutritious

yíng rào 萦绕 *v* haunt

yíng 赢 *iv* win

yíng dé 赢得 *v* enlist

yíng qǔ 赢取 *v* win back

yǐng jù yuàn 影剧院 *n* theater

yǐng shè 影射 *n* innuendo, insinuation

yǐng shè 影射 *v* insinuate

yǐng xiǎng 影响 *v* affect, impact

yǐng xiǎng 影响 *n* affection, effect, impact

yǐng xiǎng lì 影响力 *n* influence

yǐng yìn 影印 *n* photocopy

yǐng zi 影子 *n* shadow

yìng biàn 应变 *v* strain

yìng biàn 应变 *n* strain

yìng dá de 应答的 *adj* responsive

yìng fu 应付 *v* cope, deal

yìng yòng 应用 *n* application

yìng 硬 *adj* hard

yìng bì 硬币 *n* coin

yìng dù 硬度 *n* hardness, stiffness

yìng jiàn 硬件 *n* hardware

yìng mù 硬木 *n* hardwood

yòng jīn 佣金 *n* commission

yōng bào 拥抱 *v* cuddle, embrace, hug

yōng bào 拥抱 *n* embrace, hug

yōng dǔ 拥堵 *n* congestion

yōng hù 拥护 *v* champion

yōng hù zhě 拥护者 *n* defender

yōng jǐ 拥挤 *n* congestion

yōng jǐ de 拥挤的 *adj* congested, crowded

yōng yǒu 拥有 *v* own, possess

yōng lǎn de 慵懒的 *adj* mellow

yǒng héng 永恒 *n* eternity

yǒng héng 永恒 *adj* timeless

yǒng héng de 永恒的 *adj* everlasting

yǒng jiǔ de 永久的 *adj* permanent

yǒng shēng 永生 *n* immortality

yǒng yuǎn 永远 *adv* forever

yǒng yuǎn de 永远的 *adj* immortal

yǒng gǎn 勇敢 *n* manliness

yǒng gǎn de 勇敢的 *adj* brave, courageous

yǒng gǎn de 勇敢地 *adv* bravely

yǒng qì 勇气 *n* courage

yǒng rù 涌入 *n* influx

yòng 用 *v* employ

yòng bēng dài bāo zhā 用绷带包扎 *v* bandage

（**yòng bèng**）**chōu**（**shuǐ**）（用泵）抽（水）*v* pump

yòng chē zhuāng zài 用车装载 *v* cart

yòng fǎ 用法 *n* usage

yòng fān bù fù gài 用帆布覆盖 *v* canvas

yòng fān bù zhuāng bèi 用帆布装备 *v* canvas

yòng gùn bàng lián xù dǎ 用棍棒连续打 *v* bludgeon

yòng hù 用户 *n* user

yòng jìn 用尽 *v* wear down, wear out

yòng jù 用具 *n* appliance

yòng lì guān 用力关 *v* bang

yòng lǔ zhī pào 用卤汁泡 *v* marinate

yòng luó dīng gù dìng 用螺钉固定 *v* screw

yòng mó shù biàn chū 用魔术变出 *v* conjure up

yòng pǐn 用品 *n* supplies

yòng（**qián**）用（钱）*iv* spend

yòng tàn shāo kǎo 用炭烧烤 *adj* charbroil

yòng tuī tǔ jī tuī 用推土机推 *v* bulldoze

yòng wán 用完 *v* run out

yòng yào wù 用药物 *v* drug

yòng zhuǎ zi zhuā 用爪子抓 *v* claw

yōu diǎn 优点 *n* virtue

yōu huì quàn 优惠券 *n* coupon

yōu róu guǎ duàn 优柔寡断 *n* indecision

yōu shèng zhě 优胜者 *n* winner

yōu shì 优势 *n* advantage, ascendancy, superiority

yōu xiān 优先 *n* priority

yōu xiù 优秀 *n* distinction

yōu xiù de 优秀的 *adj* excellent, outstanding

yōu yǎ 优雅 *n* elegance, grace

yōu yǎ de 优雅的 *adj* elegant, graceful

yōu yuè 优越 *n* ascendancy

yōu chóu 忧愁 *n* gloom

yōu lǜ 忧虑 *v* apprehend

yōu lǜ 忧虑 *n* distress, misgiving, worry

yōu bì de 幽闭的 *adj* pent-up

yōu líng 幽灵 *n* apparition, phantom

yōu mò 幽默 *n* humor

yōu mò de 幽默的 *adj* humorous

yóu qí 尤其 *adv* especially, particularly

yóu qí 尤其 *adj* particular

yóu 由 *pre* by

yóu yú 由于 *adv* owing to

yóu tài de 犹太的 *adj* Jewish

yóu tài jiào 犹太教 *n* Judaism

yóu tài jiào jiào shì 犹太教教士 *n* rabbi

yóu tài jiào táng 犹太教堂 *n* synagogue

yóu tài rén 犹太人 *n* Jew

yóu yù 犹豫 *v* falter, hesitate, vacillate

yóu yù 犹豫 *n* hesitation

yóu yù bù dìng de 犹豫不定的 *adj* hesitant, indecisive

yóu chāi 邮差 *n* posterity

yóu chuō 邮戳 *n* postman

yóu dì yuán 邮递员 *n* mailman

yóu fèi 邮费 *n* post office

yóu jì 邮寄 *v* mail

yóu jiàn 邮件 *n* delivery, mail

yóu piào 邮票 *n* stamp

yóu zhèng 邮政 *n* post

yóu zhèng biān mǎ 邮政编码 *n* zip code

yóu zhèng jú 邮政局 *n* postmark

yóu mò 油墨 *n* ink

yóu nì 油腻 *n* grease

yóu nì 油腻 *adj* greasy

yóu qī 油漆 *v* varnish, fry

yóu qī 油漆 *n* varnish

yóu yān 油烟 *n* fumes

yóu zhá 油炸 *adj* fried

yòu zi 柚子 *n* grapefruit

yòu zi shù 柚子树 *n* grapefruit

yóu 疣 *n* wart

yóu dàng 游荡 *n* loin

yóu jī duì 游击队 *n* guerrilla

yóu lǎn 游览 *n* excursion, tour

yóu lè chǎng 游乐场 *n* fair, playground

yóu shuì 游说 *v* lobby

yóu tǐng 游艇 *n* yacht

yóu xì 游戏 *n* game

yóu xíng 游行 *v* march

yóu xíng 游行 *n* march, procession

yóu yǒng 游泳 *iv* swim

yóu yǒng 游泳 *n* swimming

yóu yǒng zhě 游泳者 *n* swimmer

yóu yú 鱿鱼 *n* squid

yǒu hǎo 友好 *n* goodwill

yǒu hǎo de 友好的 *adj* nice, sociable

yǒu yì 友谊 *n* companionship, friendship

yǒu 有 *iv* have

yǒu ài xīn de 有爱心的 *adj* caring

yǒu bǎ wò de 有把握的 *adj* confident

yǒu bāng zhù 有帮助 *adj* helpful

yǒu bào chóu de 有报酬的 *adj* rewarding

yǒu bìng de 有病的 *adj* sick

yǒu cái néng de 有才能的 *adj* gifted

yǒu cái qì de 有才气的 *adj* brilliant

yǒu tán xìng de 有弹性的 *adj* elastic

yǒu dào dé de 有道德的 *adj* ethical, moral

yǒu diǎn 有点 *adv* somehow, somewhat

yǒu dú de 有毒的 *adj* noxious, poisonous, toxic

yǒu dú lì zhǔ quán de 有独立主权的 *adj* sovereign

yǒu fēn cùn de 有分寸的 *adj* decent

yǒu fēng xiǎn de 有风险的 *adj* risky

yǒu gòng 有供 *n* availability

yǒu guān xì de 有关系的 *adj* pertinent

yǒu guò shī de 有过失的 *adj* delinquent

yǒu hài 有害 *adj* harmful

yǒu hài de 有害的 *adj* hurtful, injurious, pernicious

yǒu hēi mù de 有黑幕的 *adj* shady

yǒu hú zi de 有胡子的 *adj* bearded

yǒu jī tǐ 有机体 *n* organism

yǒu jì liǎng de 有伎俩的 *adj* tricky

yǒu jià zhí de 有价值的 *adj* worth

yǒu jiān guǒ de 有坚果的 *adj* nutty

yǒu jù dú de 有剧毒的 *adj* virulent

yǒu kòng de 有空的 *adj* available

yǒu lǐ mào de 有礼貌的 *adj* courteous, polite

yǒu lì 有力 *adj* forceful

yǒu lì de 有力的 *adj* telling

yǒu lì 有利 *adj* favorable

yǒu lì de 有利的 *adj* beneficial, profitable

yǒu luó jí de 有逻辑的 *n* logic

yǒu mèi lì de 有魅力的 *adj* catching

yǒu míng de 有名的 *adj* renowned, well-known

yǒu nài xīn de 有耐心的 *adj* patient

yǒu néng lì de 有能力的 *adj* capable

yǒu qí yì de 有歧义的 *adj*
ambiguous

yǒu qǐ dí zuò yòng de 有启迪作
用的 *adj* revealing

yǒu qián lì de 有潜力的 *adj*
potential

yǒu qíng gǎn de 有情感的 *adj*
emotional

yǒu qíng yù 有情欲 *v* lust

yǒu qū bié de 有区别的 *adj*
distinctive

yǒu qù 有趣 *n* fun

yǒu qù de 有趣的 *adj* amusing,
interesting, intriguing

yǒu quē xiàn de 有缺陷的 *adj*
defective, deficient

yǒu què bān 有雀斑 *adj* freckled

yǒu rǔ rén gé 有辱人格 *v* degrade

yǒu rǔ rén gé de 有辱人格的 *adj*
degrading, demeaning

yǒu shēng yù de 有声誉的 *adj*
renowned

yǒu shí 有时 *adv* sometimes

yǒu shù fù lì de 有束缚力的 *adj*
binding

yǒu tè sè de 有特色的 *adj*
distinctive

yǒu tiáo bù wěn 有条不紊 *adj*
methodical

yǒu tiáo jiàn de 有条件的 *adj*
conditional

yǒu tiáo jiàn tóu xiáng 有条件投
降 *v* capitulate

yǒu tóng qíng xīn de 有同情心的
adj compassionate

yǒu wén huà de 有文化的 *adj*
literate

yǒu wèn tí de 有问题的 *adj*
problematic

yǒu xī yǐn lì 有吸引力 *adj*
appealing

yǒu xī yǐn lì de 有吸引力的 *adj*
attractive

yǒu xī wàng de 有希望的 *adj*
hopeful

yǒu xī zhài quàn 有息债券 *n* bond

yǒu xiào de 有效的 *adj* effective,
telling, valid

yǒu xiào xìng 有效性 *n* validity

yǒu xìn xīn de 有信心的 *adj*
confident

yǒu xìng qù de 有兴趣的 *adj*
interested

yǒu xíng 有形 *adj* tangible

yǒu xióng xīn de 有雄心的 *adj*
ambitious

yǒu yā lì de 有压力的 *adj* stressful

yǒu yě xīn de 有野心的 *adj*
ambitious

yǒu yí wèn de 有疑问的 *adj*
skeptic

yǒu yì yì de 有异议的 *adj*
dissident

yǒu yì de 有益的 *adj* conducive,
rewarding

yǒu yì jiàn kāng de 有益健康的
adj wholesome

yǒu yì shēn xīn jiàn kāng de 有益
身心健康的 *adj* wholesome

yǒu yì shí de 有意识的 *adj*
conscious

yǒu yì yì de 有意义的 *adj*
meaningful

yǒu yǐng xiǎng de 有影响的 *adj*
influential

yǒu yìng ké de 有硬壳的 *adj*
crusty

yǒu yòng de 有用的 *adj* useful

yǒu yòng xìng 有用性 *n*
usefulness

yǒu zé rèn de 有责任的 *adj*
accountable, responsible

yǒu nián xìng de 有粘性的 *adj*
adhesive

yǒu zhēng yì de 有争议的 *adj*
contentious

yǒu zhù de 有助的 *adj* conducive

yǒu zī gé 有资格 *v* qualify

yǒu zī gé de 有资格的 *adj* eligible

yǒu zī wèi de 有滋味的 *adj*
tasteful

yǒu zuì 有罪 *n* culpability

yǒu zuì de 有罪的 *adj* guilty

yǒu zuì niè 有罪孽 *v* sin

yòu bian 右边 *adv* right

yòu shòu 幼兽 *n* cub

yòu zhì de 幼稚的 *adj* puerile

yòu ěr 诱饵 *n* bait

yòu guǎi 诱拐 *v* abduct

yòu guǎi 诱拐 *n* abduction

yòu huò 诱惑 *v* beguile, entice,
lure, seduce, tempt

yòu huò 诱惑 *n* enticement,
seduction, temptation

yòu huò de 诱惑的 *adj* enticing

yòu piàn 诱骗 *v* beguile

yòu rén de 诱人的 *adj* alluring

yòu shǐ 诱使 *v* induce

yū fǔ de 迂腐的 *adj* pedantic

yū huí lù 迂回路 *n* detour

yú 鱼 *n* fish

yú chā 鱼叉 *n* harpoon

yú chì 鱼翅 *n* fin

yú lè 娱乐 *n* amusement,
entertainment

yú lè 娱乐 *v* entertain

yú lè de 娱乐的 *adj* entertaining

yú fū 渔夫 *n* fisherman

yú kuài 愉快 *adj* enjoyable

yú kuài de 愉快的 *adj* merry

yú qī de 逾期的 *adj* overdue

yú chǔn 愚蠢 *n* numbness,
stupidity

yú chǔn de 愚蠢的 *adj* moron

yú chǔn de cuò wù 愚蠢的错误
n goof

yú chǔn de rén 愚蠢的人 *n* goof

yú nòng 愚弄 *v* deride, fool

yú shù 榆树 *n* elm

yǔ 与 *c* and

yǔ ……máo dùn 与……矛盾 *v*
contradict

yǔ cǐ tóng shí 与此同时 *adv*
meantime, meanwhile

yǔ qíng kuàng yǒu guān de 与情
况有关的 *adj* circumstantial

yǔ háng yuán 宇航员 *n* astronaut,
cosmonaut

yǔ zhòu 宇宙 *n* universe

yǔ zhòu de 宇宙的 *adj* cosmic

yǔ máo 羽毛 *n* feather

yǔ 雨 *n* rain

yǔ péng 雨篷 *n* awning

yǔ yī 雨衣 *n* raincoat

yǔ fǎ 语法 *n* grammar

yǔ yán 语言 *n* language

yù mǐ 玉米 *n* corn

yù mǐ bàng 玉米棒 *n* cob

yù féi 育肥 *v* fatten

yù jīn xiāng 郁金香 *n* tulip

yù jǐng 狱警 *n* jailer

yù gāng 浴缸 *n* bathtub

yù pén 浴盆 *n* tub

yù shì 浴室 *n* bathroom

yù yī 浴衣 *n* bathrobe

yù bèi de 预备的 *adj* preliminary

yù cè 预测 *iv* forecast, predict

yù cè 预测 *n* prediction

yù fáng 预防 *n* prevention

yù fáng de 预防的 *adj* preventive

yù fù dìng jīn 预付定金 *n* down payment

yù gǎn 预感 *n* premonition

yù jì 预计 *v* project

yù jiàn 预见 *iv* foresee

yù jiàn 预见 *n* foretaste

yù jǐng 预警 *v* forewarn

yù lǎn 预览 *n* preview

yù móu 预谋 *v* premeditate

yù móu 预谋 *n* premeditation

yù qī 预期 *v* anticipate

yù qī 预期 *n* anticipation, expectancy

yù shè 预设 *n* presupposition

yù shè de 预设的 *adj* predisposed

yù shì 预示 *v* foreshadow

yù suàn 预算 *n* budget

yù yán 预言 *n* prophecy

yù zhào 预兆 *n* portent

yù zhī 预知 *v* foretell

yù zhì 预制 *v* prefabricate

yù yán 寓言 *n* allegory, fable, parable

yù yán zhōng de 寓言中的 *adj* fabulous

yù dào 遇到 *v* encounter

yù dào 遇到 *n* encounter

yù hé 愈合 *v* heal

yù liáo zhě 愈疗者 *n* healer

yuán shuài 元帅 *n* marshal

yuán sù 元素 *n* element

yuán yīn 元音 *n* vowel

yuán gōng 员工 *n* personnel

yuán dīng 园丁 *n* gardener

yuán 原 *adv* formerly

yuán běn 原本 *adv* originally

yuán chǎn dì 原产地 *n* origin

yuán gào 原告 *n* plaintiff

yuán liàng 原谅 *v* forgive, pardon

yuán liàng 原谅 *n* pardon

yuán shǐ de 原始的 *adj* original, primitive

yuán xíng 原型 *n* prototype

yuán yě 原野 *n* wilderness

yuán yì de 原义的 *adj* literal

yuán yīn 原因 *n* cause, reason

yuán zé 原则 *n* principle

yuán zǐ 原子 *n* atom

yuán zǐ de 原子的 *adj* atomic

yuán de 圆的 *adj* circular, round

yuán guī 圆规 *n* compass

Y

yuán huán 圆环 *n* ring
yuán pàng de 圆胖的 *adj* chubby
yuán quān 圆圈 *n* circle
yuán tǒng 圆筒 *n* cylinder
yuán wū dǐng 圆屋顶 *n* dome
yuán xíng jù chǎng 圆形剧场 *n* amphitheater
yuán zhù 援助 *n* aid, assistance
yuán zhù 援助 *v* aid, bolster
yuán yú 源于 *v* originate
yuán 猿 *n* ape
yuǎn 远 *adv* far
yuǎn fāng 远方 *adj* faraway
yuǎn háng 远航 *v* voyage
yuǎn jiàn 远见 *n* foresight
yuǎn lí 远离 *adv* away
yuǎn lí zhōng xīn de 远离中心的 *adj* outer
yuǎn zhēng 远征 *n* expedition
yuàn hèn 怨恨 *n* grudge
yuàn hèn 怨恨 *v* resent
yuàn qì 怨气 *n* resentment
yuàn zhǎng 院长 *n* dean
yuàn wàng 愿望 *n* desire, wish
yuàn wàng 愿望 *v* wish
yuàn yì 愿意 *n* readiness
yuàn yì de 愿意的 *adj* willing
yuàn yì de 愿意地 *adv* willingly
yuē dìng 约定 *n* appointment
yuē huì 约会 *v* date
yuē shù 约束 *n* constraint
yuē shù 约束 *v* tie
yuè 月 *n* month
yuè jīng 月经 *n* menstruation
yuè liang 月亮 *n* moon

yuè shí 月食 *n* eclipse
yuè duì 乐队 *n* band
yuè pǔ 乐谱 *n* notation
yuè tuán 乐团 *n* orchestra
yuè fù 岳父 *n* father-in-law
yuè mǔ 岳母 *n* mother-in-law
yào shi 钥匙 *n* key
yào shi kòu 钥匙扣 *n* key ring
yuè guǐ 越轨 *n* aberration
yuè guǐ xíng wéi 越轨行为 *n* escapade
yuè guò 越过 *v* cross
yún 云 *n* cloud
yǔn xǔ 允许 *v* allow, permit
yǔn xǔ jìn rù 允许进入 *v* admit
yùn qī 孕期 *n* trimester
yùn dòng 运动 *n* campaign, move, movement
yùn dòng de 运动的 *adj* athletic, sporty
yùn dòng yuán 运动员 *n* athlete, sportsman
yùn hé 运河 *n* canal
yùn qi 运气 *n* luck
yùn shū 运输 *n* transit
yùn shū 运输 *v* transport
yùn xíng 运行 *iv* run
yùn chuán de 晕船的 *adj* seasick
yūn dǎo 晕倒 *v* faint
yūn dǎo 晕倒 *n* faint
yūn dǎo 晕倒 *adj* faint
yùn hán 蕴涵 *n* implication

Y

Z

zá cǎo 杂草 *v* weed

zá huò 杂货 *n* groceries

zá jì yǎn yuán 杂技演员 *n* acrobat

zá luàn de 杂乱的 *adj* promiscuous

zá wén 杂文 *n* essay

zá zhì 杂志 *n* journal, magazine

zá kāi 砸开 *v* break open

zāi huò 灾祸 *n* scourge

zāi nàn 灾难 *n* calamity, cataclysm, disaster

zāi nàn xìng de 灾难性的 *adj* disastrous

zāi péi 栽培 *n* cultivation

zài bǎo zhèng 再保证 *v* reassure

zài chōng diàn 再充电 *v* recharge

zài chuàng zào 再创造 *v* recreate

zài cì 再次 *adv* again

zài huí dá 再回答 *v* rejoin

zài hūn 再婚 *v* remarry

zài jiā rù 再加入 *v* rejoin

zài jiàn 再见 *e* bye

zài jìn rù 再进入 *n* reentry

zài shēng 再生 *n* regeneration

zài shēng chǎn 再生产 *v* reproduce

zài shēng chǎn 再生产 *n* reproduction

zài shēng de 再生的 *adj* retroactive

zài tǐ yàn 再体验 *v* relive

zài xiàn 再现 *v* reappear

zài xiàn 再现 *n* recurrence

zài zhì dìng 再制定 *n* reenactment

zài zhì zào 再制造 *v* refurbish

zài 在 *pre* at, upon

zài ……hòu 在……后 *pre* after, behind

zài ……páng 在……旁 *pre* beside

zài ……páng biān 在……旁边 *pre* alongside

zài ……qián 在……前 *pre* before

zài ……shàng 在……上 *pre* above

zài ……xià 在……下 *pre* below

zài ……xià fāng 在……下方 *pre* beneath

zài ……zhī jiān 在……之间 *pre* between

zài ……zhōng jiān 在……中间 *pre* amid, among

zài ……zhōu wéi 在……周围 *pro* around

zài …shàng shǐ guò 在…上驶过 *v* run over

zài àn biān 在岸边 *adv* ashore

zài àn shàng 在岸上 *adv* ashore

zài chuán shàng 在船上 *adv* aboard

zài fēi jī shàng 在飞机上 *adv* aboard

zài guó wài 在国外 *adv* abroad

zài hòu mian 在后面 *adv* back

zài huǒ chē shàng 在火车上 *adv* aboard

zài lǐ miàn 在里面 *pre* in, inside

zài lóu shàng 在楼上 *adv* upstairs

zài nǎ li 在哪里 *adv* where

Z

zài nèi 在内 *adv* inwards

zài páng biān 在旁边 *adv* aside

zài qī jiān 在期间 *pre* during

zài qián 在前 *pre* ahead

zài qián mian de 在前面的 *adj* preceding

zài shàng mian 在上面 *pre* on

zài shí zì jià shàng dìng sǐ 在十字架上钉死 *n* crucifixion

zài shí zì jià shàng dìng sǐ 在十字架上钉死 *v* crucify

zài sì chù 在四处 *pro* around

zài xià mian 在下面 *adv* down

zài xià mian 在下面 *pre* under, underneath

zài yuǎn fāng 在远方 *adv* afar

zài zhī nèi 在之内 *pre* within

zài zhī qián 在之前 *v* precede

zàn dìng de 暂定的 *adj* tentative

zàn duǎn 暂短 *adj* fleeting

zàn shí bō duó 暂时剥夺 *n* suspension

zàn shí de huǎn hé 暂时的缓和 *n* respite

zàn shí píng xī 暂时平息 *n* lull

zàn tíng 暂停 *v* suspend

zàn tíng 暂停 *n* suspension

zàn zhù 暂住 *v* stay

zàn chéng 赞成 *n* approval

zàn měi 赞美 *v* exalt, glorify

zàn měi shī 赞美诗 *n* chant

zàn tóng 赞同 *v* assent, endorse

zàn tóng 赞同 *n* favor

zàn yáng 赞扬 *n* compliment

zàn zhù rén 赞助人 *n* patron

zàn zhù shāng 赞助商 *n* sponsor

zāng wù 赃物 *n* booty, spoils

zàng lǐ 葬礼 *n* burial, funeral

zāo shòu 遭受 *v* suffer from

zāo yù 遭遇 *v* confront

zāo gāo de 糟糕的 *adj* lousy

zāo tà 糟蹋 *v* botch

záo zi 凿子 *n* chisel

zǎo 早 *adv* early

zǎo cān 早餐 *n* breakfast

zǎo chǎn de 早产的 *adj* premature

zǎo shú de 早熟的 *adj* precocious

zǎo wǔ cān 早午餐 *n* brunch

zào chéng 造成 *v* inflict

zào chéng sǔn hài de 造成损害的 *adj* hurtful

zào yīn 噪音 *n* noise

zé bèi 责备 *v* censure, chide, condemn, reproach

zé bèi 责备 *n* reproach

zé dǎ 责打 *n* spanking

zé guài 责怪 *n* blame

zé guài 责怪 *v* blame

zé mà 责骂 *v* chide

zé rèn 责任 *n* responsibility

céng jīng 曾经 *adv* ever

zēng zhǎng 增长 *n* growth

zēng dà 增大 *v* augment

zēng gāo 增高 *n* raise

zēng jiā 增加 *v* augment, compound, enhance, increase

zēng jiā de 增加的 *adj* increasing

zēng liàng 增量 *n* increment

zēng qiáng 增强 *n* reinforcements

zēng rèn 增韧 *v* toughen

Z

zēng wù 憎恶 *v* detest

zēng wù 憎恶 *n* disgust

zèng kuǎn 赠款 *v* grant

zèng kuǎn 赠款 *n* grant

zèng sòng 赠送 *v* give away

zèng yǔ rén 赠与人 *n* donor

zhā 扎 *n* bunch

zhā yíng 扎营 *v* camp

zhá 轧 *v* mangle

zhá mén 闸门 *n* floodgate

zhǎ yǎn 眨眼 *v* blink, twinkle

zhà piàn 诈骗 *n* fraud

zhà lán 栅栏 *n* barricade

zhà dàn 炸弹 *n* bomb, bombshell

zhāi 摘 *v* pick

zhāi yào 摘要 *v* brief

zhāi yào 摘要 *n* summary

zhài quán rén 债权人 *n* creditor

zhài wù 债务 *n* debt

zhài wù rén 债务人 *n* debtor

zhān 粘 *v* duck

nián de 粘的 *adj* adhesive, sticky

zhān fù 粘附 *v* adhere

zhān shàng 粘上 *v* affix

zhǎn 斩 *iv* slay

zhǎn shǒu 斩首 *v* behead, decapitate

zhǎn chū 展出 *v* exhibit

zhǎn kāi 展开 *v* unfold

zhǎn lǎn 展览 *n* exhibition

zhǎn shì 展示 *n* display

zhǎn shì 展示 *iv* show

zhǎn wàng 展望 *n* outlook, prospect

zhàn jù 占据 *n* occupation

zhàn jù 占据 *v* occupy

zhān xīng jiā 占星家 *n* astrologer

zhān xīng shù 占星术 *n* astrology

zhàn yōu shì 占优势 *v* dominate

zhàn yǒu 占有 *v* possess

zhàn zhǔ dǎo dì wèi 占主导地位 *v* predominate

zhàn dòu 战斗 *n* battle, combat, fight

zhàn dòu 战斗 *v* battle, combat

zhàn dòu jī 战斗机 *n* fighter

zhàn dòu yuán 战斗员 *n* combatant

zhàn dòu zhě 战斗者 *n* fighter

zhàn háo 战壕 *n* trench

zhàn jiàn 战舰 *n* battleship

zhàn lì 战利 *v* loot

zhàn lì pǐn 战利品 *n* booty, loot

zhàn lì 战栗 *n* shudder

zhàn lì 战栗 *v* shudder

zhàn shèng 战胜 *v* prevail

zhàn shi 战士 *n* warrior

zhàn shù 战术 *n* tactics

zhàn shù shàng de 战术上的 *adj* tactical

zhàn wú bù shèng de 战无不胜的 *adj* invincible

zhàn yì 战役 *n* campaign

zhàn zhēng 战争 *n* war, warfare

zhàn fáng 栈房 *n* depot

zhàn 站 *n* station, stop

zhàn bù zhù jiǎo de 站不住脚的 *n* invalid

zhàn lì 站立 *iv* stand

zhàn lì 站立 *n* standing

Z

zhàn fàng 绽放 *v* bloom

zhāng 章 *n* chapter

zhāng yú 章鱼 *n* octopus

zhāng láng 蟑螂 *n* cockroach

zhǎng luò 涨落 *v* fluctuate

zhǎng duò 掌舵 *n* helm

zhǎng shēng 掌声 *n* applause

zhǎng wò 掌握 *iv* hold, master

zhàng fū 丈夫 *n* husband

zhàng hù 帐户 *n* account

zhàng peng 帐篷 *n* tent

zhàng 胀 *n* bulge

zhàng dà 胀大 *iv* swell

zhàng dān 账单 *n* bill

zhàng ài 障碍 *n* barrier, handicap, hindrance, obstacle

zhāo dài huì 招待会 *n* reception

zhāo dài yuán 招待员 *n* receptionist

zhāo mù 招募 *v* recruit

zhāo mù 招募 *n* recruitment

zhāo shēng 招生 *n* enrollment

zhāo zhì 招致 *v* incur

zháo dì 着地 *v* land

zháo jí de 着急的 *adj* anxious

zhǎo chū 找出 *v* find out

zhǎo dào 找到 *iv* find

zhǎo jiè kǒu 找借口 *v* excuse

zhǎo zé 沼泽 *n* bog, swamp

zhào huàn 召唤 *v* beckon

zhào huàn 召唤 *n* calling

zhào jí 召集 *n* roundup

zhào kāi 召开 *v* convene

zhào gù 照顾 *v* look after, minister

zhào liàng 照亮 *v* illuminate

zhào liào 照料 *n* care, oversight

zhào míng 照明 *n* lighting

zhào piàn 照片 *n* photo

zhào yào 照耀 *v* gleam, shine

zhào zì miàn de 照字面的 *adj* literal

zhē shì 蜇 *iv* sting

zhē shì 蜇 *n* sting

zhē yīn de 遮荫的 *adj* shady

zhé dié de 折叠的 *adj* pleated

zhé jiù 折旧 *n* depreciation

zhé kòu 折扣 *n* discount, rebate

zhé mó 折磨 *v* afflict, torment, torture

zhé mó 折磨 *n* torment, torture

zhé wān 折弯 *iv* bend

zhé zhuǎn de 折转的 *adj* reflexive

zhé xué 哲学 *n* philosophy

zhé xué jiā 哲学家 *n* philosopher

zhě 褶 *n* pleat

zhě fèng 褶缝 *n* crease

zhě hén 褶痕 *n* crease

zhè 这 *adj* this

zhè lèi 这类 *adj* such

zhè lǐ 这里 *adv* here

zhè xiē 这些 *adj* these

zhè gū 鹧鸪 *n* partridge

zhēn jié 贞洁 *n* chastity

zhēn jié de 贞洁的 *adj* chaste, virtuous

zhēn 针 *n* needle, pin, stitch

zhēn 针 *v* stitch

zhēn duì de 针对的 *adj* pointed

zhēn xiàn 针线 *n* thread

zhēn zhī 针织 *v* knit

Z

zhēn chá 侦查 *n* inquisition

zhēn chá chū 侦查出 *v* detect

zhēn tàn 侦探 *n* detective

zhēn guì de 珍贵的 *adj* precious, valuable

zhēn pǐn 珍品 *n* treasure

zhēn qí de 珍奇的 *adj* rare

zhēn xī 珍惜 *v* cherish

zhēn zhū 珍珠 *n* pearl

zhēn chéng 真诚 *adj* sincere

zhēn jūn 真菌 *n* fungus

zhēn shí de 真实的 *adj* authentic, genuine, real

zhēn shí xìng 真实性 *n* authenticity

zhēn xiàng 真相 *n* truth

zhēn xīn shí yì de 真心实意的 *adj* wholehearted

zhēn zhèng de 真正的 *adj* genuine

zhēn zhèng de 真正地 *adv* really

zhēn zhì de 真挚地 *adv* dearly

zhēn zi 榛子 *n* hazelnut

zhěn duàn 诊断 *v* diagnose, defame

zhěn duàn 诊断 *n* diagnosis

zhěn suǒ 诊所 *n* clinic

zhěn tào 枕套 *n* pillowcase

zhěn tou 枕头 *n* pillow

zhěn 疹 *n* rash

zhèn fēng 阵风 *n* gust

zhèn liè 阵列 *n* array

zhèn dòng 振动 *v* vibrate

zhèn dòng 振动 *n* vibration

zhèn zhèn yǒu cí de 振振有词的 *adj* plausible

zhèn 镇 *n* town

zhèn dìng 镇定 *n* composure

zhèn jìng 镇静 *n* sedation

zhèn jìng de 镇静的 *adj* composed

zhèn chàn 震颤 *n* shudder, tremor

zhèn chàn 震颤 *v* shudder

zhèn dàng 震荡 *n* concussion

zhèn dòng 震动 *v* quake

zhèn ěr yù lóng de 震耳欲聋的 *adj* deafening

zhèn jí 震级 *n* magnitude

zhèn jīng 震惊 *n* consternation, shock

zhèn jīng 震惊 *v* stun

zhèn jīng de 震惊的 *adj* shattering, startled

zhèn shè 震慑 *n* deterrence

zhēng biàn 争辩 *v* argue

zhēng chǎo 争吵 *n* altercation, brawl, hassle

zhēng duān 争端 *n* dispute

zhēng duān 争端 *v* dispute

zhēng lùn 争论 *n* argument, debate, disagreement

zhēng lùn 争论 *v* debate

zhēng yì 争议 *n* controversy

zhēng bīng 征兵 *n* conscript

zhēng fú 征服 *v* conquer, subdue, vanquish

zhēng fú 征服 *n* conquest

zhēng fú zhě 征服者 *n* conqueror

zhēng mù 征募 *v* enlist

zhēng qiú 征求 *v* solicit

zhēng shōu 征收 *v* levy

zhēng tú 征途 *n* journey

Z

zhēng yòng 征用 *v* expropriate

zhèng tuō 挣脱 *v* break free

zhēng fā 蒸发 *v* evaporate

zhēng liú 蒸馏 *v* distill

zhēng qì 蒸汽 *n* steam

zhěng jiù 拯救 *v* save

zhěng dùn 整顿 *v* reorganize, straighten out

zhěng gè 整个 *adj* entire

zhěng gè de 整个的 *adj* whole

zhěng jié de 整洁的 *adj* tidy

zhěng lǐ 整理 *n* ordination

zhěng lǐ 整理 *v* sort out

zhěng qí 整齐 *adv* neatly

zhěng qí de 整齐的 *adj* neat

zhěng xiū 整修 *n* renovation

zhèng cháng de 正常的 *adj* normal

zhèng cháng huà 正常化 *v* normalize

zhèng dāng de 正当地 *adv* justly

zhèng guī de 正规的 *adj* normal

zhèng guī huà 正规化 *v* formalize

zhèng lái lín de 正来临的 *adj* incoming

zhèng miàn 正面 *n* frontage

zhèng miàn 正面 *adj* positive

zhèng pài de 正派的 *adj* chaste

zhèng qiē 正切 *n* tangent

zhèng què de 正确的 *adj* correct, right

zhèng shì 正式 *n* formality

zhèng shì de 正式的 *adj* formal, official

zhèng shì de 正式地 *adv* formally

zhèng shì xuān bù （sǐ zhě） **wéi shèng tú** 正式宣布（死者）为圣徒 *v* canonize

zhèng zhí de 正直的 *adj* rigid

zhèng zhí de 正值的 *adj* upright

zhèng zōng de 正宗的 *adj* authentic

zhèng cí 证词 *n* testimony

zhèng jù 证据 *n* evidence

zhèng míng 证明 *v* attest, manifest, prove

zhèng míng 证明 *n* proof, verification

zhèng míng wú zuì 证明无罪 *v* exonerate

zhèng shí 证实 *v* authenticate

zhèng shí de 证实的 *adj* proven

zhèng shū 证书 *n* certificate

zhèng biàn 政变 *n* coup

zhèng cè 政策 *n* policy

zhèng fǔ 政府 *n* government

zhèng quán 政权 *n* regime

zhèng zhì 政治 *n* politics

zhèng zhì jiā 政治家 *n* politician

zhèng zhuàng 症状 *n* symptom

zhī chēng 支撑 *v* bolster

zhī chí 支持 *v* back, back up, support

zhī chí 支持 *n* backing, countenance

zhī chí zhě 支持者 *n* supporter

zhī chū 支出 *n* expenditure

zhī fù 支付 *v* defray, disburse

zhī fù de 支付的 *adj* payable

zhī liú 支流 *n* branch

Z

zhī lù 支路 *n* bypass
zhī pèi 支配 *v* dominate
zhī pèi 支配 *n* domination, dominion
zhī piào 支票 *n* check
zhī piào bù 支票簿 *n* checkbook
zhī qì guǎn yán 支气管炎 *n* bronchitis
zhī zhù 支柱 *n* pillar
zhī yè 汁液 *n* sap
zhī zhī shēng de 吱吱声的 *adj* squeaky
zhī xíng diào dēng 枝形吊灯 *n* chandelier
zhī dào 知道 *iv* know
zhī dào de 知道的 *adj* aware
zhī shi 知识 *n* knowledge
zhī 织 *v* loom, weave
zhī jī 织机 *n* loom
zhī wù 织物 *n* fabric
zhī tǐ 肢体 *n* limb
zhī fáng 脂肪 *n* fat
zhī zhū 蜘蛛 *n* spider
zhī zhū wǎng 蜘蛛网 *n* cobweb, spider web
zhí shì 执事 *n* deacon
zhí xíng 执行 *v* carry out, execute
zhí xíng guān 执行官 *n* bailiff
zhí yè 执业 *v* practice
zhí zhèng 执政 *v* reign
zhí nǚ 侄女 *n* niece
zhí zi 侄子 *n* nephew
zhí bō 直播 *v* televise
zhí cháng 直肠 *n* rectum
zhí chǐ 直尺 *n* ruler

zhí dào 直到 *adv* till
zhí dào 直到 *v* till
zhí dào 直到 *pre* until
zhí de 直的 *adj* straight
zhí jiē de 直接的 *adj* direct
zhí jié liǎo dàng de 直截了当的 *adj* forthright
zhí jìng 直径 *n* diameter
zhí jué 直觉 *n* hunch, intuition
zhí shuài 直率 *n* bluntness
zhí shuài de 直率的 *adj* blunt, brusque
zhí shuài de（de） 直率的（地）*adj* forthright
zhí shēng jī 直升机 *n* helicopter
zhí dé 值得 *v* deserve, merit
zhí dé 值得 *n* merit
zhí dé chēng dào de 值得称道的 *adj* praiseworthy
zhí dé chóng bài de 值得崇拜的 *adj* adorable
zhí dé de 值得的 *adj* deserving, rewarding, worthwhile, worthy
zhí dé yōng yǒu de 值得拥有的 *adj* desirable
zhí dé zhù yì de 值得注意的 *adj* notable, noteworthy
zhí wèi 职位 *n* position
zhí yè 职业 *n* calling
zhí yè 职业 *n* career
zhí yè 职业 *n* occupation
zhí yè 职业 *n* vocation
zhí zé 职责 *n* duty
zhí bèi 植被 *n* vegetation
zhí rù 植入 *v* implant

Z

zhí wù 植物 *n* plant
zhí wù xué 植物学 *n* botany
[zhí]zǐ fáng [植]子房 *n* ovary
zhí mín 殖民 *n* colonization
zhí mín de 殖民的 *adj* colonial
zhí mín dì 殖民地 *n* colony
zhí mín dì de 殖民地的 *adj* colonial
zhǐ tòng yào 止痛药 *n* painkiller
zhǐ zhù 止住 *v* snub
zhī 只 *adv* merely, only
zhǐ zài 旨在 *v* aim
zhǐ 纸 *n* paper
zhǐ bǎn 纸板 *n* cardboard
zhǐ jiāng 纸浆 *n* pulp
zhǐ jīn 纸巾 *n* tissue
zhǐjuǎn 纸卷 *n* scroll
zhǐ chū 指出 *v* pinpoint
zhǐ dǎo 指导 *n* conduct, guidance
zhǐ dǎo 指导 *v* direct, guide
zhǐ dǎo fāng zhēn 指导方针 *n* guidelines
zhǐ dǎo yuán 指导员 *n* instructor
zhǐ diǎn 指点 *v* point
zhǐ dìng 指定 *v* designate, earmark
zhǐ huī 指挥 *v* command
zhǐ huī 指挥 *n* conductor
zhǐ huī bàng 指挥棒 *n* baton
zhǐ huī guān 指挥官 *n* commander
zhǐ jia 指甲 *n* fingernail, nail
zhǐ jiān 指尖 *n* fingertip
zhǐ kòng 指控 *n* accusation, charge

zhǐ kòng 指控 *v* charge
zhǐ nán 指南 *n* guide, guidebook
zhǐ pài 指派 *v* assign
zhǐ pài 指派 *n* assignment
zhǐ shì 指示 *v* instruct
zhǐ shì qì 指示器 *n* marker
zhǐ shù 指数 *n* index
zhǐ wén 指纹 *n* fingerprint
zhǐ xiàng biāo 指向标 *n* marker
zhǐ zé 指责 *v* accuse, denounce
zhǐ jiǎ 趾甲 *n* toenail
zhì 至 *pre* to
zhì cǐ 至此 *adv* hitherto
zhì gāo wú shàng de 至高无上的 *adj* paramount, sovereign
zhì shǎo 至少 *adj* least
zhì yuàn zhě 志愿者 *n* volunteer
zhì biǎo zhě 制表者 *n* watchmaker
zhì cái 制裁 *v* sanction
zhì cái 制裁 *n* sanction
zhì dìng 制定 *v* constitute
zhì dòng 制动 *v* brake
zhì dòng qì 制动器 *n* brake
zhì fú 制服 *v* subdue
zhì fú 制服 *n* uniform
zhì mú 制模 *adj* mold
zhì zào 制造 *v* manufacture
zhì zào shāng 制造商 *n* maker
zhì zuò 制作 *n* make
zhì zuò mú jù 制作模具 *v* mold
zhì lǐ 治理 *v* govern
zhì liáo 治疗 *n* treatment
zhì yù 治愈 *v* cure
zhì yù 治愈 *n* cure

Z

zhì dì 质地 *n* texture
zhì liàng 质量 *n* quality
zhì wèn 质问 *v* heckle
zhì cán 致残 *v* maim, mutilate
zhì jìng 致敬 *n* tribute
zhì lì 致力 *v* dedicate
zhì lì 致力 *n* dedication
zhì mìng 致命 *adj* fatal
zhì mìng de 致命的 *adj* deadly,
　lethal
zhì mìng xìng 致命性 *n* mortality
zhì zhù jiǔ cí 致祝酒辞 *v* toast
zhì zhù jiǔ cí 致祝酒辞 *n* toast
zhì mèn de 窒闷的 *adj* stuffy
zhì xī 窒息 *v* asphyxiate, choke,
　suffocate
zhì xī 窒息 *n* asphyxiation
zhì huì 智慧 *n* wisdom
zhì lì chí dùn de 智力迟钝的 *adj*
　retarded
zhì lì fā yù chí huǎn de 智力发育
　迟缓的 *adj* retarded
zhì 痣 *n* mole
zhōng chǎn jiē jí de 中产阶级的
　adj bourgeois
zhōng děng de 中等的 *adj*
　medium
zhōng dù de 中度的 *adj* moderate
zhōng duàn 中断 *v* break off,
　disrupt, interrupt
zhōng duàn 中断 *n* disruption,
　interruption
zhōng hé 中和 *v* counteract
zhōng jí de 中级的 *adj* secondary
zhōng jiān 中间 *n* middle

zhōng jiān rén 中间人 *n*
　middleman
zhōng jiè 中介 *n* intermediary
zhōng lì 中立 *v* neutralize
zhōng lì de 中立的 *adj* neutral
zhōng shì jì de 中世纪的 *adj*
　medieval
zhōng wèi 中尉 *n* lieutenant
zhōng wǔ 中午 *n* midday, noon
zhōng xīn 中心 *n* center
zhōng xīn de 中心的 *adj* central
zhōng yāng de 中央的 *adj* central
zhōng yōng 中庸 *n* moderation
zhōng zhuǎn 中转 *v* relay
zhōng chéng 忠诚 *adj* faithful
zhōng chéng 忠诚 *n* loyalty
zhōng chéng de 忠诚的 *adj*
　committed, loyal
zhōng zhǐ 终止 *v* terminate
zhōng bǎi 钟摆 *n* pendulum
zhōng lóu 钟楼 *n* belfry
zhōng xīn 衷心 *adj* heartfelt
zhǒng kuài 肿块 *n* bump
（zhǒng）kuài （肿）块 *n* lump
zhǒng liú 肿瘤 *n* tumor
zhǒng zhàng 肿胀 *n* swelling
zhǒng zhàng de 肿胀的 *adj*
　swollen
zhǒng 种 *iv* sow
zhǒng lèi 种类 *n* type
zhǒng xìng zhì dù 种姓制度 *n*
　caste
zhòng zhí 种植 *v* plant
zhǒng zi 种子 *n* seed
zhǒng zú 种族 *n* race

Z

zhǒng zú miè jué 种族灭绝 *n* genocide

zhǒng zú zhǔ yì 种族主义 *n* racism

zhǒng zú zhǔ yì zhě 种族主义者 *adj* racist

zhòng dú 中毒 *n* poisoning

zhòng jiǎng 中奖 *n* jackpot

zhòng fēng 中风 *n* stroke

zhòng shāng 中伤 *v* malign

zhòng shǔ 中暑 *n* heatstroke

zhòng cái 仲裁 *v* arbitrate

zhòng cái 仲裁 *n* arbitration

zhòng cái rén 仲裁人 *n* umpire

zhòng cái zhě 仲裁者 *n* arbiter, referee

zhòng dà de 重大的 *adj* momentous

zhòng dà shì jiàn 重大事件 *n* watershed

zhòng de 重的 *adj* heavy

zhòng diǎn 重点 *n* emphasis

zhòng fàn 重犯 *n* felon

zhòng jī 重击 *v* pound

zhòng lì 重力 *n* gravity

zhòng lì xī yǐn 重力吸引 *v* gravitate

zhòng liàng 重量 *n* weight

zhòng yào de 重要的 *adj* vital

zhòng yào xìng 重要性 *n* importance

zhòng yīn 重音 *n* accent

zhòng zuì 重罪 *n* felony

zhōu 州 *n* state

zhōu zhǎng 州长 *n* governor

zhōu cháng 周长 *n* perimeter

zhōu dào de 周到的 *adj* thoughtful

zhōu mò 周末 *n* weekend

zhōu nián 周年 *n* anniversary

zhōu qī 周期 *n* cycle, period

zhōu rì 周日 *n* Sunday

zhōu wéi 周围 *n* surroundings

zhōu yī dào zhōu wǔ 周一到周五 *adj* weekday

zhōu 洲 *n* continent

zhōu de 洲的 *adj* continental

zhóu 轴 *n* axis

zhǒu 肘 *n* elbow

zhòu 咒 *v* cuss, damn, spell

zhòu yǔ 咒语 *n* spell

zhòu méi 皱眉 *v* frown

zhòu wén 皱纹 *n* wrinkle

zhòu jiàng 骤降 *v* plummet

zhū rú 侏儒 *n* midget

zhū bǎo diàn 珠宝店 *n* jewelry store

zhū bǎo shāng 珠宝商 *n* jeweler

zhū 猪 *n* hog, pig

zhū ròu 猪肉 *n* pork

zhū yóu 猪油 *n* lard

zhú zi 竹子 *n* bamboo

zhú tái 烛台 *n* candlestick

zhú chū 逐出 *v* dislodge

zhú zì de 逐字地 *adv* verbatim

zhǔ 主 *n* lord

zhǔ bō 主播 *n* anchor

zhǔ chí 主持 *v* preside

zhǔ chí mù shī 主持牧师 *n* dean

zhǔ chí rén 主持人 *n* host

zhǔ guǎn 主管 *n* executive

zhǔ jiào 主教 *n* bishop, synod

zhǔ móu 主谋 *n* mastermind

zhǔ móu 主谋 *v* mastermind

zhǔ quán 主权 *n* sovereignty

zhǔ rén 主人 *n* host, master, owner

zhǔ rèn 主任 *n* director

zhǔ shí 主食 *n* staple

zhǔ tí 主题 *n* subject, theme

zhǔ xí 主席 *n* chairman, president

zhǔ xiū 主修 *v* major in

zhǔ yào 主要 *adv* mainly, primarily

zhǔ yào de 主要的 *adj* leading, main, major, principal

zhǔ yì 主义 *n* doctrine

zhǔ yì 主意 *n* idea

zhǔ zhāng 主张 *v* advocate, allege, stand for

zhǔ zhāng 主张 *n* allegation

zhǔ zhóu 主轴 *n* linchpin

shǔ xìng 属性 *v* attribute

shǔ yú 属于 *v* belong, pertain

zhǔ fèi 煮沸 *v* boil

zhù 住 *v* lodge

zhù chù 住处 *n* residence

zhù sù 住宿 *n* lodging

zhù yuàn 住院 *v* hospitalize

zhù zhái 住宅 *n* dwelling, residence

zhù shǒu 助手 *n* aide

zhù 注 *v* note

zhù cè 注册 *v* register

zhù cè 注册 *n* registration

zhù dìng de 注定的 *adj* doomed, fateful

zhù jiě 注解 *n* annotation

zhù rù 注入 *n* infusion

zhù rù 注入 *v* inject

zhù shè 注射 *n* injection, shot

zhù shè qì 注射器 *n* syringe

zhù shè wù 注射物 *n* injection

zhù shì 注视 *iv* behold

zhù shì 注释 *v* annotate

zhù xiāo 注销 *v* log off

zhù yì 注意 *v* beware, notice

zhù yì 注意 *n* care

zhù yì dào de 注意到的 *adj* aware

zhù yì de 注意的 *adj* attentive, watchful

zhù yì lì 注意力 *n* attention

zhù jūn 驻军 *n* garrison

zhù liú 驻留 *n* presence

zhù dǎo 祝祷 *n* benediction

zhù fú 祝福 *v* bless

zhù fú 祝福 *n* blessing

zhù hè 祝贺 *v* congratulate

zhù hè 祝贺 *n* congratulations

zhù jiǔ rén 祝酒人 *n* toaster

zhe míng 著名 *adj* famous

zhe míng de 著名的 *adj* notable

zhe zuò 著作 *n* writing

zhù zào 铸造 *n* foundry

zhù zào 铸造 *v* mint

zhù zào chē jiān 铸造车间 *n* foundry

zhuā 抓 *v* grab, grip

zhuā 抓 *n* grip

zhuā hén 抓痕 *n* scratch

zhuā jǔ 抓举 *v* snatch

zhuā yǎng 抓痒 *v* tickle

Z

zhuā zhù 抓住 *iv* catch, come over, seize

zhǎo 爪 *n* claw

zhuān gōng 专攻 *v* specialize

zhuān hèng de 专横的 *adj* arbitrary

zhuān hèng de rén 专横的人 *n* tyrant

zhuān jiā 专家 *adj* expert

zhuān kē 专科 *n* specialty

zhuān lán 专栏 *n* column

zhuān lì 专利 *n* patent

zhuān lì de 专利的 *adj* patent

zhuān mài 专卖 *n* monopoly

zhuān tí 专题 *n* feature

zhuān yè 专业 *n* major, profession

zhuān yè de 专业的 *adj* professional

zhuān zhèng 专政 *n* dictatorship

zhuān zhì de 专制的 *adj* despotic, domineering

zhuān zhù 专注 *v* preoccupy

zhuān tou 砖头 *n* brick

zhuān wǎ gōng 砖瓦工 *n* bricklayer

zhuǎn 转 *v* turn

zhuǎn 转 *n* turn

zhuǎn huàn 转换 *n* conversion

zhuǎn huàn 转换 *v* convert, transform

zhuǎn ràng 转让 *v* convey, transfer

zhuǎn ràng 转让 *n* transfer

zhuǎn ràng fáng chǎn 转让房产 *n* demise

zhuǎn tǐ 转体 *v* swivel

zhuǎn wān 转弯 *v* twist

zhuǎn wān 转弯 *n* twist

zhuǎn xiàng 转向 *n* diversion

zhuǎn xiàng 转向 *v* veer

zhuǎn xíng 转型 *n* transformation

zhuǎn yí 转移 *n* diversion

zhuǎn yí 转移 *v* relegate

zhuàn dòng 转动 *v* rotate

zhuàn dòng 转动 *n* rotation

zhuàn 赚 *v* earn

zhuāng yán 庄严 *n* dignity

zhuāng yán de 庄严的 *adj* solemn

zhuāng 桩 *n* stake

zhuāng bèi 装备 *v* equip, furnish

zhuāng dìng hǎo de 装订好的 *adj* bound

zhuāng huáng 装潢 *n* décor

zhuāng píng 装瓶 *v* bottle

zhuāng shì 装饰 *v* adorn, decorate, emboss, garnish

zhuāng shì 装饰 *n* garnish

zhuāng shì de 装饰的 *adj* decorative, ornamental

zhuāng shì huà 装饰画 *n* poster

zhuāng tián 装填 *n* filling

zhuāng yùn 装运 *n* shipment

zhuāng zài de 装载的 *adj* laden

zhuāng zhì 装置 *n* device

zhuàng guān de 壮观的 *adj* majestic

zhuàng jǔ 壮举 *n* feat

zhuàng lì de 壮丽的 *adj* splendid

zhuàng měi de 壮美的 *adj* sublime

zhuàng kuàng 状况 *n* circumstance

Z

zhuàng tài 状态 *n* state
zhuàng jī 撞击 *n* bump
zhuī 追 *n* chase
zhuī 追 *v* chase
zhuī bǔ 追捕 *n* manhunt
zhuī qiú 追求 *v* pursue
zhuī qiú 追求 *n* pursuit
zhuī shàng 追上 *v* overtake
zhuī suí zhě 追随者 *n* follower
zhuī gǔ 椎骨 *n* vertebra
zhuī tǐ 锥体 *n* cone
zhuì luò 坠落 *iv* fall
zhǔn bèi 准备 *n* preparation
zhǔn bèi 准备 *v* prepare
zhǔn bèi hǎo 准备好 *adj* ready
zhǔn bèi jiù xù 准备就绪 *n* readiness
zhǔn què de 准确的 *adj* accurate
zhǔn què wú wù de 准确无误的 *adj* unmistakable
zhǔn shí de 准时的 *adj* punctual
zhǔn zé 准则 *n* guidelines, norm
zhuó yuè 卓越 *n* excellence
zhuó yuè de 卓越的 *adj* remarkable
zhuō nòng 捉弄 *v* tease, trick
zhuō zhù 捉住 *v* seize
zhuō bù 桌布 *n* tablecloth
zhuō zi 桌子 *n* desk, table
zhuó 啄 *v* peck
zhuó 啄 *n* peck
zhuó shǒu （on）着手 *v* embark
zhuó shǒu 着手 *v* get down to, set about
zhuó zhuāng 着装 *n* dress

zhuó zhuāng 着装 *v* dress
zhuó shēng 擢升 *v* exalt
zī xún 咨询 *v* consult
zī xún 咨询 *n* consultation
zī shì 姿势 *n* gesture, pose
zī běn 资本 *n* capital
zī běn huà 资本化 *v* capitalize
zī běn zhǔ yì 资本主义 *n* capitalism
zī chǎn 资产 *n* asset
zī gé 资格 *n* competence, pretension
zī xùn 资讯 *n* information
zī yuán 资源 *n* resource, source
zī zhì 资质 *n* aptitude
zī rùn 滋润 *v* moisten
zī yǎng 滋养 *v* nourish
zǐ dàn 子弹 *n* bullet
zǐ gōng 子宫 *n* womb
zǐ gōng tǐ 子宫体 *n* uterus
zǐ jù 子句 *n* clause
zǐ xì de 仔细的 *adj* careful
zǐ luó lán sè 紫罗兰色 *n* violet
zǐ sè de 紫色的 *adj* purple
zì 字 *n* letter
zì diǎn 字典 *n* dictionary
zì jūn dōng qīn 字军东侵 *n* crusade
zì mí 字迷 *n* puzzle
zì mǔ biǎo 字母表 *n* alphabet
zì mù 字幕 *n* subtitle
zì bái zhě 自白者 *n* confessor
zì cóng 自从 *pre* since
zì dòng de 自动的 *adj* automatic
zì dòng fú tī 自动扶梯 *n* escalator

Z

zì fā de 自发的 *adj* spontaneous

zì fā xìng 自发性 *n* spontaneity

zì fǎn de 自反的 *adj* reflexive

zì fù de 自负的 *adj* conceited, vain

zì fù de 自负地 *adv* vainly

zì gào fèn yǒng 自告奋勇 *v* come forward

zì háo de 自豪的 *adj* proud

zì háo de 自豪地 *adv* proudly

zì jǐ 自己 *pre* oneself

zì jǐ de 自己的 *adj* own

zì jué de 自觉的 *adj* self-conscious

zì lái shuǐ 自来水 *n* tap

zì lì yuán zé 自利原则 *n* self-interest

zì rán 自然 *n* nature

zì rán de 自然的 *adj* natural; spontaneous

zì rán de jié guǒ 自然的结果 *n* corollary

zì rán de 自然地 *adv* naturally

zì shā 自杀 *n* suicide

zì shēn lì yì 自身利益 *n* self-interest

zì sī 自私 *n* selfishness

zì sī de 自私的 *adj* selfish

zì xíng chē 自行车 *n* bicycle, bike

zì xuán 自旋 *iv* spin

zì yóu 自由 *n* freedom, liberty

zì yuàn 自愿 *n* willingness

zì zhì de 自制的 *adj* homemade

zì zhì 自治 *n* autonomy

zì zhì de 自治的 *adj* autonomous

zì zhì de shì zhèn 自治的市镇 *n* borough

zì zhù cān tīng 自助餐厅 *n* cafeteria

zì zūn 自尊 *v* esteem

zì zūn 自尊 *n* self-esteem, self-respect

zōng jiào 宗教 *n* clan, religion

zōng jiào de 宗教的 *adj* religious

zōng jiào lǐ bài shì 宗教礼拜式 *n* rite

zōng jiào zhàn zhēng 宗教战争 *n* crusade

zōng lú 棕榈 *n* palm

zōng sè de 棕色的 *adj* brown

zǒng bù 总部 *n* headquarters

[zǒng chēng] rén yuán [总称]人员 *n* personnel

zǒng de 总的 *adj* gross

zǒng dū 总督 *n* governor

zǒng gòng 总共 *adj* altogether

zǒng hé 总和 *n* sum

zǒng jì 总计 *v* amount to, reckon, reckon on

zǒng jì dá 总计达 *v* aggregate

zǒng jì de 总计的 *adj* total

zǒng jià 总价 *n* lump sum

zǒng jié 总结 *v* sum up, summarize

zǒng lǐ 总理 *n* chancellor

zǒng shì 总是 *adv* always

zǒng tǐ 总体 *adv* overall

zǒng tǐ 总体 *n* totality

zǒng tǒng de zhí wù 总统的职务 *n* presidency

zǒng zhàng 总帐 *n* ledger

zòng héng zì mí 纵横字谜 *n* crossword

zòng huǒ 纵火 *n* arson
zòng huǒ zhě 纵火者 *n* arsonist
zòng huǒ zuì 纵火罪 *n* arson
zòng róng 纵容 *v* connive, pamper
zǒu dào 走道 *n* hallway
zǒu kāi 走开 *v* go away
zǒu láng 走廊 *n* corridor
zǒu sī fàn 走私贩 *n* smuggler
zǒu sī pǐn 走私品 *n* contraband
zū 租 *v* rent
zū fèi 租费 *n* rent
zū lìn 租赁 *v* lease
zū lìn 租赁 *n* lease
zú gēn 足跟 *n* heel
zú gòu 足够 *adv* enough
zú jì 足迹 *n* footprint
zú qiú 足球 *n* football
zú zhì duō móu de 足智多谋的 *adj* tactical
zú zhǎng 族长 *n* patriarch
zǔ zhòu 诅咒 *v* curse
zǔ zhòu 诅咒 *n* damnation
zǔ ài 阻碍 *v* counteract, hinder, obstruct
zǔ ài 阻碍 *n* obstruction
zǔ ài wù 阻碍物 *n* impediment
zǔ sè 阻塞 *v* bar, block, choke, clog, obstruct
zǔ zhǐ 阻止 *v* baffle, deter, foil, hold up, restrain
zǔ chéng 组成 *n* composition, makeup
zǔ chéng 组成 *v* make up
zǔ chéng jù lè bù 组成俱乐部 *v* club

zǔ hé 组合 *n* combination
zǔ jiàn 组件 *n* component
zǔ zhī 组织 *n* organization; texture; tissue
zǔ zhī 组织 *v* organize
zǔ zhuāng 组装 *v* assemble
zǔ fù mǔ 祖父母 *n* grandparents
zǔ mǔ 祖母 *n* grandmother
zǔ sūn 祖孙 *n* grandchild
zǔ xiān 祖先 *n* ancestor, ancestry
zuàn 钻 *v* drill
zuàn shí 钻石 *n* diamond
zuàn zi 钻子 *n* drill
zuì ài 最爱 *adj* favorite
zuì chū 最初 *n* outset
zuì chū de 最初的 *adj* initial
zuì dà de 最大的 *adj* utmost
zuì duō de 最多的 *adj* most
zuì gāo（dà）de 最高（大）的 *adj* maximum
zuì gāo de 最高的 *adj* supreme
zuì gāo diǎn 最高点 *n* apex
zuì gāo jí huì yì 最高级会议 *n* summit
zuì hòu 最后 *adj* final
zuì hòu 最后 *adv* lastly
zuì hòu de 最后的 *adj* conclusive, ultimate
zuì hòu de jué zhàn 最后的决战 *n* showdown
zuì hòu tōng dié 最后通牒 *n* ultimatum
zuì huài de 最坏的 *adj* worst
zuì jiā de 最佳的 *adj* best
zuì jìn de 最近的 *adj* recent

Z

zuì jīng cǎi de bù fen 最精彩的部分 *n* highlight

zuì shǎo 最少 *n* minimum

zuì tū chū de dì wèi 最突出的地位 *n* foreground

zuì xīn de 最新的 *adj* latest, up-to-date

zuì zhōng 最终 *adv* eventually

zuì zhōng jiě jué 最终解决 *v* clinch

zuì è 罪恶 *n* evil

zuì è gǎn 罪恶感 *n* guilt

zuì fàn 罪犯 *n* culprit

zuì kuí 罪魁 *n* ringleader

zuì niè 罪孽 *n* sin

zuì niè shēn zhòng 罪孽深重 *adj* sinful

zuì rén 罪人 *n* sinner

zuì 醉 *adj* drunk

zuì jiǔ 醉酒 *n* drunkenness

zūn jìng 尊敬 *n* homage, respect

zūn jìng 尊敬 *v* regard, respect

zūn jìng de 尊敬的 *adj* respectful

zūn yán 尊严 *n* dignity, sanctity

zūn zhòng 尊重 *n* reverence

zūn shǒu 遵守 *v* adhere, comply, conform, abide by

zūn yú 鳟鱼 *n* trout

zuō fang 作坊 *n* workshop

zuó tiān 昨天 *adv* yesterday

zuó wǎn 昨晚 *adv* last night

zuǒ lún shǒu qiāng 左轮手枪 *v* revolver

zuǒ liào 佐料 *n* sauce

zuò bì 作弊 *v* cheat

zuò biāo jì 作标记 *v* mark

zuò fèi 作废 *v* invalidate

zuò guài 作怪 *n* mischief

zuò jī chǔ 作基础 *v* base

zuò jiā 作家 *n* writer

zuò jiǎn bào 作简报 *v* brief

zuò pǐn 作品 *n* piece; writing

zuò qǔ 作曲 *v* compose

zuò qǔ jiā 作曲家 *n* composer

zuò wéi 作为 *c* as

zuò wén 作文 *n* composition

zuò wù 作物 *n* crop

zuò yè bù 作业簿 *n* workbook

zuò zhàn 作战 *v* campaign

zuò zhě 作者 *n* author

zuò zhèng 作证 *v* attest, testify

zuò 坐 *iv* sit

zuò diàn 坐垫 *n* cushion

zuò gōng jiāo chē 坐公交车 *v* bus

zuò láo 坐牢 *n* jail

zuò láo 坐牢 *v* jail

zuò luò 坐落 *adj* situated

zuò xià 坐下 *adj* seated

zuò zhě huò tǎng zhe qǔ nuǎn 坐着或躺着取暖 *v* bask

zuò wèi 座位 *n* pew

zuò yǐ 座椅 *n* seat

zuò yòu míng 座右铭 *n* motto

zuò 做 *iv* do, make

zuò bái rì mèng 做白日梦 *v* daydream

zuò chǔn shì 做蠢事 *v* goof

zuò hǎo zhǔn bèi 做好准备 *v* brace for

zuò jié lùn 做结论 *v* conclude

Z

zuò mù lù 做目录 *v* catalog
zuò shǒu shì biǎo dá 做手势表达
  v gesticulate

Word to Word® Bilingual Dictionary Series

All languages are two-way:
English-Language / Language-English.
More languages in planning and production.

Order Information

To order our Word to Word® Bilingual Dictionaries or any other products from Bilingual Dictionaries, Inc., please contact us at (951) 296-2445 or visit us at **www.BilingualDictionaries.com**. Visit our website to download our current Catalog/Order Form, view our products, and find information regarding Bilingual Dictionaries, Inc.

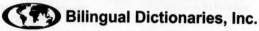 **Bilingual Dictionaries, Inc.**

PO Box 1154 • Murrieta, CA 92562 • Tel: (951) 296-2445 • Fax: (951) 461-3092
www.BilingualDictionaries.com

Special Dedication & Thanks

Bilingual Dicitonaries, Inc. would like to thank all the teachers from various districts accross the country for their useful input and great suggestions in creating a Word to Word® standard. We encourage all students and teachers using our bilingual learning materials to give us feedback. Please send your questions or comments via email to support@bilingualdictionaries.com.